Varaha Mihira's

Brihat Jataka

ENGLISH TRANSLATION
With Original Slokas in Devanagari

BANGALORE SURYANARAIN RAO

Revised by
B. LAKSHMINARAIN RAO
Mysore Educational Service (Retd.)

Edited by
BANGALORE VENKATA RAMAN

MOTILAL BANARSIDASS PUBLISHERS
PRIVATE LIMITED ● DELHI

Fifth Edition: Bangalore, 1986
Reprint: Delhi, 1996, 1998, 2001, 2005

ISBN: 81-208-1395-2 (Cloth)
ISBN: 81-208-1396-0 (Paper)

MOTILAL BANARSIDASS

41 U.A. Bungalow Road, Jawahar Nagar, Delhi 110 007
8 Mahalaxmi Chamber, 22 Bhulabhai Desai Road, Mumbai 400 026
236, 9th Main III Block, Jayanagar, Bangalore 560 011
120 Royapettah High Road, Mylapore, Chennai 600 004
Sanas Plaza, 1302 Baji Rao Road, Pune 411 002
8 Camac Street, Kolkata 700 017
Ashok Rajpath, Patna 800 004
Chowk, Varanasi 221 001

Printed in India
BY JAINENDRA PRAKASH JAIN AT SHRI JAINENDRA PRESS,
A-45 NARAINA, PHASE-I, NEW DELHI 110 028
AND PUBLISHED BY NARENDRA PRAKASH JAIN FOR
MOTILAL BANARSIDASS PUBLISHERS PRIVATE LIMITED,
BUNGALOW ROAD, DELHI 110 007

PREFACE TO FIFTH EDITION

It is with feelings of considerable pride that I present the fifth edition of my grandfather's English translation of *Brihat Jataka*.

There are several translations of this matchless book into English available in the market. But Prof. Rao's translation has been acclaimed not only as authentic, based mainly on the commentaries of *Bhattopala* but also as embodying in the notes, Prof. Rao's vast practical experience in the field of astrology.

It is hoped that this translation, out of print for a long time, will supply a long-felt want to the vast number of astrological students and savants, for an authoritative presentation of Varaha Mihira's treatise in simple English.

I must record my appreciation of the helpful attitude displayed by my good friend Mr. G. K. Ananthram in readily coming forward to publish the book in an attractive manner. My thanks are due to him.

Bangalore
8–9–1986

B. V. RAMAN

FOREWORD

This translation of Brihat Jataka by my revered father, the late Prof. B. Suryanarain Rao, was commenced as early as 1908, when I was in the College classes and it was given as a supplement to *The Astrological Magazine* and then got up in a book form. It was not till 1918 that the first edition was issued and owing to change of residence and settlement at a village, many of the books were lost and a second edition was issued by about 1921. It was also sold out and circumstances did not permit the issue of the third edition immediately. When my nephew Prof. B.V. Raman had established *The Astrological Magazine* on a sound basis and began the reprint of some of my father's works like 'Jaimini Sutras', 'Stree Jataka', etc., he asked me to revise 'Brihat Jataka' so that a third edition of the book may be placed before the public. What with the scarcity of paper, printers, and war conditions, the book is seeing the light of the day in 1948, after a lapse of more than 25 years. I have carefully revised the translation and have added many concrete examples while discussing the Yogas and Bhavas and have tried my best to make it as intelligent as possible to a layman who takes it up for the first time to study. Brihat Jataka from time immemorial has been considered as the standard text-book on Astrology and all other works like Jataka Chandrika, Sarvartha Chintamani, etc., come only next to Brihat Jataka. More than the text, the commentaries by Bhattotpala have made Brihat Jataka immortal and a standard work. A brief summary of Bhattotpala's life is given under Chapter IV on page 119 of this work. *The Astrological Magazine* has also devoted many pages to his work and times. This English version of Brihat Jataka by my father is not a mere translation as is found in the other editions of Brihat Jataka but the ripe experience of Mr. B. Suryanarain Rao for over 60 years in the field of Astrology and his sound judgment on doubtful points with as clear and as convincing language as ever written in astrological literature and to which standard very few have come up so far as my humble knowledge goes. As one who sat at his feet and learnt a few invaluable gems of astrological principles, I have placed this fourth edition, through the kind solicitude of my nephew Prof. B. V. Raman. The inclusion of the original slokas in Devanagari, will it is hoped appeal to a wider circle of astrological students.

B. LAKSHMINARAIN RAO, B.A.

BANGALORE
2-5-1957.

PREFACE

In presenting the English translation of Brihat Jataka, to the educated public of the world, I make no appeal for their indulgence. This is a monumental work, where the difficulties in translating a beautiful, technical and suggestive work in Sanskrit had to be surmounted by hard labour, profound research, want of adequate expressions in a poor and non-constructive language like the English by the selection of the most comprehensive expressions and by laborious mental analysis, which would have a tendency to minimise the linguistic incongruities so difficult to reconcile. How far I have succeeded in my attempts to simplify the technicalities by my notes is a matter for decision by the succeeding generations.

In my introduction to the English translation of Sarvartha Chintamani I have plainly referred to these difficulties and doubts and would refer the readers to that work for greater explanations. The priceless commentaries of Bhattotpala in Sanskrit on Brihat Jataka have been fully utilised by me in the course of my work and if I am to express my sense of gratitude to anybody I have to do so to him. Most of the English works on astrology are sorry performances and no reliance can be placed upon them. If Varaha Mihira is to be respected as the author of Brihat Jataka, his matchless commentator deserves even greater credit for the splendid way in which he has not only made clear many of the obscure passages but also for the valuable quotations he has given so copiously and so aptly in the course of his work. Envy and meanness are the index of lower minds and appreciation and generosity are the indications of a nobler psychic development. I shall close this preface with a simple request to my readers that when they read through my notes they can never complain of wasting their time. Their intellects will be sharpened and their knowledge will be expanded.

Hunsamaranahalli,
Mysore Province,
India.   B. SURYANARAIN RAO.
21-5-1919

CONTENTS

BRIHAT JATAKA

ENGLISH TRANSLATION

BY

Prof. B. SURYANARAIN ROW, B.A., M.R.A.S., F.R.H.S.

(Fourth Edition)

INTRODUCTION

I propose to give a very liberal translation of this famous work on horoscopy written by the learned Varaha Mihiracharya, a native of Kapitha village, in the country of Avantika. His father was Adityadasa and both, father and his illustrious son, seem to have had very comprehensive intellects. In my translation of this ancient Sanskrit work I have tried my best to keep to the spirit of the illustrious author more than to his letter, and in this particular, I am very ably supported by the immortal commentaries of Bhattotpala, but for whose special labours in this field, the works of Varaha Mihira probably would not have attained to such wide celebrity and to have been so useful as they have been now. Dr. H. Kern in Bibliotheca Indica (Brihat Samhita, p. 61, Preface) thus observes on the merits of this great commentator. " We owe the knowledge of nearly all the particulars about the predecessors of Varaha Mihira to Bhattotpala. This astronomer seems to have earned his great reputation, less by his original compositions than by his commentaries on Varaha Mihira. An original work of his is Bhattotpala Horasastra,

a very short treatise in 75 stanzas. A greater reputation
has been earned by him in his capacity of commentator.
The merits of Bhattotpala as a commentator are held high
and methinks deservedly so. To an unusual knowledge of
the astronomical and astrological writings before his time,
he had the acquaintance with some authors in other branches
of learning like Charaka : With a stupendous memory, he
combines judgment. Where he knows his deficiency he tells
us so with a candour, rarely met with among persons of his
class. So he admits for instance, that he is only superficially
acquainted with the technicalities of perfumery (*Gandha-
yukthi*). With a profound reverence for his author, whom
he considers to be an incarnation of the Sun, he earnestly
endeavours to explain and to elucidate the text without
taking it as a mere pretext for pouring forth his own wisdom.
When a passage is ambiguous, he has recourse to the sound
method of comparing the words of Varaha Mihira, with
those passages of more ancient authors, whom he thinks him
to have immediately imitated. This method has the addi-
tional value, that thereby precious fragments of authors now
utterly forgotten, and perhaps never to be recovered, have
been preserved."*

The principal works of Varaha Mihira are : (1) Pancha-
siddhantica, (2) Brihat Samhita, (3) Brihat Jataka, (4)
Laghu Jataka, and (5) Yogayatra.

Bhattotpala has written commentaries on all of these
works as well as on Shat-Panchasika, the author of which
Prithuyasas was the son of the famous Varaha Mihira.

---

* The life of Varahamihira by Prof. B. S. Rao has been published
recently and throws much light on the life of the author rarely found
in any book published so far.

" The original text in Brihat Jataka extends over 407 stanzas and upon these Bhattotpala has written 7,500 (*slokas*) stanzas as commentaries in the Anustap, excluding the vast number of quotations which may be taken to be at least, not less than one thousand." Thus, for about 400 stanzas of the original text, this illustrious commentator has given more than 8,500 *slokas,* or for every verse in the original, he has given more than 21 verses in his commentaries by way of explanation and illustration. Brihat Jataka contains 27 Chapters and the Sanskrit used therein is flowing, graceful and highly expressive of astrological ideas.

With the help of the learned commentaries of such a profound scholar as Bhattotpala, the translation of Brihat Jataka, becomes a possibility with the present generation of astrological scholars. Being thoroughly technical, and highly compressed in Sanskrit, the translation becomes extremely difficult, even with the advantage of possessing these full commentaries and when the Sanskrit words admit of two or three different interpretations it is really difficult to say what was the exact meaning which the author of Brihat Jataka attached to it himself.

These difficulties will be pointed out in their suitable places in the course of this book. I shall now give the names of the Chapters contained in Brihat Jataka before I begin to translate the stanzas themselves. The First Chapter is called Rasiprabhadodhyaya, or that which explains technicalities of the subject and it contains *20 slokas* (stanzas). The Second Chapter is called Grahayoni Bhedadhyaya or that which explains many of the peculiarities of the planets, their sexes, characteristics, positions, the senses they control, their metals, qualities, different names, natures, the places they command and so forth. This contains 20 stanzas.

The Third is called Viyonijanmadhyaya or the combinations of planets which produce insects, birds, trees and so forth.

This contains only 8 stanzas. This seems to have been a very important subject which, in my humble opinion, required more elaborate treatment, than that which Varaha Mihira has given to it in his Brihat Jataka. The births of animals, birds and vegetables are certainly more numerous than those obtained among the human species and although they may not be so important as man is, still, the subject required fuller explanation to prevent ordinary students from falling into hopeless confusions when making predictions in the different bhavas. It is now difficult to say why the learned author has not written more than 8 *slokas* for it. Even Bhattotpala is not so explanatory as one might expect on such an abstruse and difficult subject as the horoscopy of animals and vegetables. In the course of his commentaries in this chapter he quotes only a few *slokas* from *Saravali* which seems to have been a work of great merit before his time.

Then in Fourth Chapter he treats of Nisheka Adhyaya, or the attainment of puberty, appearance of menses, sexual connection, conception, and so forth and this contains 22 stanzas. In the Fifth Chapter comes the Janmakala Lakshanadhyaya or the relation of marks, moles, cowls, peculiarities in birth, chastity and vicious nature of the mother, etc., and this extends over 26 stanzas. A description of the nature of the house where the birth takes place, peculiarities of delivery, and the character and position of the females who collect at the critical time, are also given with a view to correct the inaccuracies of birth time, with reference to actual surroundings on that important occasion. The Sixth Chapter is called the Balarista or the treatment of planetary conjunctions for early deaths, and those peculiar positions of the planets which prevent early death and prolong the life to greater periods. This chapter is very important.

The age of the child is first to be determined and then only, other events should be consulted. If good periods or conjunctions of planets come after the man's death they serve no earthly purpose and therefore Varaha Mihira, first gives the principal combinations for early death, after an examination of which, if the child is found to possess long life, he asks the readers to read the other chapters and ascribe the principal events to their proper periods and sub-periods. This important chapter contains 12 stanzas, but the learned commentator has added very valuable and extensive quotations, which would be of great use to the students of astrology. The Seventh Chapter is called Ayurdayadhyaya, and it treats of the terms of life, which each planet is able to give at the time of birth, by its position, direction, collateral strength, exaltation, retrogression, etc., and how to find out the total number of years of the life of man whose horoscope forms the subject of examination. This contains 14 stanzas, but the commentator has given a very elaborate account, which clearly and definitely explains, what must be considered the most important part of the man's horoscope. In the Eighth Chapter the subject is called Dasantardasa Adhyaya, and it treats of the major and minor periods of planets, with the influences they are capable of exerting during their controlling times. This contains 23 stanzas, and has been largely

commented upon by Bhattotpala. In the Ninth Chapter, he
treats of Ashtakavarga or the relative strengths of the planets
and the rising sign (Lagna) by their occupation of peculiar
positions, and the extent of good and evil they are capable of
producing while they are moving by *gochara* in the various
signs. This is a sort of balance sheet of the planetary influences, which should be carefully studied by the astrological
readers, as it would enable them to measure the quantity of
good which may be expected from the planetary positions
during the future career of the native. This extends over
8 stanzas but is full of technical language.* The Tenth
Chapter goes under the name of *Karmajiva Adhyaya* and is
one of the most imporant in the field of astrology, as it
determines the means of livelihood and what will be the
success of the man in his earthly career. This chapter
contains only 4 *slokas* which are very suggestive and which,
when properly understood, give the astrological adepts a
good clue to the finding out of the avocation or line of business which would best pay a man and the extent to which
he can hope to inherit any property. But I must say that
Varaha Mihira, could have, with greater advantage, written
something more about a matter, which is of paramount
importance to all terrestrial creatures, like men. Venkatesa,
on the other hand, in his Sarvartha Chintamani expands his
observation on this subject and takes the readers to great
many details which are of the utmost value to the reader of
astrology. Chapter † Eleventh gives combinations for

* This may be studied with advantage with the help of the latest
publication on this subject, viz. *Hindu Predictive Astrology* by B.V.
Raman.

† Readers are advised to go through the II and X Chapters of
Sarvartha Chintamani, English translation by Prof. B. Suryanarain Rao .

Rajayogas and hence it is called Rajayogadhyaya. These are all combinations, which give men political or kingly power, and as such, have little significance for the ordinary masses, most of whom even in their wildest dreams, do not aspire to royal position or power. But this chapter is very important for all these ambitious souls—whether born in royal families or not—who have a great desire to become political leaders, and who aspire to become Chiefs or Kings in course of time. This chapter contains 20 *slokas*, and is well worth a careful study. There are Neechabhanga Rajayogas, and Rajabhanga Neechayogas. In the first case, there are some men, who have humble birth, and subsequently rise to the kingly power. Hitler, Napoleon and Hyder afford examples for these kinds of luck. The second contains combinations, where mighty Kings loose their power and become humble men. History gives many examples, where rulers have lost their territories, and have sunk to the level of ordinary men or pensioners.

Then we have Chapter Twelve, called Nabhasa Yogadhyaya in which according to various permutations and combinations of planets and their relative positions towards each other, about 1,800 varieties of conjunctions have been shown to be possible by Bhattotpala in his commentaries. This extends over 19 stanzas. The Thirteenth Chapter is denoted as Chandrayoga Adhyaya, and explains the results of the position of Moon from the Sun, the position of beneficial planets with reference to Moon and the occupation of the 2nd and 12th houses from the Moon and this contains 9 stanzas. The Fourteenth Chapter goes under the name of Dwigrahayogadhyaya or the results to be ascertained when two or three planets join together in a house. This comprises only five *slokas*. The Fifteenth Chapter is called *Pravarrajja Yoga Adhyaya*, in which combinations are sketched out for giving great religious merit, and explaining the various Sanyasa (ascetic) yogas. This contains four stanzas. The Sixteenth Chapter bears the name of Rukshasiladhyaya and explains the principal characteristics, which result in the body and mind of man by the influences exercised by the rising constellation at the time of birth. The Seventeenth Chapter takes the reader to the influences resulting from the position of Moon in each of the twelve zodiacal signs and is called Rasisiladhyaya. The former contains 13 *slokas* while the latter counts 12 stanzas one for each house occupied by the Moon. The Eighteenth Chapter is also called Rasisila, from the fact that it explains the results of the occupation of each of the houses (*rasis*) by the Sun, Mars, Mercury, Jupiter, Venus and Saturn. This is an important chapter and extends over 20 stanzas. The Nineteenth Chapter goes under the name of Dristi Phaladhyaya and it explains the results of the planetary aspects upon each other and upon the lagna and other houses. This contains 9 *slokas*. The Twentieth Chapter is called Bhavadhyaya, and contains explanations for finding out the results of the planets occupying the different bhavas or significations from the birth or rising sign and this contains 11 stanzas. Chapter Twenty-one is called Ashrayayogadhyaya, and contains directions to estimate the relative position of the native, both with reference to his own community and that of the society where he lives. Ten stanzas compose this chapter. Twenty-second Chapter goes under the name of Prakeernadhyaya and explains the Karakas of each of the planets, in their positions relative to the others and contains 6 stanzas. Chapter

Twenty-three is called Aristadhyaya or that which explains combinations for all misfortunes, that humanity is subjected to and contains 17 *slokas*. Chapter Twenty-four goes under the name of Streejatakadhyaya and treats of the special combinations, which affect the feminine classes. Here the author gives some combinations, which are peculiar to females, and which cannot be applied to males. Pregnancy, chastity, certain bodily peculiarities, etc., can only be attributed to females and they are all given here. This chapter extends over 16 stanzas. Then we have the important Chapter Twenty-five which is called Niryanikadhyaya which explains the combinations of planets for death, mode of death and other circumstances connected with that final event of human existence on this earth. This contains 15 stanzas. Chapter Twenty-six is equally important. There are many who have no horoscopes and who are anxious to know their future in the light of astrology. This is called Nastajatakadhyaya and gives directions to find out the year, month, date and time of the person's birth. Seventeen stanzas are devoted to explain these principles for finding out lost horoscopes. Chapter Twenty-seven is devoted to the explanation of the *Drekkanas* which are 36 in number and whose knowledge will be useful for various astrological purposes. This contains 36 *slokas*. Chapter Twenty-eight is called Oopasamharadhyaya and contains enumeration of the twenty-seven chapters the author has written, and also the contents of the chapters, he has explained in his Yatra, a work on the solution of questions put and predictions based upon the time at which they are moved. Remembering all these chapters and the contents they speak of I shall now take my readers to a liberal translation of the stanzas

in Brihat Jataka, dwelling particularly at considerable length
where the meaning is obscure, or difficult, and where without explanations the spirit of the author cannot be properly
grasped. The last Chapter contains ten verses and the total
therefore exceeds a little more than four hundred *slokas*.
The work is very suggestive and requires very high intellects
to properly understand it. The translation simply speaks
of the original stanzas as I have grasped them and therefore, may not correctly represent the true meanings of the
author. In all works of translation from one language to
another, readers should specially remember that the translation gives the purport as understood of the original by the
translator and not perhaps as the original author meant.
This work of translation becomes extremely difficult, when
one has to present his ideas from a richer constructive
language like Sanskrit, in a progressive and yet imperfectly
formed language like that of English. The compounding
of words, their abbreviations, the various meanings into
which words are capable of being interpreted, and the short.
pithy and suggestive *Sutras*, which are in the Sanskrit works,
can never be appropriately represented in a poor language
like the English. Added to this the extensive developments
in Astrology, Vedantha, Yoga, Sankhya and Mimamsa
philosophies, which the ancient Sanskritists had made during their earliest periods of existence, throw considerable
obstacles in the way of good and appropriate English translation, for the fact that in the English language, most of
those ideas, are absent and such of those which are just
now beginning to be introduced, are done so in their original forms for want of proper English words and syllables.
We have nothing like *Sutras* in the English language and

so long as it remains in its present form it is not possible
to conceive that any *Sutras* can possibly be spun out of it.
The word *Hari* in Sanskrit has about 20 different meanings,
and so also many other words. So far as I have known
of the English language, there is hardly any word which,
with the same spelling, has even four different meanings.
The *Adhyaharas* (words, sentences, verbs or ideas to be
understood) are many in the original Sanskrit, and they
cannot be properly represented by any suitable words in the
English language. Under these linguistic, shastraic and
sutraic difficulties it is absolutely impossible to either
properly understand the original Sanskrit texts, or to put
them before the intelligent public in a way that would be
free from faults or criticism.

॥ श्री गणेशाय नमः ॥

॥ बृहज्जातकम् ॥

BRIHAT JATAKA

राशिप्रभेदोऽध्यायः

मूर्तित्वे परिकल्पितः शशभृतो वर्मांऽपुनर्जन्मना-
मात्मेत्यात्मविदां ऋतुश्च यजतां भर्तामरज्योतिषाम् ।
लोकानां प्रलयोद्भवस्थितिविभुश्चानेकधा यः श्रुतौ
वाचं नः स धात्व नैकाकिरणस्त्रैलोक्यदीपो रविः ॥ १ ॥

CHAPTER I

EXPLANATION OF TECHNICALITIES USED

Stanza 1.—The Sun, who is one of the Ashta-Murthies of Siva, who forms the path for those who go to Moksha, who represents Atma for those who are well versed in Atmavidya, who accepts the results of the sacrificial rites, who is the master of Amaras and Jyotishas ; who destroys, creates and protects the Lokas, who is praised in the Vedas in various forms, who is possessed of many rays and who is the lamp of the three worlds, may he grant us speech ?

NOTES

The amplification of these passages will take us to any
extent as Varaha Mihira has condensed in the course of this
stanza, a world of scientific ideas which it would be impossible to explain in brief notes.   Usually all Hindu works
are addressed to Brahma, Vishnu, Maheswara, or to any
one of the three grandest forces in Nature, Saraswathi,
Lakshmi or Parvati.   The learned author takes a departure
from this usual custom, and justifies in this stanza, his
choice of the glorious Sun, in whom all the greatest visible
and invisible agencies, are combined for creation, protection
and destruction of the worlds.   The Ashta (8) Murthies of
Rudra are—(1) Surya (Sun), (2) Jalam (Water), (3) Mahi
(Earth), (4) Vayoo (Air), (5) Vahni (Fire), (6) Akasa (Sky),
(7) Yayajuka (Sacrificial Performer) and (8) Soma (Moon).
These are the principal agencies in the formation of the
worlds.   The first part also means with a slight variation
from Sasi to Sasa that the Sun gives light to the body of the
Moon, as it is composed of water and will otherwise be
lustreless.   Sasi Brit will mean Siva as he is represented as
bearing the Moon on his head ; Sasa Brit means who bears
a rabit-like shade in his globe.   Bhattotpala, the learned
commentator of Varaha Mihira's works, considers Sasi Brit
as the (Sadhu) approved reading.   Moksha is the emancipation from all future births, and final incorporation with
the Supreme Intelligence.   Atma represents the essential
principle in man roughly translated into soul.   Atmavidam
are those who are acquainted with the knowledge relating to
soul and who are after Para Brahma.   Amaras are those
who have no Marana or *mortis* (death) hence the Devatas
of the Hindu philosophy.   Jyoitisham represent the stars

and planets, who are shining with light (Jyoitis). Yajats
are those who perform Yagnas or sacrificial rites, according
to the dicta contained in the Vedas; for those sacrificial
rites, the presiding deity is the Sun as all Ahuits or offerings
are to be made to him (Fire is another form of the Sun) and
he distributes their fruits among the various Devatas to
whom they are offered. Lokas are fourteen in number :
(1) Atala, (2) Vitala, (3) Sutala, (4) Mahatala, (5) Talatala,
(6) Rasatala, . (7) Patala, (8) Bhuloka, (9) Bhuvarloka,
(10) Suvarloka, (11) Mahaloka, (12) Janoloka, (13) Tapo-
loka, and (14) Satyaloka. Vedas are four : (1) Rig Veda,
(2) Yajur Veda, (3) Sama Veda, and (4) Atharvana Veda.
The Sun is called Sahasra Kirana (Thousand rayed).
Thrilokas are : (1) Swarga, (2) Martya and (3) Patala.
Varaha Mihira invokes the help of the glorious and mighty
Sun to grant him speech to complete his work without any
difficulties and breaks. He uses the editorial (we) in his
book.

भूयोमिः पटुबुद्धिभिः पटुधियां होराफलज्ञतये
शब्दन्यायसमन्विनेषु बहुशः शास्त्रेषु दृष्टेष्वपि ।
होरातन्त्रमहार्णवप्रतरणे भयोद्यमानामहं
स्वल्पं वृत्तविचित्रमर्थबहुलं शास्त्रप्रत्रं प्रारभे ॥ २ ॥

Stanza 2.—Although there are great many
works ably written by intelligent men in accordance with excellent literary style, many
people get dispirited in trying to cross the vast
ocean of horoscopic knowledge ; to such I offer

a small boat, constructed with metre of various
kinds, short but very suggestive and full of instructive ideas, to enable them to cross this ocean.

NOTES

Varaha Mihira here tries to justify his publication. He
admits the existence of grand and elaborate works before
his time, but thinks that from their colossal nature, many
who approach them (oceans of science) get dispirited when
they look to the vast ocean of Astrological science, which
they want to cross. The works which were before him
were those composed by Vasista, Gargi, Parasara, Vyasa,
Badarayana, Chanikya, Mandavya, Pulisa, Romaka, Surya,
Brahma, Soma, and Kasyapa. The most versatile
works on horoscopy were those of Gargi, Badarayana, Satyacharya, Maya, Yavana and Vishnugupta or
Chanikya. He also declares, that his work is short but very
suggestive and written in such varied and rich Sanskrit
prosody (metre) that the readers of his work will find it highly
interesting and instructive. I do not know how far this
statement of Varaha Mihira can be supported by actual facts.
On the other hand, Varaha Mihira's boast that *Swalpam
vritta vichitra martha bahulam* may most advantageously
and appropriately be attributed to the Sutras on astrology
composed by Maharishi Jaimini, who was the disciple of
Veda Vyasa and the author of the immortal Purvamimamsa.
But we are not to find fault with his motto. There is no
doubt whatsoever that his Sanskrit metre is excellent, his
ideas grand and his language as concise as possible, which
may be classified in merit inferior only to the Sanskrit
Sutras.

होरेत्यहोरात्रविकल्पमेके वाञ्छन्ति पूर्वापरवर्णलोपात् ।
कर्मार्जितं पूर्वभवे सदादि यत्तस्य पंक्तिं समभिव्यनक्ति ॥३॥

Stanza 3.—The science of astrology is called
Hora Sastra from the compounding of the two
words Aho and Ratri and the dropping of the
first and last letters; and it speaks of the
results of the good and bad deeds done by men
in their previous births.

NOTES

Ahas in Sanskrit means day and Ratri means night.
The author here suggests that this Hora Sastra or the
influence of time is indicated by the positions of planets
at the time of birth.

The words, horoscope, horologue (clock) and hour are
derived from this Sanskrit root and signify the influence of
time on men and objects. Some people, not understanding
the original word *Vanchanti* properly, think that Varahamihira borrowed this science from the Greeks where Hora
means a portion of time as also in Latin. They cannot commit
a greater mistake. I have shown by elaborate and irrefutable
arguments that astrology was far more ancient than the
age ascribed to Grecian and Roman civilisation, that the
Egyptians, Assyrians, Chaldeans and Abyssinians had
borrowed their civilising influences from the Aryans of India
in remote antiquity and that many thousands of years before
Varaha Mihira appeared, the science of astrology had been
perfected and left to the succeeding generations for study and
guidance. Parasara and Vyasa are well known Maharishis

and if Vasista was the Purohit of Sri Rama, Parasara was
the grandson of the venerable sage. Vyasa was the son of
Parasara and Vyasa plays an important part in the Mahabharata. It was he who composed it, and brought the Vedas
together which had been probably gathered and collected by
Garga, also a famous astronomer and astrologer. Parasara
must at least be more than 5,000 years old. The word
Horasastra was applied to his astrological works and we
are now mostly guided by Parasara Horasastra. Therefore
Vanchanthi used in this stanza which means they say,
should not be taken in a contemptuous sense. Varaha
Mihira pays profound respect to Garga, Parasara, Vyasa
and Suryasiddhantas, and when he uses " they say " he
simply means that the greatest men in the field of astrology
derived the word Hora by Ahoratri being cnmpounded and
the first and last syllables dropped out. Bhattotpala explains
that the zodiac and all its divisions are enclosed in the Womb
of Time and the word Hora therefore means the influence
of time as indicated by the planets, zodiacal divisions
and the stellar influences at the time of birth of any
person or object. In the " Introduction to the study of
Astrology " I have clearly stated about the theory of Karma
and the indications of the Karmaic results by the planctary
conjunctions and aspects at the time of birth. I refer my
readers to my other works for a very full explanation of
this all absorbing topic. Hora in Sanskrit is compounded of
two letters Ho and Ra, the former implying the earthly
attractions and the latter indicating the solar influences.
Thus Hora means and includes all terrestrial and planetary
influences and the results which one can predict from their
work in any given direction. Hora also means 2½ ghaties

or 1/24th of a day (sunrise to sunrise) as the Hindu day is divided into 60 equal divisions called ghatikas. Hora further means one's personal influence or magnetism as we say, and the way in which it works. All these definitions are correlated, and signify more or less the influence of time upon men and their careers here and hereafter.

Bhattotpala raises the vital question about the use of this knowledge of our past and future and says that by knowledge of the future we will be able to read the existing evil influences and we can also adopt remedial measures recommended in the shastras, to alleviate the miseries. He clearly indicates that astrology has no fatalism about its doctrines. It simply reveals the penalties for breaches of proper conduct in the previous states of births, and that it is in a man's power to know the evil, and nip it in the bud before it takes root and produces miserable results.

कालाङ्गानि वराङ्गमाननमुरो हृत्क्रोडवासो भृतो
वस्तिर्व्यञ्जनमूरुजानुयुगले जंघे ततोंऽघ्रिद्वयम् ।
मेषाश्विप्रथमा नवर्क्षचरणाश्चक्रस्थिता राशयो
राशिक्षेत्रगृहर्क्षभानि भवनं चैकार्थसंप्रत्ययाः ॥ ४ ॥

Stanza 4.—In the celestial Chakra (globe) the signs commencing with Mesha and Aswini, are each formed by nine padams (quarters) of stars and govern the following organs of Kalapurusha, namely, head, face, chest, heart, belly, waist, lower belly, sexual organ, thighs, knees, buttocks and feet respectively. Rasi, Kshetra, Griha, Ruksha,

Bha and Bhavana refer to and signify the zodiacal signs.

NOTES

This stanza is beautifully expressed in the original
Sanskrit and cannot be so concisely put into English.
Varaha Mihira says begin with Mesha and the first nine
quarters of constellations from Aswini to form each of the
twelve houses of the zodiac. This celestial circle is divided
into 360 equal divisions called Bhagas or degrees, 30
degrees make a rasi and 2¼ constellations one zodiacal
house. These twelve rasis from Mesha to Meena govern
the following organs of Kalapurusha (Time and Space
Personified).

There are twenty-seven constellations named in the
astrological works and each of these is divided into four
quarters or padams. We get therefore 27 × 4=108 Nakshatra padams. These divided by the twelve zodiacal
houses give nine quarters for each rasi or house and therefore each padam of a star will roughly comprise 3⅓ degrees
of the zodiacal circle. The following are the constellations
and signs named in ancient works and Garga and Vyasa
give correct definition of them.

CONSTELLATIONS

(1) Aswini, (2) Bharani, (3) Krittika, (4) Rohini.
(5) Mrigasira, (6) Aridra, (7) Punarvasu, (8) Pushyami,
(9) Aslesha, (10) Makha, (11) Pubha, (12) Uttara, (13)
Hasta, (14) Chitta, (15) Swati, (16) Visakha, (17) Anuradha, (18) Jyeshta, (19) Moola, (20) Poorvashada, (21)
Uttarashada, (22) Sravana, (23) Dhanishta, (24) Satabhisha, (25) Purvabhadra, (26) Uttarabhadra, (27) Revati.

ZODIACAL SIGNS

1.	Mesha	...	Aries	...	Ram
2.	Vrishabha	...	Taurus	...	Bull
3.	Mithuna	...	Gemini	...	The twins or couple
4.	Kataka	...	Cancer	...	Crab
5.	Simha	...	Leo	...	Lion
6.	Kanya	...	Virgo	...	Virgin
7.	Thula	...	Libra	...	Balance
8.	Vrischika	...	Scorpio	...	Scorpion
9.	Dhanus	...	Sagittarius	...	Centaur
10.	Makara	...	Capricorn	...	Crocodile
11.	Kumbha	...	Aquarius	...	Water-bearer
12.	Meena	...	Pisces	...	The fish

The English equivalents of the constellations have been given in my * *Astrological Mirror*, to which I refer my kind readers. Mesha is always considered as the first zodiacal sign in Hindu Astrology and Aswini as the first constellation for all calculations. When a house is equal to nine quarters of constellations and each constellation furnishes four padams or quarters, it is easily seen that each house is measured with reference to 2¼ stars. Thus Aswini (4 quarters), Bharani (4 quarters) and the first quarter of Krittika making nine quarters compose the first sign of the Zodiac, Mesha or Aries. Then proceeding further it is seen that Vrishabha (Taurus) is composed of the remaining three quarters of Krittika, the four quarters of Rohini and the first two quarters of Mrigasira or $3 + 4 + 2 = 9$ quarters. Mithuna (Gemini) is composed of the two last quarters of

---

* See also *Hindu Predictive Astrology* by B.V. Raman.

Mrigasira, the four quarters of Aridra and the first three
quarters of Punarvasu or $2 + 4 + 3 = 9$ quarters of the
constellations. Kataka (Cancer) is composed of the last
quarters of Punarvasu, four quarters of Pushyami and the
four quarters of Aslesha or $1 + 4 + 4 = 9$ quarters. Thus
in nine constellations we get naturally four houses and the
rest of the houses must be similarly treated with reference
to the remaining constellations.

The different organs of the body are given here :

Aries—governs	...	The Head
Taurus	...	Face
Gemini	...	Chest
Cancer	...	Heart
Leo	...	Belly
Virgo	...	Waist
Libra	...	Lower Belly (that part of the stomach which lies below the navel and above the sexual organ).
Scorpio	...	Sexual organ
Sagittarius	...	The Two Thighs
Capricorn	...	The Two Knees
Aquarius	...	The Buttocks
Pisces	...	The Two Feet

Bhattotpala quoting from *Saravali (a learned astrological work) says that those organs of the Kalapurusha which are occupied by evil planets indicate want
of development or deformity or total loss or absence
while those houses which are occupied by benefic planets

---
*The English translation of this famous work by B. V. Raman
is under preparation.

indicate good development, beauty, health and strength
to the organs governed by them. Mesha indicates head.
Sani in it without beneficial aspects will be debilitated. He
represents evil influences and is called a malefic. The
person who has this combination will have some disorder
in the head, according to the intensity of the strength of
the evil planet who occupies it. The disorder may be
giddiness, paralysis, wounds, scars, derangement, idiotic
traces, brain fever, monomania, peevishness, stupidity and
so forth. If Sani joins Kuja in Mesha, then the combination indicates complicated complaints in the head.
Suppose a person has Sani and Kuja in Vrischika and
without any good aspects, the result will be deformation in
the sexual organs, disease, impotency, or something abnormal and unpleasant. If Kuja and Sani occupy Cancer
without good aspects or conjunctions then there will be
irregular development of the heart pain or disease there
and some chest disorders which trouble the man. The
six sources of strength of the signs as well as the planets
who are there, must be taken into consideration and if the
balance is evil, then the organ suffers much or will be
marked by its absence or rottenness.

मत्स्यौ घटी नृमिथुनं सगदं सवीणं
चापी नरोऽश्वजघनो मकरो मृगास्यः ।
तौली ससस्वदहना ध्रुवगा च कन्या
शेषाः स्वनामसदृशाः स्वचराश्च सर्वे ॥ ५ ॥

Stanza 5.—Meena is represented by two fishes
lying close to each other with their heads pointing

in opposite directions ; Kumbha is shown by a
person bearing a water pot ; Mithuna is indicated
by a man with a club and a woman with a lute,
in close embrace ; Dhanus is described as a
Centaur with the hind part resembling that of a
horse and the front of an archer ; Makara bears
the representation of the face of a deer with the
hinder part of a crocodile ; Thula represents the
appearance of a man with a balance in hand ;
Kanya is shown by a virgin seated in a boat with
a crop in one hand and with a light in the other,
and the other signs are represented by their names
and move in places congenial to their nature.

NOTES

    Pisces is formed of one fish with its tail against the head
of the other and *vice versa*. The sign will be later on called
Ubhayodaya or that which can rise either way, for we see a
head and a tail on each side of the figure. Kumbha
in Sanskrit means a pot and Makara means a crocodile.
Thula means balance and Kanya means a virgin. Dhanus
means a bow and the rest are easy to understand. The places
most congenial to their natures will be controlled by them and
they also have a great likeness for such regions and the products of those regions. Watery surfaces are liked by fish and
crab, ordinary jungles and grassy plains are for ram and bull.
Deep forests and caves are for lion. Streets in the cities are
for balances. Towns are for men and women or the couple.
Military grounds are for archers.

Crocodiles are fond of watery places. Scorpions are fond of underground crevices and holes. The representations of these creatures are very familiar to our readers to require any further explanations.

क्षितिजसितज्ञचन्द्ररविसौम्यसितावनिजाः
सुरगुरुमन्दसौरिगुरवश्च गृहांशकपाः ।
अजमृगतौलिचन्द्रभवनादिनवांशविधि-
भवनसमांशकाधिपतयः स्वगृहात्क्रमशः ॥ ६ ॥

Stanza 6.—Kuja, Sukra, Budha, Chandra, Ravi, Budha, Sukra, Kuja, Guru, Sani, Sani and Guru are respectively the lords of the signs and their divisions from Mesha ; the navamsas commence from Mesha, Makara, Thula and Kataka, etc., Dwadasamsas commence from the houses themselves.

NOTES

This is an important stanza and requires explanation. The whole celestial circle is divided into 12 equal parts each composed of 30 degrees. A sign or such division of 30 degrees is called a zodiacal house, Bha, Bhavana, Ruksha, Lagna, Rasi, etc.

When this is divided into 2 equal parts each part is called a hora (15 degrees). When it is divided into 3 equal parts each part is called a Drekkana or decanate (10 degrees), when a house is divided into 9 equal divisions each is called a navamsa ($3\frac{1}{3}$ degrees), when a rasi is divided into 12 equal divisions each is called a Dwadasamsa ($2\frac{1}{2}$ degrees). When a house is divided into 30 equal divisions each is called a

Trimsamsa (1 degree). There is a beautiful order given for
navamsas. As there can be no break in the counting of
the zodiacal circle we must reckon always continually
round. Divide Mesha into 9 parts each of which is a
navamsa of course.

Taking the divisions regularly we have the 1st navamsa
of Mesha owned by the lord, Mars. The second is governed
by the lord of the 2nd house from Mesha, viz., Vrishabha or
Venus. Then the third is governed by the lord of Mithuna
or Mercury, fourth by the Moon, fifth by the Sun, sixth
by Mercury, seventh by Venus, eighth by Mars and the ninth
by Jupiter. Thus we have had the nine divisions of Mesha
regularly governed by the lords of the houses, consecutively
from it. After the completion of Mesha we begin with
Vrishabha and as Makara commences after Dhanus the last
navamsa of Mesha, the first navamsa of Vrishabha will
be begun by Makara, 2nd by Kumbha, 3rd by Meena,
4th, 5th, 6th, 7th, 8th and 9th by Mesha, Vrishabha, Mithuna, Kataka, Simha and Kanya respectively. The
rulers of these houses are also the lords of their navamsas. Then the last navamsa of Vrishabha ends with Kanya
and the first navamsa of Mithuna should commence with
Thula. From Thula we take the 9 houses respectively as
navamsas of Mithuna and the last navamsa of it will be
Mithuna itself. Then for Kataka we begin with itself and
its ninth navamsa falls in Meena. Then for Simha we have
to begin the first navamsa again from Mesha. Thus for
Mesha, Simha and Dhanus begin the navamsa from Mesha.
For Vrishabha, Kanya and Makara begin with Makara ; for
Mithuna, Thula and Kumbha from Thula and for Kataka,
Vrischika and Meena begin with Kataka. The six divisions,

Rasi, Hora, Drekkana, Navamsa, Dwadasamsa and Trimsamsa constitute Shadvargas or six-fold divisions. For
Dwadasamsas, the process is easy. Divide Aries into 12
parts and the first Amsa is governed by Mars, the second by
Venus, etc. till we get to the 12th, *i.e.*, Pisces and this will be
governed by Jupiter. Take Taurus.   The 1st, 2nd, 3rd, 4th,
5th, 6th, 7th, 8th, 9th, 10th, 11th and 12th are respectively
governed by Venus, Mercury, the Moon, the Sun, Mercury,
Venus, Mars, Jupiter, Saturn, Saturn, Jupiter and Mars.
For Mithuna it begins with Mithuna and ends with the 12th
house from it, namely, Vrishabha.   The other divisions are
detailed in the next few verses.

Varaha Mihira seems to follow Satyacharya.   Parasara,
Gargi and Badarayana considerably differ from him and his
great teacher.   There are some other writers in astrology
who have given Shodasavargas or 16 divisions for each
house, and base their results on the relative strength which
these divisions of time furnish the planets. Each planet
seems to possess a peculiar body whose composition differs
from those of the others and which possesses peculiar properties of attracting and repelling the component parts of
the solar rays.   The solar ray seems to contain all the in-
gredients humanity wants but in its radiation and reflection
it seems to undergo material changes and often produces
results which are quite antagonistic in their nature to their
parental rays.   Take the pure solar ray as opposed to the
ray which is reflected by the body such as Saturn.   In the
first case, the ray produces biliousness, energy, generosity
and good health.   But when the same ray is reflected by the
body of Saturn, it becomes darkish in colour, produces
inactivity and peevishness, misery and darksome thoughts

and an indescribable abhorrence for all good works. Take
the 5th degree of Aries as the birth time. Then we get the
following Shadvargas for this lagna. Mesha is governed
by Kuja. The lord of lagna is therefore Kuja I. The
birth has taken place within the first half of Mesha. It is
an odd sign and the first half of Hora in Mesha is governed
by Ravi. The lord of the Hora is therefore Ravi II. The
birth degree falls within the first 5 degrees of Mesha and
therefore the lord of the 1st Drekkana is its own lord Kuja.
The lord of the Drekkana is therefore Kuja III. The navamsa of Mesha extends over 3½ deg. and therefore the birth
has fallen in Taurus governed by Venus. The lord of the
navamsa is Sukra IV. The birth is in the 5th degree. Each
Dwadasamsa will be 2½ degrees. The birth has taken place
in the 2nd Dwadasamsa. The lord of the Dwadasamsa has
fallen in the 5th degree. The lord of the Dwadasamsa is
Venus V. In odd signs the first 5 degrees in the Trimsamsa
are governed by Mars and therefore the lord of Trimsamsa
is Kuja VI.

Thus summarised we get the following results in the
Mesha Shadvarga :

Lord of Rasi is Kuja, lord of Hora is Ravi, lord
of Drekkana is Kuja, lord of Navamsa and Dwadasamsa is Sukra and lord of Trimsamsa is Kuja. Thus
in the Shadvarga or six-fold sources of energy 3 divisions are governed by Kuja, one by Ravi and two by
Sukra. The evil predominates and results must be judged
as such.

The lord of the Trimsamsa is Kuja as Mesha is an odd
sign, and as the birth has fallen within the first 5 Bhagas or
degrees, it is governed by Kuja as will be stated in the next

stanza 6.   The *six sources of strength for a lagna that fall
for example in the fifth degree of Mesha are : I House lord
is Mars ; II Hora lord is the Sun ; III Drekkana lord is
Mars ; IV The Navamsa lord is Venus ; V The Dwadasamsa lord is Venus ; and VI The Trimsamsa lord is
Mars. Analysing we find three sources are governed by the
house lord which is good, two sources are governed by
Venus, a benefic, this is also good but Venus is inimical to
the lord of lagna, Mars and one source is governed by the
Sun, which is bad, but as the Sun is a friend of Mars the
evil is partly mitigated.

कुजरविजगुरुज्ञशुक्रभागाः
पवनसमीरणकौर्पिज़ूकलेयाः ।
अयुजि युजि तु मे विपर्ययस्थाः
शशिभवनालिझषान्तमृक्षसंधिः ॥ ७ ॥

Stanza 7.—Mars, Saturn, Jupiter, Mercury
and Venus govern five, eight, seven and five
Bhagas (degrees) respectively in the Trimsamsas
of the odd signs while the order is reversed in
those of the even signs. The last part of Cancer,
Scorpio and Pisces goes under the name of Riksha-
sandhi (junction of two rasis or constellations).

NOTES

Trimsamsa implies in Sanskrit 30th division. When a
house of the zodiacal circle is divided into 30 equal divisions

---

*This is only a rough classification. The methods for finding
the exact sources of strength are discussed in *Graha and Bhava Balas*
by B. V. Raman.

each is technically called a Bhaga or degree of the Western
astronomers. In odd signs like Mesha, Mithuna, Simha,
Thula, Dhanus and Kumbha the arrangement is as follows :

   5   5   8   7   5

Mars, Saturn, Jupiter, Mercury, Venus, = 30 degrees.

In even signs like Vrishabha, Kataka, Kanya, Vrischika, Makara and Meena this is reversed, *viz.* :—

   5   7   8   5   5

Venus, Mercury, Jupiter, Saturn, Mars, = 30 degrees.

The learned Bhattotpala refers to the last navamsa of Kataka, Vrischika and Meena as *Rikshasandhis*,
and children born during these junctional periods
hardly live unless powerfully aspected by or joined with
energetic benefics.

Riksha means in Sanskrit both a zodiacal house (Rasi)
and also a constellation (Nakshatra).

As already explained, the end of Kataka is completed
by the last padam (quarter) of Aslesha, the end of Vrischika
by the last padam of Jyeshta and the end of Meena by the
last padam of Revati. Thus the double signification of
Riksha is most appropriately used by Varahamihira. In a
future chapter the author gives sandhis as dangerous to the
prolongation of a child's life.

क्रियतावुरिजितुमकुलीरलेयपाथोनजूककौप्र्यार्ल्या: ।
तौक्षिक आकोकेरो हृद्रोगश्चान्त्यभं चेत्थम् ॥ ८ ॥

Stanza 8.—Kriya, Thavuri, Jitheema, Kulira,
Laya, Pathona, Juka, Kowrpi, Thaukshika, Ako-
kero, Hridroga and Anthya are names for Mesha,
Vrishabha, Mithuna, Kataka, Simha, Kanya,

Thula, Vrischika, Dhanus, Makara, Kumbha and
Meena respectively.

NOTES

Varahamihira in the first chapter has given some curious names occurring in astrology and which are not usually
found in the ordinary Nighantus or dictionaries. This
simple fact seems to have been taken advantage of by some
ignorant and ill-informed Astrologers, Translators and
Orientalists and several crude theories have been advanced
with the object of showing that Varahamihira borrowed his
astrologico-astronomical knowledge from the Greek and
Chaldean works. This is an important question which
cannot be solved in a few sentences devoted to the explanatory notes of an English translation.

I have already pointed out the merit of Bhattotpala, the
creditable commentator of all the works of Varahamihira in
THE ASTROLOGICAL MAGAZINE, Vol. VIII, but for whose
valuable explanations, quotations, criticisms and collections,
the world should have known very little of Varahamihira,
and what is more fortunate, the works of a host of most
eminent astrologers who preceded Varahamihira, in this
noble science. Parasara, a voluminous writer on astrology
and other shastraic works in Sanskrit, was the father of
Veda Vyasa, and he must have been at least 5,000 years old
as we find Vyasa figuring prominently in the war of Mahabharata and the subsequent horse sacrifice performed by the
victorious Pandus to exculpate themselves from the famous
butchery we see in the wars between the Kurus and the
Pandus. Mahabharata was written by Vyasa. Apart from
this we have now a few copper plate grants made to Brahmins by the Emperor Janamejaya and these have the Kaliyuga

year clearly given on them, thus placing their own venerable
age beyond the least shadow of doubt. These are more than
4,000 years old. Chidambara Aiyar, B.A., who made a
hasty and ill-digested translation of Brihat Jataka in 1885
was neither a good Sanskrit scholar, nor a good astrologer.
He possessed considerable capacity in real mathematics and
with the help of Sundaresa Shrouti, he began his work of
English translation of Varahamihira's difficult and technical
works.   Under notes to this stanza he thus observes—" All
the above names, excepting Kulira and Antyabha are evi-
dently Greek names—a circumstance clearly indicating that
the intercourse between the learned men of India and Helias
was more than superficial ".   If a reader carefully peruses
the commentaries of Bhattotpala *re.* this stanza, he is struck
with the absence of any reference about these terms either
to the origin of Greek or Persian astrological sciences.
This famous commentator was no way inferior in capacity or astronomical ability to Varahamihira. He is
original and to a critical mind he even shows greater
acumen and comprehensiveness of this difficult subject than
his author. If really these terms were of Greek origin, he
would have made a note of these significant facts in his
excellent commentaries.   Laya is purely a Sanskrit word for
Lion and the Latin word Leo (Simha) probably derived its
form from the more perfected sister Sanskrit. Then again
Chidambara Aiyar is entirely wrong when he says that Hrid
Roga is a Greek term. Hrid or Hridaya refers to heart in
Sanskrit and Roga means disease. This is specially applied
to Kumbha, whose lord Sani is also the lord of the 12th
house Makara from it and a child born in Kumbha suffers
from heart disease. The term Kriya refers to a goat or

sheep in Sanskrit and it is a great pity that even a Brahmin
gentleman, through ignorance, should have run away, in these
philological matters, on wrong lines like those of his less
informed brethren, the orientalists engaged in such
works.

In Chapter VII.—Varahamihira clearly refers to Maya,
Yavana, Manitha and Parasara and Bhattotpala says that
Yavana was a learned Mlechha (Mussalman). The question
here naturally arises whether Mlechha can be interpreted
as a mussalman since the date of Varahamihira is first
century A.D. or prior, he being one of the nine gems of
Vikramaditya's Court (B.C. 57) *vide* life of Varahamihira by
me and Mahamud's date is 6th century A.D.   I think that
the word Yavana may be taken to mean as a person belonging to Ivan (Persia).   Wherever there was a necessity to
acknowledge the source of information, these authors did so
with a grace and frankness which is simply admirable.
There is no use of passing off-hand remarks and we cannot
so easily accept foreign origin for Sanskrit words as Col.
Todd could do in his Rajasthan for, he confounds Hercules
with Harikulas (from his own imagination) and Maharishi
Atri with the Greek Artius. Such hasty conclusions are
dangerous and are greatly misleading. Helios or Hellas
was the name for the Sun God and He is styled in Sanskrit
as Heli. The Egyptians and Greeks, who borrowed their
civilisation from the ancient Hindus, must have necessarily
taken large number of their words and scientific ideas and
the true explanation for these similarities seems to lie in the
fact that the tide of civilisation which flowed from the East
to the West, also carried many words and ideas which were
incorporated (with such local modifications as was needed)

4

in their religious and philosophical works. Hora itself has been beautifully derived by Varahamihira and his predecessors, in the science and the whole of Parasara's work in this branch is called Parasara Horasastra.

द्रेष्काणहोरा नवभागसंज्ञास्त्रिंशांशकद्वादशसंज्ञिताश्च ।
क्षेत्रं च यद्यस्य स तस्य वर्गो होरेति लग्नं भवनस्यचार्द्धम् ॥ ९ ॥

Stanza 9.—If a planet is in its Drekkana, Hora, Navamsa, Trimsamsa, Dwadasamsa and Rasi, it is said to be in its Varga.

NOTES

The six sources of strength seem to be only for lagna and not for all the planets. For Kuja, Budha, Guru, Sukra and Sani there is no lordship in hora. Ravi and Chandra command no Trimsamsas. Varahamihira here means that when a planet is in its above divisions it occupies a Varga and obtains great strength. Hora means a Lagna as well as half of it as explained in stanza 6.

गोजाश्विककर्किमिथुनाः समृगा निशाख्याः
पृष्टोदया विमिथुनाः कथितास्त एव ।
शीर्षोदया दिनबलाश्च भवन्ति शेषा
लग्नं समेत्युभयतः पृथुरोमयुग्मम् ॥ १० ॥

Stanza 10.—Vrishabha, Mesha, Dhanus, Kataka, Mithuna and Makara are Ratribala Rasis or signs powerful during night. With the exception of Mithuna these same rasis are called Prustodayas. The other rasis, *viz.*, Simha, Kanya, Thula, Kumbha and Vrischika are called Dinabala Rasis. These with Mithuna are called Sirshodayas. Meena is called Oobhayodaya.

NOTES

Prustodayas are those which are supposed to rise with their Prusta or tail and Sirshodayas are those which rise with their *sirus* or head. Oobhayodaya is that which rises both with head and tail. Meena is represented as composed of two fishes one with the tail of the other towards its head. Thus, in either way, in Meena there will be one head and one tail on each side of it. The zodiacal signs are all not uniformly strong at all times and these timely influences are indicated in this manner by explanation with a view to help the student in judging of the powers of planets and houses in their future predictions.

कूर: सौम्य: पुरुषवनिते ते चरागढिदेहा:
प्रागादीशा: क्रियवृषनृयुक्ककर्कटा: सत्रिकोणा: ।
मार्तंडेन्द्रोरयुजि समभे चन्द्रभान्वोश्च होरे
द्रेष्काणा: स्यु: स्वभवनसुतत्रित्रिकोणाधिपानाम् ॥ ११ ॥

Stanza 11.—The signs are cruel and beneficial regularly, they are also masculine and feminine, the same are also movable, fixed and common; the lords of the cardinal points are the lords of the triangular houses from Mesha, Vrishabha, Mithuna and Kataka. In odd signs, the first hora

is governed by Ravi and the second hora by
Chandra and the reverse holds good in the even
signs.   The lords of the Drekkanas are the lords
of the 1st, 5th and 9th in a rasi.

NOTES

The stanza is very suggestive and confirms the declara-
tion made by the author in stanza 2, *viz.*, that he would
write little and suggest much.   The first words *krura* (cruel)
and *soumya* (beneficial) indicate that the 1st, 3rd, 5th, 7th,
9th and 11th signs are cruel and the rest 2nd, 4th, 6th, 8th,
10th and 12th are beneficial.   Then again, he says all these
are regularly masculine and feminine.   All cruel signs therefore become masculine, and all beneficial signs become
feminine.   The same rasis again become movable, fixed
and common or double bodied.   Mesha, Kataka, Thula and
Makara become movable signs.   Vrishabha, Simha, Vrischika
and Kumbha are fixed signs.   The rest Mithuna, Kanya,
Dhanus and Meena are common or double-bodied signs.
Mesha, Simha and Dhanus represent East ; Vrishabha,
Kanya and Makara represent South ; Mithuna, Thula and
Kumbha indicate West ; while Kataka, Vrischika and Meena
show North.   All the twelve signs are odd and even.   In
Mesha, Mithuna, Simha, Thula, Dhanus and Kumbha the
first hora (or the first half of the sign) is governed by the
Sun and the second by the Moon.   In even signs Vrishabha,
Kataka, Kanya, Vrischika, Makara and Meena the first
hora is governed by the Moon while the second hora is
governed by the Sun.

When a sign is divided into 3 equal parts (each part
gets therefore about 10 degrees) each part is called a Drek-

kana.   The first Drekkana in a sign is governed by the lord
who rules that sign.   The second part is under the control
of the lord of the 5th house from it and the master of the
3rd Drekkana is the lord of the 9th house from it. If we
take Mesha and divide it into 3 equal divisions then we get
3 Drekkanas.   The first Drekkana is governed by Mars the
lord of Mesha.   The second is governed by the Sun the lord
of the fifth house and the third is governed by Jupiter the
lord of the 9th.   Similarly for Vrishabha, Venus, Mercury
and Saturn are the lords of the 1st, 2nd and 3rd Drekkanas
respectively.   For differences of opinion on these points see
my elaborate notes on the English translation of Sarvartha
Chintamani.

केचित्तु होरां प्रथमां भपस्य वाञ्छन्ति लाभाधिपतेर्द्वितीयाम् ।
द्रेष्काणसंज्ञामपि वर्णयन्ति स्वद्वादशैकादशराशिपानाम् ॥१२॥

Stanza 12.—Some writers on astrology say
that the first hora is governed by the lord of that
house while the second hora is governed by the
lord of the eleventh from that house. They further
say that the lords of the Drekkanas are : (1) the
lord of the first, (2) the lord of the 12th, and (3)
the lord of the eleventh houses respectively.

NOTES

The author Varahamihira, whose reading seems to have
extended to all the extant works on astrology during his
time, here and there uses the word *Kaychit*, which means
some others, etc.   He appears to attach some sort of

contempt, but at the same time he seems to admit that they were men of great reputation from whom quotations by him were not considered disgraceful or beneath his dignity as a writer of great merit. The commentator Bhattotpala, occasionally puts in the names of Yavana, Manitha and Yavanacharya for this term. This shows that in the opinion of this great and learned commentator these abovenamed writers existed before Varahamihiracharya and attained to great reputation as astrological writers. This is also confirmed by Varahamihira's own verse in Chap. VII of *Brihat Jataka*. These writers were therefore in the field of astrology long before Varahamihira, and were authors of no despicable reputation, to have been quoted by him as authorities, and also by his illustrious commentator the learned Bhattotpala. But some of the views expressed by them were not in agreement with those of the author of the book, who seems to have held the Rishies of India in the highest esteem and regard. The first hora, according to these authors, is governed by the lord of the house itself. Here there seems to be a great divergence in views which it is difficult to defend or reconcile. While Varahamihira and his school of astrologers give the lordship of horas only to the two planets, the Sun and the Moon, the other school of astrologers give these lordships to all the seven planets. In the above instance of Mesha, the first hora would be governed by Mars while the second hora is ruled by Saturn the lord of the eleventh house. The Drekkanas of Mesha then would be governed (1) by Mars the lord of the first house Mesha, (2) by the lord of the 12th house Jupiter, and (3) by the lord of the eleventh house Saturn. It is really difficult to reconcile these theories and it is more difficult to offer any opinion upon a matter like this, where modern

astrologers of whatever fame and name they may be, have no
data known to them by which they can examine these planetary influences and say thus or thus in contradiction to or in
confirmation of, the views held by the different schools of
ancient astrology promulgated by the Indian Maharishis.
Experience along, must be, our test and basis ; it confirms
more of Varahamihira's views than anything else. The readers are quite welcome to take or accept any theory they like.

[My father's experience of nearly 60 years in the field
of astrology, specially with regard to predictive and remedial measures and his study of thousands of horoscopes, and
wide travel and discussions, have enabled him to give sound
and valid judgments in all cases, where doubts arise and
it is this aspect of his translation of original works that have
enhanced his reputation as an astrologer.   As he says
Varahamihira's views seem more valid re. Drekkanadhipathis
than the other verisons.]

अजवृषभमृगाङ्गनाकुलीरा
झषवणिजौ च दिवाकरादि तुङ्गः ।
दशशिखिमनुयुक्तिथींद्रियांशे-
स्त्रिनवर्कर्विंशतिमिश्च तेऽस्तनीचाः ॥ १३ ॥

Stanza 13.—Aries, Taurus, Capricorn, Virgo,
Cancer, Pisces and Libra are signs of exaltation
for the Sun, etc., respectively. The 10th, 3rd, 28th,
15th, 5th, 27th and 20th degrees of the above
signs are deep exaltations for the Sun, etc., respectively. The seventh from these are the signs
and degrees of debilitations for those planets.

NOTES

The Sun is exalted is Mesha and his *Paramoccha* will be the 10th degree or Bhaga there. The Moon is exalted in Vrisbabha and his deep exaltation falls in its 3rd degree. Mars is exalted in Makara and his deep exaltation occurs in its 28th Bhaga (degree). Mercury is exalted in Kanya and has his deep exaltation in its 15th degree. Jupiter has his exaltation in Kataka and his highest elevation falls in the 5th degree. Venus finds his exaltation in Meena and has the highest elevation in its 27th degree. Saturn is exalted in Libra or Thula, and gets his deep exaltation in the 20th degree there. If Aries is the exaltation of the Sun, the seventh from it will be Libra and it becomes his sign of debilitation. The exact seventh house or division of a house of a planet or sign will be the 180th degree of the position he or it occupies. If the Sun is *Paramoccha* in the 10th degree of Aries then his *Paramaneecha* or greatest fall will be in the 10th degree of Libra. A few facts require some explanation. Exaltation is different in its results from deep exaltation, the last being the most powerful position for a planet to occupy. Rahu and Kethu are not mentioned here. It would be interesting to know why their exaltations and debilitations have not been mentioned by Varahamihira. This author mentions Rahu twice only in his book (Stanzas 3 and 5 of Ch. II) and Kethu only once in Stanza 3 of Ch. II and in the latter part of this verse he refers the readers to other well-known works on astrology, for more detailed information. The general consenses of opinion about Rahu and Kethu shows that Rahu is exalted in Taurus or Vrishabha and Kethu in Scorpio or Vrischika. Bhattotpala quotes Maharishi Gargi on the uses of these exaltations of planets, *viz.*, the Sun and

the Moon. " If the Sun and the Moon occupy exaltation the
person becomes rich and famous." He also quotes Yavaneswara to the same effect. In dealing with this verse, Bhattotpala points out a grammatical inaccuracy of the author, when
he says Dasa, ten, instead of Dasama the 10th. Sikhi (fires)
three instead of the 3rd and so forth. Of course if we take
the author as he has put it, then the words may be interpreted to mean that the first 10 degrees in Mesha are Oochha
for Ravi (Sun) and so on. The commentator quotes
Yavaneswara on this point, where that author clearly says
Dasama the 10th degree as the deepest exaltation for the
Sun. Various other authors have also been distinct upon
this point and Varahamihira in his anxiety to be brief, has
introduced for metrical purposes shorter forms, which, to
a less cultivated mind, may appear to be misleading or a
little against the grammatical rules.

वर्गोत्तमाश्वरगृहादिषु पूर्वमध्य-
पर्यन्ततः शुभफला नवभागसंज्ञः ।
सिंहो वृषः प्रथमषष्ठहयाङ्गतौलि
कुंभास्त्रिकोणभवनानि भवन्ति सूर्यात् ॥ १४ ॥

Stanza 14.—The first navamsa of movable,
the middle navamsa of the fixed and the last
navamsa of the double-bodied signs are technically
called Vargottama. Leo, Taurus, Aries, Virgo,
Sagittarius, Libra and Aquarius are Moolathrikonas for the Sun, Moon, Mars, Mercury, Jupiter,
Venus and Saturn respectively.

NOTES

We have already seen that when a zodiacal sign is divided into nine equal divisions, each is called a navamsa. All the navamas do not seem to possess the same efficiency. Later on certain combinations of planets are given by this author in which he lays great stress and value upon the Vargottama navamsa. *Varga* means divisions of a sign and *Oottama* means best. This simply means the best among the divisions in a sign. The signs of the zodiac have already been divided into Chara—movable, Sthira—fixed, and Dwiswabhava—common or double-bodied. In Mesha, Kataka, Thula and Makara, the first navamsa goes under the name of *Vargottama*. The middle or the 5th navamsa of Vrishabha, Simha, Vrischika and Kumbha becomes Vargottama, and the Anthya or the 9th navamsa of Mithuna, Kanya, Dhanus and Meena goes under the name of Vargottama. Thus on a careful examination it will be seen that if the navamsa of a sign becomes the same as the sign itself, it is called Vargottama. If Mesha navamsa rises in Mesha Lagna, if Vrishabha navamsa rises in Vrishabha Lagna, if Mithuna navamsa comes in that lagna and if Katakamsa falls in Kataka Lagna they become Vargottamas. This will be so in all the signs. Satyacharya says that those born in Vargottamamsa will attain to the chief positions among their communities. Therefore if the navamsa is the same as the rasi, then it becomes Vargottama and this can easily be identified. Thrikona means the angles of an equilateral triangle. *Moola* means original or final. Probably this ranks in power next to exaltation for the planets, Simha for the Sun, Vrishabha for the Moon, Mesha for Mars, Kanya for Mercury, Dhanus for Jupiter, Thula for

Venus and Kumbha for Saturn are considered as Moolathrikonas.   A few facts require more clearer explanation.
Varahamihira in his over-anxiety to express ideas briefly
sometimes, does not give all the information, which he ought
to give, to clear the doubts of his readers. If he simply says
that Leo is the Moolathrikona for the Sun the reader is
misdirected, for he has already been told in a previous
verse, that Leo is owned by the Sun.   Are we to take Leo
as his own house or *Swakshetra* or his Moolathrikona or as
both, and if the latter, what portion of Leo will be his own
house and what portion of it should be classed as his
Moolathrikona.   Then again take Mercury.   Virgo has
Mercury as its lord, then again it becomes his sign of
exaltation, and yet again he also has his Moolathrikona
there. The different degrees of Virgo which go to constitute
exaltation, Moolathrikona and own house, have not been
detailed here and the beginners will get not a little confused
over such apparent misdirections. Take Taurus.   The Moon
's exalted there and he has also his Moolathrikona.   But
Varahamihira has explained these clearly, in his *Laghu
Jataka* from which I shall give the details, to avoid confusion
to my astrological readers. The Moon has the first 3 degrees
as exaltation in Taurus and the remaining 27 degrees form
his Moolathrikona.   Venus has the first 10 degrees in Libra
as his Moolathrikona and the rest as his own house. The Sun
has the first 20 degrees in Leo as his Moolathrikona and the
remaining 10 degrees form his own house. Saturn has the first
20 degrees as his Moolathrikona, in Acquarius, while the
remaining 10 degrees form his own rasi.   Mars has the first
18 degrees in Aries as his Moolathrikona and the remaining
12 degrees form his own house. Jupiter has the first 13

degrees in Sagittarius as his Moolathrikona while the next 17 degrees form his own house (*Swakshetra.*)   Mercury has his Moolathrikona in Virgo from the 16th to 20th degrees, inclusive, his exaltation in the first 15th degrees and the remaining degrees, *viz.*, 21st to 30th inclusive form his own sign.   But the author of Saravali, a valuable astrological work of old reputation, gives a different version.

In Aries, Mars has his Moolathrikona in the first 18 degrees and the last 12 degrees form his own house.

In Sagittarius, Jupiter has the first 10 degrees as his M.T. and the rest as his own house.

In Libra, the first 15 degrees form his M.T. for Venus and the rest his own house.

होरादयस्तनुकुटुम्बसहोत्थबन्धु-
पुत्रारिलिमरणानि शुभास्पदायाः ।
रिःफास्यमित्युपचयान्यरिकर्मलाभ-
दुश्चिक्यसंज्ञितगृहाणि न नित्यमेके ॥ १५ ॥

Stanza 15.—The twelve houses from lagna have been given the following names : (1) Thanu, (2) Kutumba, (3) Sahotha, (4) Bandhu, (5) Putra, (6) Ari, (7) Patni, (8) Marana, (9) Shubha, (10) Aspada, (11) Aaya, and (12) Ripha.   The Oopachayas are the 3rd, 6th, 10th and 11th houses from lagna, while the rest are Apachayas.   Some say that these should not be taken as permanent.

NOTES

The first house or lagna is called (1) Thanu—body, (2) Kutumba—family, (3) Sahotha—brother, (4) Bandhu—relation, (5) Putra—child, (6) Ari—enemy, (7) Patni—wife, (8) Marana—death, (9) Shubha—happiness, (10) Aspada—state, (11) Aaya—gain, and (12) Ripha—loss. Oopachaya means improvement or increase but there seems to be some difference of opinion on this point. Bhattotpala very clearly tries to justify his author but I myself see that his justification is a poor apology. Some say that Oopachaya houses or planets in them do not always give increase but only indicate improvement under certain definite conditions. The 6th house, for instance, is an Oopachaya. It denotes debt, enemy and disease. A good planet in any Bhava increases that significance, while a bad planet destroys it. In the 6th house, Saturn, for instance, destroys its significance, *viz.,* enemy, debt and disease. For any man a planet, that destroys the above three dire misfortunes in this life, becomes the most auspicious; for which of us does not feel exhilirated by the destruction of our enemies, our debts and our diseases? "Thus, there is improvement in a man's position says the commentator." But if good planets occupy the 6th, they increase the Bhava (significance) and therefore there is improvement to the 6th house. Thus in the case of evil planets, there is improvement in the man's future and health while in the case of good planets there is improvement of the sign itself and hence its signification." This looks to me more a quibble that cannot be justified, than a real explanation which offers satisfactory solution by a learned scholar. But Bhattotpala is a great commentator and I leave the readers to draw their own inferences. Some

plead that when evil planets or those who are inimicable to
the lords of the Oopachayas combine or aspect them, they
cannot give improvement and therefore the Oopachaya is
not a permanent signification, but changeable with the
condition of the houses and planets in them. This view is
supported by the quotation of Bhattotpala from Gargi.
But Varahamihira and his great authority Satyacharya
consider that these four houses are Oopachayas, irrespective
of their conjunctions or aspects, and this view is also
supported by quotations from Yavanacharya. Here Bhattotpala cleverly escapes from a dilemma where his own view
was generally expected. With due deference to Varahamihira,
Satyacharya and Yavanacharya, I beg to differ from them
and say with Bhagavan Gargi, that some modifications must
be made with the condition of houses and those of the
planets who occupy or aspect them. Take an example.
Suppose a man is born in Meena. Then the 11th from it
will be Makara. If it is occupied by Mars, he will be exalted and will be in an Oopachaya. Suppose Kanya is the
Lagna of a man and Kuja is in Kataka. He will also be in
the 11th from it and therefore in an Oopachaya. Suppose
in the first case he has the aspect of Guru in the 7th house
occupying Kataka, where he is exalted, and in the second
instance Guru is in Makara debilitated and aspects Kuja in
Kataka ; what would be the results in these two Oopachaya
cases ? Varahamihira and his school of astrologers would
have us believe that the results which Kuja would give in
his occupation of an Oopachaya Rasi will be similar or
same in both these cases ? Gargi and his school on the
other hand, tell us to differentiate between these two sets of
Oopachaya combinations and ascribe good results to the

first, where the planet is exalted and aspected by another benefic, also in exaltation, while in the second set, much less good should be ascribed on account of the debilitations of planets and their mutual aspects.

Common sense and general principles of astrology revolt against the first explanation while the second set, stands to reason and rhyme. There may be truth in both.

कल्पस्वविक्रमगृहप्रतिभाक्षतानि
चित्तोत्थरन्ध्रगुरुमानभवव्ययानि ।
लग्नाच्चतुर्थनिधने चतुरस्रसंज्ञे
द्यूनं च सप्तमगृहं दशमर्क्षमाज्ञा ॥ १६ ॥

Stanza 16.—Kalya, Swa, Vikrama, Griha, Pratibha, Kshata, Chitthotha, Randhra, Guru, Mana, Bhava, Vyaya are names of birth, second, third, etc., houses, respectively. The fourth and eighth from lagna are technically called Chaturasra, the seventh goes under the name of Dyuna and the tenth is Agnya.

NOTES

Birth house (Lagna) is called Kalya denoting strength, Swa means wealth, Vikrama indicates courage, Griha shows house, Pratibha means intelligence, Kshata denotes wounds or sores, Chitthotha signifies cupid, or that which is born of mind, Randhra means accidents, or breaks in life, Guru denotes preceptor, Mana indicates respect, Bhava shows domestic concerns, and Vyaya indicates loss.

The fourth and eighth together technically go under the name of Chaturasra and Dyuna signifies the seventh and the tenth house shows *Agnya* or command.

कण्टककेन्द्रचतुष्टयसंज्ञाः सप्तमलग्नचतुर्थखभानाम् ।
तेषु यथाभिहितेषु बलाढ्याः कीटनराम्बुचराः पशवश्च ॥१७॥

Stanza 17.—Kantaka, Kendra and Chatustaya
denote quadrants and these are Saptama (7th),
Lagna (1st), Chaturtha (4th) and Kha (10th)
Bhanam Rasis (signs). The Nara Rasis (masculine
signs) are Mithuna, Kanya, Thula, the first half
of Dhanus and Kumbha and these are powerful
when they happen to be birth signs. The Jala-
chara Rasis (Aquatic) are Kataka, Meena, the
second half of Makara, and these become powerful in the fourth. Kita Rasi (Vrischika) becomes
powerful in the 7th, and Pasu Rasis (quadruped)
Mesha, Vrishabha, Simha, the 2nd half of
Dhanus and the 1st half of Makara become potent
when they become the 10th houses.

NOTES

If we draw a square in the zodiacal circle, it will have
angles of equal dimensions and each of them is called a
quadrant. Thus the 1st, 91st, 181st and 271st degrees
become the kendras or angular points or if we take the
0, 90, 180 and 270 degrees they indicate kendras for any
house or signification. The 1st, 4th, 7th and 10th houses
are technically called kendras and they have other names
like Kantaka (enemies or pricks) and Chatustaya meaning
four places. The others are denoted here with a view to show
the technicalities which are used in the astrological works.

केन्द्रात्परं पणफरं परतश्च सर्वे-
मापोक्किमं हिबुकमम्बु सुखं च वेश्म ।
जामित्रमस्तभवनं सुतभं त्रिकोणं
मेषूरणं दशममत्र च कर्म विद्यात् ॥ १८ ॥

Stanza 18.—Those houses next to kendras are
called *Panaparas* and those next to Panaparas
are designated *Apoklimas.* Hibuka, Ambu, Sukha
and Vesma denote 4th house, Jamitra denotes
7th, Suthabham, Thrikona shows 5th, Meshurana
and Karma are names for Dasama (10th).

NOTES

Further on we have Badarayana stating that quadrants are the most powerful, the next in strength are
the Panaparas and the least powerful are Apoklimas.
Panaparas as being next houses to the kendras will be the
2nd, 5th, 8th and 11th houses from lagna. Apoklimas will
then be their next houses or the 3rd, 6th, 9th and 12th
houses. The other names are some of the technicalities which
occur in the astrological works quoted here for reference.

होरास्वामिगुरुज्ञवीक्षितयुता नन्यैश्च वीर्योत्कटा
केन्द्रस्था द्विपदादयोऽह्नि निशि च प्राप्ते च सन्ध्याद्वये ।
पूर्वार्द्धे विषयादयः कृतगुणा मानं प्रतीपं च त-
द्श्रिक्यं सहजं तषश्च नवमं न्याद्यं त्रिकोणं च तत् ॥ १९ ॥

Stanza 19.—If the lord of the birth, Jupiter
or Mercury occupy or aspect lagna (birth) it becomes most powerful.   If other than these planets

5

aspect or occupy it, it will not be so. All signs
in kendras are powerful. **Signs in Panaparas
are of moderate strength while signs in Apoklimas
are powerless.** Biped signs are powerful during
day, Quadruped signs in the night and Kita Rasi
during the two twilights. The measure of the
rasis from Mesha to Kanya inclusive is 5–6–7–8–9
and 10 multiplied by four, respectively, the other
half from Thula to Meena in the reverse order.
Sahaja (3rd) is called Duschikya, Navama (9th)
is denoted as Thapas and Trikona.

NOTES

The most important question here dealt with by Varaha
Mihira is his statement about the measurement of the
zodiacal signs. But for the invaluable services of collection,
collation and explanation offered by Bhattotpala, the stanza
should have been very obscure, as it makes no reference to
any division of time, beyond the suggestion offered by him
to multiply 5–6–7–8–9 and 10 by four. But what these
20–24–28–32–36 and 40 could mean it would not have
been easy to say. Quoting Satyacharya the commentator
makes a distinction between a Bhaga of a rasi, and its equivalent of the *Chashakas*. Thus the Bhagas of the rasis
multiplied by 10 will give the extent of the rasis in vighatikas
or 1/60th of a ghatika, which in itself would be 1/60th of a
day or 24 minutes of English Time. Mesha and Meena
would get 200 v.ghts. or $3\frac{1}{3}$ ghts.; Vrishabha and Kumbha
will measure 4 ghts. or 240 v.ghts.; Mithuna and Makara
get 280 v.ghts. or $4\frac{2}{3}$ ghts.; Kataka and Dhanus would get
320 v.ghts. or $5\frac{1}{3}$ ghts.; Simha and Vrischika would get

360 v.ghts. or 6 ghts.; and Kanya and Thula would get
400 v.ghts. or 6⅔ ghts. This makes the zodiac as of oval
shape, with one end sharpened while the other end is
broadened. The measurements given here must not be mis-
taken for those which actually represent their durations or
extension. For it would be absurd to suppose that a profound mathematician like Varaha Mihira would arbitrarily
fix the measurements of the rasis (signs) when they are
certainly changeable with the latitudes and longitudes of
places, whose knowledge can be determined by the works on
Jyotisha Siddhantas. The learned commentator explains
that the author has given these *Manas* (measurements) with a
view to enable the students to find out the proportions of the
limbs of persons born in the different signs and of the distances to which stolen articles have been removed from their
proper places. Whichever organ or part of the body is
occupied by the longest sign will be longer and whichever
is occupied by short signs will be proportionately short.
If it is of middle size then the organ will also be similar.
The author of Saravali says Meena, Vrishabha, Mesha and
Kumbha are Hraswa Rasis or short signs. Mithuna,
Dhanus, Karki and Makara are Sama or moderately sized.
Vrischika, Kanya, Simha and Thula are Dirgha Rasis or
long signs. These measurements must only be employed
to find the proportions of the bodily organs, distances and
the sizes of the stolen articles, etc., and not for measuring
the extent of the zodiacal signs. This part of the work
should be entirely learnt from the mathematical portion of
astrology or Ganitha Skanda. Dwipada (bipeds) Rasis are
Mithuna, Thula, Kumbha, Kanya and the first half of
Dhanus, Chatushpada (quadruped) Rasis are Mesha, Vrisha-

bha, Simha, the first half of Makara and the second half of Dhanus. Kita denotes in Sanskrit insects and these are Vrischika, Meena, Kataka and the second half of Makara. Varaha Mihira has omitted the name of an important planet Sukra (Venus) as giving great strength to the lagna by his conjunction and aspect. Other writers including Gargi and Badarayana clearly give him great prominence when Venus occupies lagna or birth.

A great point of interest here, is the quotation he gives from Brahmagupta, who is titled here as a Bhatta and who certainly preceded as a famous astrological writer, Bhattotpala. Bhattotpala finished his priceless commentaries of the Brihat Jataka in the Salivahana Saka 888, to which we have to add 78 years to bring it on to the Christian Era. [*Vide* Chapter on Bhattotpala]. Thus we see that Bhattotpala completed his important commentaries in 966 A.D. He must have been in the prime of life and not much advanced in years and probably was born about the early part of the tenth century. Varaha Mihira's works were already eleven hundred years old, and they must have been the most famous during Bhattotpala's time, which remained without suitable commentaries until this erudite writer took up the difficult task of writing commentaries. This desideratum he supplied with a knack, erudition, comprehensiveness and diligence, which entitle him to our greatest respect and love.

रक्तः श्वेतः शुकतनुनिभः पाटलो धूम्रपाण्डुः
चित्रः कृष्णः कनकसदृशः पिङ्गलः कर्बुरश्च ।
बभ्रुः स्वच्छः प्रथमभवनाधेषु वर्णाः प्लवत्वं
स्वाम्याशाख्यं दिनकरयुताद्राद्वितीयं च वेशिः ॥ २० ॥

Stanza 20.—Blood-red, white, green, whitish red, smoky, variegated, black, golden, reddish yellow, whitish yellow, darkish white, and fish tint are the colours of Aries, etc., respectively. The signs of planets get *Plava* in the direction of their lords. The second from the Sun becomes *Vasi.*

NOTES

Bhattotpala has here exhibited great depth of knowledge and gives long commentaries. The colours are :

1.	Mesha	...	blood-red
2.	Vrishabha	...	white
3.	Mithuna	...	green, parrot colour
4.	Kataka	...	whitish red
5.	Simha	...	smoky white
6.	Kanya	...	variegated or many coloured
7.	Thula	...	black
8.	Vrischika	...	golden
9.	Dhanus	...	reddish yellow
10.	Makara	...	whitish yellow
11.	Kumbha	...	darkish white
12.	Meena	...	the colour of the fish

This may be of many colours but generally the fish colour may be yellowish dark. For aught we know, it may also mean all the colours which may be seen among the finny tribe. *Plava* means hollow or pit. Mars owns Aries and Scorpio and he governs south. In the south, therefore, these two signs Aries and Scorpio get the technical name of *Plava.* Sukra rules Taurus and Libra and his direction is Son-East. So these two rasis are Plava for S.E. Budha rules Gemini and Virgo and these are *Plavas* for North. Jupiter

rules Sagittarius and Pisces and these are *Plavas* for N.-East.
Saturn rules Capricorn and Aquarius—these are *Plavas* for
West. Ravi rules Leo and this is *Plava* for East. Kataka
is ruled by Chandra and he governs North-West. In this
direction the sign Kataka gets the *Plava* technicality. This
technicality will be useful for giving the directions taken
by thieves and missing articles. Also this will be useful for
conquering enemies, if the kings or their generals follow in
the direction of *Plava*, for that means hollow and the oppo-
nents will be cornered and conquered there. As regards the
colours of the signs, the use will be, with reference to the
identification of the colours of animals and planets in dealing with the *Viyoni* janmas or those which are not born
through the human sexual organs. The 2nd house from the
Sun is denoted as *Vasi* and this lagna is recommended for
all travelling purposes. If that is adopted then the Sun will
occupy the 12th house. If this house is also occupied by a
good planet, it denotes fortune to the *Native*. In closing
this first Chapter the clever commentator thus summarises
his remarks which may be quoted here for ready reference,
as they clear many doubts and difficulties in the path of
progress in the astrological studies. In this first Chapter,
which goes under the name of *Samgnyadhyaya* (Chapter on
Techncalities) many names are given, some of which have
root meanings, while others simply convey a technical sym-
bol. The following are mere symbols : Hora for Lagna ;
Duschikya for 3rd ; Hibuka for 4th ; Trikona for 5th ;
Dyunam for 7th ; Meshurana for 10th ; Ripha for
12th ; Chaturasrya 4th and 8th ; Kantaka, Kendra, Chatustaya for 1st, 4th, 7th and 10th ; Panapara for 2nd, 5th,
8th and 11th ; and Apoklima for 3rd, 6th, 9th and 12th.

The first sign is called Thanu and Kalya and from these the body and health of the man must be consulted.

The second is denoted as Kutumba and Swa—and from this must be examined the condition of the general family and wealth.

The third goes under the names of Sahaja and Vikrama— the physical strength and brothers must be examined from this sign.

The fourth has the names of Bandhu, Vesmi and Sukha—and from this must be known relations, houses and happiness of the person.

The fifth denotes Putra and Buddhi and reveals the state of children and intelligence.

The sixth has the names of Ari, Vrana and Kshata and gives clue to enemies and wounds or sores.

The seventh is called Dara, Chitthotha and Jamitra and therefore denotes wife, passions and marriage.

The eighth denotes Marana and Randra or death and sins.

The ninth is called Shubha, Guru and Thapas.

Shubha means Dharma or charities, Guru means parents, preceptors, etc., and Thapas denotes rituals and religious contemplation.

All these items have to be examined with reference to the ninth.

The tenth house is called Aspada, Karma, Agnya or residence, profession or calling, and command or authority respectively.

The eleventh house is called Bhava and Aaya. The first means education, character, etc. The second signifies gains or pecuniary earnings.

The twelfth is called Vyaya and signifies expenditure.

The 3rd, 6th, 10th and 11th houses are termed Oopa-chayas for their power of improving men's fortune. In these houses even evil planets give good results. The benefics increase the events or objects indicated by the houses except in the 6th house, where they produce the reverse effect, *viz.*, they destroy or suppress the events indicated by that Bhava. The evil planets destroy those events signified by the 1st, 2nd, 4th, 5th, 6th, 7th and 9th houses and increase the results in the rest of the houses, namely, 3rd, 8th, 10th, 11th and 12th. Thus it will be seen that benefics as well as male-fics in the 6th produce good, because both of them there, destroy the results indicated by that house. 6th indicates debts, enemies and diseases. The good planets cut these short as also the evil planets and a man who has less or none of these three significations, certainly will be a very happy man. The names of the Bhavas are indicative of the results. The 3rd house is called Parakrama or strength and courage and planets increase that Bhava ; 8th house denotes death and sins and that is increased by evil and beneficial planets and so also the twelfth. This is support-ed by a good quotation from Sri Devakirthi. These are the general principles. But when any special combination or result therefrom is foretold or mentioned, these do not interfere with such special cases, and the readers are warned not to think they are contradictions in astrology. For beginners in astrology almost all points appear debatable and contradictory. One planet is said to give gold, while another is said to take it away. Even the broad principles of this science often appear to be confusing. All this dis-appears before the dawn of knowledge and experience and I would ask patience, application and diligence from the students and readers, to dispel these doubts.

CHAPTER II

GRAHAYONI PRABHEDA

ग्रहयोनिप्रभेदोऽध्यायः

कालात्मा दिनकृन्मनस्तुहिनगुः सत्त्वं कुजो ज्ञो वचो
जीवो ज्ञानसुखे सितश्च मदनो दुःखं दिनेशात्मजः ।
राजानौ रविशीतगू क्षितिसुतो नेता कुमारो बुधः
सुरिदानवपूजितश्च सचिवौ प्रेष्यः सहस्रांशुजः ॥ १ ॥

Stanza 1.—The Sun represents the Atma, the
Moon mind, Mars strength, Mercury speech,
Jupiter wisdom and happiness, Venus passions,
and Saturn sorrow, of Kalapurusha respectively.
The Sun and the Moon are Rajas, Mars is Com-
mander-in-Chief, Mercury is Yuva Raja, Jupiter
and Venus are ministers, and Saturn is the
servant.

NOTES

The movable and immovable universe has been
represented to be the organs of Kalapurusha or *Time
Eternal* personified in the shape of zodiacal signs and constellations. From this it will be seen, that the planets
form part of His body and therefore the different characteristics of that Divine body are now enumerated or indicated
by the heavenly planets.

When there are many planets, it may be pertinently asked why Varaha Mihira, a great Astonomer and Mathematician, should have taken the influence of only seven planets.
I beg to refer my readers to my lengthy and learned disser-
tations upon these points in THE ASTROLOGICAL MAGAZINE
published by me.   In Vols. II and III, the matter has been
discussed at full length and in the Bhoutika Kalanidhi which
was being published in 1910, 1911 and 1912 a lengthy article
appeared in its columns. The sutra says ' *Grahaparam Kota-*
yaha, Mukhya Sapta', meaning that there are millions of planets, but the chief ones are only 7.   Seven seems to be a very
important number in human affairs, beginning with the seven
stages, seven-ten span of life, seven dhatus and seven sorrows
(Sapta Vyasana).   Sun is composed of seven colours.   We
have seven worlds, seven seas, seven *kulachalas* (mountains),
seven days, seven Maharishis, seven secred cities and so on.
Hence probably the conception of seven important planets
and the days of the week in their names. As only seven principal planets have been known to exercise direct and tangible
influence on the earth and its numberless phenomena, the
ancient astrologers confined their researches to them.   The
Sun   represents the soul or vitality of the Kalapurusha,
Moon represents his mind, Mars indicates physical strength,
Mercury the power of speech, *Gno* is Budha, while *Gna* is
knowledge ; Jupiter, knowledge and happiness arising from
that knowledge, Venus denotes sensual pleasures and Saturn
represents sorrow.   As all creation is embedded in the womb
of time, and as its influences on phenomena are detailed in
the astrological works under the guise of planetary bodies,
the author calls the Sun *Kalatma* or the soul of the Kalapurusha.   Readers have to be careful in differentiating

between knowledge and wisdom.   Knowledge may be proud that it knows so much while wisdom is humble that it knows so little.   Budha represents knowledge while Guru denotes wisdom.

The various characteristics indicated here for the planets show their influences on men born under their direct control and their strength or weakness will be a guide to judge of the strength or weakness of the bodily organs as well as the characteristics enumerated above pertaining to men.   " In the case of all the planets " says the author of Saravali " when they are strong, they produce strength in the results indicated by them, and when they are weak, they produce weakness in such results.   But with Saturn the results must be reversed."   The Sun and the Moon represent royalty or protective agency, Mars indicates the military power, Mercury the power wielded by heir-apparent or *Yuva Raja*, Jupiter and Venus indicate counselling or ministerial influence and Saturn represents menial services.   This affords some clue to the means to be employed in securing power or advantage. Whichever planets occupy the Oopachayas, at the time of birth, the personages, indicated by those planets, would become instrumental in furthering the interests of the individual or he will be successful in life, if he makes applications to them.   Suppose, Mars powerfully occupies one of the Oopachayas, then the man will be patronised by military authorities or he should attempt to push on his interests through such commanders.   It is well known that while some patronise people, others without any ostenible reason, throw obstacles in their way.   This is due to such planets occupying unfavourable positions in the horoscope without power and against Oopachaya planets.

हेलिः सूर्यश्चन्द्रमाः शीतरश्मि-
हेंम्रो विज्ञो बोधनश्चेन्दुपुत्रः ।
आरो वक्रः क्रूरदृक् चावनेयः
कोणो मन्दः सूर्यपुत्रोऽसितश्च ॥ २ ॥

Stanza 2.—Heli and Surya are names for
the Sun. Chandrama and Sitarasmi stand for
the Moon. Hemno, Vit, Gno, Bodhana and
Induputra are names for Mercury. Ara, Vakra,
Kruradrik, Avanaya denote Mars ; Kona, Manda,
Suryaputra and Asita stand for Saturn.

जीवोऽङ्गिराः सुरगुरुर्वचसांपतींज्यौ
शुक्रो भृगुर्भृगुसुतः सित आस्फुजिच् ।
राहुस्तमोऽगुरसुरश्च शिखीति केतुः
पर्यायमन्यदुपलभ्य वदेच्च लोकात् ॥ ३ ॥

Stanza 3.—Jiva, Angira, Suraguru, Vacha-
sampathi and Ijya are terms for Jupiter.

Sukra, Bhrigu, Brigusuta, Sita and Aspujit
are names for Venus.

Thamas, Agu and Asura are names for Rahu.
Sikhi stands for Kethu.

Their other names must be learnt from well-
known works in the world.

NOTES

Amara Kosha gives 37 names to the Sun and these are
indicative of the various phenomena he causes   The author
gives only a few names here, not much in use, and desires

the readers to learn the rest from well-known works in Sanskrit. Rahu is called Agu and Bhattotpala derives it as one
who has *a* no and *gu* bright rays. This means Rahu has no
bright rays. Varahamihira, his predecessors and Bhattotpala speak of Rahu as a planet who has dark rays. The
discoveries of modern science are yet in their infancy, and
the means, which are at their command are certainly composed of glasses by whose medium they do their work of
examining the planetary phenomena. On the other hand,
the ancient Rishis claim great mental development and they
have recorded in technical language what they actually saw
with superior sight. All discoveries are made with the help
of instruments constructed by the development of mind.
Mind is constructed by the invisible energies in the
atmosphere as fecundated by the rays of the Sun. Tele-
scopes and microscopes, spectroscopes and helioscopes,
cannot penetrate certain objects when they offer resistance
or obstruction. Mind, the most subtle and invisible energy
yet discovered in nature, can conceive of no objects through
which it cannot pass, and can imagine no obstacles which
it cannot surmount. In fact, when it is purified from its
gross earthly surroundings, when it is elevated by the study
of sublime subjects like astromy, and when it is ennobled
and expanded by deep contemplation and concentration on
the Infinite Intelligence, it becomes the grandest power.
Mahatma or expanded atma or soul will acquire a power
before which, the word impossible, in the physical or planetary planets, would be found meaningless. Therefore we
have two sets of philosophers. Those who expand their
intellects with reference to external earthly phenomena by
the construction and use of terrestrial machinery and those

who have gone into the very root and cause of mind, and
who consequently soar far higher than the first set can ever
hope to do·   The first set can only see through what it
arranges in the shape of machinery. The second, more purified, will soar far higher and see the very essence of all phenomena. If some theories are explained here against the
accepted views of· modern sciences, the readers are not to
run away prejudiced, and shelve the older theories as anti-
quated; on the other hand, the modern views must be
accepted with the greatest suspicion, for they are highly
tentative and at best in an experimental stage, liable to be
frequently modified. These views of modern astronomers
are being so rapidly replaced by their own admirers and
students that people are in great bewilderment as to what
would be the fate of the today theories ten years hence. The
ancient theories have been uniformally recognised and
respected by the succeeding generations so much so, that
even today they comprehend all the latest discovered facts
and fancies and still leave ample room for contemplation
and original research.

रक्तश्यामो भास्करो गौर इन्दु-
र्नात्युच्चाङ्गो रक्तगौरश्च वक्रः ।
दूर्वाश्यामो ज्ञो गुरुगौंरगात्रः
श्यामः शुक्रो भास्करिः कृष्णदेहः ॥ ४ ॥

Stanza 4.—The Sun is dark-red, the Moon
white, Mars blood-red, Mercury green, Jupiter
yellow or golden, Venus neither white nor black,
Saturn black.

NOTES

The use for these colours will be found in identifying the thieves, etc., in questions affecting lost persons or articles. As there is some difference in the colours attributed to the planets they may be noted here for the information of my readers. The Sun has copper colour, while Mars has purple red. Moon and Venus are represented by some to be pure white, while Jupiter is given a deep golden colour.

वर्णास्ताम्रासितातिरक्तहरितव्यापीतचित्रासिता
वह्वयम्ब्वग्निजकेशवेन्द्रशचिकाः सूर्यादिनाथाः क्रमात् ।
प्रागाद्या रविशुक्रलोहिततमः सौरेन्दुवित्स्वरयः
क्षीणेन्दुर्कमहीसुतार्कतनयाः पापा बुधस्तैर्युतः ॥ ५ ॥

Stanza 5.—Copper colour is governed by the Sun, while white by the Moon, blood-red by Mars, green by Mercury, yellow by Jupiter, variegated colours by Venus and black by Saturn. The Sun has Agni as *adhidevata*. The Moon *Ambu*, Mars has *Kumara*, Mercury has *Kesava*, Jupiter has *Indra*, Venus has *Indrani*, and Saturn has *Kaha*. The east, etc., is governd by the Sun, Venus, Mars, Rahu, Saturn, Moon, Mercury and Jupiter respectively. Waning Moon, Sun, Mars, Saturn and Mercury in conjunction with them, are malefics.

NOTES

In the preceding and this stanza, a distinction is made. There the colours of the planets are given to identify persons, etc., and in this to identify the objects, etc. Also the gains and losses of objects with the colours above named, during the periods and sub-periods of planets and the flowers to be used in the worship of planets* in the remedial measures adopted for lessening the evil influences of planets. In the invocation of planets the Gods and Goddesses named for them, should be worshipped. Yavaneswara says to the same effect. When a thief takes away an article, his name will be one of the names of the God or Goddess who governs the planet of the rising sign at the time of question. In travelling, a person is advised first to worship that diety which governs the planet who is the lord of that direction. Saravali says to a similar effect. The directions given about the cardinal points, enable a person to find out which side, the door of the room of confinement

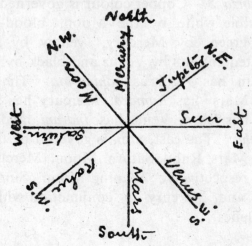

* *Vide* Introduction to the Study of Astrology.

faced, at the birth of a child. The Sun, Venus, Mars,
Rahu, Saturn, Moon, Mercury and Jupiter indicate the
East, South-East, South, South-West, West, North-West,
North and North-East, respectively.

Moon when full is a benefic.   When weak (as on
Amavasya day) a malefic.   Mercury is good when in good
conjunction and evil when he joins evil planets. The
commentator says that Chandra is Kshina (weak)
from the 8th lunar day of the dark half to the 8th day
of the bright half of the lunar month and that he will be
Poornima (Full Moon) on other days.   This is for general
consideration. But for Ayurdaya (longevity), the Moon will
be Kshina (lean or powerless) from the end of the 13th day
of the dark half of every lunar month to the end of
Amavasya, till he has not passed the solar globe. Yavaneswara maintains that the Moon is never a *papa* or malefic
planet. He says that the Moon is moderately strong from
the 1st to the 10th day of the bright half of the lunar
month, from the 10th of the bright half to the 5th of the
dark half of the lunar month, he is Full Moon or very
powerful, and from the 5th to the last of the dark half of
the lunar month, he is powerless. But he is never a malefic.
The use for this knowledge is, that if evil planets predominate, the man becomes evil natured ; and when the
benefics are powerful, he becomes good and with the
mixture of good and evil planets the nature of the man
will also be mixed.

The question of Devatas and Adhi Devatas is an
important one. A full discussion of this here is out of
tune in a short note like this. *Devatas* may be explained
as the essence of events or objects, and Adhi Devatas

are the adjunctional energies which help the essential forces. There is a difference between active forces and passive energies. The active forces are called *Gods* while the passive ones are styled *Goddesses. Agni* is the essence of fire and controls the solar disc. Ambu is water and the *Force* representing it governs Moon. Kumara or Shanmukha is the reputed son of Siva and represents the essence of martian strength. He governs Mars. Kesava represents the protective agency or energy and governs Mercury. Indra represents the Devata energy, and he controls Jupiter. *Indrani* or *Sachi* is the feminine energy of Indra and this Goddess rules Venus. *Kaha* is Brahma and he represents the creative energy. Saturn is under his control. Saturn represents life, means of livelihood and death and he is aptly placed under the creative force designated Brahma. The above are agencies of the several planets to whom remedial measures must be dedicated in our attempts to soften the rigour of evil influences.

बुधमन्दयसुतौ नपुंसकाख्यौ शशिशुक्रौ सुवती नराश्च शेषाः ।
शिखिभूखपयोमरुद्घणानां वशिनो भूमिसुतादयः क्रमेण ॥६॥

Stanza 6.—Saturn and Mercury are impotent, Venus and Moon are females and the rest are masculine. Fire, earth, sky, water and air are ruled by Mars, etc.

NOTES

Eunuchs are those who have no potency to copulate with the opposite sex, on account of some defect in the organs or whose sexual organs are not capable of having

any intercourse.   Persons who have Saturn or Mercury
aspecting the body or in its conjunction will have this defect.
Powerful Moon and Venus give the feminine sex and the
Sun, Mars and Jupiter represent masculine power and make
the person male and manly.   By this the sex of the thieves,
etc., can also be ascertained.   Mars rules the fire, Mercury
rules the earth, Jupiter the sky, Venus the water, and Saturn
the air.   Varaha Mihira has not named the lordship of the
Sun and the Moon.   But that the Sun rules the fire and the
Moon the water, has already been stated by the author in
Stanza 5.   In the periods of the planets the colour of the
person will be predominated by the influence of the
planet and the corresponding Mahabhoota. (See *St. 21,
Ch. VIII.*)

विप्रादितः शुक्रगुरू कुजार्कौं शशीबुधश्चेत्यसितोऽन्त्यजानाम् ।
चन्द्रार्कजीवा असितौ कुजार्कीं यथाक्रमं सत्वरजस्तमांसि ॥७॥

Stanza 7.—Sukra and Guru represent Vipras,
Kuja and Ravi Kshatriyas, Chandra Vaisya,
Budha Sudra, and Sani represents Antyajas.
Chandra, Ravi and Guru represent Satwa, Kuja
and Sani Thamasa, and Budha and Sukra re-
present Rajasa.

NOTES

This is a very difficult stanza for translation as it apparently deals with the different castes found in the Indian
Peninsula and also as it refers to the characteristics most
famously known as Satwika, Rajasa and Thamasa. If astrology is to be taken as a universal science, then it may be

questioned that in this verse it betrays a narrowness of
vision that would quite unfit it to be a comprehensive science, applicable to all nations. Like medicine, astrology
has its universality as well as its particular locality.

It is in this way. When Guru and Sukra are called
Vipras, they represent Brahmins in India and when these
are powerful the horoscope may be attributed as belonging
to a Brahmin in India. But when Guru and Sukra are
strong in the horoscope of an African, an American or an
European, where the particular kind of castes found in India
are not existing, how should the astrologer be guided in his
prediction about the caste of the native? The answer is
simple. *Vipra* in Sanskrit means one who is pure, that is
one who is entirely devoted to the service of God. In countries where Brahmins as a caste, do not exist, then it applies
to all those persons who devote their time to the contemplation of God, and who are priests of real merit and pious
living. When there is no caste as Kshatriya, the planets
include all men who pass muster under the military orders.
Vaisyas are to be similarly interpreted. All those who have
mercantile instincts and who depend upon commerce for
livelihood may be called Vaisyas. Sudras are agriculturists,
servants and industrial men. Antyajas are those who are
pariahs or outcastes in India and in other parts who follow
pariah occupation of killing and removing dirt. Principles
of science are always applicable to all countries and all
nations alike, but with local or general modifications. A
man may be called a king in one country, a president in
another and a dictator in the third. Functions performed
by them will almost be similar, and a real adept in any science looks more to the spirit of the verse than to its letter ;

and quarrelling over technicalities without catching their spirit, will be like nursing a body when the soul has passed away.

The following are characteristics for *Satwa*.

A man, who has Daya (kindness), Sthiratwam (fixed purpose), Satya (truthfulness), Arjava (straight-going), Brahmana and Deva *Bhakti* (regard and respect with faith in good people and Gods.)

Rajas—one who performs sacrifices, who is fond of poetry and general literature, of women and possesses courage.

Thamas—deceitful, stubborn, lazy, cruel, revengeful and sleepy.

In *Bhagavadgita*, a work of immortal merit for which the greatest Adwaitha Philosopher Sankaracharya has written invaluable commentaries as also the other famous Acharyas, we have a clear description of what these characteristics denote, what acts constitute them and what results could be produced by adhering to them. (*See Bhag. Chs. XIV, stanzas 6, 7 and 8 and XVII, stanzas 20, 21 and 22.*)

Thec reative energy of Brahma called *Prakriti*, has given three principal characteristics to humanity called Satwa, Rajas and Thamas and with these binds, the permanent Atmas, a ray of Para Brahma or Supreme Intelligence. Satwa is pure and causes light to others. It gives happiness and wisdom to mankind. Rajas denotes desire for objects, and binds the Atma by the ropes of Karmaic results. Thamas is denoted by ignorance, makes the people passionate and avaricious, and causes laziness, sleepiness and negligence in doing good work. Satwa gives moral happiness, Rajas makes him do Karma and Thamas causes

him to do bad work. When Satwa supercedes and controls
Rajas and Thamas, then he will be elevated and will,
therefore, be able to see the grand and glorious bliss of
Para Brahma. When a person dies, when Satwa predominates, he gets into heavenly bliss; when Rajas prevails
at the time of death, he will have Karma and get birth
again under Karma conditions ; and when Thamas prevails
at the time of death, the person will take births again in
lower orders of creation.

Actions done when *Satwa* predominates, result in
knowledge and happiness. Deeds done when *Rajas* prevails
result in sorrow and misery and acts done under the control
of *Thamas* result in producing ignorance and debasement
of mental faculties.

Men, with developed Satwa, attain to blissful regions,
men with development of Rajas take birth as mortals and
men whose Thamas predominates go down to infernal
regions or lower orders in creation. Satwikas worship or
satisfy Devatas or higher forms of beneficial energies,
Rajasas worship Rakshasas and Yakshas while Thamasas
worship the Devils and low Spirits. Under these,
therefore comes, the classification of food so necessary to
man but so prejudicial to him when promiscuously
consumed. People seem to laugh at the idea when
Vedantists lay down rigorous restrictions on the food we
consume, the clothing we wear, and the surroundings we
select. This is a grand mistake, the neglect of which,
leads men to most injurious results. The composition of
different vegetables and animals differs most radically,
in the various species and genera and to say that men get
the same blood and flesh, same energy and mental strength,

same morality and nervous capacity, without reference to
the various kinds of foods used, would be asserting
a principle more stupid than which we can hardly conceive
anything in the logic of any nation.

Worship includes contemplation and concentration.
These powers produce result as per objects upon which
they work and this distinction must be kept clearly
under our vision. An executioner and a highly developed
Yogi are both capable of great concentration. A beneficient
King and a tyranical sovereign possess great power of
concentration, but with different results. The first con-
centrates his thoughts upon the minutest details of bad
administration and grants redress to them and thus benefits
humanity and gets merits.

The second bestows great attention upon the very same
details with a view to extortion from the people under all
circumstances and introduces misery and ruin to his nation
and indirectly to himself. It should be the noble attempt of
every man to select the best place, the best clothing, the best
climate, the best subject for contemplation, and direct his
best energies to attain good name here and eternal salvation
in the life beyond. Therefore at the time of birth, planets
indicate the nature of the child, and it is for the parents
and guardians to afford it all the facilities to suppress evil
propensities and to increase good tendencies. Man is a most
curiously formed compound, where the component parts,
while under some dominating, uniting power, are still possessed of various degrees of independence, and capacity to
act on their own responsibility. This is a Vedantic question
of the greatest importance and cannot be fully discussed in
this note.

मधुपिङ्गलदृक् चतुरस्रतनुः पित्तप्रकृतिः सवितात्पकचः ।
तनुवृत्ततनुर्बहुवातकफः प्राज्ञश्च शशी मृदुवाक् छुभदृक् ॥ ८ ॥

क्रूरदृक् तरुणमूर्तिरुदारः पैत्तिकः सुचपलः कृशमध्यः ।
श्लिष्टवाक् सततहास्यरुचिर्ज्ञैः पित्तमारुतकफप्रकृतिश्च ॥ ९ ॥

बृहत्तनुः पिङ्गलमूर्धजेक्षणो बृहस्पतिः श्रेष्ठमतिः कफात्मकः ।
भृगुः सुखी कान्तवपुः सुलोचनः कफानिलात्मा सितवक्रमूर्धजः॥

मन्दोलसः कपिलदृक् कृशदीर्घगात्रः
स्थूलद्विजः परुषरोमकचोऽनिलात्मा ।
स्नाय्वस्थ्यसृक्त्वगथ शुक्रवसेचमज्ञा
मन्दार्कचन्द्रबुधशुक्रसुरेज्यभौमाः ॥ ११ ॥

Stanzas 8 to 11.—The Sun has a well proportioned body, is bilious and possesses pingala
eyes, has short hairs, coloured eyes.

The Moon has a well rounded body, much
wind and phlegm, intelligent, sweet speech and
good eyes.

Mars is youthful, liberal, bilious, fickle-
minded and possesses a thin waist.

Mercury has gurgling speech, fond of joking
and has a mixture of air, phlegm and bile.

Jupiter has a corpulent body, golden locks
and eyes, moral and is phlegmatic.

Venus is fond of happiness, handsome, fine
eyes and black ringlets and a temperament
compounded of wind and phlegm.

Saturn is lazy, has yellowish eyes, lean tall body, stout teeth and rough hairs. He is of a windy temperament. Saturn governs nerves, the Sun rules bones, the Moon controls the blood, Mercury the skin, Venus the sperm, Jupiter the brain, and Mars the marrow.

NOTES.

The characteristics of the planets are given here and there is some difficulty. A question may be asked as to whether the planets really possess these characteristics, or whether they influence the persons to assume these varieties when they are under the strong control of these planetary influences. Astrology is a science which deals with men and their surroundings being directly influenced by the planets and so we are not much concerned as to what the planets may be really in their own places, but are highly concerned with their direct influences on men and their environments. We have to understand these characteristics as being possessed by men who are born under the direct influences of the several planets. Further on, we have Varaha Mihira speaking to the same effect (*Ch. V, Verse 23*) The characteristics of a man may be determined either by the lord of the navamsa rising in lagna or by the most powerful planet in the horoscope. The last portion of the stanza is also very important. Men have good or bad health. When evil planetary periods and sub-periods come in, such diseases may be predicted which arise from the Dhatus (nerves, blood, etc.), directly controlled by the evil planet or planets as the case may be. In questions affecting loss of persons or properties the rising sign and its lord furnish details for their identification. So also in questions about diseases, the lord of the navamsa rising in the lagna may determine the kind and extent of disease by which the person suffers at the time.

For a careful observer of human nature, these verses are of immense value as furnishing landmarks in the science of astrology by which they will be able to identify the people of all grades and place them under the control of the particular planet whose special characteristics, he most possesses. Thus if a man is ordinary in height, fair in complexion, royal in nature, bilious in temperament, having short hairs and honey-coloured eyes, an astrologer at once places him under the presidency of the Sun. That is, the man will be born in the lagna ruled by the Sun or occupied or aspected by him or he may be the lord of the navamsa, which rises at the time of his birth. Where a man is all bristly with stout bones and teeth generally lazy in habits, dark in complexion and prematurely old in appearance he may be placed at once under the influence of Saturn.

देवाम्बुविधिविहारकोशशयनक्षितियुत्करेशाः क्रमात्
वस्त्रं स्तूलमभुक्तभस्मिकहतं मध्यं दृढं स्फाटितम् ।
ताम्रं स्यान्मणिहेमयुक्तिरजतान्यर्काञ्च मुक्तायसी
द्रेष्काणैः शिशिरादयः शशुरुचन्द्रग्वादिषूघटत्सु वा ॥ १२ ॥

Stanza 12.— The Sun controls Devastana, the Moon watery place, Mars the fire place, Mercury the gaming place, Jupiter the treasury, Venus the bed room, and Saturn the heap of dirt.

The Sun governs rough cloth, the Moon rules new clothes, Mars controls burnt clothes, Mercury rules soaked clothes, Jupiter controls neither old nor new clothes, Venus controls strong clothes, and Saturn rules rags. Sun governs copper, Moon precious stones, Mars gold, Mercury bellmetal, etc., Jupiter silver, and when he is in his own house he governs gold, Venus pearls and Saturn governs iron, lead, etc.

Saturn controls Sisira, Venus Vasanta, Mars Grishma, Moon Varsha, Mercury Sarat, Jupiter Hemanta, and the Sun Grishma. These seasons may also be indicated by the lord of the Drekkana rising in the lagna at the time of question or consultation of lost horoscopes.

NOTES

The Sun governs all places of worship in a house or elsewhere and by this the birth place may be identified. The Moon controls bath rooms, wells, tanks and all watery places, while Mars rules over fire places (kitchens, furnaces), Mercury controls playgrounds, Jupiter rules over treasure rooms.

Venus control places of sexual enjoyment and bed-rooms, and Saturn rules over heaps of dirt and filth. These two chapters are the keys to the whole study of astrology and a careful analysis of the various planetary characteristics is needed to indicate the results, which a man enjoys under their periods and sub-periods. The different kinds of clothes governed by the planets are named here, and during their periods and sub-periods the man either wears such clothes or deals with them. The metals serve the same purpose.

The Hindu astronomers have divided the cyclic year into 6 divisions called Vasanta (Chaitra and Vaisakha)—April and May, Grishma (Jyeshta and Ashada)—June and July, Varsha (Sravana and Bhadrapada)—August and September, Sarat (Aswija and Karthika)—October and November, Hemanta (Margasira and Pushya)—December and January, and Sisira (Magha and Phalguna)—February and March. As lunar and English months differ, I have given the seasons roughly in English months. Occasionally there may be slight differences. First refer to the planet in the lagna for predicting the Ruthu or season, if there are more than one planet in the rising sign the season must be determined by the most powerful among them. If there is no planet in the lagna then the planet which governs the rising Drekkana in the lagna determines the season. Bhattotpala quotes Manitha on this subject. The commentator points out an omission of the author here in not stating the divisions of the Vedas called Sakhas (branch). He quotes from Varaha Mihira's Laghu Jataka about this. Rig Veda is governed by Guru, Athar Veda is ruled by Budha, Sama Veda is controlled by Kuja and Yejur Veda is ruled by Sukra. When plantes are powerful they give the native inclination in their own Sakas and these are also useful in remedial measures where evils indicated by planets must be averted by those mantras (incantations) which are found in the Vedas ruled by them.

त्रिदशत्रिकोणचतुरस्रसप्तमा-
न्यवलोकयन्ति चरणाभिवृद्धितः ।
रविजामरेज्यरुधिराः परे चये
क्रमशो भवन्ति किल बीक्षणेऽधिकाः ॥ १३ ॥

Stanza 13.—Planets aspect ¼, ½, ¾ and full in the 3rd and 10th, in the 5th and 9th, in the 4th and 8th and in the 7th respectively. Saturn, Mars and Jupiter have special sights and are powerful in aspecting 3rd and 10th, 4th and 8th and 5th and 9th respectively.

NOTES

These planetray aspects have been very minutely described in THE ASTROLOGICAL MAGAZINE as well as in my translation of Sarwartha Chintamani to which I refer my readers. All planets aspect the 7th house in full. But the aspecting of Sani is the most powerful in the 3rd and 10th houses from him. Mars aspects most powerfully in the 4th and 8th houses and Jupiter in the 5th and 9th houses. Their aspecting is consequently not so powerful in the 7th house. In the case of other planets 7th aspect is the best for them.

अयनक्षणवासरर्तवो मासार्द्धं च समाश्र भास्करात् ।
कटुकलबणतिक्तमिश्रिता मधुराम्लौ च कषाय इत्यपि ॥१४॥

Stanza 14.—An Ayana, a Kshana, a Wasara, a Ruthu, a Masa, an Ardha and a Sama will be the time allotted to the Sun, etc., respectively, for the fulfilment of any act or deed indicated in a question. Pungent, salt, bitter, mixture, sweet, sour and acid are the tastes attributed to the Sun, etc., respectively.

NOTES

Ravi—*Ayana*—6 months.

Chandra—*Kshana*—minute or short time.

Kuja—*Wasara*—week.

Budha—*Ruthu*—two months.

Guru—*Masa*—one month.

Sukra—*Ardha*—half of a month—a fortnight.

Sani—*Sama*—one full year.

Find the lord of the navamsa at the time of the question and also calculate how many signs he is from his navamsa. This number denotes the Ayanas, etc., according as the navamsa lord is the Sun, etc. Take an example. In Mesha at the time of question, rises the navamsa of Thula. The lord of this is Sukra. Suppose Sukra is in Meena in the navamsa. Then from Thula he is 6 signs from himself. For Sukra the time allotted is a fortnight. Therefore the success of an enterprise, if it is so, must be predicted within 6 fortnights or about 3 months from the date of question. Suppose a man is sick and a question is put to an astrologer about the patient. After proper calculations he fixes the lagna and the navamsa and by their strength, etc., he says either the man dies or lives as the case may be. The next question would be if he lives, when will he be cured, if he dies within how many months or days or hours he dies. To such questions this stanza will give a clear explanation; and so also for the recovery of stolen articles, for the return of lost or missing persons and so forth. Some astrologers say (Manitha) that the Ayanas, etc., will have to be determined by the number of the navamsa which rises at the time of question. The tastes here given are—

Ravi—pungent.

Chandra—salt.

Kuja—bitter.

Budha—mixed taste.

Guru—sweet.

Sukra—sour.

Sani—acid.

According to the strength of the planets at the time of birth will be the tastes of the man or when a powerful planet rules he will introduce his own taste to the man under his control. (See also *Bhavartha Ratnakara*, English Translation by B.V. Raman.)

जीवो जीवबुधौ सितेन्दुतनयौ व्यर्का विभौमाः क्रमा-
द्रीन्द्रकौ विकुजेन्द्रिनाथ सुहृदः केषांचिदेवं मतम् ।
{सत्योक्ते सुहृदस्त्रिकोणभवनात्स्वात्स्वान्त्यधीधर्मपाः
स्वोच्चायुःसुखपाः स्वलक्षणविधेर्नान्यैर्विराधादिति ॥ १५ ॥

Stanza 15.—According to some, Sun has Jupiter, Moon has Mercury and Jupiter, Mars has Venus and Mercury, Mercury has all except the Sun ; Jupiter has all except Mars ; Venus has all except the Sun and the Moon ; and Saturn has all except Mars, Moon and the Sun as friends. But according to Satya from the thrikona of the planet the 2nd, 12th, 5th, 9th, the lord of his exaltation, 8th and 4th lords, are friends. The rest are not friends.

NOTES

The first part of the verse contains the Matam (doctrine) of Yavaneswara.

Bhattotpala observes rightly that according to Yavaneswara there are only friends and foes but not neutrals or acquaintances. According to Satyacharya, whom the author of Brihat Jataka holds in great admiration and respect, all the various shades of friendship and enmity are clearly traceable. The commentator here gives lengthy explanations with a view to simplify matters. I may quote here one or two cases so that the rest may easily be grasped. The Sun has his Moolatrikona in Leo. The 12th from Leo is Cancer. Its lord is the Moon and as he owns only one house he becomes the best friend of the Sun. The 4th from Leo is Scorpio, and 9th is Aries : their lord is Mars. The Sun is exalted in Aries. Therefore Mars is a friend of the Sun. The 5th and 8th from Leo are Sagittarius and Pisces. Their lord is Jupiter. Therefore Jupiter is an intimate friend of the Sun. The 2nd and 11th from Leo are Virgo and Gemini. Their lord is Mercury. The 2nd rasi is mentioned but the 11th is not named, therefore Mercury is a neutral of the Sun. The 6th and 7th from Leo are Capricorn and Aquarius, and as both of those houses are not mentioned in the rule, their lord Saturn is a bitter enemy of the Sun. The 3rd and 10th from Leo are Libra and Taurus. Their lord is Venus. Both of these houses are not mentioned in the Sutra, and therefore Venus is a bitter enemy of the Sun. Take now Moon. His Moolatrikona is in Taurus. The 4th is Leo, its lord is the Sun, and therefore he is a friend of the Moon. The 2nd and 5th houses from Taurus are Gemini and Virgo. Mercury is their lord. Therefore he

is a friend of the Moon. The 7th and 12th from Taurus are
Scorpio and Aries. Their lord is Mars, 7th house is not mentioned but the 12th is named. Mars therefore is a neutral of
the Moon. The 8th and 11th from Taurus are Sagittarius and
Pisces. Their lord is Jupiter, as the 11th is not mentioned
but the 8th is named and therefore Jupiter becomes neutral
to the Moon. Moon is exalted in Taurus. The 6th from
it is Libra, its lord is Venus. The 6th is not mentioned and
therefore Venus becomes a neutral of the Moon. The 9th
and 10th houses from Taurus are Capricorn and Aquarius.
Their lord is Saturn. 10th is not named and therefore Saturn
becomes a neutral of the Moon. For Mars, Aries is Moolatrikona. The fourth from it is Cancer, with Moon as its lord.
He owns only one house and therefore Moon is the friend of
Mars. The 5th from Aries is Leo. Its lord is the Sun,
he owns only one house and as it is named the Sun becomes
the friend of Mars. Similarly find out for all the planets
from their moolathrikonas. There are planets who own two
houses while the Sun and the Moon own only one house
each. If the planet owns two houses named in the sutra
(text), then he becomes a friend. If he owns two houses
but one of them falls in the numbers named above and the
other does not, then the planet becomes a neutral. But if a
planet owns two houses and none of them is named in the
sutra then he becomes an enemy.

शत्रू मन्दसितौ समश्च शशिजो मित्राणि शेषा रवेः ।
तीक्ष्णांशुर्हिमरश्मिजश्च सुहृदौ शेषाः समाः शीतगो ।
जीवेन्दूष्णकराः कुजस्य सुहृदो ज्ञोऽरिःसिताकीं समौ
मित्रे सूर्यसितौ बुधस्य हिमगुः शत्रुः समाश्चापर ॥ १६ ॥

7

घ्वरेः सौन्यसितावरी रविसुतो मध्योऽपरे त्वन्यथा
सौन्यार्की सुहृदौ समौ कुजगुरू शुक्रस्य शेषावरी ।
शुक्रज्ञौ सुहृदौ समः सुरगुरुः सौरस्य चान्येऽरयो
येऽोक्ताः स्वत्रिकोणभादिषु पुनस्तेऽमी मया-
                        कीर्त्तिताः ॥ १७ ॥

Stanzas 16 and 17.—

PLANETS	FRIENDS	NEUTRALS	ENEMIES
Sun ...	Moon, Mars and Jupiter.	Mercury ...	Saturn & Venus.
Moon ...	Sun & Mercury ...	Mars, Jupiter, Saturn and Venus.	None.
Mars	Jupiter, Moon & Sun.	Saturn & Venus...	Mercury.
Mercury ...	Sun and Venus ...	Saturn, Mars and Jupiter.	Moon.
Jupiter ...	Sun, Moon and Mars.	Saturn ...	Mercury & Venus
Venus ...	Mercury and Saturn.	Mars & Jupiter...	Moon and Sun.
Saturn ...	Mercury & Venus	Jupiter ...	Mars, Moon and Sun.

NOTES

This is the purport of what is stated in the previous stanza, as the results of the Sutraic information contained in Verse 15. Varaha Mihira summarises the purport of Satya's doctrine in clear language here. As I have given the friendship, etc., in a tabular form further notes will be quite unnecessary.

अन्योन्यस्य धनव्ययायसहजव्यापारबन्धुस्थिता-

स्तत्काले सुहृदः स्वतुङ्गभवनेऽप्येकेऽरयस्त्वन्यथा ।

द्वैकानुक्तभपान् सुहृत्समरिपून् संचिन्त्यनैसर्गिकां-

स्तत्काले च पुनस्तु तानधिसुहृन्मित्रादिमिः कल्पयेत् ॥१८॥

Stanza 18.—The planet in the 2nd, 12th,
11th, 3rd, 10th, or 4th from any other planet at
the time of birth, becomes his temporary friend.
Some say the lord of the house in which a planet
is exalted also becomes his friend. The rest
(unnamed here) are enemies. The lords of two
houses, the lord of one house named and the
lord of house not named become friend, neutral,
and enemy, respectively. These relations
(temporary) must be taken along with the
Nisargika (permanent) relations named in the
previous stanzas and then friendship, etc., must
be finally determined.

NOTES

A few examples will determine these results and bring
home the processes easily before the understanding of the
readers. Take a horoscope.

	Moon Rahu	Birth	Saturn
Sun Jupiter Mercury	RASI Diagram		
Venus		Mars Kethu	

According to Nisargika relationship Mars is the friend of Jupiter. But according to the Tatkalika (temporary) Jupiter is in the 5th house from Mars in the horoscope given here. Thus 5th house is not named as friendly in St. 18 and therefore Jupiter becomes an enemy of Mars. Again take Jupiter. Mars is his friend in the Nisargika. But in the present diagram Mars is in the 9th house from Jupiter. 9th is not named as friendly. Therefore Mars becomes an enemy to Jupiter. The result is that according to the Nisargika, Mars and Jupiter are friends. But in this horoscope, both of them, by their unnamed positions to each other, have become enemies. In the one case both of them are friends. In the other both of them become enemies. The result is they become neutrals and much good ought not to be expected from them. Thus seven states of relationship are mentioned and they show the delicacy of mutual feelings which men entertain towards one another.

The perfections of a science are only known when we read its literature and apply its rules to the existing order of human relationships. This will be a very good lesson for the Western presumptious astrologers to learn. What do we find in their works, so much boasted of by them and pretended to have been written by the Chaldeans, whom they are so prone to worship without rhyme or reason? Are

there any grounds given for the friendship and enmity among
their works, if so they may bring forth their authorities.
Varaha Mihira borrows his ideas from the illustrious predecessors in this field of research.

The seven states of relationship are :—

1. Mitra—friend.
2. Adhi Mitra—intimate friend.
3. Sama—neutral or acquaintance.
4. Samasatru—less than neutral and better than
   enmity.
5. Satru—enemy.
6. Adhi Satru—bitter enmity.
7. Sama Mitra—better than acquaintance, but less
   than real friendship.

स्वोच्चसुहृत्स्वत्रिकोणनवांशैः स्थानबलं स्वगृहोपगतश्च ।
दिक्षु बुधाङ्गिरसौ रविभौमौ द्र्यर्यसुतः
                                     सितशीतकरौ च ॥ १९ ॥

Stanza 19.—By Swochha, Suhrut, Swa
Thrikona, Navamsa, the planets get Sthanabala.
In the East Jupiter and Mercury, in the North the
Sun and Mars, in the West Saturn, and in the
South Venus and Moon get Digbala.

NOTES

Planets have four sources of energy or bala, *viz.*, Sthana,
Dik, Chesta and Kala, and in this verse he names the first
two sources of strength or power for the planets. A planet

in exaltation, in a friendly house, in his own house, in his Thrikona, in his navamsa gets what is called Sthanabala or strength from the locality. The birth sign represents the East and Jupiter and Mercury are powerful there. The North represents the 10th house and the Sun and Mars are powerful there. The West represents the 7th house and Saturn is powerful there, and the South represents the 4th house and the Venus and the Moon are powerful there. This is called Digbala or strength arising from the direction of the planet. A general principle by which the astrological readers are to be guided is that all planets become powerless in the 7th house from that in which they are held to be mos powerful.

Aries is the house of Mars and he attains some power as he is in his own house. The seventh from it will be Libra. Here he loses that power which he is given in Aries. Mars is exalted in Capricorn. The 7th from it is Cancer. He loses in Cancer that power which he attains in Capricorn. The rules must be similarly applied with reference to all other planets. Planets in signs between their power and debility, must be given such quantity of strength, which they get by simple rule of three Thus the Sun attains his highest elevation in the 10th degree of Aries and his lowest debilitation in the 10th degree of Libra. Suppose he is in the 20th degree of Cancer. Then what strength does he get there? If the highest elevation is represented as X then the lowest debilitation will have to be represented by a zero. This he attains in 180 degrees, the distance between the 10th degree of Aries and the 10th of Libra. But the 20th degree of Cancer is the 10th degree

from his highest elevation in Aries; therefore if the
Sun had full strength in the 10th degree of Aries he will
have.

$1 - \frac{100}{180}$ of that energy = 4/9th in the 20th degree of Cancer. This holds good in all their positions and must be
carefully worked out by simple rule of three. Suppose
Jupiter is in the 2nd house from lagna in a horoscope. We
are tempted to say that he will give great wealth. That is
what astrology says. If that 2nd house becomes Cancer
and Jupiter occupies the 5th degree in it then he gives
great wealth provided he has no evil conjunctions or
aspects. But suppose he is in Capricorn occupying the
5th degree there. The wealth that he gave in Cancer,
will not find place in Capricorn and the man loses his
wealth or will be a pauper, because Jupiter has there zero
strength. But if he is in the 10th degree of Scorpio and
that happens to be the second house, then what wealth
he gives there (Scorpio) would be in proportion to that
which he gave in Cancer. The 10th of Scorpio is the 125th
degree from the 5th of Cancer. The distance from Jupiter's
greatest elevation to his lowest fall is 180 degrees. Therefore he gives $1 - \frac{125}{180}$th part of the wealth he would have
given in Cancer. The rule of proportion must be carefully
worked out. Suppose in Cancer he gave the unit result,
equivalent to say about 100 rupees. Then the wealth he
would give in the 10th degree of Scorpio would be
$(1 - \frac{125}{180}) \times 1000 = \frac{55}{180} \times 1000 = \frac{2750}{9}$ or Rs. 305 5/9. By
travelling 125 degrees from his greatest elevation he
has lost $\frac{25}{180} \times 100 = $ Rs. 694 4/9.

But the supposition here is subjected to various other calculations arising from other sources of strength and therefore ought not to be literally taken. This is given as an example to work out the method. Besides, any planet does not give a zero result at any house as he is subjected to so many other influences all of which have to be taken into consideration in determining his strength.

Similarly work out for other planets according to their falls or elevations from places of strength.

उदगयने रविशीतमयूखौ वक्रसमागमगाः परिशेषाः ।
विपुलकरा युधि चोत्तरसंस्थाश्चेष्टितवीर्ययुताः परिकल्प्यः ॥२०॥

Stanza 20.—Ravi and Chandra have chestabala in Oottarayana. The rest will have chestabala when they have Vakra or Samagama. Those who are in the North of the planetary fight, and those whose rays are bright also possess chestabala.

NOTES

Months from Capricorn to Gemini constitute Oottarayana. The Sun here attains his northern most elevation. Months from Cancer to Sagittarius inclusive compose Dakshinayana when the Sun attains his highest southernmost elevation. The Sun and the Moon are possessed of chesta (action) bala (power) during Oottarayana. This will be generally from the 13th or 14th January to about 14th or 15th of July. The Sun

attains peculiar power here and it is considered good
for doing all beneficial work. The reverse holds good in
Dakshinayana. The other planets, viz., Kuja, Budha, Guru,
Sukra and Sani, get *Chestabala* when they are retrograde
(*Vakra*) or when they are joined by Moon (*Samagama*).
Vipulakara or brightness in rays comes to these planets
before they get retrograde, and when they get retrograde, and
when they are Sigrakendras. Bhattotpala quotes *Acharya
Vishnu Chandra*, who says—that planets with the Sun
are Astha (combust), with the Moon *Samagama* (lunar
conjunction) and *Kusutadinamyuddham* and the rest of
planets with each other get into planetary fight.

*When the Moon is with the Sun he gets no Astha, and
when the Sun is with the Moon there is no Samagama. In
fact, *Astha* and *Samagama* are only states for other planets.
North should be interpreted as full of lustre and that planet
whose rays are full is to be considered as victorious in the
planetary fight. When two are more planets join, he who
has the most southern position there, who shakes, who
appears small and whose rays are lustreless, and who has
deviated from his orbital line and whose color has
changed, is said, by astrological adepts, as the planet who
has suffered defeat in the planetary conjunction. When
the reverse is the case the planet must be considered as
victorious. Pulisacharya says that Venus even when he is
in the South, may be victorious.

---

*The method of finding the numerical strength of planets and
houses and the Shadbalas have been fully elaborated in *Graha and
Bhava Balas* by B. V. Raman.

निशि शशिकुजसौराः सर्वदा ज्ञोऽद्धि चान्ये
बहुलसितगताः स्युः क्रूरसौम्याः क्रमेण ।
द्वयचयनदिवसहोरामासपैः कालवीर्यम्
शरुबुगुशुचसाध्या द्विद्वितो वीर्यवन्तः ॥ २१ ॥

Stanza 21.—The night gives Moon, Mars
and Saturn Kala Bala. Mercury has it always.
The rest are powerful during the day. Benefics
have Kalabala during the bright half of the lunar
month, while malefics get it during the dark half.
The lord of the year, of the day, of the hora, of
the masa also gets Kalabala. Sa, Ku, Bu, Gu,
Su, Cha, Ra, are respectively stronger than each
other.

NOTES

Kala means time, and Mars, Saturn and Moon are
strong during the nights. The Sun, Jupiter and Venus are
strong during the day while Mercury has this time-influence
always. The lord of the year will be the planet, whose
week day commences on the 1st of that cyclic lunar year.
During Parabhava (1906 and 1907) the lunar year commenced on a Sunday and this is controlled by the Sun. He
gets kalabala. This is to be applied to the lord of the year
during which a person is born. The lord of the day is so
well known that it requires no explanation. The *hora*
refers to that division of the time (measuring 2½ ghaties)
which rises at the time of birth. On Sunday a child is born

at 12-30 p.m. The horas for a day are 24 (*corresponding to exact English hours*) and on Sunday the first hora is governed by the Sun, the 2nd by Venus, the 3rd by Mercury, the 4th by Moon, the 5th by Saturn, the 6th by Jupiter. With the completion of the first 6 hours, 12 o'clock or noon is completed. The child is born at 12-30 p.m. The next *hora*, *i.e.*, from 12 o'clock noon to 1 o'clock p.m. the hora is governed by Mars, and as the birth has taken place in the 7th hora on that day Mars in that horoscope gets kalabala. Masadhipathi is the lord of the week day with which the lunar month commences and if it happens to be Friday, then Venus who governs it gets kalabala as the lord of that month. All these powers are called Nisargika and have permanent influences while all other sources of power named in the book must be superseded or modified by these permanent powers. For the sake of brevity Varaha Mihira uses in the last part of the verse the first letters of the planets to show their relative strength, *Sa*—stands for Sani and he is the weakest of the planets. This must be, I suppose, for doing good and certainly not for doing evil. He holds tremendous power to give evil. *Ku*—stands for Kuja and he is stronger than Sani. *Bu*—stands for Budha and he is stronger than Kuja. *Gu*—stands for Guru and he is stronger than Budha in power. *Su*—stands for Sukra and he is stronger than Guru. *Cha*—stands for Chandra and he is stronger then Sukra. *Ra*—stands for Ravi and he is the strongest of the whole lot. Bhattotpala quotes from other works the results for these four principal sources of power the planets get, *viz*, *Sthana*, *Dig*, *Chesta*, and *Kala*. Saravali says Occha planet gives much wealth. Moolatrikona planet makes a man minister or commander.

A planet in his own house gives joy, wealth, grain and happiness.

A planet in a friendly house gives reputation, courage, happiness, fixed and royal wealth.

A planet in his own navamsa makes a man well known. Varaha Mihira says also to a similar effect in his Laghu Jataka.

A planet subjected to beneficial aspects, makes a man wealthy, reputed, handsome, principal and agreeable.

If benefics in masculine signs aspect a planet the person becomes respected, learned, and if they do so in feminine signs, the person becomes frank-hearted, courageous and god-fearing. This is for Sthanabala.

Now the reader is taken to Digbala or directional strength.

Planets with Digbala take the person to their directions and get him clothes, conveyances, ornaments and happiness.

Planets with Chestabala give a man some territory or land, some respect, some money and some education. This means that they give in small quantities these beneficial results and probably not in their completeness.

Benefics in Vakra are powerful and give territories. If malefics are in Vakra they give vain travelling and useless troubles.

Victorious planet gives good health, happiness through friends and general prosperity, and lands without enemies.

Planets with nocturnal and diurnal powers give elephants, courage, lands, destruction to enemies and wealth.

The lords of the year, of the month, of the day and of the hora give good results in double proportion respectively. This means that the lord of the month gives double the good which the year-lord gives. The lord of the day gives double of what the lord of the month gives and the hora-lord gives double of the lord of the day. Planets in bright and dark halves of lunar months give destruction to enemies, precious gems, clothes, elephants, gold, females and lands, clean reputation. Those planets whose rays are full of lustre give happiness, territory and all mental desires. If the above sources of strength are possessed by benefics they give good manners, prosperity, beauty, lustre, reputation, gratefulness, faith in God and saintly persons, clothes, gems, garlands and men. But if the malefics possessed these sources of strength, they make man miserly, fond of evil work, selfish, join evil company, quarrelsome, ignorant, cruel and ungrateful. Powerful planets in masculine signs make men warlike, courageous, strong, friendless, cruel, stubborn. Powerful planets in feminine signs make men timid in war, quarrelsome and fond of water, flowers and clothes.

CHAPTER III

Viyoni Janmadhyaya

वियोनिजन्माध्यायः

क्रूरग्रहैः सुबलिभिर्विंबलैश्च सौम्यैः
क्लीबे चतुष्टयगते तदवेक्षणाद्वा ।
चन्द्रोपगद्विरसभागसमानरूपं
सत्वं वदेद्यदि भवेत्स वियोनिसंज्ञः ॥ १ ॥

Stanza 1.—When benefics are powerless and
malefics are powerful, and when impotent planets
are in *kendras*, the birth must be foretold of
objects which have resemblance to the nature of
the Dwadasamsa occupied by the Moon at the
time ; or when under similar conjunctions the
birth sign is aspected by impotent planets the
birth of *Viyonis* must be predicted.

NOTES

Varaha Mihira uses the term *Viyoni* or *Vividhayonis*
for various kinds of female sexual organs, through which
births take place other than those of the human species.
Cows, goats, birds, reptiles, insects and plants are meant
here. The author gives in this Chapter only 8 verses while
one expects an able and exhaustive treatment in an important
division of the terrestrial phenomenon like this. In Chapter II
he has shown clearly what is meant by power and weakness

for planets, and also who are masculine, and who are impotent. At the time of birth or query, the Moon must rise in some Dwadasamsa. If it is a Viyoni Rasi, then alone the birth must be predicted of some other creatures than human but not when it represents Nara Rasis or human signs. If the Dwadasamsa is Aries, occupied by the Moon at birth or question, the birth of goats, etc., must be determined. If it is Vrishabha, cows, bulls, buffaloes, etc. If it is Kataka, crabs, etc. If it is Simha, lions tigers, cats, etc. If it is Vrischika, serpents, reptiles and insects. If it is the second half of Dhanus, predict horses, asses, etc. If it is the first half of Makara, deers, etc., others, say frogs, crocodiles, etc. are also born. If it is Meena, fishes, etc. The cruel planets Ravi, Kuja, Sani, bad Mercury and weak Moon must be powerful, while Guru, Sukra, Poornachandra and good Budha must be powerless and if Saturn and Mercury (impotent planets) are in the kendras then predict Viyoni creatures. Under the above conditions if the birth is aspected by Saturn then the same result happens. These facts are fully quoted from *Saravali by* Bhattotpala, which are given here for ready reference. " Malefics must be powerful, benefics powerless, Chandra must occupy Viyoni Bhaga, Budha and Sani must be in kendras, or these must aspect the rising sign, then predict viyonis. If Chandra occupies Mesha or its amsa goats, etc. ; if Vrishabha, cows and buffaloes ; if Mithuna, human species ; if Kataka, tortoises, crabs, etc. ; if Simha, lions, tigers, etc. ; if Kanya, men ; if Thula, human species; if Vrischika, serpents, etc. ; if Dhanus, asses, horses, etc. ; if Makara, deer, peacocks, varieties of trees and grasses and if Kumbha, human species, and if Meena, fishes and other aquatic animals must be predicted. In dogs, cattle, horses, etc., the number of young ones has to be determined by the number of Dwadasamsas, which has passed in lagna at the time.

This is an important aspect of knowing whether the horoscope that is given belongs to a human being or a *Viyoni* Janma and students of Astrology would do well to test these with practical experience by noting the Dwadasamsa and the position and aspect of planets there, to cause Viyoni Janma. Many a time such test inspections come up and an astrologer has to be careful.

पापा बलिनः स्वभांगगाः पारक्ये विबलाश्च शोभनाः ।
लग्नं च वियोनिसंज्ञकं दृष्ट्वात्रापि वियोनिमादिशेत् ॥ २ ॥

Stanza 2.—If powerful malefics occupy their navamsa, if powerless benefics occupy others' navamsas and if lagna is Viyoni then Viyoni creatures must be predicted.

NOTES

The species must here also be predicted, of those creatures which are represented by the Dwadasamsa occupied by Chandra.

क्रियः शिरोमेषवगले वृषान्ये
पादांशकं पृष्ठमुरो'थ पार्श्वे ।
कुक्षिस्त्वपानांध्रयथ मेढ्रमुष्कौ
स्फिक्पुच्छमित्याह चतुष्पादाङ्गे ॥ ३ ॥

Stanza 3 —Aries represents head, Taurus face and neck, Gemini front legs, Cancer back, Leo chest, Virgo two sides, Libra belly, Scorpio anus, Sagittarius hind legs, Capricorn sexual organ and testicles, Aquarius the buttocks and upper legs, and Pisces tail.

NOTES

The author uses *chatushpada* or quadruped in the verse, but the learned commentator and others say that it is used in a general sense and includes birds and reptiles. If birds are taken then they have no front or hind legs. Wings are meant when the term front legs is used and legs to be taken when hind legs are meant. In Ch. I, verse 4, the author has given the various organs of Kalapurusha, with a view to enable the student to find out the proper development or deformity or non-growth of human organs by the directions he has given there, but here he enables the student to find out the growth, etc., of the various animal organs.

लग्नां शकाद्रहयोगेक्षणाद्धा
वर्णान्वदेद्द्रलयुक्ताद्रियोनौ ।
दृष्ट्वा समानां प्रवदेत्स्वसंख्यया
रेखां वदेत् समरसंस्थैश्च पृष्ठे ॥ ४ ॥

Stanza 4. —The color must be predicted by the birth sign, its amsa, by planets in it or by their aspects. The intensity of the color by the

powerful conjunctions or aspecting of the many
planets. By the planets in the 7th the lines or
spots on the buttocks or back must be identified.

NOTES

The planets, as well as the rasis, have already been given
different colors in Chapter II. The color of the animal or
reptile must be that which is ascribed to the birth sign or
the navamsa rising in it or by the conjunction or aspecting
of planets there.   If there are more planets than one in the
birth the most powerful of them will impart his color, while
others give traces of their lines. The same holds good with
reference to their aspects. If the navamsa is that which
rises in a lagna, whose lord conjoins or aspects it, then that
color must be prominent in the creature. The various organs
of these creatures have been sketched in Stanza 3 and the
colors of these organs will be adjusted according to the
colors of the planets occupying those signs which govern
them. Saravali says that while planets cause their colors in
the different organs of the creatures they conjoin or aspect,
the brightness of the color will depend upon their occupation of their own houses or navamsas. But when they are
in others' houses, the colors are there but greatly modified
by the strength or weakness of the planets. Jupiter gives
yellow color, Moon white, Venus variegated, Sun and Mars
red, Saturn dark, and Mercury a mixture of colors.

खगे दृगाणे बलसंयुतेन वा ग्रहेण युक्ते चरभांशकोदये ।
बुधांशके वा विहगाः स्थलाम्बुजाः
                    शनौश्चिरेन्द्रीक्षणयोगसंभवाः ॥ ५ ॥

Stanza 5.—If birth is Pakshi Drekkana, if Saturn joins or aspects it, the birth of birds must be predicted. If this Drekkana is joined or aspected by the Moon then water-birds must be predicted.

If the navamsa is movable, if a powerful planet occupies it, and if Saturn conjoins or aspects it, then the birth of birds must be predicted. If the Moon is there or aspects it, then predict the birth of water-birds. If the navamsa falls in Mercurial signs with Saturn in conjunction or aspecting, then ordinary birds, but if the Moon joins or aspects it, aquatic birds must be predicted.

NOTES

Each sign is divided into 3 equal divisions called Drekkanas. Thus we have 36 Drekkanas. These are treated of elaborately in Ch. XXVII of this work and they are to serve a number of useful purposes which will be explained later on. The 1st Drekkana of Simha, the 2nd of Mithuna, the 2nd of Thula, and the 1st of Kumbha are called Vihanga or bird Drekkanas. If one of these Drekkanas rise at the time, conjoined or aspected by Saturn or Moon, the birth of birds and aquatic birds must be predicted. The Mercurial signs are Gemini and Virgo. Several combinations are given here and the students must carefully watch them. Land birds are different from water-birds and this is shown distinctly by the influences of Saturn and the Moon. The last is a watery globe lit up by the rays of the Sun. Saravali supports this theory entirely.

होरेन्दुखरिरविर्बिर्बिंदलैस्तरूणां
तोयस्थले तरुभवां ा कृतः प्रभेदः ।
लग्रार्द्वहः स्थलजलर्क्षपतिस्तु यावां-
स्तावन्त एव तरवः स्थलतोयजाताः ॥ ६ ॥

Stanza 6.—When birth sign, Moon, Jupiter
and the Sun are powerless, the birth of trees
must be predicted. The nature of the plants
(*land or aquatic*) must be identified by the rising
navamsa, and the number of the trees, by the
number of the navamsas, the lord of the navamsa
has passed from his rising amsa in the lagna.

NOTES

The watery signs are Cancer, Meena and the latter half
of Makara. When these signs rise with watery navamsas,
then aquatic plants must be determined ; otherwise ordinary
trees. Or this may also refer to the trees growing in watery
places as opposed to trees growing in dry lands. Bhattotpala
suggests that the number of the amsas passed by the
navamsa lord may be multiplied as in the case of Ayurdaya
(*longevity, see St. 2, Ch. VII*).

अन्तः सारान् जनयति रविर्दुभगान् धूर्यसूनुः
क्षीरोपेतांस्तुहिनकिरणः कण्टकाढचांश्च भौमः ।
वागीशङ्क्रौ सफलविफलान्पुष्पवृक्षांश्च शुक्रः
स्निग्धानिन्दुः कटुककविटपान् भूमिपुत्रश्च भूयः ॥ ७ ॥

Stanza 7.–The Sun produces internally strong trees, Saturn raises ugly trees, the Moon makes milky trees, Mars produces dry plants, Mercury and Jupiter produce fruitless and fruitful trees, respectively, Venus makes flowery trees, the Moon makes bright plants, and Mars makes bitter plants.

NOTES

From the previous stanza the reader learns the nature of the tree, and from this he can identify the class to which the tree belongs and the characteristics it possesses. Jupiter makes trees, which bear fruit while Mercury produces them without fruit. When the Sun happens to be the lord of the amsa, then trees which have heartwood or which are strong inside are produced by his influence. Saturn produces plants like aloes, etc., which are not pleasing to sight or mind. The Moon gives juicy plants like sugarcane and pelluliferas. There are some plants which give only flowers but give no fruits and these are under the influence of Mercury. Venus gives rise to flowery trees like champaca, jasmine, etc

शुभोऽशुभर्क्षे रुचिरं कुभूमिजं
करोति वृक्षं विपरीतमन्यथा ।
परांशके यावति विच्युतः स्वकाद्
भवन्ति तुल्यास्तरवस्तथाविधाः ॥ ८ ॥

Stanza 8.—If a benefic occupies a bad sign, then a good tree grows in a bad place, if otherwise it is reversed. The number of trees is

determined by the amsas the lord has passed
from his.

NOTES

There are good and bad trees and so also good and bad
localities. This verse enables the astrologer to say whether
a beautiful tree grows in a dirty place or a dirty tree grows
in a grand place. Take the rising navamsa as Cancer. The
lord of it is Moon. Suppose he occupies Meena. He will
be in the 9th amsa between the rising amsa and the place
occupied by its lord. If we take Moon as in exaltation then
this intervening number may be multiplied by three and if
Jupiter occupies Cancer it may still be increased. The
astrologer has been given some principles for guidance. He
must possess capacity to examine the time, nature, circumstances, and the places and then say what the trees are and
what their number may be.

CHAPTER IV
NISHEKA OR CONSUMMATION OF MARRIAGE

निषेकाध्यायः

कुजेन्दुहेतुप्रतिमासमार्तवं गते तु पीडर्धमनुष्णदीधितौ ।
अतोऽन्यथास्थे शुभपुंग्रहेक्षिते नरेण संयोगमुपैति-
कामिनी ॥ १ ॥

Stanza 1.—Mars and the Moon are the cause
for monthly menses. When the Moon is in
anupachaya rasis the menses for conception occurs.
When the reverse is the case, and the masculine
benefics aspect, the woman gets sexual union with
man.

NOTES

This is an important chapter. Conception and the
previous states preparatory for this event are here described.
Nisheka means to soak well; that is to have nuptials
needed for conception and child-bearing. Mars represents
blood and the Moon water. These two planets in certain
conjunctions and positions cause menses and their regular
or irregular appearances. The health of the women, and
thus the health of the community, depends upon the
auspicious planetary influences exerted during the act of
sexual union. Every male or female must come through a
female, and therefore woman occupies the highest rank in
the order of creative agencies. *Upachayas* are 3rd, 6th, 10th
and 11th houses, and the rest, *viz.,* 1st, 2nd, 4th, 5th, 7th
8th, 9th and 12th are *anupachayas* or not *upachayas.* When

the Moon occupies these non-upachaya signs the menses appear. When the Moon occupies the anupachaya from the birth sign of a woman aspected by Mars, menses appear, which facilitate conception. This must not be predicted in the case of young girls, old women, women suffering from diseases and barren women. Badarayana (*Vyasa*) is clear on this point and says that only such menses must be predicted in the case of child-bearing women. Saravali explains that the Moon causes water and blood is formed out of water Mars represents fire and fire is developed by bile or heat. Such blood influenced by the bile causes menses. Such menses when well formed, give occasion for the development of the seed in the ovary. But when the Moon is in upachaya, there may be menses each month and although Mars may aspect him, there will be no conception or menses which facilitates conception. After finding out such menstrual times, the astrologer must then consider the combinations which give the woman sexual union with man. Bhattotpala explains by the term *reverse* used in the stanza as the combination affecting men who are to couple with the women. When the Moon is in *upachaya* houses from the birth sign of a man aspected by the masculine benefic Jupiter, the woman has connection with him. Badarayana clearly refers to men. But Saravali says that the Moon in the upachayas of a man's horoscope aspected by Jupiter or Moon's friends, causes union with a female and this is certain if Venus aspects him.

Manitha says, that if woman, after bathing on the 4th day, has the Moon in the *upachayas* aspected by powerful Jupiter, she will have connection with her husband, if the Sun aspects such Moon, she will have sexual union with a royal

personage, if Mars aspects. she will have a lover's embrace,
if Mercury aspects she will have a fickle-minded man, if
Venus aspects Moon she will have a handsome person, if
Saturn aspects she will have a servant to join her, and if
there are many evil planetary aspects she will behave like a
prostitute. The words used in Sanskrit are difficult to translate. The combinations may be meant for a man or a woman.
If a woman should have an evil combination to commit
adultery, she must also have the man to do that offence.
Badarayana clearly refers to males' horoscopes. Saravali
refers to *upachayas* and uses *they*. This may refer to male
or female. Even Manitha escapes in a quibbling fashion
from this difficulty. Since a great Maharishi like Vyasa is
quoted by Bhattotpala, I have to interpret it as referring to
males. The woman after bathing on the 4th day of such
menses wants some man to couple with her. Who will be
such a man is determined by the male's horoscopic conjunctions at the time.

यथास्तराशिर्मिथुनं समेति तथैव वाच्यो मिथुनप्रयोगः ।
असद्ग्रहालोकितसंयुतेऽस्ते सरोष इष्टैः सविलासहासः ॥ २ ॥

Stanza 2.—The sexual union resembles the
nature of the *Astha rasi*. If malefics conjoin or
aspect the 7th, union will be consummated under
quarrelling, if benefics join or aspect the 7th, the
sexual union will be happy.

NOTES

Astha means the 7th house from birth or query and
denotes setting.

The process or act of sexual union resembles the nature of the 7th house, from the sign rising at the time of union or query.

If the 7th is a quadruped sign, then the copulation will resemble beasts, if it is human, then it will be natural to mankind. If it represents reptiles, then sexual union will resemble their process. Man and woman may join in sexual union, but if evil planets occupy or aspect the 7th, then they will unite and do the work in a quarrelling mood. When good and evil planets occupy, the union will be under half quarrelling and pleasure mixed up. But when benefics aspect or join the 7th, the union takes place under very pleasant circumstances. Saravali supports this view and refers to a chapter in Vatsyayana called Samprayagikam.

Vatsyayana is a great Rishi who has written many works, not the least important among them being his *Kama Sutras* or full treatises on sexual union. This commonly goes under the name of *Kokkokam*. The art of love making, of sexual union and of remedies to be applied in these processes, are all admirably stated by him and show great skill in medicine, chemistry, physiology and psychology.

Books on sex-matters are not new nowadays. There are hundreds of books and Vatsyayana's *Kama Sutras* have been translated and published and boys who are in their teens have easy access to sexual knowledge. How far this has helped the present generation and how far such knowledge is useful to students to lead a more moral and better life, is a doubtful point and we have our own fears in the matter.

रवीन्दुशुक्रावनिजैः स्वभागगै-
गुरौ त्रिकोणोदयसंस्थितेऽपि वा ।
भवत्यपत्यं हि विबीजिनामिमे
करा हिमांशोर्विद्धशाभिचाफलाः ॥ ३ ॥

Stanza 3.—If Ravi, Chandra, Sukra and Kuja occupy their own navamsas, if Guru is found in lagna or thrikona, conception takes place. If this combination is present in impotent cases, it will be useless as moonlight is to a blind man.

NOTES

This combination must be present either at the time of sexual union or at the rising sign of the query. Thrikona means 5th or 9th houses from the rising sign. Ravi, Chandra, Sukra and Kuja may be in any sign, in the union lagna or Prasna Lagna but they must be in their own navamsa. If even all these planets are not in their own navamsas, if the Sun and Venus are in the upachayas of the male and have their own amsas, then conception takes place. If, in the female's horoscope, Moon and Mars occupy upachayas and join their own navamsas conception takes place. These combinations will be of no avail in the case of eunuchs and impotent men and sterile women, just as a blind man cannot enjoy moonlight. These ideas are quoted by the commentator from *Laghu Jataka* of Varaha Mihira.

दिवाकरेन्द्रोः स्मरगौ कुजार्कजौ
गदप्रदौ पुंगलयोषितोस्तदा ।
व्ययस्वगौ मृत्युकरौ युतौ तथा ।
तदेकदृष्ट्या मरणाय कल्पितौ ॥ ४ ॥

Stanza 4.—If Kuja and Arkaja occupy the seventh from Ravi and Chandra, they make the man and the woman sick respectively. If they occupy the 12th and the 2nd from Ravi and Chandra, the man and woman will meet with Mrityu respectively. If Kuja and Arkaja join Ravi and Chandra, and has one of their aspects, death may be foretold for the man and woman respectively.

NOTES

If Kuja (Mars) occupies the 7th from Ravi (Sun) then sickness happens to the man. If Arkaja (Sun's son or Saturn) occupies the 7th from the Moon, the woman gets sick.

If the Sun has Mars and Saturn in the 12th and the 2nd houses respectively the person dies in the month governed by that planet who is the stronger of the two. (*Vide* Stanza 16 for lords who govern the respective months of pregnancy). If Mars and Saturn occupy the 12th and 2nd from the Moon, death happens to the woman. If the Sun joins Mars and has the aspect of Saturn or *vice versa* the man dies, while the same conjunction and aspect with the Moon sends the woman to the grave.

दिवार्कशुक्रौ पितृमातृसंज्ञितौ शनैश्वरेन्दु निशिताद्रिपर्ययात् ।
पितृव्यमातृष्वसृसंज्ञितौ च तावथौजयुग्मर्क्षगतौ-
तयोः शुभौ ॥ ५ ॥

Stanza 5.—During the day the Sun stands for father and Venus for mother; during the night Saturn and Moon. Paternal uncles and maternal aunts are to be judged in the reverse order, and if they are in odd and even signs respectively they become beneficial to the parties concerned.

NOTES

I am afraid the brevity of Sanskrit expression, throws the translator off his head and makes him reel back for putting the ideas so finely in English which presents poor constructive capacity for expressing grand ideas. For those who are born during the day Saturn governs the paternal uncles and the Moon indicates the maternal aunts. Persons born during the night have Ravi to govern the paternal uncles and Venus the maternal aunts. For those who are born during the day, if the Sun occupies odd signs, he gives prosperity to father and if he is so situated in the night, he gives good to paternal uncles. If Venus occupies even signs for a person born during the day he gives good to mother, and during the night he gives prosperity to maternal aunts. If Saturn occupies odd signs during the night (*i e., for one who is born in the night*) he gives good to father and during the day to paternal uncles. If the Moon occupies even signs during the night he favours the mother, and during the day maternal aunts. If, in the above conjunctions of planets, they are found in the reverse order then they indicate evil to the presons named. In this stanza, the rising sign refers to the birth of the child and not to the time of conception or query.

अभिलषद्विरुदयर्धं मसद्विर्मरणमेति शुभदृष्टिमयति ।
उदयराशिसहिते च यमे स्त्री विगलितोऽडुपतिभूसुतदृष्टे ॥ ६॥

Stanza 6.—If malefics are approaching the
rising sign without beneficial aspects the woman
dies. If Saturn occupies the rising sign aspected
by Mars or weak Moon she dies.

NOTES

The rising sign here refers either to the time of conception
of the woman, or to the time of query put to the astrologer
with a view to know the results of such conception. About
the desire of the planets to go to the rising sign, some say
that malefics in the 2nd house from it have this desire of
going back to the house which is close to them.

Bhattotpala rightly condemns this strained meaning and
says that planets in the 12th house have a desire to go to the
rising sign which is their next destination and the verse
therefore means that when evil planets are in the 12th without
beneficial aspects to the rising sign, the woman dies. Gargi
clearly refers to the 12th house with malefics, and this is more
reasonable.

पापद्वयमध्यसंस्थितौ लग्नेन्दू न च सौम्यवीक्षितौ ।
युगपत्पृथगेव वा वदेन्नारीगर्भयुता विपद्यते ॥ ७ ॥

Stanza 7.—If the rising sign and the Moon are
betwixt two evil planets unaspected by benefics
jointly or separately the woman dies in pregnancy.

NOTES

The rising sign may be conjoined with Moon and thus be
between two evil planets or they may be separately placed
between two evil planets. The commentator gives clear

explanations. Take an example. If Aries rises at the time of conception, with Moon there, having Mars in the 12th and Saturn in the 2nd, the women dies in pregnancy as in No. I But suppose Aries rises and the Moon is in Virgo with Mars in Pisces and Saturn in Libra, without any planets between the rising sign and the Moon then also they may be said to be betwixt two malefics as in No. II.

Mars	Conception Moon	Saturn		Mars	Conception 1	2	3
	No. I Conception sign (Aries)				No. II Conception sign (Aries)		4
							5
						Saturn	Moon

In No. I all other planets may be placed anywhere but benefics must not be in such houses as would make them aspect the rising sign or the Moon.

Mars	Conception	Saturn	Moon	Saturn	Conception	Sun	
	No. III Conception sign (Aries)		Sun	Moon	No. IV Conception sign (Aries)		
				Mars			

In No. III we see that the rising sign as well as the Moon are betwixt malefics, so also in No. IV. Bhattotpala observes, that even if either the rising sign or the Moon singly has this evil conjunction in the 12th and 2nd, death must be predicted for the woman in pregnancy.

कूरे शशिनश्चतुर्थगे लग्नाद्वा निधनाश्रिते कुजे ।
बन्ध्वन्त्यगयोः कुजार्कयोः क्षीणेन्दौ निधनाय पूर्ववत् ॥ ८ ॥

Stanza 8.—If from the rising sign or the Moon the 4th house is joined by evil planets and Mars is in the 8th house, she suffers death. If from lagna, the 4th and 12th houses are occupied by the Sun and Mars and the Moon is weak, she suffers death as before.

NOTES

There are three cases stated here : (1) The 4th house from lagna joined by evil planets and the 8th conjoined by Mars, (2) the 4th from the Moon should have evil planets and the 8th occupied by Mars, and (3) the lagna should have the 4th occupied by Mars and the 12th by the Sun with Kshina Chandra or weak Moon. In all these cases, the female dies, as before in pregnancy.

उदयास्तगयोः कुजार्कयोर्निधनं शस्त्रकृतं वदेत्तथा ।
मासाधिपतौ निपीडिते तत्कालं स्रवणं समादिशेत् ॥ ९ ॥

Stanza 9.—If Kuja and Ravi are in the 1st and 7th respectively, death occurs to her by weapons. The abortion takes place in the month, whose lord is powerless or afflicted.

NOTES

In Stanza 16 the author gives the names of the lords of the months who govern pregnancy. Abortions or miscarriages take place in such months as those whose lords are powerless or are otherwise afflicted. Those planets are *Nipiditha* or afflicted, who are defeated in planetary fight, conjoined by Kethu or who suffer from the fall of meteors. For the Sun and the Moon they must either be eclipsed by Rahu and Kethu or be in conjunction with malefics. Mars in the lagna, and the Sun in the 7th, cause death from weapons. This may be by being killed by fighting men or by thieves or by enraged relations or by falling on dangerous weapons.

शशाङ्कलग्नोपगतैः शुभग्रहैस्त्रिकोणजायार्थसुखास्पदस्थितैः ।
तृतीयलाभर्क्षगतैश्च पापकैः सुखी तु गर्भो गुरुणा-
निरीक्षितः ॥ १० ॥

Stanza 10.—If benefics are in conjunction with lagna and Chandra, or if the 5th, 9th, 2nd, 7th, 4th and 10th houses from them are occupied by benefics or if the malefics occupy 3rd and 11th houses, and aspected by the Sun she will have a safe and happy pregnancy.

NOTES

The author says that both the rising sign as well as the Moon must have beneficial conjunctions with the aspect of the Sun, and good planets must be found located in the 5th, 9th, 2nd, 7th, 4th and 10th houses from lagna or Chandra to give good growth and keep the woman happy in her

9

pregnancy. Lagna here means, the rising sign at the time of sexual union when conception takes place, as also the lagna which rises at the time of the query on her behalf. Some writers read *Guruna* and say that the lagna and Chandra must have Jupiter's aspects. The author uses *Ravina, i.e.,* the Sun's aspect. Bhattotpala quotes Saravali which clearly mentions *Ravina, i.e.,* the Sun's aspect.

It is extremely difficult to justify such readings. What the solar ray may do to the development of the fœtus, as opposed to what the ray of Jupiter may do, I am not in a position to explain. General principles give Jovian aspect great strength but these general laws may and must be superseded by special combinations. The real influences must have been watched by Maharishis by Divya Drishti or divine vision and it is possible to think that in this particular instance the solar ray may be absolutely needed for the development of the fœtus in the womb. Saravali supports it and I have no option of my own to choose. Recent scientific books on the development of the embryo and certain scientific investigations, go to show that the influence of the Sun's ray is more powerful than the Jovian ray. Pregnant women are rarely allowed to come out during solar or lunar eclipses and those who have dared these, have been blessed with deformed children. The connection between these has not been fully established as yet.

ओजर्क्षे पुरुषांशकेषु बलिभिर्लग्नार्कगुर्बिन्दुभिः
पुंजन्म प्रवदेत्समांशकगतैर्युग्मेषु तैर्योषितः ।
गुर्वर्कौं विषमे नरं शशिसितौ वक्रश्च युग्मे स्त्रियं
द्व्यंगस्था बुधवीक्षणाच्च यमलौ कुर्वन्ति पक्षे स्वके ॥ ११ ॥

Stanza 11.—If powerful lagna, Ravi, Chandra and Guru occupy odd signs or navamsas, they cause masculine birth. If these occupy even signs and amsas, they produce feminine birth. If Guru and Ravi are found in odd signs, then a male, if Sukra, Kuja and Chandra are in even signs, a female is born. If these planets are in double-bodied signs aspected by Budha, there will be twins after the sex of the zodiacal sign.

NOTES

This may be applied to identify the sex of the children either from the nuptial time or conception time or the question time. Here the purport seems to be, that all these must be powerful, must be in odd signs and navamsas and then they produce male children. If all these are in even signs and even navamsas then they give rise to female children. The double-bodied signs are Gemini, Virgo, Sagittarius and Pisces. He has given four items namely, birth sign, Jupiter, the Sun and the Moon. Suppose two of them are found powerful, then the sex must be determined with reference to them. If two planets are powerful for male and two for female, then the sex must be determined by the most powerful among these two sets. If Jupiter and the Sun occupy odd signs, without reference to their occupation of the amsas, and are otherwise powerful, they produce male. Similarly, if the Moon, Venus and Mars are in even signs, without reference to amsas, then they produce female. There are four common signs (Dwiswabhava) of which Gemini and Sagittarius are masculine and Virgo and Pisces are feminine. If Jupiter and the Sun

join masculine navamsas, aspected by Mercury, then male
twins must be predicted. When Venus, Mars and the Moon
occupy the feminine common signs, Virgo and Pisces
aspected by Mercury, then female twins must be predicted.
If the first and the second set of conjunctions, both exist
and have Mercurial aspect, then of the twins, one will be
a male and the other will be a female. Bhattotpala
interprets the last portion of the sloka, as meaning the
planets in the double-bodied amsas, and supports this view
by quoting from Varahamihira's *Laghu Jataka*.

विहाय लग्नं विषमर्क्षंसंथः सौरोऽपि पुंजन्मकरो विलग्नात् ।
प्रोक्तग्रहाणामवलोक्य वीर्यं वाच्यः प्रसूतौ घुरुपोऽङ्गना वा ॥१२॥

Stanza 12.—If Saturn occupies odd signs
from the lagna (excepting lagna), he causes
male birth. Examine the relative strength of
the various planets and predict the birth of males
or females.

NOTES

In the previous stanza *odd* refers to signs from Aries,
etc., but now odd refers to signs from the lagna, from
which they have to be counted. If Ravi and Guru are in
Aries, and lagna and Chandra are in Gemini, and all these
are powerful, then as per directions given above, predict
the birth of a male. But if Taurus is lagna and Saturn is in
Cancer, what is the result? Taurus is, by the general
division, an even sign and so also Cancer where Saturn is.
But under this stanza, the lagna becomes an odd figure one,
because we count from it and Cancer becomes odd also,

because it is the third from lagna. But suppose Saturn occupies lagna, then it may be left out of consideration.

अन्योन्यं यदि पश्यतः शशिरवी यद्यार्किसौम्यावपि ।
वक्रो वा समगं दिनेशमसमे चन्द्रोदयौ चेत् स्थितौ ।
युग्मौजर्क्षगतावपीन्दुशशिजौ भूम्यात्मजेनेक्षितौ
पुंभागे शितलयशीतकिरणाः स्युः क्लीब्ययोगाश्च षट् ॥ १३ ॥

Stanza 13.—If the Moon and the Sun aspect mutually, if Saturn and Mercury aspect mutually; if Mars, in an odd sign, aspects the Sun in an even sign; if the Moon and lagna are in odd, and have the aspect of Mars in even sign; if the Moon is in even and Mercury in odd, and have the aspect of Mars; if Venus, lagna and the Moon are posited in masculine amsas; in all these six cases, eunuchs will be born.

NOTES

The author gives here 6 sets of combinations, in each of which, the birth of eunuchs or impotent men must be predicted. Impotency varies considerably and is difficult to define. There are some who are neither male nor female in formation and they are incapable of sexual intercourse and cannot reproduce their own species. There are others who have ordinarily developed sexual organs, but rarely they feel any inclination for want of erectile capacity. Then again there are some who by abuse in the earlier stages, become thoroughly impotent, when they grow up to manhood and come to married life. Sudden joys and sorrows and sexual union with certain women, sometimes take away these virile powers in man and he becomes thoroughly impotent. But the author here clearly means *Cliba* or Napumsaka yogas and refers apparently to born eunuchs, or persons with defective organs for these purposes. The study of astrology is the most sublime, and it makes provision for all kinds of human experience and existence. The Sun in odd and the Moon in even sign, with mutual aspects, produce a eunuch. Saturn in even and Mercury in odd sign with mutual aspects, produce a eunuch. The Sun in even and Mars in odd sign with mutual aspects, produce similar results. The other cases are clearly stated and require no further explanation. The verse is defective as some words are not used and by which the meaning becomes obscure or doubtful. Bhattotpala clears these doubts by quotations from Saravali, where the meaning is plainly expressed. If the combinations sketched in verses 11 and 12 are not present, then these combinations must be given prominence. But when they are present, they must be given preference, even if combinations sketched here may also be present. Probably if all these *yogas* are present, the potency of the male or female may be considerably affected. Eunuchs may also be found among females. They develop the external signs of womanhood, and will have a complete feminine outfit, but the sexual organ, being defective, they can neither enjoy the sexual pleasure, nor are they capable of bearing any children. A few cases are recorded in medical works, where an individual may have, both male and female organs, ordinarily developed, and it is extremely doubtful, under what planetary conjunctions, they should be placed. Astrology

may contain references even to such abnormalities. Its
pages must be carefully examined.

युग्मे चन्द्रसितौ तथौजभवने स्युर्ज्ञारजीवोदया
लग्नेन्दू नृनिरीक्षितौ च समगौ युग्मेषु वा प्राणिनः ।
कुर्युस्ते मिथुनं ग्रहोदयगतान्द्वयगांशकान् पश्यति
खांशे ड्रे त्रितयं ज्ञकांशकवशाद्युग्मं त्वमिश्रे समम् ॥ १४ ॥

Stanza 14.—If the Moon and Venus are in
signs, and if Mercury, Mars, Jupiter and lagna
are in odd signs, twins are born, of whom one
will be male and the other female. Lagna and
the Moon in even houses aspected by male planets,
produce twins, as above. If powerful Budha,
Kuja, Guru and lagna are in even signs, then
predict the same result. If planets and lagna are in
common amsas, aspected by Mercury in his amsa,
three children will be born, of whom two will
partake of the sex of the amsa occupied by
Mercury and the other of the opposite sex. If
planets, lagna and Budha are in similar amsas,
then three children of that sex will be born.

NOTES

The first two combinations are easy   The third requires
a little explanation. If all the planets (except Budha)
occupy common navamsa, aspected by Budha in his own
navamsa there will be three children, whose sex has to be
determined in the following manner. If Mercury is in the

amsa of Gemini, and aspects all planets in Sagittarius, then
the birth of two males and one female should be predicted.
But if Mercury occupies the amsa of Virgo and aspects all
the planets in Pisces, then two females and one male should
be predicted.   In the last combination, as it is stated in the
verse, I cannot make any difference in meaning.   But by
reading the invaluable commentaries of Bhattotpala and
specially his quotation from Saravali, the difference may
thus be made out.   If all the planets and lagna are
in Mithuna and Dhanus with Budha in Mithuna,
then all the three children should be males.   But if
all the planets and lagna are in Kanya and Meena
with Budha in Kanya, then the birth of three females,
should be predicted.   In the former half, the idea
seems to me to be that all the planets and lagna, must
be in Dhanus, with Mercurial aspect from Mithuna, to have
two male and one female and in Meena with Mercurial aspect from Kanya to have two female and one male births.
In the latter case all the planets and birth may be in Dhanus
and Mithuna with the aspect of Budha in the same to have
three male and in Meena and Kanya with Budha in Kanya
to have three female children.   It may be questioned that
if some planets are in Dhanus and some in Mithuna with
Budha in Mithuna, then Budha from Mithuna aspects
those in Dhanus, but not those which are in Mithuna as
they will be in conjunction with him.   So also he can aspect
planets in Meena from Kanya, but not the planets in Kanya
itself.   This question may be easily solved.   Where a planet
remains, it aspects all those who are with it as well as those
who are in its seventh house, and in such other houses,
where a planet has been given special sight.   Budha has full

aspect in the 7th house, and we are to understand the author here, as referring to full aspects and not to any fractional aspects.

धनुर्द्धरस्यान्त्यगते विलग्ने ग्रहैस्तदंशोपगतैर्बलिष्ठैः ।
ग्रेनार्किणा वीर्ययुतेन दृष्टैः सन्ति प्रभूता अपि कोशसंस्थाः ॥१५॥

Stanza 15.—If lagna is in Dhanus, or falls in that amsa, if all the planets are powerful and occupy that amsa, and if they are aspected by powerful Sani and Budha, then predict many children at one birth.

NOTES

The planets may be in any rasis but if they all occupy the navamsa of Dhanus, and are powerful, and if these planets are aspected by powerful Sani and Budha, then more than three children must be predicted. Of course here, only one possible combination is given. All the planets, (except Budha and Sani) must be found occupying Dhanur navamsa, as also the amsa of the lagna, and Sani and Budha must be found in Mithuna, to produce this yoga for many children. Bhattotpala suggests that as many as 10 children may be born at one time, provided the strength of the planets is not in any way impaired. From the quotation of the commentator, the births of more than 4 or 5 children at a time was a well established fact and he even suggests that as many as 10 children may be predicted at a time from a single conception. Now and then we read of the birth of as many as 5 or 6 children at a time in a woman, and there is nothing strange in such births although they are rare.

The examples of quintuplets of America and the birth of
seven children at a time in 1937, are well known.

कललघनांकुराखिचर्मांङ्गजचेतनताः
सितकुजजीववख्र्यचन्द्रार्किबुधाः परतः ।
उदयपचन्द्रखर्यनाथाः क्रमशो गदिता
भवन्ति शुभाशुभं च मासाधिपतेः सद्दशम् ॥ १६ ॥

Stanza 16.—*Kalala, Ghana, Ankura, Asthi,
Charma, Angaja, Chetanatha* are governed by
Sukra, Kuja, Guru, Ravi, Chandra, Sani and
Budha respectively. The lord of lagna, Chandra,
and Ravi are rulers of the next three months
respectively. The fœtal growth depends upon
the strength and weakness of the planets, who
govern the particular month.

NOTES

Kalala in Sanskrit means the united fluid of the male
and the female after sexual union and the discharge of
the sperm. When a male joins sexually with a female,
vital essence is discharged from the male organ into the
ovum of the female. At the time of discharge from the
male, the female organ receives it, but it does not enter
the ovum and hence proves useless. But after menstruation
and at the time of fecundity this discharged sperm
from the male organ, is directly received into the ovum
of the female and mixes with the discharged essence
of the female. The sperm of the man is generally
yellowish white, but the fluid discharged by the female, at

time of conception, will be reddish white. The male's
sperm is called Sukra or Sukla (white) and that of the female
is called Shonitha or blood-like fluid. As soon as they are
mixed in the ovum, fecundation begins, and what is technically called pregnancy commences. Vedas openly declare
that the sex of the child may be changed before delivery and
before the formation of the sex-organs in the foetus by
certain rituals, which are full of medical and chemical significance. A ceremony called the *Pumsavanam* is specially
recommended in the 5th month of pregnancy, and if we take
the trouble of examining the real purport of the incantations
(mantras), therein chanted, we will be struck by the vastness
of chemical and physical knowledge, the ancient Rishis
possessed, about the process of conception, and the gradual
development of the foetus in the womb. When in the union
and discharge of the essences of the male and female, if the
fluid discharged by the male is greater in quantity, a male
child is formed and if the female discharge is greater, a girl's
birth takes place, but when both fluids are equal in quantity,
the birth of a eunuch must be predicted. Charaka, one of
the greatest Ayurvedic writers in India on medicine, thus refers to *Pumsavanam* in his immortal Samhita. The learned
Sage observes, " Instructions will be laid down about those
Vedic rites, by which the sex of the child (in the womb) before
its manifestation may be changed observing that a woman has
conceived, the medicines (with proper rites) called *Pumsavanam* should be administered to her before the manifestation
of the sex of the child in the womb." (*See* Pp. 824 and 825,
English Trans. of "Charaka Samhita" by Avinash Chandra
Kaviratna). The translator says that *Pumsavanam* is performed just after the expiration of 3 months, from the date

of conception. Therefore, studying these delicacies and secrets of birth, foetal development and sex, the joining couple are strictly recommended to follow, certain regulations, laid down, by Dharmasastras, containing the essence of Vedic teachings with a view to give every advantage, for the birth of a good and healthy male child. These ceremonies are not meaningless and ought not to be neglected. During the sexual union and the first month of conception, the whole process will be under the control of Venus and hence he is also called *Sukra* or one who controls sperm and vital essence. *Ghana* (solidified) is the state of this united fluid, in the second month, governed by Mars, when it condenses and becomes thick, and takes the form of a kidney bean. *Ankura* means sprouting, or budding when all the different bodily organs, will begin to show themselves during the third month governed by Jupiter. In the fourth month *Asthi* or bones are formed and it is governed by the Sun. In the fifth month *Charma* or skin begins to gather on the body under the control of the Moon. In the sixth month hairs are formed (Angaja) under Saturn. During the seventh month consciousness (Chetanatha) or knowledge begins to develop in the foetus governed by Mercury or Budha. In Sanskrit Budha, (knowing) is derived from *Budha, bodhana* or consciousness. In the eighth month, the foetus takes through the umbilical cord, the essence of the food consumed by the mother, and this is governed by the lord of conception time (sign) In the ninth month, *udvega* or the desire to get out of the mother's womb, actuates the foetus and is governed by the Moon. During the tenth month *Prasava* or delivery takes place and this important month is governed by the Sun. In this work, the lords of the 8th, 9th and 10th

months are given, but not the state of the foetus and the
development. Horasara gives a quotation about this more
clearly, *Kalila* in the first month governed by Sukra, *Ping-
aksha bija* in the second under Kuja, *Garbhankura* in the third
by Guru, *Majja* and *Asthi* in the fourth by Ravi, *Twak,
Medha, Raktha* in the fifth by Moon, all organs in the sixth by
Sani, consciousness or *Gnanendriya* in the seventh by Budha,
hunger and thirst in the eighth by lord of conception time,
Udvega in the ninth by Moon, and *Prasuti* or delivery in the
tenth by Ravi. Bhattotpala quotes his authority from the
Laghu Jataka of Varaha Mihira. There is some slight
difference between Varaha Mihira and Yavaneswara, who
says that the first month is under the control of Mars while
the second is governed by Venus. Yavaneswara is more
to the point and gives greater details as regards the foetal
development. In the fourth month, bones, blood vessels
and nerves are formed. In the fifth *Majja* (marrow) and
skin are developed. In the sixth, blood, hair, nails and
Ekruta are formed. The last term has two significations :
(1) Some fleshy part developed in the head, and (2) some
kosha in the left side of the stomach, which has its opposite
pleha in the right side of the stomach ; when there is any
disturbance to these two, *mahodara* or dropsy results and the
man dies. In the ninth month the foetus feels the touches
which affect its mother. In the tenth month all nerves, all
blood vessels and all other necessaries in the body will be
fully developed, and the child will be born in complete
human shape. At the time of conception the strength and
weakness of planets should be specially noted, and there
will be miscarriage in that month, which is governed by an
afflicted planet. The foetus suffers much during that

month, which is governed by a lustreless, or contracted planet, but when the planet is strong and possesses its natural brilliancy, the development will be what is most desirable. Bhattotpala quotes some special points from Saravali, which deserve reproduction here, not only to give instruction to the readers of this work, but also to show, how deeply the ancients had grasped the minutest details of this important and all absorbing question of human reproduction. The bad and good Karma of the Atma (soul) during its states of previous existence, lie encumbered upon it, and join the fluid at the time of male and female union by the decrees of Karma. The child partakes of the nature of the mental composition, which rules supreme over the parties at the time of sexual union before conception. The child partakes of the nature of *Vata*, *Piththa*, or *Sleshma* or wind, bile, and phlegm which is elevated in the couple at the time of sexual union. If the Sun is powerful at the time of birth, the child takes resemblance after the father, but if the Moon is powerful, then the child resembles more its mother. A few references to grand medical ideas may be made here. Saravali, which succeeded Varaha Mihira, knows the important medical and Vedic idea, that the child is greatly influenced, by the mental attitude of the joining couple at the time of conception. The Karma theory is directly supported by astrological works. The Atma encumbered with its good and evil acts in the previous births or states of existence, will be driven, as it were, by invisible energies, by the decrees of Karma, and will be attracted to such male and female and such environments, as are suitable to its orders, and the results which it has to endure, during the present state of existence. In short notes, such as these, a colossal

question like that of Karma, and its decrees cannot be raised
and satisfactorily solved.   I refer my readers to some of my
own contributions, in THE ASTROLOGICAL MAGAZINE, Vol. IX,
for fuller information on these vital points. (*Vide*
ASTROLOGICAL MAGAZINE, January 1945, p. 33).   The idea
of fixing a very auspicious time for the first contact of the
couple in nuptials, shows the anxiety of the earlier astrological writers to afford good opportunities for the birth and
breeding of healthy, well behaved, intelligent and long lived
children. The time was not confined to only the first
occasion. Even on ordinary days, when the couple felt a
desire to have sexual correspondence, they were religiously
enjoined to avoid connection on all such evil lunar days and
week days as were governed by malefic planets. The lagna
for sexual contact should be clean in the 8th house and good
planets must aspect it or occupy other favourable positions.
New Moon days, evil constellations and unsuitable times are
to be scrupulously avoided. When carefully examined, these
show that the sole object of the Maharishis in laying down
such injunctions was to minimise the chances of producing
undesirable and deformed children, and afford every possible
chance for improving the physical and mental breed of the
future generations.

त्रिकोणगे ज्ञे विबलैस्ततोपरै मुखांत्रिहस्ताद्विगुणस्तदा भवेत् ।
अवाग्गवीन्द ।वशुमैर्भसान्निघनैः शुभेक्षितैश्चेत्कुरुते-
गिरं चिरात् ॥ १७ ॥

Stanza 17.—If Budha is in thrikona, and
other planets are powerless, then the child will
have two faces, four hands, and four legs with one

face. If the Moon is in Taurus, and evil planets are in Ruksha Sandhis, predict a dumb child. If, in this conjunction, the Moon has beneficial aspect, the child begins to speak very late in life.

NOTES

If Budha occupies 5th and 9th with powerless planets in other houses, a double body joined in stomach will be the result. Some say that Budha must be in Moolathrikona, but this view is directly negatived by the authoritative quotation from Maharshi Gargi. If Chandra is in Vrisha-bha and evil planets occupy the last navamsas of Kataka, Vrischika and Meena, then a dumb child is produced, but when Chandra is subjected to beneficial aspects, the child may begin to speak after some years. The planets may be in one or two or three last navamsas of the signs stated above. Gargi says, that if the two sets of planets, evil and good, aspect Moon and if benefics are stronger than malefics, the speech comes after a long time, but if malefics are stronger than benefics, the child becomes dumb. Ruksha Sandhis are the last navamsas of Kataka, Vrischika and Meena, and this is clearly stated so by Gargi.

सौम्यर्क्षांशे रविजरुधिरौ चेत्सदन्तोऽत्र जातः
कुब्जः स्वर्क्षे शशिनि तनुगे मन्दमाहेयदृष्टे ।
पङ्गुर्मीने यमशशिकुजैर्वीक्षिते लग्नसंस्थे ।
सन्धौ पापे शशिनि च जडः स्यान्नचेत्सौम्यदृष्टः ॥९८॥

Stanza 18.—If Sani and Kuja occupy Budha's houses or navamsas, the child will be born with teeth. If Kataka is lagna with Chandra in it, having the aspects of Sani and Kuja, the child will be dwarf. If Meena becomes lagna aspected by Sani, Chandra and Kuja, the child becomes a cripple. If the Rasi Sandhis are occupied by malefics and the Moon, the child will be deaf. In all these cases there must be no beneficial aspects.

NOTES

There are some children who are born defective or with abnormal developments. Children generally get their teeth after some months. But here is a combination which brings in a child with teeth already present at the time of birth. Hyder from a tradition current at Budicota his birth place is said to have been born with all the teeth and his

			Rahu
	HYDER'S RASI		
Sukra			
Kethu	Ravi Chandra Budha Guru Kuja Sani	Birth	

mother could not bear to look at the child. The above noted horoscope is the rasi diagram of Hyder. Budha's rasis or amsas are Mithuna and Kanya. If these are

10

occupied by Sani and Kuja, then this abnormal development occurs. Some are of opinion that both Sani and
Kuja must be in Mithuna as well as in that navamsa or
in Kanya and also in that navamsa. The full aspects of
the benefics negative these results while partial beneficial
aspects may produce traces of such defects or deformities.
When there are no beneficial aspects these results will be
fully realised. Geographical researches have established
that there are some nations of dwarfs, the tallest of whom
will be about 18 inches in height while the shortest is under
a foot. In Central Africa, such a nation has been recently
discovered. Their women, although not higher than 16
inches, are graceful, handsome, attractive and well proportioned and they are intelligent and advanced fairly in
the arts of civilised life.

सौरशशाङ्कदिवाकरदृष्टे वामनको मकरान्त्यविलग्ने ।
धीनवमोदयगैश्च दगाणैः पापयुतैर्भुजाङ्घ्रिशिराः स्यात् ॥१९॥

Stanza 19.—If the last navamsa of Makara
is lagna aspected by Sani, Chandra and Ravi
then a dwarf is born. If malefics occupy the 5th,
9th and 1st drekkanas, handless, feetless and
headless child respectively must be predicted.

NOTES

The last navamsa of Makara is Kanya and if this
happens to be the birth and Saturn, the Sun and the Moon
aspect it, the birth of a dwarf will be the result. The second
half of this verse is the subject of some discussions by
Bhattotpala.

Referring to these drekkanas there are some who say that as the 5th house is the 2nd drekkana, and if that forms the lagna, occupied by a malefic and aspected by Sani, Chandra and Ravi, the child will have no arms. As the 9th is the 3rd drekkana, and similar combinations as above are present the child will have no feet, and as the 1st drekkana is the first itself and similar conjunctions are present the child will be headless. This last may be simply a lump of round flesh and may live for a short time. *Vide* Kabhandu's description in the Ramayana. In the division of drekkanas we have seen that the lords of the drekkanas are (1) the lord of the house itself, (2) the lord of the 5th, and (3) the lord of the 9th. Reference is made in the light of this information. The malefic refers to Mars as the other two evil planets the Sun and Saturn are required to aspect the lagna. Some other astrologers even go to the length of simply saying that if these drekkanas are occupied by evil planets, the results may be predicted even when, unaspected by Saturn, the Sun and the Moon. Some say that the word *respectively* need not be considered at all as any one of these deformities may be predicted by any one of these combinations sketched above. Others say that if lagna falls in the first drekkana then the fifth will be the first division in the fifth from it or the second drekkana and the first in the 9th will be the first in the 3rd drekkana. If every one of these 3 divisions is occupied by a malefic then deformities must be predicted. Bhattotpala explains his own views thus. If, at the time of conception, drekkana in the fifth house is occupied by Kuja and aspected by Sani, Chandra and Ravi, then armless person will be born. If the drekkana which rises in the 9th house is occupied by Kuja having similar aspects by Sani, Chandra and Ravi, then the child will have no feet. If the drekkana which rises in the lagna is occupied by Kuja aspected by Sani, Chandra and Ravi then predict a child without a head. This is supported by Bhagavan Gargi, and the author of Saravali, both of whom are simple and clear on this point.

रविशशियुते सिंहे लग्ने कुजार्किनिरीक्षिते
नयनरहितः सौम्यासौम्यैः सबुद्धदलोचनः ।
व्ययगृहगतश्चन्द्रो वामं हिनस्त्यपरं रवि-
र्ने शुभगदिता योगा याप्या भवन्ति शुभेक्षिताः ॥ २० ॥

Stanza 20.—If Leo is birth occupied by the Sun and the Moon, aspected by Mars and Saturn the child will be blind. If in the above combination there is also beneficial aspect the vision will be dim. The Moon in the 12th house causes loss to the left eye and the Sun there causes loss to the right eye. Beneficial aspects give some relief in these combinations.

NOTES

Ravi and Chandra must be in Simha, the birth sign, having the evil aspects of Sani and Kuja to produce blindness. Blindness is of many sorts. A child may be born perfectly blind or it may have dim sight and then lose it later on or it may have good sight early in life, and lose it by accident, small-pox or other disease. Beneficial aspects to lagna, Chandra and Ravi there, will greatly modify this

blindness and a child will be born with Budbudaksha or
some defective vision in the sight.   Budbudaksha means a
cataract eye or what in ordinary language is called a flower
in the eye.   If the Sun is in Leo, as birth and has
aspects of Mars and Saturn, the child will have the right
eye blind.   If the Moon is there and has these evil aspects,
the left eye will become blind.   If one of the two planets,
the Sun or the Moon, is in birth which is Leo, then the
blindness will be partial.   In these and the previous
recorded combinations, care should be taken to gauge the
intensity of the misfortune by the strength of the evil
planets and the absence of the beneficial influences.   When
evil influences are attributed to aspects or malefics, their
conjunctions will, of course, intensify the evil, although
this has not been hinted at by the diligent commentator.
Suppose Simha is the lagna and Ravi, Chandra, Kuja and
Sani are also there without any beneficial aspects or conjunctions.   What would be the result? I believe that the
blindness will be there, though no mention of this is made
in the commentaries. Although this is my view it is possible
to imagine that results predicted from aspects of planets may
not be produced by their conjunctions and those results which
they give in conjunction may not be attributed to their aspects. These are difficult astrological points whose solution
can only be offered when we have any authority in the ancient
works. Those who base certain inferences on their personal
experiences will be doing very little credit by placing too
much confidence on such knowledge and twisting the plain
texts of ancient astrological literature to support their
limited experience and pride.   Till now Varahamihira refers
to the time of conception and birth therefore refers to the

birth of the child in the mother's womb or the time of conception when the seed enters the womb. Vatsyayana says an intelligent lady generally knows and feels it. Very few care to know it.

तत्कालमिन्दुसहितो द्विरसांशको य-
स्तुल्यराशिसहिते पुरतः शशाङ्के ।
यावानुदेति दिनरात्रिसमानभाग-
स्तावद्धृते दिननिशोः प्रवदन्ति जन्म ॥ २१ ॥

Stanza 21.—The birth of a child takes place in the sign occupied by the Moon, which is represented by the number, in which Dwadasamsa, the Moon is fixed at the time. The day or the night and the ghaties of the birth time must be known by the number of the ghaties at the time of the question and the nature of the sign whether diurnal or nocturnal.

NOTES

From here either actual birth or question time is discussed. The wording in the original Sanskrit is simply untranslatable. The author subjects his verse to so many *omissions* and *understandings* that in a poorly constructed language like English, it is almost impossible to reproduce the brevity of expression stated in the original Sanskrit. I shall however explain the verse in clear and simple language by examples. It is desired to know when a child will be born after conception, either by reference to that event or to a query or to the actual birth. The directions

given here explain the time and the division of the day or
the night. The Moon occupies some sign or rasi at the
time of conception, query or birth. Find which Dwadasamsa the Moon occupies and then count from there by that
number of the Dwadasamsa and find out what sign it will
be. The birth takes place in the tenth month under
normal conditions, when that sign is occupied by the
Moon. Take Aries as the rasi for conception with the
Moon in the 9th house Sagittarius and in its tenth Dwadasamsa. The tenth Dwadasamsa in Sagittarius will be
Virgo or Kanya. The birth takes place in the tenth month
of conception when the Moon occupies the tenth from
Virgo, *i.e.*, Gemini. The commentator wisely restricts the
time of birth to be predicted to the tenth month, as students
in their ignorance of higher knowledge of astrology may
predict the birth in any of the other months. As Chandra
moves in a rasi in 2¼ days he will be found in each of
the rasis every month. Take another example as the
question is very important. Suppose the conception takes
place in Libra when the Moon is in Gemini in its fifth
Dwadasamsa. The fifth Dwadasamsa of Gemini is the fifth
house from it, namely, Libra. The birth of the child must
be predicted in the *10th month*, when the Moon moves in
Aquarius which is the fifth from Libra, the Dwadasamsa
occupied by the Moon at the time of conception. It
means that when the Moon moves in the constellations of
Dhanishta (last two quarters), Satabhisha (four quarters)
and Purvabhadra (three quarters) birth takes place. There is
some difference here between Saravali and Varaha Mihira.
And Bhattotpala wisely quotes Bhagavan Gargi in the
explanation above offered and considers that as the best

interpretation. Saravali says thus. " The Moon is found in
some Dwadasamsa at conception time. Take the number
of the Dwadasamsa and count it from the first sign Aries,
and say that the child will be born in the 10th month on
that day when the Moon occupies that sign." This seems to
make some difference. Take the above example. The
Moon was found in the 5th Dwadasamsa of Gemini, the
birth happens at that time in the 10th month, when the
Moon moves in Leo, for that is the 5th sign counted from
Aries the number to the Dwadasamsa occupied by the
Moon at the conception time. Bhattotpala here suggests a
way to find out the constellation, about which the author is
quite silent in the verse. The Moon moves $2\frac{1}{4}$ days in a
rasi and therefore this verse enables one, when rightly
understood, to fix the time of birth within $2\frac{1}{4}$ days. Each
rasi contains 30 divisions called bhagas or degrees and
each of these bhagas again is divided into 60 ghaties or
nadis. Thus for a rasi we get $30 \times 60 = 1800$ kalas or
ghaties. When the whole rasi is represented by 1800 kalas
and also by $2\frac{1}{4}$ constellations, we get by division 800 kalas
for each star. 1800 kalas represent the full rasi and this
divided by 12 gives 150 kalas for each Dwadasamsa. Thus
150 kalas make one Dwadasamsa. In the above example
Chandra is found in the 5th Dwadasamsa. He will be
moving in that part of the zodiac which is represented by
kalas 600 to 750 in Mithuna. This must be divided by 800
kalas, the value of a star. To get one star complete we
have still to pass 50 kalas more. Therefore the Moon is
within the first constellation which composes Gemini. But
Gemini is composed of the last two padams of Mrigasira,
the four padams of Aridra and the 3 padams of Punarvasu

or 9 padams in all.   The Moon therefore is within the first
800 kalas or within the 2nd padam of Aridra.   But the
kalas passed by the Moon is 600 and say he is in the 700th
kala.   Thus as each Nakshatrapadam gets 200 kalas he
has passed 3 padams and is in the 4th padam.   He is just
in half of the 2nd padam of Aridra or the birth of the
child takes place when Aridra has passed 22½ ghatikas on
that particular day.   If the conception or query sign is
nocturnal the time of birth will be night, if it is diurnal,
it will be day and the ghati will be the time of the ghaties
passed over by the rising sign above referred to.   But this
point will also be easily found by the measure of the
constellation explained   by Bhattotpala.   In the first
example given above, the lagna is Mesha, and it is a
nocturnal sign. (*See* St. 10, Ch. I). Suppose the month
was the 1st of Kanya.   The first degree of Meena sees the
sunset on that day.   Suppose 2 ghaties of Mesha elapsed
before the rise of conception time.   Then we have four of
Meena and two of Mesha=6 ghaties.   The birth will take
place at 6 ghaties after sunset on that day when the Moon
is moving in Kanya during the tenth month of conception.
Bhattotpala omits one question.   The author uses *Tatkala*
in the verse and this is explained by the commentator as
referring to (1) Prasnakala (question time).   The above
explanation will be consistent if the data is conception
time, for then we may wait for the tenth month and find
out the movement of the Moon and fix the birth, etc.   But
how to regulate the 10th month with reference to question
time.   Suppose the woman is full nine months pregnant
and the question, when she would deliver, is put to the
astrologer without giving him any reference to the time of

sexual union or conception; how should the astrologer
proceed? This vital question wants solution. In St. 2 of
this Chapter, Varaha Mihira explains combinations at query
to find out the nature of the sexual union. The astrologer
must proceed safely as follows. Either find out the fact
of conception and its proper development (1) by the
combinations of planets at the time of query and predict
from that knowledge the birth of the child in the tenth
month when the Moon is moving in a particular sign, or
(2) by the nature of the conjunctions of the planets at the
time of question in the light thrown in Ch. II, St. 14. This
enables the astrologer, to say when the child will be born.
Manitha says clearly to this effect—" the happening of
a result has to be fixed with reference to such time as is
indicated by the lord of navamsa rising in the question
time, multiplied by that number which the navamsa has
moved in that sign ". Take an example. Suppose Leo is
the sign and the 7th navamsa rises in it. The lord of the
7th navamsa in Leo is the lord of Libra, viz., Venus. He
is given a fortnight as his time. But the navamsa has
moved to the 7th division; therefore this (fortnight) or
more correctly paksha must be multiplied by 7, and it
gives us 3½ months. The astrologer may say that the child
will be born after 3½ months.

उदयति मृदुभांशे सप्तमस्थे च मन्दे
यदि भवति निषेकः क्षतिरब्दत्रयेण ।
शशिनि तु विधिरेषद्वादशेऽब्दे प्रकुर्या-
न्निगदितमिह चिन्त्यं क्षतिकालेऽपि युक्त्या ॥ २२ ॥

Stanza 22.—If Makara or Kumbha navamsa rises at the time of conception, aspected by Sani, the child will be born after 4 years. If Kata-kamsa rises at the time of conception, aspected by Chandra, then the birth occurs after 12 years of pregnancy. The details in this chapter must be carefully understood and applied with sense and judgment.

NOTES

Pregnancy is supposed to last generally for 9 months after conception and then usually in the 10th month the child is born. But there are certain cases (gajagarbham) in which pregnancy is supposed to last for 3 years, and even for 12 long years. There are of course special and peculiar cases which must have happened in the world to make the astrological adepts to record these combinations. The elephants have the same age as men but their pregnancy lasts for 3 years. A caution is given to students here both by the author and his illustrious commentator. When questions are asked and the combinations denote conditions inconsistent with the events, the man should study the problem well and answer it. The astrologer must be careful, prudent and well versed in the nature of times, conditions, classes and the circumstances before he ventures into the fields of future predictions. Is fact a high intellectual development, practice in yoga and excellent mathematical and predictive skill, must be combined in a man to make him a successful astrologer. Blind fools, who study only a few stanzas and whose general education is most ordinary, can never hope to become successful astrologers, in whose prediction people can place implicit confidence. (*Vide Life of Varahamihira* by me). Bhattotpala thus summarises his advice. Such events as defects in organs, parents, uncles and aunts must be predicted from birth combination. That which is inconsistent must not be predicted. For instance, miscarriage ought not to be predicted in a case where a child is born and so forth. The three methods of gauging the influence of time should be carefully compared and such of the results which are reasonable should be predicted. The three methods are birth time, conception time and question time.

BHATTOTPALA
(His work and age)

Bhattotpala calls himself us Utpala, in his commentaries of Varahamihira's Brihat Samhita, and as Bhattotpala in his Prasna work entitled *Prasna Gnyana*. It is not clear to what country he belonged, but it seems certain that he belonged to North India. He has written commentaries on all the works of Varahamihira excepting his Pancha Siddhantika and also for Shat Panchashat by Varahamihira's son *Prithuyasas*. He seems to have composed an original work on *Prasna* (query) called *Prasna Gnyana* and also completed the missing or unfinished portions of Saravali.

There is a stanza which runs to this effect and which is well-known to the learned in astrology. It says :—The work *Saravali*, which was largely used by the Chinese and which remained unfinished for one hundred years, was taken up by Bhattotpala and completed. Some strong colour is given to this passage by Bhattotpala quoting largely from

Saravāli in support of his interpretations of the texts in *Brihat Jataka*. It is difficult to say that Bhattotpala did not write commentaries on the Pancha Siddhantika of Varahamihira. Bhattotpala has also written commentaries on *Khanda Khadya* of Brahma Gupta, one of the famous earlier astrological writers. The following are the works of Varahamihira :—

1. Brihat Samhita.
2. Samasa Samhita.
3. Brihat Jataka.
4. Laghu Jataka.
5. Pancha Siddhantika.
6. Vivaha Patala.
7. Yoga Yatra.

Commentaries by Bhattotpala for all these (except Pancha Siddhantika) are available.

There are also two works, named by Bhattotpala, as having been written by Varahamihira, entitled Brihat Yatra and Laghu Yatra. Whether these are the same as Yoga Yatra or different, it is not easy to say, because no copies of such separate works are yet before the public.

As regards the age during which this illustrious commentator lived, the readers are referred to Pp. 135 of THE ASTROLOGICAL MAGAZINE, Vol. X, Feb. issue. There the suggestion seems to be a little wide off the mark. The writer refers to Salivahana and converts 888 years which Bhattotpala gives for the completion of his invaluable commentaries on Brihat Jataka, and also suggests that it may refer to Samvat or Vikramarka Saka. There is no necessity to convert them into Salivahana at all, as Bhattotpala clearly refers the Saka to Vikramaditya and not to Salivahana.

In Ch. VIII, St. 20 of Brihat Samhita Bhattotpala converts the Saka years from the era established by Vikramaditya after his conquest of Sakas or Mlechas. Thus he finished his commentaries of *Brihat Jataka* in April 832, A.D. Therefore it is clear that Vikrama Saka is meant and not Salivahana. The commentaries of Bhattotpala are always to the point and are expressed in clear and simple language. His power of quotation is hardly surpassed by any other writer, on astrology and indirectly he has conferred a great boon on the succeeding generations, by handing over to them fragments of astrological works many of which now seem to have been either lost or have not yet been brought before the public. His scholarship and reading must have been simply colossal, to have enabled him to deal with the original texts in the masterly way in which he has explained their hidden truths. We cannot think there is another commentator in the whole field of astrological literature, who could equal Bhattotpala in the valuable services he has rendered to the public and so long as the astrological literature stands in the world, his name is likely to be cherished with affection and reverence. Learned as Varahamihira is, it is certain that he would not have been so well-known to the public as he is now, but for the commentaries of Bhattotpala. Throughout the length and breadth of India, and now by English translations, in other countries, Varahamihira's works have been popularised by these commentaries, and placed within the reach of ordinary intellects. A splendid and authoritative work on Varahamihira and his times by the present translator is also available and therein he has clearly and authoritatively shown how, why and when Varahamihira, who was called merely Mihira, became

' Varahamihira '. Varahamihira lived during the I Century B.C. in the Court of Vikramaditya. Kalidasa's Jyotirvida-bharanam quotes the following stanza :

" 1. Dhanvantari, 2. Kshapanaka, 3. Amarasimha, 4. Bhetalabatta, 5. Sankha, 6. Ghatakarpura, 7. Kalidasa, 8. Khyato Varahamihira, Nripatesabhayam Ratnanivy, 9. Vararuchir Nava Vikramasya " meaning that these nine literary gems graced the Court of Vikramaditya of whom Varaha Mihira alone had the epithet Khyato or famous.

CHAPTER V

JANMA KALA LAKSHANA

जन्मकाललक्षणाध्यायः

(Peculiarities of Birth)

पितुर्जातः परोक्षस्य लग्नमिन्दावपश्यति ।
विदेशस्थस्य चरमे मध्यान्द्दष्टे दिवाकरे ॥ १ ॥

Stanza 1.—If birth sign is unaspected by the
Moon, father will be absent at the birth. If the
Sun occupies a movable sign (*pathitha*) from the
10th, the father will be away in a foreign country
at the birth of child.

NOTES

Pathitha (*fallen*) is explained by Bhattotpala as a fall
for the Sun, on either side of the 10th house upto two
houses, *i.e.,* when the Sun is in the 11th or 12th he will
be fallen from the 10th in front and when he is in the 9th
8th he will be fallen in the rear. He must occupy one
of these which should be a movable sign to keep the father
away in a foreign country. If the Sun is in a fixed sign the
father will be in the country but absent from home and if he
is in a common sign, the father will be on his return from a
foreign place. If birth is not aspected by the Moon and the
Sun is in the signs as stated above, the child will be born
when the father is away. Saravali runs to the same tune.

उदयस्थेऽपि वा मन्दे कुजे वास्तं समागते ।
स्थिते वान्तः क्षपानाथे शशाङ्कसुतशुक्रयोः ॥ २ ॥

Stanza 2.—If Saturn occupies lagna or if Mars is in the 7th or if the Moon is between Mercury and Venus, the father will be absent at the birth of the child.

NOTES

Three combinations are given here to show the absence of the father at the time of birth. He may be in his own country or in a foreign country or may be on his way back. Venus and Mercury may be on both sides of the Moon, in the same sign, or they may be in the next house on either side of the Moon, *i.e.*, 2nd or 12th house. Venus and Mercury follow close upon the movements of the Sun, and have constant combusts, risings and settings. This is specially so with Mercury. Therefore this conjunction can only take place on Amavasya (New Moon) or a day or two on either side of it. Between the Moon and Venus and Mercury on either side there must be no other planet. In these 3 combinations, the Moon should not aspect lagna. Laghu Jataka also quotes the same combination, *viz.*, Moon between Venus and Mercury and Mars in the 7th.

शशाङ्के पापलग्ने वा वृश्चिकेशत्रिभागगे ।
शुभैः स्वायस्थितैर्जातः सर्पस्तद्वेष्टितोऽपि वा ॥ ३ ॥

Stanza 3.—If the Moon occupies Mars drekkana and benefics are in the 2nd and 11th houses, predict a serpent's birth. If an evil sign falls in Kuja's drekkana and has benefics in the 2nd and the 11th, the child will be bound by a serpent-like bandage.

11

NOTES

The drekkanas of Mars are the 1st of Aries, the 2nd of Cancer, the 3rd of Leo, the 1st of Scorpio, the 2nd of Sagittarius and the 3rd of Pisces. In the 2nd half, the evil sign referred to which possesses a Kuja drekkana will be one of Aries, three of Leo and one of Scorpio. Then all the benefics must occupy 2nd and 11th houses. Gargi supports this view. It strikes me as most strange that while Chandra occupies a Kuja drekkana and has benefics in the 2nd and 11th houses, he produces a serpent while an evil sign rising in Kuja drekkana with similar beneficial combinations produces a child bound with a serpent-like appendage.

The intensity of evil appears to me to be greater in the 2nd than in the first set of combination. But the text is plain and it is supported by Maharishi Gargi and also by Saravali. Readers would do well to test a few horoscopes, before venturing on such predictions, since such births are rare. A case of a serpent's birth in the author's own family has been handed over by tradition and even now in the village once a year, a serpent worship is being done by some member of the family who is settled in the village and every scion of the family has a child named after Tirupathi Venkataramana, who is called Seshadri Vasa or Lord of the Serpent's hill.

चतुष्पादगते भानौ शेषैर्वीर्यसमन्वितैः ।
द्वितनुस्थैश्च यमलौ भवतः कोशवेष्टितौ ॥ ४ ॥

Stanza 4.—If the Sun occupies a quadruped sign and if other powerful planets occupy common

signs, twins will be born covered with a common
hood.

NOTES

The quadruped signs are Mesha, Vrishabha, Simha, the
2nd of Dhanus and the first half of Makara. The twins will
be enclosed in one common bag.

छागे सिंहे वृषे लग्ने तत्स्थे सौरेऽथवा कुजे ।

राश्यंशसद्दशे गात्रे जायते नालवेष्टितः ॥ ५ ॥

Stanza 5.—If Mesha, Simha or Vrishabha
falls as lagna, occupied by Sani or Kuja, the child
will be born with a cowl or cord in that organ
which is represented by the rising navamsa.

NOTES

In Chapter I, Stanza 4, the different organs of *Kalapurusha* have been stated. The child born will have a cord
or nerve-like appendage in that organ which is represented
by the navamsa rising at the time of birth. For instance
take Aries as the birth and the navamsa of Leo rises at the
time. Leo represents stomach or belly of Kalapurusha
and the child will have Nala (Nadi) about the belly.

न लग्नमिन्दुं च गुरुर्निरीक्षते न वा शशाङ्क रविणा समागतम् ।

सपापकोऽर्केण युतोऽथवा शशी परेण जातं प्रवदन्ति-

निश्चयात् ॥ ६ ॥

Stanza 6.—If Jupiter does not aspect birth and
Moon, or if he does not aspect the Sun, in con-

junction with the Moon, if the Moon with a malefic combines with the Sun then say certainly the child is born to another person or of adultery.

NOTES

This is a very important stanza where the question of the mother's character arises and the students should not hastily run away with misinterpretations and thus throw blame upon the character of innocent women. Every astrologer must, in the first place, confine himself to predict such events as are particularly referred to by the consulter. Even if, from stupidity or neglect the native puts a senseless or ungentlemanly question, the astrologer must be careful and must decline to answer it in case it is likely to disturb the harmony of the person's life or that of his family or relations. Suppose a man in his youthful vagary and inexperience asks an astrologer whether his wife is adulterous. The astrologer should decline to answer such a silly question and give him better advice. Similarly many horoscopes show, want of chastity on the part of their mothers, wives or sisters. Although the astrologer first notices this point he must be reticent on this head and omit the point altogether unless he has very grave necessity to express his views upon such delicate question as the chastity of females or the morality of males. The world is a world of great diversities, of tastes, morals and position, whether public or private. Prostitution is so strongly rooted in the nature of human beings that it is found in all countries, in all nations, during all times and in all sects and families where the number of members assumes a respectable figure. " It is a mere absurdity to assert " says Dr. W. Sanger " that prostitution can ever be eradicated. Strenuous and well-directed efforts for this purpose have been made at different times. The whole power of the Church (religious and political) has been in vain directed against it. Nature defied the mandates of the clergy and the threatened punishment of an after life were futile, to deter men from seeking and women from granting, sinful pleasures in this world. Monarchs, victorious in the field and unsurpassed in the council chamber, have bent all their energies of will and brought all the aids of power to crush it, but before these the vice has not quailed. The guilty women have been banished, scourged, branded, executed, their partners have been subjected to the same punishments, held up to public opinions as immoral, denuded of their civil rights, have seen their offences visited upon their families, have been led to the stake, the gibbet and the block, and still prostitution exists. The teachings of morality and virtue have been powerless here. In some cases they restrain individuals, but upon the aggregate they are inoperative. The researches of sciences have been unheeded. They have traced the physical results of vice and have foreshadowed its course. They have demonstrated that the suffering parents of their generation will bequeath to their posterity a heritage of the ruined powers, that the malady which their illicit pleasure communicates, is destructive to the hopes of man, that the human frame is perceptibly and regularly deteriorating by the operation of this poison and have shown that even the desire for health and long life, one of the most powerful motives that ever influences a human being, has been of no avail to stem the torrent ". (*See* Pp. 19 and 20. *The History of Prostitution by William W. Sanger, M.D., New York, 1859 A.D.*)

Therefore many horoscopes give room for such combinations as would show adultery on the part of men and women and the astrologer has no option, but to be silent on this point.   Further on, the character of the wife comes in, and the astrologer will be in a nice funk, when he is asked by a gentleman whose children are all born to adultery and who wishes to know, by the examination of his children's horoscopes, when the father would die. In some horoscopes, under our observation, the paramour of the woman dies early, if the combination is unfavourable to the progenitor while her so-called husband puts the question, as regards the longevity of himself.   A merchant's wife gave birth to a son.   The planets indicated immediate death to the father. His wife had connection with a washerman and the child was the result of this illicit intercourse. The astrologer consulted, told the man that the father would be drowned in a day or two. The time passed and he learnt that his washerman had died by drowning as predicted and inferred that, in that particular instance, he was not the father and it was good for him that he was not so, as death would have snatched him away.   Jupiter's aspect of the lagna or Moon or his aspect of the Sun and Moon combined is favourable and no imputation should be made.   Even if the birth or the Moon occupies beneficial amsas or divisions, the result is favourable and the mother will be chaste.   The Sun and the Moon join on the Amavasya day (New Moon) and if they have malefic associations or aspects without beneficial conjunction or aspects there will be a strong presumption of guilt on the part of the mother.   The astrologer should see whether in the rasi and amsa kundalis, the Sun and the Moon are not aspected by Jupiter or are not situated in his houses.

Yavaneswara, Gargi and Saravali are all unanimous that
when Jupiter aspects the question of immorality does not
arise. But Bhattotpala says that when the Sun and the Moon
are in the same sign with other evil planets, the morality
of the mother has to be doubted even though Jupiter aspects. But the benefit of the doubt should be given and the
astrologer should always be careful. Discretion is necessary
in such matters.

कूरर्क्षगतावशोभनौ द्व्याद् द्यूननवात्मजस्थितौ ।
बद्धस्तु पिता विदेशगः स्वे वा राशिवशादयो पथि ॥ ७ ॥

Stanza 7.—If malefics occupy the signs of
cruel planets and are in the 7th, 9th or 5th from
the Sun, the father will be imprisoned when the
child is born. The sign occupied by the Sun
determines the locality of his bondage.

NOTES

Malefics are Mars and Saturn and the signs of the
cruel planets are Aries, Leo, Scorpio, Capricorn, Aquarius
and Cancer, when the Moon is weak in the dark half of the
month and Virgo and Gemini, when Mercury is in evil
conjunction. If the Sun occupies a movable sign, the
father suffers from imprisonment in a foreign land, if in a
fixed sign in his own country and if in a common sign on
his way home.

पूर्णे शशिनि स्वराशिगे सौम्ये लग्नगते शुभे सुखे ।
लग्ने जलजेऽस्तगेऽपि वा चन्द्रे पोतगता प्रभूयते ॥ ८ ॥

Stanza 8.—If Full Moon is in Cancer, if
Mercury is in lagna and benefics are in the 4th,

the delivery takes place in a boat or steamer, or in a sea-voyage. If birth is watery with the Moon in the 7th the same result happens.

NOTES

Some read *Shubhaihi* as benefics and think that as the plural is used three or more benefics must be understood. The text reads *Shubhay* in the singular and Bhattotpala interprets this as Jupiter in the 4th. Since shubha means benefic it may also refer to Venus. But when Mercury occupies birth, Venus cannot be placed in the 4th from it. When the Moon is full and in Cancer, then necessarily the Sun must be in the 7th from it, namely, Capricorn. If Mercury is in lagna and three benefics are in the 4th then we must take birth as Aries with Mercury in it and the three benefics as in Cancer, namely, Full Moon, Venus and Jupiter. This view of some astrologers is quite untenable as when the Sun is in Capricorn, Mercury can never be in Aries and much less could Venus be in the 7th from him. Bhattotpala therefore rightly renders the verse by taking the text as *shubhay* (singular) and referring it to only Jupiter. But some say that in ancient times such combinations may have occurred and the authors who recorded such facts—now impossible—may have been perfectly true. Later on some combinations of such stamp are also recorded by the learned Varahamihira and he says that although they may look now as absurd, they may not have been so in the earlier times and the recorded combinations of the Maharishis cannot be rejected as untrue. It is very difficult to make remarks on such events, as in the numberless revolutions of the planets, universal phenomena undergo such changes during immense cycles of time and produce such inconsistent and contradictory phenomena that nobody has any right to condemn them as impossible. What is absurd now may have been perfectly consistent in times remote and what was absurd then may now become perfectly true and practicable. Those who affirm dogmatically that such and such events could not have happened in the world, at any time, simply expose the shallowness of their brains and the weak comprehension they have on matters terrestrial and celestial. They may be absurd at one time, but possible at another age. Here combinations are given to denote the delivery of the child in ships or boats or on watery surfaces. Watery signs are Cancer, the second half of Capricorn, and Pisces. The fact that there are the two systems now Sayana and Nirayana, with a difference of nearly 23 degrees, shows that the positions of planets from the respective positions of their original starting, have changed and hence what might have been possible in remote ages, may not be possible now and *vice versa*.

आप्योदयमाप्यगः शशि सम्पूर्णः समवेक्षतेऽथवा ।
मेषूरणबन्धुलग्नगः स्यात्स्तुतिः सलिले न संशयः ॥ ९ ॥

Stanza 9.—If birth falls in a watery sign as also the Moon, the delivery will be close to water. If lagna (a watery sign) has Full Moon's aspect the same result happens. If, for such lagna, the Moon is there or in the 5th or 10th then similar results happen.

NOTES

These refer to births close to watery surfaces like lakes, seas, large tanks or rivers. If a watery sign is lagna possessing Full Moon's aspect delivery occurs near watery surfaces. Weak Moon's aspect may not have this effect. If birth is watery and the Moon occupies it or is in the 5th or 10th from it delivery occurs near water. Some texts read 4 and 10.

उदयोडुपयोर्व्ययस्थिते गुप्त्यां पापनिरीक्षिते यमे ।
अलिकर्कियुते विलग्ने सौरे शीतकरेक्षितेऽवटे ॥ १० ॥

Stanza 10.—If Saturn occupies the 12th, and a malefic aspects the Moon, the woman delivers the child when in bondage or jail. If Saturn is in Scorpio or Cancer one of which is the birth aspected by the Moon, the delivery takes place in a hole or hollow or pit.

NOTES

This denotes that birth and the Moon must be in the same sign to have Saturn in the 12th. Malefics here may refer to Mars and the Sun who should aspect Saturn. The text also reads Saturn in the 12th from birth and the Moon aspected by evil planets. There are many women who are imprisoned and who deliver while they are in jail or they may be captured by vagabonds and kept in bondage or confinement and the delivery may take place there.

मन्देऽज्जगते विलग्ने बुद्ध्येन्दुनिरीक्षिते क्रमात् ।
क्रीडाभवने सुरालये प्रसवं सोषरभूमिवृद्दिशेत् ॥ ११ ॥

Stanza 11.—If birth is watery with **Saturn in** it, aspected by Mercury, the Sun and the **Moon,** the birth takes place in playgrounds, temples **and** uncultivated fields, respectively.

NOTES

Three combinations are sketched here. If the rising sign is watery with Saturn in it aspected by Mercury, the delivery occurs on playgrounds or pleasure resorts. If similar Saturn has the Sun's aspect the birth takes place in temples or places of worship and if similar Saturn has the Moon's aspect the delivery occurs in barren or uncultivated ground. This also applies to lost property and sex union questions.

नृलग्नगं प्रेक्ष्य कुजः श्मशाने रम्ये सितेन्दू गुरुरग्निहोत्रे ।

रविनरेन्द्रामरगोकुलेषु शिल्पालये ज्ञः प्रसवं करोति ॥१२॥

Stanza 12.—If birth with Sani falls in a **Nara** Rasi aspected by Kuja the birth happens in a grave-yard ; aspected by Sukra and Chandra in pleasant places ; aspected by Guru in sacrificial places ; aspected by Ravi in royal mansions, cowsheds, or temple premises ; aspected by **Budha** in libraries, art colleges or carpenters' premises.

NOTES

Nara Rasis are Gemini, Virgo, Libra, the first **half of** Sagittarius and Aquarius. Saturn must be in birth in **any** one of these signs and have the aspects of planets referred to above, to produce the results indicated there. The birth

happens in places indicated by the rising sign and its
navamsa. If it is movable the delivery occurs in travelling,
if fixed at a house and if the amsa is the same as the rasi at
her own home. The result must be ascertained according
to the strength of the sign and its navamsa.

राश्यंशसमानगोचरे मार्गे जन्म चरे स्थिरे गृहे ।
स्वर्क्षांशगते स्वमन्दिरे बलयोगात्फलमंशकर्क्षयोः ॥ १३ ॥

Stanza 13.—Place of birth happens to be
according to the nature of the rasi and navamsa,
either at home or outside. The birth place should
be determined according to the strength of the
lagna either in rasi or navamsa.

NOTES

For places represented by the different signs refer to
St. 5, Chap. I. If the birth sign and its navamsa are
movable, then the delivery takes place congenial to such
signs. If they both are fixed there, she delivers at places
similar to their nature in her own house. If both of these
are common signs then in places, congenial to those signs
outside the premises of her house. If the navamsa falls in
the same sign as the rasi (that is if it falls in its
Vargottama) the birth takes place in her own house, even if
they are movable or double-bodied. The nature of the
place of birth must be determined by the lagna or its
navamsa according to the strength they possess. This
stanza, Bhattotpala remarks, will apply only when the
previous planetary combinations are not found. He means

that if such combinations are present then the results named
in this stanza should not be predicted.

आरार्कंजयोस्त्रिकोणगे चन्द्रेऽस्ते च विसृज्यतेऽम्बया ।
दृष्टेऽमरराजमन्त्रिणा दीर्घायुः सुखभाक् च सत्कृतः ॥१४॥

Stanza 14.—If the Moon or the Sun is in the
9th or 5th from Saturn and Mars, the child will
be forsaken by its mother. If in that combination
Jupiter aspects it, the child lives long and prospers
although forsaken by its mother.

NOTES

Here Saturn and Mars combined in any house, have the
Moon in the 5th, 9th or 7th houses from them to make the
mother forsake her infant. In this combination if the Moon
is aspected by Jupiter the forsaken babe will be taken care of
by others, will live long and be happy and prosperous.
Some read here only the Moon as indicated above though
the original says ' Chandre Arkacha ' while the other version
is ' Chandre Asthecha ' meaning the 7th from the Moon,
i.e., including the 7th in addition to 5 or 9. Readers should
judge for themselves.

पापेक्षिते तुहिनगावुदये कुजेऽस्ते
त्यक्तो विनश्यति कुजार्कंजयोस्तथाये ।
सौम्येऽदपि पश्यति तथाविधहस्तमेति
सौम्येतरेषु परहस्तगतोऽप्यनायुः ॥ १५ ॥

Stanza 15.—If the Moon is in birth aspected
by a malefic and has Mars in the 7th the forsaken

babe will perish. If in this combination Mars
and Saturn are in the 11th, the child dies, if aspected by a benefic, the child gets protection by
such casteman as is indicated by the benefic; if
aspected by malefics, the child falls to different
hands and dies.

NOTES

If the Moon occupying birth, has the aspect of the Sun
or Saturn with Mars in the 7th the child is forsaken by the
mother, and it dies. If the Moon occupies birth aspected by
the Sun with Saturn and Mars in the 11th, the forsaken child
dies. If the Moon occupying the birth as above stated, has also
the aspect of a benefic, the forsaken child will be taken care
of by such casteman as is indicated by the benefic who
aspects the Moon and the child lives long and prosperously.
Bhattotpala clearly declares this benefic to be Jupiter to
make the child live and prosper on the strength of the combinations given by Saravali. Other benefics are Mercury
and Venus but their aspect of the Moon will not protect the
life of the infant. The caste of the person who takes care of
the mother—forsaken child—will be that which is governed
or indicated by the most powerful of the aspecting planet.
Here even if Jupiter is very weak and aspects the Moon the
child lives and thrives although it may be taken care of by a
Brahmin, Kshatriya, Vaisya, Sudra or Antyaja. The significations conveyed by these caste divisions have already been
explained by me in Stanza 7, Ch. II.

पितृमातृगृहेषु तद्बलात् तरुशालादिषु नीचगैः शुभैः ।
यदि नैकगतैस्तु वीक्षितौ लभेन्दू विजने प्रसूयते ॥ १६ ॥

Stanza 16.—The birth takes place in the house of the father or mother according to the strength of their lords. If benefics occupy debilitated places, birth will be under trees, roads, etc. If benefics occupy neecha and if the Moon and birth are unaspected by other planets occupying one house, the birth occurs in lonely places.

NOTES

In St. 5, Ch. IV, reference has already been fully made as to the lordship of the planets about father, mother and other relations. If the planet representing father (the Sun during the day and Saturn during the night) is stronger, then the birth must be predicted in the paternal house. Here paternal means not only the child's father, but the brothers of the father and father's relations. Similarly maternal means mother's relations, etc. If Venus in the day and the Moon in the night are stronger, then delivery takes place in mother's house, *i.e.*, mother's parent's house. If the order is changed that is if Saturn in the day and the Sun in the night are stronger, then delivery would be in father's younger or elder brother's house or in father's sister's house. Similarly in case of mother. All the benefics must be debilitated to produce birth in open places and road-sides. The word *Adi* used by the author makes the meaning much wider and includes rivers, wells, tanks, gardens and mountains where there is no covering. In the last case of birth in lonely places, the benefics must be debilitated, all the other planets must be in one house and they should not aspect birth and the Moon. But if the Moon and birth are aspected, then predict delivery in a crowded place. Probably this refers

to birth in wilderness and other unfrequented places where
the woman may have stayed away or left alone by others.
Saravali supports this view and is quoted by Bhattotpala.

मन्दक्षोंशे शशिनि हिबुके मन्दद‍ृष्टेऽज्जगे वा
तद्युक्ते वा तमसि शयनं नीचसंस्थैश्च भूमौ ॥
यद्द्राशिर्व्रजति हरिजं गर्भमोक्षस्तु तद्वत्
पापैश्चन्द्रस्मरसुखगतैः क्लेशमाहुर्जनन्याः ॥ १७ ॥

Stanza 17.—If the Moon joins Saturn's
amsa or is in the 4th or has the aspect of Saturn
or occupies watery signs or conjoins with Saturn,
then birth takes place in darkness. If there are
three or more debilitated planets, birth takes
place on the ground. The birth takes place
similar to the rasi which rises on a level with the
equator. If malefics occupy the 4th or the 7th
from the Moon or join the Moon the delivery is
attended by much pain.

NOTES

Certain characteristics pertaining to the birth are given
here with a view to find out the correct time of the birth
and the sign which rises then. Theories must be supported
by practice while practice must also be confirmed by theory.
By carefully reading this stanza, the astrologer will be able
to predict whether the birth occurred in darkness or on the
ground and whether the head or foot of the child came first.
Zodiacal signs have already been described as rising with

head or tail or both and the birth of the child takes place
similar to the process represented by the rasi which rises
on a level with the earth's equator.

Bhattotpala says that that place where the earth and the
sky appear to meet is called *Harija* and directs the student
to watch the birth sign which rises in the horizon.
Probably the English word *horizon* is derived from the
Sanskrit word *Harija*. The birth takes place say in Aries.
Aries rises in the horizon with prusta and therefore, says
the learned commentator, the child comes out of the yoni
(sexual organ) with first showing its middle part.   In
Sirshodayas the head presents itself first and the birth
takes place.   In Oobhayodaya the sides will be first visible
and then the birth occurs.   Saturn's amsas are Capricorn
and Aquarius.   The watery signs are Cancer and Pisces.
Birth takes place in dark rooms or places without any light
when the Moon occupies the navamsas of Saturn or joins
him or watery signs or has Saturn's aspect.   Saturn is a
dark planet capable of absorbing all light and reflecting
back dark rays.   Three or more neecha planets deprive
the woman of any bedding or clothes and at the time of
delivery she lies down on the plain ground or that covered
with grass.   In the following horoscope, note how 3 planets
debilitated caused immediate delivery on the ground in a
dark room.   The mother finished her cooking by about
10-30, and as labour pains set in, she was immediately
taken to a dark room and delivery immediately took place
and a female child was delivered.   Note here Kuja, Guru
and Chandra are debilitated and Sani an evil planet aspects
birth as well as the Moon.   If evil planets are with the
Moon or in the 4th or 7th from him the delivery is attended

with great pain and suffering for the mother.　Bhattotpala quotes in this connection Saravali, Yavaneswara and Manitha.　In all the above cases, if the Moon has the aspect of the Sun, there will be no darkne s and many lamps will be burning at the time of birth.　What will the result be, when the Sun is with the Moon ? Manitha differs

	Ravi Budha	Sukra Sani	
Rahu	RASI		Birth Kuja
Guru			Kethu
	Chandra		

from the author about the manner of the birth. He observes that if the lord of navamsa is retrograde the process of birth will be reversed.　He remarks that if the lord of the birth is retrograde then the child will be born the reverse of what it would do ordinarily. In ordinary delivery the child presents its head first and it is thus thrown out. But when any of the planets above named is retrograde the child comes out with feet or back first.

स्नेहः शशाङ्कादुदयाच्च वर्तिर्दीपोर्कयुक्तर्क्षवशाच्चराधः ।
द्वारं च तद्वास्तुनि केन्दूसंस्थैर्ज्ञेयं ग्रहैर्वीर्यसमन्वितैर्वा ॥ १८ ॥

Stanza 18.—The quantity of oil by the Moon, the wick by the birth sign and the light by the Sun,

the door by the planets in the kendras or by the
most powerful of the planets must be ascertained.

NOTES

This verse enables one to have an idea of the quantity
of oil in the lamp at the time of birth. If the Moon is full
then the lamp is full of oil, if it is new then there will
hardly be any oil.   It may be asked that as on the
Amavasya day the Moon is not visible, the lamps in the
rooms of all those who are born on that day, should have
no oil in them.   Bhattotpala anticipates this question and
observes that if the Moon is in the beginning of the rasi
then the quantity will be full. When he is in the last
degree of it, there will hardly be any oil.   If the birth
takes place in the beginning of the rasi then the wick was
just lighted. If half the rasi has advanced then half of
the wick had been burnt and so on the measurement is to
be determined by the simple rule of three.   If the Sun is
in a movable sign the light will be moving, if in a fixed
sign it will be fixed in one place and if he is in a double-
bodied sign the light will be moved now and then.   The
direction of the lamp is determined by the cardinal direction
shown by the rasi occupied by the Sun.   If the Sun is in
Aries, the light is kept in the eastern part of the room as
the sign indicates East.   There are some who maintain
that the direction of the lamp will be determined by the
position of the Sun to be located by dividing the day into
8 Yamas and by finding out where the Sun is at the time
of birth.   This is a little difficult and I shall give an
example.   Say that a child is born on a Sunday at 25
ghatikas after sunrise.   The day contains 60 ghatikas and

this divided by 8 will give $\frac{60}{8} = 7\frac{1}{2}$ ghatikas for a Yama or three English hours. The day has advanced 25 ghatikas and therefore $\frac{25}{7\frac{1}{2}}$ will give us the Yama passed. Birth, we find, falls in the 4th Yama on that day. The fourth from the East will be the direction in which the Sun is to be located for that purpose.

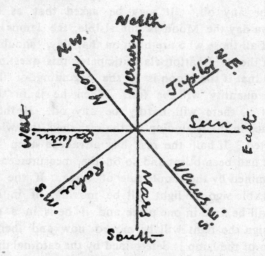

The fourth from the East is the South-west and the Sun should be placed there. The lamp must be represented to have been placed in the S.-W. in the delivery room. The door has to be determined by the planets in the kendras or if there are none there, by the most powerful of the planets in the horoscope. (*See* Chap. II, St. 5). These are ably supported by quotations from Manitha and Saravali. Manitha says that the direction of the door may be determined by the direction indicated by the rising

Dwadasamsa in sign. Since the origin and development
of astrology is not clearly known and since the Maharishis
gave out these facts by their Divya Drishti or divine sight
evolved by long meditation we have to simply record here
these differences without being in a position to affirm or
contradict them.

जीर्णं संस्कृतमर्कजे क्षितिसुते दग्धं नवं शितगौ ।
काष्ठाढयं न दृढं रवौ शशिसुते तन्नैकशिल्प्युद्भवम् ।
रम्यं चित्रयुतं नवं च भृगुते जीवे दृढं मन्दिरं
चक्रस्थैश्च यथोपदेशरचनां सामन्तपूर्वो वदेत् ॥ १९ ॥

Stanza 19.—If Saturn is the strongest, the
house will be one newly repaired having become
old, if Mars is so it is partly burnt; if the Moon,
new ; if the Sun, the house contains much wood ;
and if Mercury, built by many artists; if Venus,
handsome, painted and new; if Jupiter, strong
house; the adjoining houses must be indicated
similarly by the planets in the rasis.

NOTES

The author enables the readers to predict or to know
the nature of the house where the delivery takes place. If
Saturn is the most powerful among the planets at the time,
then the house will be old, but newly repaired. If Mars is
the strongest then it will be partly a burnt house. If the Moon
is the strongest then the house will be quiet new. If the Moon
is waxing then the house will be whitewashed. If the Sun

is the most powerful the house contains a lot of timber work but in a weak condition ; if Mercury is the strongest the house will have been built by many good artists and masons. If Venus is the strongest the house will be beautiful, new, and adorned with pictures and paintings. If Jupiter is the strongest then the house will be strong. He now gives an idea of the neighbouring houses. Having found out the strongest planet and determined the nature of the delivery house, take this planet as the lagna and proceed to divide the 12 houses by four cardinal directions. Take an example·

	Chan-dra Rahu	Birth	Sani
Ravi Budha Guru	RASI		
Sukra		Kuja Kethu	

For argument's sake we shall consider Mercury as the strongest of the planets. Then as per above rule the person must have been born in a house well built by various skilful workmen. Thus we have a knowledge of the delivery house but what about the adjacent houses. As Budha has been found to be the most powerful, take him as the first or lagna the ascendant. Then Kumbha, Meena and Mesha—the first three houses from Budha form the eastern direction and the houses indicated by the planets

will be found situated to the east of the house where delivery
took place. The next three houses, *viz.*, Vrishabha, Mithuna
and Kataka represent the houses adjoining the delivery house
in the southern direction and the planets there show the
nature of those houses. The next three houses, *viz.*, Simha,
Kanya and Thula represent the west and the planets there
will show the nature of the houses adjoining the western
direction. The next three houses, *viz.*, Vrischika, Dhanus
and Makara represent the north and the nature of the planets
there shows the nature of the houses to the north. Thus the
zodiac has been divided into four equal divisions commencing with the most powerful planet as the starting point.
Bhattotpala cites from Laghu Jataka and explains rules to find
out whether the house is single, double or treble storied. If
Jupiter occupies degrees in Kataka before his deep exaltation,
and this forms the 10th house, then the house will be three
storied. If he is in deep exaltation there, then it will be
four storied. If Jupiter has fallen from his deep exaltation
the house will be double storied. If Dhanus is strong in
conjunction with Jupiter and happens to be the 10th house
will be treble in extent. If Mithuna, Kanya or Meena forms
the 10th house with Guru there, it will be double in extent.
The extent probably refers to partition or accommodation
for two or three families.

मेषकुलीरतुलालिघटैः प्रागुत्तरतो गुरुसौम्यगृहेषु ।
पश्चिमतश्च वृषेण निवासो दक्षिणभागकरौ मृगसिंहौ ॥२०॥

Stanza 20.—If birth falls in Mesha, Kataka,
Thula, Vrischika and Kumbha, or in these
navamsas the delivery will be in the eastern part

of the house. If the birth falls in Guru's or
Budha's houses or amsas the delivery happens in
the northern part of the house. If it falls in
Vrishabha or its amsa the birth takes place in the
west and if it falls in Makara or Simha or their
navamsas the birth place will be in the southern
side.

NOTES

Hitherto the house and its nature have been shown.
Now the author explains in what direction of the house the
birth takes place. If the rising sign is Aries, Cancer, Libra,
Scorpio or Aquarius, the delivery must be predicted in the
eastern part of the house. If birth occurs in the houses
or navamsas of Jupiter or Mercury, the delivery occurs in
the northern portion of the house. Taurus and its amsa
indicate the western portion as in the horoscope, Kanya
Lagna navamsa is Taurus and the signs Capricorn and
Leo as well as their navamsas denote delivery in southern
portion of the house. These suggestions help the astrological
adepts in finding out the true time and thus enable him to
cast the future results of the individual with tolerable
certainty. They will also prove the value of the science in
knowing the minute details of the important events of birth.

प्राच्यादिगृहे क्रियादयो द्वौ द्वौ कोणगताद्विमूर्तयः ।
शत्यास्वपि वास्तुब्धदेत् पादैः षट्त्रिनबान्त्यसंस्थितै ॥२१॥

Stanza 21.—The cardinal direction of the
lying down must be indicated by two signs from

Mesha, etc., and the corners by the double-bodied signs. Similarly it must be ascertained for the direction of the bed, etc. The legs of the cot or the sides of the bed must be ascertained by the 6th, 3rd, 9th and 12th houses from lagna.

NOTES

The brevity of the Sanskrit language throws great difficulties in the way of easy translations. The *etc.* of the English tongue cannot be really put as equivalent to the Sanskrit terms *Adi*. There the high development of the tongue has laid down certain rules for explanation which are wanting in the English language. Take the two signs, Mesha and Vrishabha as representing the East, then Mithuna indicates the South-east, Kataka and Simha indicate the South, and Kanya shows the South-west, Thula and Vrischika represent the West while Dhanus indicates the North-west. Makara and Kumbha represent the North while Meena shows the North-east. This is shown clearly by the kundali in the next page.

Similarly for any rasi fix up the directions as noted above. As there are 8 directions and 12 houses, the directions are adjusted accordingly. Whichever rasi happens to be the lagna then the direction indicated by it will be the direction in which the bed is placed, the front legs are indicated by the 3rd and 12th of which the 3rd is the right and 12th is the left leg. The 6th and 9th are hind legs of which the 6th is the right and the 9th is the left. The lagna and the 2nd represent head side ; 4th and 5th right side ; 7th and 8th feet side ; and 10th and 11th denote left side. The uses for these will be to judge the nature of the bed or cot, etc. If the rasis are cruel or common then there will be damage or depression on that side.

N.E.	E.	E.	S.E.
N.			S.
N.	RASI		S.
N. W.	W.	W.	S.W.

By this it seems that there can be no cot or bed whose legs are not damaged or expressed on some side - or the other. But Bhattotpala explains away this anomaly by saying that such defects are cured by the conjunction or aspecting of benefics or the lords of the houses. Even malefics occupying or aspecting such will not cause these defects, if they are exalted or are in Moolathrikona or their own houses.

चन्द्रलग्नान्तरगतैर्ग्रहैः स्युरुपषूतिकाः ।
बहिरन्तश्च चक्रार्द्धे दृश्यादृश्येऽन्यथापरे ॥ २२ ॥

Stanza 22.—The number of women to assist the delivery must be determined by the number of planets between the Moon and the lagna. Their presence inside or outside the delivery room has

to be learnt by the planets in the invisible and the
visible half of the zodiac respectively.   Some say
quite the reverse.

NOTES

Take the horoscope given under Stanza 19. Between the
lagna in Vrishabha and the Moon in Mesha we have 6
planets and therefore the number of women there will be six.
But this number is to be modified, *i.e.*, multiplied or subtracted as per directions given in the Ayurdayadhyaya (*see* Ch.
VII, St. 11). But some of the women may be in the room while
there may be others outside. This can be identified by the
number of planets in the invisible and visible halves of the
zodiac. The two halves are thus determined. Take the
number of the degree rising in the sign. From that upto the
same degree in the 7th house the division of the zodiac is
called invisible (Adrusya) half. The remaining houses upto
the degree of rising in the birth will form the visible (Drusya)
half of the zodiac. Planets in the visible half of the zodiac
denote the number of women outside the room while planets
in the invisible half of the zodiac indicate the number of
women inside the room. The features, wealth, stature and
complexion of the women will be denoted by the characteristics represented by the planets there as also their character
and caste. Jivasarma maintains this point quite contrary to
Varahamihira. He says that the planets in the visible half
of the zodiac represent the ladies in the room while planets
in the invisible half of the zodiac show their number outside.
This is quite unacceptable to the author as he has distinctly
stated so in his Laghu Jataka. But under what authority do
the two authors differ ?

Varahamihira, who had carefully studied the systems of horoscopy expounded by the greatest of the Maharishis, has always advanced views which had ample confirmation in the ancient works.   Bhattotpala has not given his opinion here. It looks reasonable to suppose with Varahamihira that the planets which are in the invisible part of the zodiac represent the women in the room, for when they are inside the room, the ladies will be invisible. Visible planets must represent the women who are visible and therefore outside the delivery room where they could be seen by others.

लग्ननवांशपतुल्यतनुः स्याद्वीर्ययुतग्रहतुल्यतनुर्वा ।
चन्द्रसमेतनवांशपवर्णः कादिविलग्नविभक्तभगात्रः ॥ २३ ॥

Stanza 23.—The body of the child will resemble the planet who is the lord of the navamsa or who is the most powerful. The color of the infant will resemble that of the lord of the navamsa occupied by the Moon. Taking the lagna as head, etc., the limbs resemble the rasis in which they fall.

NOTES

The author here gives important instructions to find out the body, its color and the proportion of the various limbs. Planetary characteristics have already been made clear in Chap. II, Sts. 8, 9, 10 and 11. Find out the navamsa and its lord and describe the body as per that planet. If this does not tally, then find out the most powerful planet in the horoscope and describe his characteristics to the child born. Judge the color by the lord of the navamsa occupied by the

Moon. In Ch. I, St. 19, Varahamihira has explained which
signs are long and which are short. He now advises his
readers to take lagna as the head, etc., and find out the
proportion of the various limbs by the length of the rasis
occupied by them. Suppose a man is born in Vrischika.
This will represent his head. As Vrischika is a long sign,
the head will be long or big. The next house represents
face. It is Dhanus and this is moderate, therefore the face
will be neither small nor long. The 3rd will be Makara and
it is long. Therefore, the chest will be long and broad.
Mithuna is the 8th from Vrischika and this represents the
sexual organ. As it is ordinary the organ will be moderately
sized. Again if the lords of the long signs be found located
in short signs, the result must be accordingly modified. If
the rasi is short and it also has a lord of a short sign then
that limb which it governs will be very short.

कन्दक्श्रोत्रनसाकपोलहनवो वक्त्रं च होरादय-
स्ते कण्ठांसकबाहुपार्श्वहृदयक्रोडानि नाभिस्ततः ।
बस्तिः शिश्नगुदे ततश्च वृषणावूरू ततो जानुनी
जंघाघ्रीत्युभयत्र वामसुदितेद्रेंकाणभागैस्त्रिधा ॥ २४ ॥

Stanza 24.—If the first drekkana rises in the
lagna ; by the Drusya and Adrusya halves of the
zodiac, left and right sides of head, eyes, ears,
nose, temples, cheeks and face must be determined
from the lagna respectively. If the second
drekkana rises in the lagna, neck, shoulders,
arms, sides, chest, belly and navel should be

similarly determined. If the third drekkana rises
in the lagna, lower stomach, sexual organ and
anus, testicles, thighs, knees, calves and feet
must be similarly delineated.

NOTES

The meaning is highly compressed and I shall explain it
fully to remove doubts and difficulties. Have the human
body divided into 3 parts. The 1st part represents head,
the 2nd part comprises all below the neck and above the
navel, and the 3rd part shows all the organs below the navel.
In order to find out any marks, cuts, scars, moles and
defects or malformations in the different organs, the author
asks the reader to take the rising drekkana. If it is the first,
it represents the head, if second it shows the organs below
the neck and above the navel and if the 3rd drekkana
commences, then the lower parts of the body from the
navel are shown. The signs to the right of the lagna represent the right side, while the signs to the left of the lagna
indicate the left side organs. Suppose the first drekkana
rises in Mesha at the birth of the child. This represents
his head. Taking this drekkana as the lagna and head we
now proceed to find out the right and left side organs.
The second house indicates right eye while the 12th shows
the left. The 3rd and 11th houses show right and left ears
respectively. The 4th and 10th houses from the lagna
show the right and left nostrils respectively. The 5th and
9th houses show the right and left temples respectively.
6th and 8th indicate the right and left cheeks respectively
and the 7th house shows the general face, some say the
mouth. Suppose the second drekkana rises. Then the

lagna shows the neck. The 2nd and 12th houses show right and left shoulders. The 3rd and 11th houses show the right and left arms. The 4th and 10th indicate the right and left sides. The 5th and 9th show the right and left side of the chest. The 6th and 8th indicate the right and left side of the stomach and the 7th house shows the navel. If the lagna has the 3rd drekkana rising at the birth, then it represents the lower stomach or waist (that region which is below the navel and above the sexual organ). The 2nd and 12th houses show sexual organ and anus. The 3rd and 11th indicate the right and left testicles. The 4th and 10th show the right and left thighs. The 5th and 9th from the lagna show the right and left knees, 6th and 8th indicate the right and left calves and the 7th shows the feet. The first half of the 7th house probably shows the right foot while the 2nd half shows the left foot.

तस्मिन् पापयुते व्रणं शुभयुते दृष्टे च लक्ष्मादिशेत्
स्वर्क्षांशे स्थिरसंयुतेषु सहजः स्यादन्यथामन्तुकः ।
मन्देऽश्मानिलजोऽग्निशस्त्रविशजो भौमे बुधे भूभवः
सूर्ये काष्ठचतुष्पदेन हिमगौ शृंग्यब्जजोऽन्यैः शुभम् ॥ २५ ॥

Stanza 25.—If those rasis are occupied by malefics there will be sores or wounds, if these are occupied or aspected by benefics there will be marks ; if such planets causing sores, etc.—are in their own rasis or navamsas or in fixed signs or navamsas, the sores, etc., will accompany birth, if not they come by accidents after birth. If such

a planet is Saturn the wounds will be caused by
stones and windy diseases; if Mars by fire,
weapons and poisons; if Mercury by the earth or
the ground ; if the Sun by wood or quadrupeds;
if the Moon by horned animals or aquatics; if
they are other planets then there will be no
wounds.

NOTES

The division of the body into 3 parts and the process to
find out the right and left side organs have already been
fully explained in the previous stanzas. If after finding
out the organs by the zodiacal houses they are occupied by
evil planets then wounds or sores must be predicted, but
if benefics are there or aspect them, then there will be
some marks or moles, but no sores. The author has
apparently omitted the aspects of evil planets. In such
cases the results will probably be lighter in intensity than
when they occupy them. Bhattotpala distinctly says that
if such rasis are not cruel and occupied by evil planets,
then the mere aspect or presence of the benefics will not
cause even these marks or moles. He means thereby that
when the rasis are occupied by evil planets without
beneficial conjunctions or aspects they will cause certainly
wounds, cuts or sores. When the evil planets are there
in conjunction with or aspected by benefics then there will
be marks or moles in these organs, but when they are
not occupied by malefics but have beneficial aspects or
conjunctions there will be no marks or moles. The
wounds, if accidental, would be inflicted during the periods

of such planets or their sub-periods. Varahamihira proceeds
to say how those wounds, etc., are caused.

समनुपतिता यस्मिन् भागे त्रयः सबुधा ग्रहाः
भवति नियमात्तस्यावासिः शुभेष्वशुभेषु वा ।
व्रणकृदशुभः षष्ठो देहे तनोर्भसमाश्रिते
तिलकमसकृद्दृष्टः सौम्यैर्युतश्च सलक्ष्मवान् ॥ २६ ॥

Stanza 26.—If Mercury joins three other
planets in any rasi he will cause wounds in that
organ which is governed by it. If an evil planet
is in the 6th from birth, there will be wound in
that organ represented by that rasi. If such a
malefic has beneficial aspect then there will be
Thilaka, Masaka, etc., there. If benefics join
him there will be Lakshma, etc.

NOTES

See Ch. I, St. 4. Find out where Budha is with 3 other
planets. This means that in any house if Budha joins 3 other
planets then that organ which is represented by that house
in the *Kalanga Vibhaga* will have wound or sore. An evil
planet in the 6th will cause wound in that organ which is
controlled by that rasi under St. 4 of Ch. I as already
described. If such an evil planet has beneficial aspect then
there will be moles and marks. If such a planet has beneficial conjunction then there will be blackmarks or other
cutaneous indications. Thilaka means a black mole or mark,
Masaka means a white spot just like leucoderma, and
Lakshma means having hairs thick in that spot.

13

CHAPTER VI

BALARISTA OR EARLY DEATH

बालारिष्टाध्यायः

सन्ध्यायां हिमदीधितिहोरा पापैर्भान्तगतैर्निधानाय ।
प्रत्येकं शशिपापसमेतैः केन्द्रैर्वा स विनाशमुपैति ॥ १ ॥

Stanza 1.—Children born during *Sandhi* or when birth is in Chandra Hora, when evil planets occupy the ends of signs or when four malefics (including the Moon) occupy the quadrants, will die.

NOTES

The importance of a chapter which deals with combinations indicating early death can hardly be overrated. In fact all events in life can only assume importance in relation to their being enacted during the life career of a man. There can be no painting without a canvas and no results can be worth detailing which do not happen to an individual when he lives. This chapter has been advanced by the author with a view to find out the longevity of the infant. *Balarista* or death in early life refers to the death of infants before they complete their 8th year. Children born during the two twilights, morning and evening, when the Moon's Hora is rising and when evil planets are found located in the last degree of the signs or when malefics occupy the four quadrants with the Moon, die early. The twilights are described in Bharadwaja Samhita clearly. About 48 minutes after the

sunset is called the evening twilight while about the same
period before sunrise is called the morning twilight. But
there are some regions where these two twilights extend for
many days or many hours. All such cases should be taken
as special and dealt with separately.

The planets in the last navamsas of the houses are said
to occupy their ends. In the second case of Balarista the
author refers to four malefics to occupy the four quadrants.
Properly speaking there are only 3 malefics—the Sun, Mars
and Saturn. The two real benefics are Jupiter and Venus.
The Moon and Mercury are changing. Weak Moon, as on
Amavasya days, and badly associated Mercury are malefics
while Full Moon and well-associated Mercury are benefics.
If so, why should the author say particularly that the Moon
and other malefics should occupy the four kendras. It will be
seen that in order to make Mercury bad, he must be in evil
company. If he is with Saturn or Mars he becomes evil but
then he cannot be in a kendra to the Sun for he never goes
beyond 23 degrees from him. The author therefore is perfectly
justified in calling for the fourth planet as the Moon. Moreover to have the Moon to be weak the birth must fall a few days
before Amavasya and a few days after it. But Chandra must at
least be in the fourth house from Ravi and he cannot be so
unless it is 7 days before or after Amavasya in which case it
is difficult to say he is Kshina. The difficulty probably does
not seem to have struck the learned commentator, for the
whole significance of this question has been entirely overlooked by him. (See Ch. II, Stanza 5.) The following horoscope may be studied with interest as indicating a powerful
'Balarista Yoga'. Born on 2-1-1934, the child died on
27-10-1936.

RASI

			Chandra Kethu
	RASI		
Sani Kuja Rahu Sukra			
Ravi Buda		Birth Guru	

AMSA

Kethu	Kuja		Budha
	AMSA		Sani Lagna
		Moon	Ravi Guru Sukra Rahu

Look at the combination in rasi and amsa. In rasi there are only 2 evil planets in the kendra ; but in amsa, we have Sani in lagna, Moon in 4, and Kuja in 10th, *i.e.,* 3 kendras. In rasi from Chandra Lagna there are 3 evil planets in the 7th, Sani, Kuja and Rahu.

चक्रस्य पूर्वापरभागगेषु क्रूरेषु सौम्येषु च कीटलग्ने ।
क्षिप्रं विनाशं समुपैति जातः पापैर्विलग्नास्तमयामितश्च ॥ २ ॥

Stanza 2.—If cruel and beneficial planets occupy the first and the 2nd halves of the zodiac respectively and the birth rises in Kita Rasi or if the birth and the 7th are placed between malefics the child dies straight.

NOTES

The first or poorvabhaga of the Bhachakra (zodiac) as well as the aparardha (later half) is described as follows. Leaving as many degrees in the 4th house as have passed in the rising sign (*Lagna*) the remaining portion of it and the 5th, 6th, 7th, 8th, 9th and as many degrees in the 10th as

have passed in the lagna, form the *parardha* or the 2nd half
while the remaining portion of the zodiac not covered by the
above houses will have to be taken as the first half or
poorvabhaga. Kita means Cancer and Scorpio. If
cruel planets occupy the first half and the second half
is combined by benefics and the birth rises in Cancer or
Scorpio the child dies at once. If there are evil planets in
the 12th and 2nd sign of the birth, as also in the 6th and 8th
the child dies at once. Quoting various authors and their
different views Bhattotpala explains these combinations in
a clear language. If there are evil planets in the 2nd, 6th,
8th and 12th, early death of course is ensured. If all the
evil planets are (1) in the 2nd and 12th ; (2) in the 6th and
8th, death should be predicted. Some writers say that
planets in the 2nd and 8th are confronting the 1st and the
7th respectively. This is opposed to facts enunciated in
Hindu Astronomy. Planets are moving from the west to the
east and therefore planets in the 12th confront the birth or
1st and planets in the 6th do so with the 7th. This is
supported by Yavaneswara. Bhagavan Gargi clearly summarises these points and says that : (1) If evil planets are
in 6th and 12th, or (2) if they are in 2nd and 8th, or (3) if
lagna is enclosed by malefics, or (4) if the 7th is enclosed by
malefics as noted in the horoscope, and (5) if the 7th from
Chandra is enclosed by Kuja and Sani, death happens to
the child. Devala says that if with these evil planets in
the houses indicated above benefics are found death should
not be predicted.

पापावुदयास्तगतों क्रूरेण युतश्च शशी ।
दृष्टश्च शुभैर्न यदा मृत्युश्च भवेदचिरात् ॥ ३ ॥

Stanza 3.—If malefics occupy birth and 7th and if the Moon joins cruel planets, unaspected by benefics, the child dies quickly.

NOTES

Here the Moon, birth and 7th must have evil conjunctions having no beneficial aspects to kill the child early.

क्षीणे हिमगौ व्ययगे पापैरुदयाष्टमगैः
केन्द्रेषु शुभाश्च न चेत् क्षिप्रं निधनं प्रवदेत् ॥ ४ ॥

Stanza 4.—If weak Moon occupies the 12th with malefics in the birth and the 8th without benefics in the kendras the child dies soon.

NOTES

If there are any benefics in the kendras, they prolong the child's life according to their relative strength.

कूरेण संयुतः शशी स्मरान्त्यमृत्युलग्नगः ।
कण्टकाद्बहिः शुभैरवीक्षितश्च मृत्युदः ॥ ५ ॥

Stanza 5.—If the Moon joins a malefic and occupies the 7th, 12th, 8th or birth and when benefics are outside kendras, and do not aspect these, the child dies.

NOTES

If a malefic in conjunction with the Moon occupies birth, 7th, 8th, or 12th possessing no beneficial aspects

and having no benefics in the kendras death comes to the
child. The principal point here is the non-occupation of
the kendras by benefics and the want of their aspect to the
Moon in conjunction with a malefic in the above enumerated houses.

शाशिन्यरिविनाशगे निधनमाशुपापेक्षिते
शुभैरथ समाष्टकं दलमतश्च मिश्रैः स्थितिः ।
असद्भिरवलोकिते बलिभिरत्र मासं शुभे
कलत्रसहिते च पापविजिते विलग्नाधिपे ॥ ६ ॥

Stanza 6.—If the Moon occupies 6th or 8th
aspected by malefics early death comes. If such
Moon has beneficial aspects the child dies before
8 years. If such Moon has mixed aspects the
child lives for 4 years. If a benefic occupies the
6th or 8th aspected by powerful malefics the
child lives for a month. If the lord of the birth
joins the 7th and suffers defeat there by malefics
similar results must be predicted.

NOTES

Mixed aspects refer to the aspect of benefics and malefics together. Planetary defeats and successes are clearly
explained in my notes on Stanza 20, Chap. II. If the Moon
occupies 6th or 8th and has no aspects beneficial or malefic,
then this combination does not apply. If the Moon joins
beneficial signs and has beneficial conjunctions, he gives
longer.life. Mandavya declares that to the child born during

the daytime in the dark half of the lunar month and to the
child born during the night in the bright half of the month,
even when the Moon occupies 6th or 8th with good and bad
aspects, there will be no death. If the benefic in the 6th or
8th has beneficial aspect there is no danger. The position of
the Moon in the 6th, 8th or 12th without beneficial aspects
or conjunctions indicates early death to the infant.

लग्ने क्षीणे शशिनि निधनं रन्ध्रकेन्द्रेषु पापैः
पापान्तःस्थे निधनहिबुकद्यूनयुक्ते च चन्द्रे ।
एवं लग्ने भवति मदनच्छिद्रसंस्थैश्च पापै-
र्मात्रा सार्धं यदि च न शुभैर्वीक्षितः शक्तिभृद्धिः ॥ ७ ॥

Stanza 7.—If weak Moon joins the lagna
with malefics in the 8th or kendras or if the
Moon is betwixt malefics occupying the 8th,
4th or 7th the child dies. If the Moon is in
lagna as above stated, malefics in the 7th and
8th without the aspect of powerful benefics, the
mother as well as the child dies.

NOTES

If Full Moon occupies birth then the danger is considerably lessened. The words "*as above*" refer to
Chandra's occupation of lagna with malefics on both sides
of it. That is if Chandra occupies lagna and evil planets
are in 12th, 2nd, 7th and 8th without beneficial aspects the
child and its mother will both die. If there are beneficial
aspects for the Moon then the child dies but not the

mother. Here also the idea of the lagna lying betwixt
evil planets seems to have been repeated.

राश्यन्तगे सद्धिरवीक्ष्यमाणे चन्द्रे त्रिकोणोपगतैश्च पपौः ।
प्राणैः प्रयात्याशु शिशुर्वियोगमस्ते च पापैस्तुहिनांशुलग्ने ॥८॥

Stanza 8.—If the Moon occupies the last
navamsa of the sign and malefics are in the 5th
and 9th without beneficial aspects, or if lagna
joins Chandra with malefics in the 7th, the child
dies immediately.

NOTES

The last amsa in every sign will be its 9th navamsa
and Chandra must be here unaspected by benefics with
malefics in the two thrikonas, *viz.,* 5th and 9th to kill the
child at once.

अशुभसहिते ग्रस्ते चन्द्रे कुजे निधनाश्रिते
जननिसुतयोर्मृत्युर्लग्ने रवौ तु सशस्त्रजः ।
उदयति रवौ शीतांशौ वा त्रिकोणविनाशगे-
निधनमशुभैर्वीर्योपेतःशुभैर्नं युतेक्षिते ॥ ९ ॥

Stanza 9.—If the Moon joins a malefic in
lagna, eclipsed with Mars in the 8th, both
mother and child will die. Similarly if the Sun
is in lagna death results from weapons. If the
Moon or the Sun occupies the lagna with

powerful malefics in thrikonas and 8th, unaspected by or uncombined with benefics, the
child dies.

NOTES

Bhattotpala has ably explained this verse. If the Moon
joins Saturn eclipsed by Rahu with Mars in the 8th the
mother and child die. The author simply says, the Moon
with a malefic and it may mean the Sun or bad Mercury.
The Moon is eclipsed on Full Moon days when the Sun is
in the 7th from him. If the Sun is in the 7th from the
Moon, Mercury cannot be with the Moon in the lagna for
he is never removed more than 23 degrees from the Sun.
Mars has been placed in the 8th. Thus the only other
evil planet left for consideration is Saturn and he must be
with the Moon in the lagna with Rahu. In the case of the
Sun, the malefics referred to, will be either Mercury or
Saturn. For Mercury with the Sun is classed as a malefic.
Weak Moon is also a malefic, but in all solar eclipses which
occur only on New Moon days (Amavasyas) the Moon will
be with the Sun. He specially uses the word *Asubhasahitay*
and it must refer to either Mercury or Saturn. In this case
the mother and child will both be killed by weapons.
Weapons refer to surgical instruments and operations which
cause the death of the child and mother. If the Sun or the
Moon occupies lagna with powerful evil planets in trikonas
and the 8th, without combination or aspect of benefics, the
child dies. A significant point brought out to light by
Bhattotpala is that, Mercury with the Sun is an evil planet.
There are many ignorant astrologers who maintain that
Budha has no astadosha or the evil of combustion. This is
wrong.

असितरविशशाङ्कभूमिजैर्व्ययनवमोदयनैधनाश्रितैः ।
भवति मरणमाशुदेहिनां यदि बलिना गुरुणा न-
बीक्षिताः ॥ १० ॥

Stanza 10.—If Saturn, Sun, Moon and Mars occupy the 12th, 9th, lagna and 8th respectively unaspected by powerful Jupiter the child dies quickly.

NOTES

Bhattotpala observes that if powerless Jupiter aspects all, or powerful Jupiter aspects some of these planets, death comes a little later. But if Jupiter in the 5th aspects all these planets there will be no death. The point may thus be illustrated.

Saturn	Birth Moon		
	RASI		
			Jupiter
Sun	Mars		

Here Jupiter aspects the Sun in the 5th and the Moon and birth in the 9th both of which are very powerfully aspected. As per Varahamihira's statement in Stanza 13,

Chap. II, all planets have quarter aspects in the 4th and 8th houses and under this method if we include the aspect of Jupiter upon Mars in the 4th and Saturn in the 8th houses, we can predict that the child lives.

सुतमदननवान्त्यलग्नरन्ध्रे-
ब्वशुभयुतो मरणाय शीतरश्मिः ।
भृगुसुतशशिपुत्रेदेववपूज्यै-
र्यदि बलिभिर्न युतोऽवलोकितो वा ॥ ११ ॥

Stanza 11.—If the Moon with malefics occupies 5th, 7th, 9th, 12th, 1st or 8th houses and not aspected by or combined with powerful Venus, Mercury or Jupiter death comes early.

NOTES

The commentator here accepts Moon as weak Moon and supports this assertion by an apt quotation from Saravali which refers to Kshina Chandra. Weak Moon therefore must occupy 1st, 5th, 7th, 8th, 9th or 12th, with malefics to produce death.

If he is aspected by any one of the powerful benefics, Mercury, Jupiter or Venus, death will be averted. Full Moon alters the case and produces good results.

योगे स्थानं गतवति बलिनश्चन्द्रे स्वं वा तनुगृहमथवा ।
पापैर्दृष्टे बलवति मरणं वर्षस्यान्ते किल मुनिगदितम् ॥१२॥

Stanza 12.—If the Moon by Gochara joins the house of the most powerful malefic in the

above yogas or joins his own place, or the lagna,
when he is strong and has strong malefic aspects
he causes death to the child within one year.

NOTES

This is greatly compressed in Sanskrit and much has
been said by the erudite commentator to offer satisfactory
explanation. The Moon moves in the 12th house of the
zodiac in about 27 and odd days. Where combinations
of planets have been clearly stated for the period of death
the student is directed to find out the time within one year
by the following methods. Certain planets have been
named in combinations as causing arista or death. Find
out which of these planets is the most powerful malefic for
causing death and take that as the powerful *arista* house.
The Moon in his rapid movements approaches that house
at a certain time and death may be predicted during that
time ; or take the house occupied by the *Moon* at the time
of birth. This will be what is technically called his rasi.
Death takes place when the Moon approaches that sign formerly occupied by him at birth or when the Moon approaches
the birth sign, predict death. The death must be predicted
within one year. But it may be questioned that as the
Moon moves in all the zodiacal signs within 27 and odd
days, how are we to find out the correct day or time of
death during the year, for the Moon approaches each planet
or his own rasi or the lagna, twelve or thirteen times in a
year. A clue is thus given. Death takes place at that time
when the Moon approaches any one of the above named
signs, powerfully aspected by malefics. Then alone death
must be foretold. All these have been stated by Varahamihira in accordance with principles of astrology, long

before enunciated by the renowned Munis of this land. He
openly disclaims all pretensions to originality or facts
deduced by his own observations. Bhattotpala now
approaches with a vast store of information on this most
vital point of early death and says that individuals with
such *arista* combinations sketched by Varahamihira have
been known to live long, within his own experience and that
it is his sacred duty to humanity to collect all such conjunctions of planets which are considered by various, strong
enough authors to protect the child, and which will enable
them to live when the *Arista yogas* are present in their
horoscopes.

Life and death are so supremely important and
interesting to mankind in all ages and climes, that I make
no apology to give the full quotations brought to bear upon
this vital question by Bhattotpala. The students should
very carefully learn these combinations and see if they are
present in horoscopes which are afflicted with Balarista
conjunctions. He gives 16 stanzas which are very necessary in judging of the Balarista yogas.

(1) If powerful Jupiter with bright rays occupies birth,
he averts all *aristas* (evils) as does Shula Dhara (Shiva)
to get rid off a man's sins when he devoutly prostrates
before that God.

(2) If the lord of birth is most powerful, unaspected
by malefics and aspected by benefics occupying the kendras,
the evils will be averted and the child lives long in wealth
and prosperity.

(3) Even when the Moon is in the 8th house, if
he occupies the Drekkanas of Mercury, Jupiter or Venus,
he will avert all evils and give long life.

(4) If the Moon is full, occupies beneficial signs with beneficial aspects, the evils will be averted, much more so when Venus aspects.

(5) If Venus, Mercury or Jupiter occupies powerfully a kendra although in conjunction with malefics, he will avert early death.

(6) Even when the Moon occupies the 6th house, if he joins the Drekkanas of Mercury, Jupiter or Venus, the child will be protected as does a serpent-bitten man by the medicine of *Siddhas*. These are men with wonderful psychic development.

(7) If Full Moon is between two benefics with bright light, the child will be protected completely as men can be protected by Garuda against all serpents.

(8) Even if Full Moon occupies 5th or 8th during the night of the bright half of the lunar month, he protects the child from all dangers.

(9) If Jupiter is bright, powerful, and lustrous and is found in a quadrant he averts all evils.

(10) If Jupiter, Moon, Venus and Mercury occupy beneficial signs or divisions they avert all evils.

(11) If the lord of the house occupied by the Moon at the time of birth joins a kendra with benefics, he protects the child from all evils as the devout prayers addressed to Vishnu protect a man from all his sins.

(12) If benefics join beneficial divisions and aspect malefics in beneficial divisions they cut away all evils as does a bad woman her husband.

(13)   If Rahu joins the 3rd, 6th or 11th house having beneficial aspects, all the evils will be blown out as cotton threads by powerful winds.

(14)   If all the planets occupy *sirshodayas*, the evils will be melted away as does the ghee placed on the fire.

(15)   If a successful benefic in the planetary fight is aspected by another benefic, the evils are blown away as do the trees by a violent storm.

(16)   If the Moon is aspected by all the planets, the evils will be conquered as a powerful emperor would conquer a petty chief opposed to him.

Apart from these planetary states which prevent Balarista, Sripathi says that the evils of Balarista dosha can be overcome by timely remedies and worship of God. There are the Durga Pujas (not in the Vamachara or evil ways, but in the Dakshinachara or Satvik ways) and Mrityunjaya Japa (the remedy that overcomes death), Mantrayamila, Havana, Homa, etc., which have been fully described in the *Santi Kamalakara* or the book of remedies and which have been dealt with in my ' Introduction to the study of Astrology '

CHAPTER VII

AYURDAYA OR LONGEVITY

आयुर्दायाध्यायः

भययवनमणित्थशक्तिपूर्वैर्दिवसकरादिषु वत्सराः प्रदिष्टाः ।
नवतिथिविषयाधिभूतरुद्रदशसहिता दशमिः स्वतुङ्गमेषु ॥ १ ॥

Stanza 1.—Sun, etc., in deep exaltation give
9+10, 15+10, 5+10, 2+10, 5+10, 11+10 and
10+10 years of life respectively according to
Maya, Yavana, Manitha and Saktipurva.

NOTES

Before he gives his own views Varahamihira quotes
previous authorities about the length of life each planet
gives to the child, when he is in deep exaltation, and
suggests that such term of life granted by each planet varies
proportionately as per a planet's fall, etc., from that place
of deep exaltation. The Sun gives 19 years, the Moon 25,
Mars 15, Mercury 12, Jupiter 15, Venus 21, and Saturn
20 years. Thus we get 19+25+15+12+15+21+20 years
or 127 years. Bhattotpala could have thrown greater
light on the lives of the famous authors quoted by Varahamihira, but he has been mercilessly short about them.
Maya was an Asura (Rakshasa or giant) who prayed
devoutly to the Sun and to whom a personification of that
God, gave the whole work of Suryasiddhanta so famous
all over the world. Yavana, an early form of Ivan in
Persia, is said to be a Mlecha Astrologer of great note.

14

Mlechas refer to Mussalmans or those who inhabit Turkey, Arabia, Persia, etc. Manitha was an acharya, a Brahmin of great astrological proficiency. Saktipurva is the son of Sakti or Parasara, the renowned father of the great Vedavyasa and the grandson of the venerable Vasishta the preceptor of Sri Rama. The views of these authors are here expressed.

नीचेस्तोऽर्द्धं हसति हि ततश्चान्तरस्थेऽनुपातो
होरा त्वंशप्रतिममपरे राशितुल्यं वदन्ति ।
हित्वा वक्रं रिपुगृहगतैर्हीयते स्वत्रिभागः
सूर्योच्छिन्नद्युतिषु च दलं प्रोज्झ्य शुक्रार्किपुत्रो ॥ २ ॥

Stanza 2.—Where a planet is debilitated he cuts away half of the term of life and in the middle rasis he gives terms of life as per rule of three. The lagna is supposed to give that number of years, which is represented by its amsa, while others say the number will be similar to the rasi. A planet in an unfriendly sign cuts one-third of his term unless he is retrograde. The combust planets except Venus and Saturn, cut off half their term of life.

NOTES

As this touches the mathematical portion of astrology to some extent the notes must necessarily be long and thoroughly explanatory. Planets in their lowest debilitation take away half the term of life granted by them while they are in deep exaltation. Thus when the Sun is at his lowest debilitations he gives $\frac{1}{2}$ of 19 or $9\frac{1}{2}$ years=114 months.

The Moon at his lowest gives $12\frac{1}{2}$ years or 150 months ; Mars gives $7\frac{1}{2}$ years or 90 months ;   Mercury gives 6 years or 72 months ; Jupiter gives $7\frac{1}{2}$ years or 90 months ;   Venus gives $10\frac{1}{2}$ years or 126 months ; and Saturn gives 10 years or 120 months.

There will be 6 signs or 180 degrees between the degree of deep exaltation and that of debilitation for a planet. Multiply the bhagas (degrees) into ghatikas (minutes) we get 1800 for each sign. This multiplied by the distance in rasi between exaltation and debilitation gives 1800 × 6 = 10800 ghatikas. When a planet falls from his exaltation take the number of degrees from it and convert them into ghatikas. When a planet has risen from his debilitation take the number of bhagas (degrees) from that and convert them into ghatikas. These are called the ghatikas gained by the planet. When the planet takes away half of his term of life for 6 signs (from his exaltation to his debilitation) or for 10800 ghatikas how much does he take away for the ghatikas he has travelled from his exaltation or debilitation ? In the case of a planet's fall he loses the term of life proportionately till he reaches his minimum in the lowest debilitation. But in the case of a planet rising from his debilitation till he approaches his exaltation, he gains proportionately above the lowest term given to him, till he gets the highest term mentioned to his credit. Take the number of ghatis gained by the planet and multiply this by the number of months it would give in its lowest debilitation.

Then divide the total by 10800. The figure obtained represents months. Take the remainder and multiply by

30, and divide the total by 10800, the figure obtained represents days. Then take the remainder and multiply it by 60 ghatis and divide the total by 10800 the figure thus obtained will be ghatis, and so on for the minuter divisions. When the figure representing the months is divided by 12, we naturally get the years. The figure obtained by this procedure must be subtracted from the total period the planet gives when it falls from its exaltation. But when the planet rises from his lowest debilitation, this figure must be added to the term of life which the planet gives at its lowest debilitation. Thus if the Sun is in Taurus, he is fallen from his exaltation in Aries. His total term in the highest elevation is 19 years and from this 19 years the total obtained by the above process must be deducted. But suppose the Sun is in Scorpio, then he has risen from the lowest fall in Libra, where he gives only 9½ years. Whatever is obtained by this process of the rule of three, that must be added to 9½ years.

Bhattotpala gives an easy method. Take any given planet and find out the degree, etc., he has gained, deduct the exaltation degrees, etc., if possible. But if the degrees he has gained cannot be deducted from the exaltation degrees then add the 12 rasis (signs) and from this total deduct the exaltation degrees and keep the remainder separate. If this remainder is less than 6 signs then deduct that from the 12 signs and keep it. But if the remainder is more than 6 signs then keep it as it is. Multiply this figure by the total number of years the planet gives in exaltation. Take the case of the Sun; here we have to multiply the rasis, degrees, ghatikas, etc., each by the total sum of 19, and convert the same into ghatis, bhagas, and rasis. Saravali gives instructions in a similar manner. Unfortunately Bhattotpala gives the theory but not the practical solution and in order to verify it, two or three examples must be given here.

Example 1.

Suppose the Sun is in 5 rasis, 15 bhagas and 20 kalas : convert the whole into kalas thus: $5 \times 30 = 150 + 15 = 165 \times 60 = 9900 + 20 = 9920$ ghatis (kalas). If the Sun loses $9\frac{1}{2}$ years for 10800 kalas, what does he lose for 9920 kalas = 10800 : 114 : : 9920 kalas to the answer =

$$\frac{114 \times 9920}{10800} = \frac{38 \times 248}{90} = \frac{19 \times 248}{45} = \frac{4712}{45} = 104 \text{ months}$$

$\frac{32}{3} \times 2$ days $= \frac{64}{3} = 21$ days and $\frac{1}{3} \times 60 = 20$ kalas (ghatis). The total of 104 months, 21 days and 20 kalas must be deducted from his total of 19 years. Thus we get 10 years, 3 months, 8 days and 40 kalas as the term of life granted by Sun.

Example 2.

Suppose the Moon is in 11 rasis, 20 bhagas and 45 kalas. Thus $11 \times 30 + 20 = 350 \times 60 = 21000 + 45 = 21045$ kalas = 21045 ghatis or kalas from his exaltation.

If the Moon gets $12\frac{1}{2}$ years for 10800 kalas what does he get for 21045 kalas $= \frac{1403 \times 15}{72}$ months $= \frac{7015}{24} = 292$ months and $\frac{7}{4} \times 5 = \frac{35}{4}$ 8 days and $3 \times 15 = 45$ ghatis or 24 years, 4 months, 8 days and 45 ghatis or kalas will be the term of life granted by the Moon = 292 months, 8 days, 45 gh.

$$= 24 y., \ 4 m., \ 8 d., \ 45 gh.$$

Take other planets in a similar way.

The birth gives the number of years denoted by the navamsa it occupies ; say birth falls in the 10th degree and 30' of Gemini. As each rasi has 9 navamsas 9 years are given.

The navamsa by calculation falls in the 4th division. The whole sign Gemini gives 9 years of life. But Gemini covers 30×60 or 1800 ghatis (minutes) and this divided by 9 gives 200 ghatis for each year. In Gemini the birth has advanced 10 degrees or $10 \times 60 + 30$ ghatis$= 630$ ghatis (minutes) this $\frac{630}{200}$ gives the number of years the birth denotes ; that is 3 years and $3/20 \times 3 = 9/5 = 1$ month and $4/5 \times 30$ days $= 24$ days.

Therefore to a person born when Gemini has advanced 10 bhagas and 30 kalas, the term of life given by that sign is 3 years, 1 month and 24 days. Similar procedure must be adopted for all birth terms of life. Manitha and others say that the number of years, etc., given by birth depends upon the rasi.

Take the same lagna. It has advanced through 2 rasis and $10\frac{1}{2}$ degrees. Two rasis give two years.

But by rule of three if 30 degrees give 1 year what would be given by $10\frac{1}{2}$ degrees? Converting the year into months we get the sum$=30 : 12 : : 10\frac{1}{2}°$ months req. $\dfrac{21 \times 5}{5}$ months$=4$ months and 6 days.

Thus according to Manitha and that school of astrology, a person born when $10\frac{1}{2}$ degrees of Gemini have passed, will be given 2 years, 4 months and 6 days of life by the birth rasi or Lagna Ayurdaya.

In the first case the birth sign cannot give more than 9 years at the most as there are only 9 navamsas in each sign, while in the second case the birth sign cannot give

anything more than 12 years. There will thus be a maxi-
mum difference of three years, and that certainly makes a
great deal of difference in fixing correctly the period of life
the man has.   Bhattotpala sides with Manitha and de-
nounces the view of Varahamihiracharya. The author of
Saravali cuts a happy medium. He says that the lagna
gives rasi longevity if its lord is powerful and amsa longevity if its lord is strong. Excepting the retrograde ones,
those planets which occupy unfriendly signs take away $\frac{1}{3}$rd
of their term of life.   The word used in the original is
Vakram Hitva which means leaving aside the Vakra
or retrograde planet or Vakra which also means Kuja
or Mars and therefore excepting Mars. This is supported by Badarayana who clearly mentions Bhumiputra.
Saravali says excepting retrograde. Varahamihira later on
says in Stanza 11 of this chapter that planets in Vakra
or retrogression become powerful and give thrice the term
of their life ; so probably he means by Vakra retrogression. Excepting Venus and Saturn the other planets when
they are in combust, take away half of their term of life.
Badarayana supports this view, *viz.*, that except Sukra and
Sani, the other planets, *viz.*, Budha, Kuja, Guru and Chandra take off, half of their term of life when in combust.

सर्वार्द्धत्रिचरणपञ्चषष्ठभागाः
क्षीयन्ते व्ययभवनादसत्सु वामम् ।
सत्स्वर्धं हसति तथैकराशिगाना-
मेकांशं हरति बली तथाह सत्यः ॥ ३ ॥

Stanza 3.—Evil planets in the 12th, 11th, 10th,
9th, 8th, and 7th take away 1, $\frac{1}{2}$, $\frac{1}{3}$, $\frac{1}{4}$, 1/6 and 1/8th

of the term of life allotted to them respectively. If
benefis occupy the same houses, they take away
only one half of that which the malefics do.
Satyacharya says that, if there are many
planets in anyone of the houses, only the most
powerful among them will eat the proportion of
life granted by it.

NOTES

A malefic in the 12th house from lagna absorbs the
whole of the term of life granted by it. In the 11th ½ of it,
in the 10th 1/3rd of it, in the 9th ¼th of it, in the 8th 1/5th of
it, and in the 7th 1/6th of it. Take on example, say Saturn in the
12th house. He absorbs all his 20 years and gives to the
child none at all as his share. If he is in the 11th he cuts
away half and gives 10 years. If he is in the 10th he cuts
away 1/3 of 20 that is 6 years and 8 months. If he is in the
9th he takes away ¼ of 20 or 5 years. If he is in the 8th
1/5 of 20 or 4 years he absorbs. If he is in the 7th he takes
away 1/6 of 20 or 3 years and 4 months.

If, on the other hand, there is Jupiter instead of Saturn in
the 12th house, he absorbs ½ of his life or ½ of 15 years. If
he is in the 11th then he takes away ¼ of his period or 3 years
9 months. If he is in the 10th he takes away 1/6th of his term
and when he is in the 9th ⅛th of his term. If in the 8th he
removes 1/10th and when he is in the 7th he removes 1/12th
of his period.

If there are, for instance Saturn, Jupiter, Mars and the
Sun in the 12th house, then the most powerful among them
will cut away the proportion or the whole of his period,
while the others do nothing at all. By quoting Satyacharya,

the author shows no difference in opinion but only as an
authority to support him.

साद्र्धोदितोदितनवांशहतात्समस्ता-
द्भागोष्ट्ययुक्तशतसंख्यमुपति नाशम् ।
क्रूरे विलग्नसहिते विधिना त्वनेन
सौम्येक्षिते दलमतः प्रलयं प्रयाति ॥ ४ ॥

Stanza 4.—If an evil planet occupies the birth
the number of amsas, etc., passed by the lagna
must be multiplied by the total of the planetary
terms of years, etc., and then divided by 108, and
deducted from the total term of life the figure
thus obtained. If a benefic aspects the above conjunction, half of this must be deducted.

NOTES

Take the time passed by the lagna and convert the
whole into kalas Divide this by 200 and we get the number
of navamsas gained by lagna. Multiply this by the total
planetary terms of life. Take the total and then divide this
by 108. The figure obtained must be deducted from the
total term of life for the malefic and half of this for the
benefic. Take an example :—

Gemini is the birth and it has passed 3 amsas and 1
bhaga and 20 kalas. Suppose Mars and Saturn are in
Gemini and the total number of years granted by all the pla-
nets is $40\frac{1}{2}$ years. Gemini has passed $3\frac{80}{200}$ navamsas$=3\,2/5$
To this add 18 amsas of Mesha and Vrishabha. This must be
multiplied by $40\frac{1}{2}$ years and divided by 108. Thus we get
$21\,2/5$ this $\times \dfrac{81}{2} \times \dfrac{1}{108}$ years $\dfrac{107}{5} \times \dfrac{1}{108} = \dfrac{107 \times 3}{5 \times 2 \times 4} = \dfrac{321}{40}$

years. 8 years and 1/40 × 12 months = 3/10 months = 3/10 × 30
days = 9 days or 8, years and 9 days.   Deduct this from the
total granted by the planets, *viz.*, 40 years, 6 months.   Thus
there will be a balance of 32 years, 5 months and 21 days.
But suppose Jupiter aspects these planets: then only half their
terms should be deducted.   That is for Saturn we have to
deduct 4 years and 4½ days, and the same for Mars if he is
that.   The author of Saravali seems to make some difference
in this connection. His process has been given here for ready
reference.   Convert the lagna into kalas, and multiply the
same by the term of life granted by each planet, and then
divide this by 21600 kalas the total of the 12 rasis.   Then
convert the quotient into years, etc.   The length of life
thus obtained for each planet will be the true measure of
life the man enjoys.   If there are malefic and benefic
planets in lagna take the term of life granted by that planet
which is close to lagna.   Thus if Saturn is 20 degrees from
the lagna and Mars 15 degrees from the lagna, then Mars
must be taken in preference to the former.   By evil planets
the Sun, Saturn and Mars alone must be understood.
Weak Moon and bad Mercury cannot be accepted.   This
is supported by a quotation from Badarayana.

समाषष्टिर्द्विघ्ना मनुजकरिणां पञ्च च निशा
हयानां द्वात्रिंशत्खरकरभयोः पञ्च च कृतिः ।
विरूपा साप्यायुर्वृषमहिषयोर्द्वादश शुनां
स्मृतं छागादीनां दशकसहिताः षट् च परमम् ॥ ५ ॥

Stanza 5.—Men and elephants have 60 × 2
years as term of life and 5 days more.   Horses
live 32 years.   Camels and asses 25 years.   Buff-

aloes and bullocks live 24 years.   Dogs have 12
years. Goats, etc., 16 years.

NOTES

This raises a great and difficult question. The utmost
limit for ordinary men is 120 years and 5 days. But there
are men who have lived for hundreds and thousands of
years. There are also instances of horses having lived for
50 years and more. So also dogs probably live to 20 years.
Much depends upon the seed, the soil, the climatic
conditions and the occupations or work in which the man
or the animal has been engaged. The limits given here are
those which ordinarily apply and these years are solar
years. In the horoscopes of horses, sheep, dogs and cattle
the same rule of three which is applied to men here must
also be applied to them. Thus if for 120 years the Sun
gives 19 years what would he give for 32 years.

$$\frac{32 \times 19}{120} \text{ years} = \frac{4 \times 19}{15} = \frac{76}{15} \text{ 5 years and } \frac{1}{15} = \frac{1}{15} \times \frac{12}{ } = \frac{12}{15}$$

$$\text{months} = \frac{12 \times 30}{15} \text{ days} = 24 \text{ days.}$$ Thus the Sun gives

in the case of the horse 5 years and 24 days, when he is
similarly situated. This enables one to fix the periods of
life for pet animals, etc. Dogs include tigers, cats and
lions according to some.

अनिमिषपरमांशके विलग्ने
शशितनये गवि पञ्चवर्गलिप्ते ।
भवति हि परमायुषः प्रमाणं
यदि सकलाः सहिताः स्वतुङ्गभेषु ॥ ६ ॥

Stanza 6.—If the last navamsa of **Meena** becomes lagna, If **Mercury** is in the 25th minute in Vrishabha and if all the rest are in their deep exaltations, the person gets the utmost limit of life, *viz.*, 120 years and 5 days.

NOTES

The following is the list of planets in their Rasis, Bhagas, and Kalas :—

	Rasi	*Bhaga*	*Kala*
The Sun	0	9	0
The Moon	1	2	0
Mars	9	27	0
Mercury	1	0	25
Jupiter	3	4	0
Venus	11	26	0
Saturn	6	19	0
Lagna	11	29	59

All these planets except Mercury now give the total number of years named against them when they are in deep exaltation. Mercury has fallen from debilitation. Therefore he has now passed one rasi, bhaga nil and 25 kalas. This must be deducted from the rasi he occupies. Thus we get 1 rasi, 15 bhagas and 25 kalas converting this into kalas we get 2725 kalas. If Budha gives 6 years for 10800 kalas what does he give for 2725 kalas $= \frac{2725 \times 6}{10800} = \frac{545}{360} = \frac{109}{72} = 1$ year $\frac{37}{72} \times 12$ months $= 6$ months and $1/6 \times 30$ days $= 5$, thus we get 1 year, 6 months and 5 days. This must be added to 6 years. We therefore get 7 years, 6 months and 5 days for Budha.

As Mars is in the 11th house he gives half of his term, *viz.*, 7½ years.

As Saturn is in the 8th house, out of his 20 years he loses 4 years or 1/5th of his term of life and gives 16 years.

The Sun, Moon, Jupiter and Venus give their full terms. As the last navamsa rises in the lagna it gives 9 years.

Birth Venus	Sun	Moon Mercury	
			Jupiter
Mars	Horoscope where 6 planets are exalted		
		Saturn	

Thus we have—

		Years	Months	Days
The Sun	...	19	...	...
The Moon	...	25	...	...
Mars	...	7	6	...
Mercury	...	7	6	5
Jupiter	...	15	...	...
Venus	...	21	...	...
Saturn	...	16	...	...
Lagna	...	9	...	...
Total	...	120	0	5

When the Sun is exalted Mercury can never occupy his exaltation in Virgo. Hence he is placed in Taurus. Bhattotpala says that even here Mercury cannot be more distant from the Sun than 4 degrees in Taurus when the latter planet is in his own deep exaltation that is in the 10th degree of Aries.   Probably Mercury did go beyond 24 degrees from the Sun during the time of Bhattotpala.   His displacement now, according to present astronomical calculation, may be carefully noted.

If Mercury is in the 4th degree of Taurus the commentator thus calculates the age of the child.   If we take Budha in the 4th degree of Taurus he gives 1 year, 7 months and 18 days. This added to 6 years of his Neecha position, he gives 7 years, 7 months and 18 days.   Thus the combination above sketched may give a term of 120 years, 1 month and 18 days.   Varahamihira's statement that a man lives to 120 years and 5 days has been shown to be erroneous by his commentator.   Man sometimes lives even to greater ages than this.

अयुर्दायं विष्णुगुप्तोऽपि चैवं
देवस्वामि सिद्धसेनश्च चक्रे ।
दोषश्चैषां जायतेऽष्टावरिष्टं
हित्वा नायुर्विंशतेः स्यादधस्तात् ॥ ७ ॥

यस्मिन्योगे पूर्णमायुः प्रदिष्टं
तस्मिन् प्रोक्तं चक्रवर्तित्वमन्यैः ।
प्रत्यक्षोऽयं तेषु दोषः परोऽपि
जीवत्यायुः पूर्णमर्धैर्विनाऽपि ॥ ८ ॥

Stanzas 7 & 8.—Vishnugupta, Devaswami and Siddhasena have given similar longevity.

There is one serious objection to the acceptance of their theory, because according to them, no children can die above 8 and below 20 years which is absurd.

They have further stated that those who have this longevity will also become emperors. This is erroneous as many men live long and still be beggars.

NOTES

Bhattotpala says that Vishnugupta was the famous Chanikya, the founder of the Mauryan Dynasty, who befriended Chandragupta and raised him to the throne formerly occupied by the Nava Nandas. Please refer to my notes on the history of Vijayanager, Pp. 30. Chandragupta ascended the throne of Magadha in B.C. 322 and ruled for 25 years. Varahamihira quotes Chanikya and therefore naturally must have come after him. The whole political record of the methods adopted by Vishnugupta to place Chandragupta on the throne of the Nava Nandas is beautifully explained in a Sanskrit Drama entitled Mudra Rakshasa. Devaswami is called an Acharya who is quoted by Varahamihira and therefore must have flourished before him.

Chanikya is a historical personage who was contemporary with Alexander the Great in the latter part of the 4th century B.C. Bhattotpala says nothing about Siddhasena and probably he was an astrologer of great fame to have been quoted by Varahamihira as an authority.

Bhattotpala points out that probably these two stanzas were not the production of his author as they are themselves subjected to severe criticism and erroneous statements. Quoting Badarayana and Yavaneswara, Bhattotpala says that if 6 planets are exalted the person will become an emperor and if seven planets are exalted then the person will be lord of the three worlds. This last statement comes from Badarayana. Probably during the earlier centuries of the world's creation such a combination may have been possible, for Vyasa maintains it and others have declared it to be frequently occurring.

But under the present mathematics as applied to planetary movements, it is impossible to have the Sun and Mercury, exalted at the same time. Mercury as above stated by Bhattotpala, never moves beyond 24 degrees of the Sun and therefore he cannot be in Virgo when the Sun is exalted in Aries. He can only be in Pisces, Aries or Taurus but never in Gemini, much less in 150 degrees from him, so also with Venus, when Mercury is in Virgo exalted and therefore the idea of ascribing results to the exaltation of seven planets at one time in a horoscope looks perfectly absurd on its face now. What the planetary movements could have been millions of years ago, it is difficult to say and dangerous to dogmatise. To get the full life, 6 planets must be in exaltation, but when they are so, the person becomes an emperor. But there are many who are poor, but who live long. This is found to be the case in practical life.

Bhattotpala first shows the error in Varahamihira's objection in Stanza 7. As per conditions laid down in Stanza 4 of this chapter it is difficult to fix the different

periods of life given by evil planets in the lagna as they
may considerably lessen the relative terms of life granted
by them and thus bring down the total to less than 20 years
and more than 8 years.   He gives an example.

Lagna gives no term of life as it has just entered
Kumbha.   We have known the relative periods given by
exalted and debilitated planets.

Sukra Budha	Ravi	Chandra	
Lagna Kuja	RASI		
Guru			
		Sani	

	Rasi	Bhaga	Kala
Ravi	0	9	...
Chandra	1	2	...
Kuja	10	28	...
Budha	11	14	...
Guru	9	4	...
Sukra	11	26	...
Sani	6	19	7
Lagna	10	0	1

These are the positions at the birth of a child given
above for illustration.

We must now find out the term given by Kuja.   He
has now fallen 30 degress from his exaltation, *viz.*, from

15

28 in Makara.   Reduce 30 degrees into kalas $30 \times 60 =$ 1800.

If he loses 90 months in 10800

$$= \frac{1800}{10800} \times \frac{90}{} = 15 \text{ kalas} = 15 \text{ months.}$$

What does he lose in 1800 ?

This must be deducted from Kuja's total period of 15 years. He gives therefore 13 years and 9 months.   We shall now give *Chakrapatha* or the terms of life to be deducted by the positions of the various planets in the horoscope.   Guru occupies the 12th from lagna and cuts half of his term.   He gives 3 years and 9 months.

The Sun gives 19 years, Moon 25, Mars $13\frac{3}{4}$, Mercury 6 years, Jupiter 3 years and 9 months, Venus gives 21 and Saturn 10 years. Lagna gives none.   Therefore the total is.

		Years	*Months*
The Sun	...	19	...
The Moon	...	25	...
Mars	...	13	9
Mercury	...	6	...
Jupiter	...	3	9
Venus	...	21	...
Saturn	...	10	...
Lagna	...	0	...
Total	...	98	6

Varahamihira, although he has not clearly stated so, had implied that the terms of life given by the exalted and debilitated planets could not be lessened either by their occupation of unfriendly or combustion houses.   For this can be easily inferred from Stanza 6 of this chapter.

For there, the Moon is in Taurus and Venus is in Pisces. From such mutual positions of 3 and 11 both of them become temporary enemies and they are also not permanent friends. If one-third of the Moon's period is deducted for his occupation of Vrishabha, then the total of 20 years, etc., given by Varahamihira cannot be obtained. The lagna in the above horoscope, in Stanzas 7 and 8 falls in the first navamsa of Kumbha and therefore is the 91st navamsa from Mesha. This must be multiplied by the terms of longevity given by all the planets.

Thus $91 \times 98\frac{1}{2}$ divided by $108 = \dfrac{91 \times 197}{2 \times 108}$ years $= \dfrac{17927}{216} =$ 82 years and $\dfrac{215}{216} \times 12$ months $= 11$ months and $\dfrac{17}{18} \times 30$ days $= 28$ days and $1/3 \times 60$ ghatis $= 20$ kalas or ghatis. Thus the presence of an evil planet in the lagna takes away 82 years, 11 months, 28 days and 20 kalas.

This must be deducted from the total Ayurdaya (term of life), viz., 98 years and 6 months. There is, therefore, a balance of 15 years, 6 months, 1 day and 40 kalas. A person having that combination given above will live only for 15 years and odd. He has shown here that Varahamihira's objection that no age comes above 8 or below 20 years according to the theories of other Acharyas fails to the ground. But others may say that with an evil planet in the lagna the term of life falls like this. Varahamihira had in view only good planets in lagna in which case no age comes below 20 years. But this is equally fallacious. When a statement is made, it must be approved of by the majority of the astrological writers and nothing can be supported which is against their declared principles. The very same Acharyas who have treated of the questions on longevity

have also treated of certain Mrityu yogas (combinations for
death) and they must be fully taken into consideration. As
the question of life and death is most significant for man,
I have thought fit to explain the whole in detail even at the
risk of profuseness. Badarayana says:

"If an evil planet joins 6th or 8th in a cruel sign,
aspected by an unfriendly planet or if he suffers defeat in
the planetary fight the person dies in his antardasa or sub-
period."

Yavaneswara observes :

" If a malefic occupies 6th or 8th, even if that is a
friendly house aspected by malefics he will kill the person
in his sub-period by ropes, imprisonment and so forth."

Saravali declares :

" If the period of a cruel planet has the sub-period of
another malefic, the person suffers death. If these malefics
have unfriendly conjunctions then the danger is enhanced.
In the dasa of Sani if the sub-dasa of Kuja intervenes
although the man may have lived long, he will be certainly
killed. If malefics join cruel signs and occupy 6th or 8th
houses or if aspected by unfriendly planets occupying 6th
or 8th, the man dies during such sub-periods. If the
period of an unfriendly planet of the lord of lagna occurs,
and the sub-period of the lagna intervenes the person dies
suddenly according to Satyacharya ". Here one point of
interest is that Satyacharya has been quoted by Saravali
and therefore he must have been earlier than that work in
the field. Varahamihira quotes often Satyacharya and does
not mention Saravali. It is plain from this that Saravali
came between Varahamihira and Bhattotpala.

Therefore the commentator triumphantly observes that according to the statements of other Acharyas—authors—longevity can be ensured both above 8 years and also below 20 years and many cases of death certainly occur during these periods. The second objection taken by Varahamihira also falls to the ground. There are many who live long but are veritable beggars.

Example.

	Rasi	Bhaga	Kala
The Sun	1	10	...
The Moon	2	3	...
Mars	10	28	...
Mercury	...	15	...
Jupiter	4	5	...
Venus	...	27	20
Saturn	10	20	...
Lagna	8	29	59

Mercury Venus	Sun	Moon
Mars Saturn	RASI	
		Jupiter
Birth or Lagna		

We shall now determine the various terms of life granted by the planets. Making the calculations we get—

		Years	Months	Days
The Sun	...	17	5	...
The Moon	...	22	11	...
Mars	...	13	9	...
Mercury	...	7	...	...
Jupiter	...	13	9	...
Venus	...	19	2	23
Saturn	...	13	4	...
Lagna	...	9	...	...
Total	...	116	4	23

Out of this Jupiter occupying the 9th house from lagna loses ⅓th of his term or 1 year, 8 months, 18 days, 45 kalas, and Chandra loses 1/7th of his term by occupying the 7th house or 3 years, 9 months, 25 days or both of these together lose 5 years, 6 months, 13 days and 45 ghatis. We get 110 years, 10 months, 9 days and 15 kalas.

None of the planets is in exaltation.

Thus a man can live for more than a hundred and ten years and still be a beggar. As there are no planets on both sides of the Moon in this diagram because Sun is not taken into consideration in considering Anapha, Sunapha, Dhuradhura and Kemadruma, there is the *Kemadruma* combination which produces dirt, sorrow, uneasiness, beggarliness, servility and vagabondism even in persons born in royal families; much more therefore will these qualities be in ordinary families. (See Stanzas 3 and 6, Chapter XIII.)   Therefore Bhattotpala has shown by example that persons can get long life without royal or affluent state. Varahamihira prefers Satyacharya's system, not because other Acharyas quoted already are false, but because Satyacharya represents the system adopted by the majority of the astrological Rishis. In Brihat Samhita Varahamihira clearly declares that " *Jyotisha is like a Veda and when different doctrines are promulgated therein we have no ability or capacity to say which is correct and which not. Therefore I shall explain the different systems*". (*Vide* ' Life of Varahamihira ' by me, Chapter V.) If this is the position taken by the learned Varahamihira, what could the ignorant modern man say about the differences in the astrological systems. Some say that there is no *Kemadruma* in the above given illustration as Chandra is in the 7th kendra but the author is clear in omitting the presence of Surya and he is supported by Bhagavan Gargi who distinctly says that the kendras with planets must be referred to from lagna excepting Chandra. Moreover when Kuja and other planets are not in 4th and 10th, there is Kemadruma according to some.

स्वमतेन किलाह जीवशर्मा
ग्रहदायं परमायुषः स्वरांशम्
ग्रहभुक्तनवांशराशितुल्यं
बहुसाम्यं समुपैति सत्यवाक्यम् ॥ ९ ॥

Stanza 9.—Jeevasarma says, on his own responsibility, that each of the planets gives one-seventh of the period of the longevity stated above. Satyacharya says that each planet gives that term of life which is indicated by the navamsa he occupies. This seems to be approved of by many astrological experts.

NOTES

Varahamihira declares that he has seen Jeevasarma's works where he distinctly lays down 1/7th of 120 years and 5 days as the longest term of life given by each of the seven planets.

Thus we get for each planet in exaltation 17 years, 1 month, 22 days, 8 kalas and 34 vikalas. Half of this will be the period given by each of the planets when in debilitation. For other rasis, the rule of three must of course be applied. In other respects Jeevasarma gives the same proportionate subtractions and additions as other authors have done in the *Chakrapatha*.

Bhattotpala gives an easy method for calculating the term of life given by any planet. Take any planet and subtract the degrees he has fallen from his deep exaltation. If the sum so subtracted is less than 6 signs, that must be subtracted from 12 rasis. Multiply the remainder by 8641 and divide the sum obtained by 504. The quotient represents days. This divided by 30 gives months and the quotient thus obtained must be divided by 12 to get years. Jeevasarma is not at all supported by any great Rishis or Acharyas and therefore the only objection against Jeevasarma's system is that he bases his authority on himself. Bhattotpala has done immense service to the chronology of various authors, although not to that extent to which we could have expected a man of his wonderful learning to do. Varahamihira refers to Maya, Yavana, Manitha and Parasara in Stanza 1 of this chapter. The commentator says that the *Yavana* referred to by the author could not be Yavanacharya who, under another name of *Sphuji Dwaja*, has composed a work after the Saka era commenced. In this work which was completely possessed by Bhattotpala. *Sphuji Dwaja* refers to some old *Yavanas* who have given various characteristics to planets in the olden times. Bhattotpala rightly infers that as this *Yavanacharya* follows Varahamihira closely, he could not have been quoted by the author, for to quote an author he must have differed from him. Unfortunately the commentator did not get a copy of the work of the older *Yavana*. He also complains that he did not get a copy of the Parasara Hora to which Varahamihira refers. But Bhattotpala says that he possessed a copy of Parasara Samhitha. He also quotes another sloka from Parasara Hora which was referred to by some early authors. Bhattotpala clearly says that he possessed full copies of the works of Maya and Manitha. Admitting for argument's sake that Bhattotpala was one of the greatest commentators on astrological works, we get a doubt about the author of *Jataka Chandrika* when he says that he has made an abstract of *Parasara Hora*. Venkateswara, the author of *Jataka Chandrika*, was the son of Yagnya Narayana, a Dikshitar or one who had performed a sacrifice and must have been certainly more recent than Bhattotpala. The age of Bhattotpala, if we take the Saka he refers to as Vikramarka's era, will be now (1936 A.D.) about 1105 years or 821 A.D. when he completed his invaluable commentaries. (*Vide* the previous chapter.)

But if Saka refers to Salivahana then it will be 955 years or 979 A.D. Anyhow Parasara Hora had not been available at that remote time and the commentator regrets the incident very naturally. Probably during the time of Varahamihira, that reputed work was well-known and respected and the author had made ample references to it.

Varahamihira now gives the terms of life given by the different planets and this system not only recommended itself to the author but was also supported by such great astrological writers as Badarayana, Satyacharya and the older Yavanas. Each planet gives the number of years which is represented by the navamsa he occupies, irrespective of the rasis occupied, by such a planet.

सत्योक्ते ग्रहमिष्टं लिप्सीकृत्वा शतद्वयेनाप्तम् ।
मण्डलभागविशुद्धेऽब्दाः स्युः शेषान्तु मासाद्याः ॥१०॥

Stanza 10.—Convert the intended planet's position into kalas; divide this by 200; the quotient, if divisable, divided by 12 represents years, etc.

NOTES

Take a planet in one rasi, 8 bhagas and 45 kalas. Convert this into kalas. One rasi has 1800 kalas.

8 bhagas × 60=480+45=2325 kalas.

Divide this by 200, and we get 11 years and $\frac{125}{200} \times 12 =$

$\frac{15}{2}$ = 7 months and $\frac{1}{2} \times 30$ days = 15 days. There is 11 as the first quotient but it is not divisible by 12, and therefore represents year. But suppose it is 14, then divided by 12, there will be a remainder of 2 and that will be the number of years given by the planet.

Badarayana gives another method. Taking the same example we have 1 rasi, 8 bhagas and 45 kalas. Multiplying this by 180 we get thus $\frac{31}{24} \times 108 = \frac{279}{2} = 139\frac{1}{2}$.

This quotient must be divided by 12, and we get years 11, and $\frac{7\frac{1}{2}}{12}$ = 7 months and 15 days. Practically the same result.

स्वतुङ्गचक्रोपगतैस्त्रिसंगुणे
द्विरुत्तमस्वांशकभत्रिभागगैः ।
इयान्विशेषस्तु भदत्त भाषिते
समानमन्यत्रप्रथमेऽप्युदीरितम् ॥ ११ ॥

Stanza 11.—A planet in exaltation or retrogression will give 3 times the term of his life. If he is in Vargottama or in his own house or navamsa or drekkana he gives double the period. This is the speciality named by Satyacharya.

NOTES

A planet in his exaltation or retrogression, gives three times the term of life obtained by the above calculation.

Vargottama is the position of the planet in the same rasi and the same navamsa. His own house in the rasi or his navamsa or drekkana enables a planet to double the quantity of life he is able to give otherwise.

किंत्वत्र भांशप्रतिमं ददाति
वीर्यान्विता राशिसमं च होरा ।
क्रूरोदये योऽपचयः स नात्र
कार्ये च नाब्दैः प्रथमोपदिष्टैः ॥ १२ ॥

Stanza 12.—Lagna gives similar number of years as it has advanced in the navamsa. If it is

very powerful it will give similar to the rasi.   If
a malefic is in lagna no deduction should be
made on this account.   Do not take the terms of
life granted by the planets as stated before.

NOTES

In this system, Satyacharya fixes one year for each of
the navamsas, with proportionate terms for fractions of
that navamsa subject to a division by the Mandala Sankhya
or 12, the remainder being represented as years. But if the
lagna is very powerful then the number of rasis passed by
the lagna may be added to the amsa longevity obtained by
the lagna. Suppose 109 kalas in the 4th navamsa in
Meena have passed at the time of birth ; if the lagna is
not powerful as per St. 19, Ch. I, then lagna gives the
term of life which is obtained by multiplying 11 rasis by
9 amsas and adding the $3\frac{1}{2}$ amsas passed in Meena to it
and then by dividing the total by the mandala figure 12,
and the remainder will be the years given. Thus convert-
ing rasis into navamsas we have $11 \times 9 = 99 + 3\frac{1}{2}$ amsas $=$
$102\frac{1}{2}$ amsas. This must be divided by 12 ; thus there is a
remainder of $6\frac{1}{2}$ years and that is the term of longevity
given by the lagna.   But suppose this Meena Lagna is
powerful, then it gives 11 years represented by the eleven
rasis passed by it *plus* the fraction of Meena passed by
the lagna. If 1800 kalas give one year what would 700

kalas give $\frac{7}{18} \times 12 = \frac{14}{3} = 4$ months and $\frac{2}{3} \times 30$ days

$$= 20 \text{ days.}$$

Thus if Meena is powerful and 100 kalas have passed in
it at the birth, it would give a total of $6\frac{1}{2}$ years *plus* 11

years, 4 months and 20 days or a total of 17 years, 10
months and 20 days.   About the *rasi* and its additions,
Varaha Mihira is vague and unconvincing.   Bhattotpala
quotes an excellent passage from Badarayana where the
whole principle is distinctly explained.

सत्योपदेशो वरमत्र किन्तु
कुर्वन्त्ययोग्यं बहुवर्गणामिः ।
आचार्यकत्वं च बहुश्रुतायां
एकं तु यद्दूरि तदेव कार्यम् ॥ १३ ॥

Stanza 13.—Satyacharya's system is excellent, but many have spoiled it by useless multiplications.

Whenever two or three figures are to be
multiplied, then multiply it by that figure which
represents the strongest factors.

NOTES

Varahamihira expresses his regret at the way in which
some astrologers have interpreted Satyacharya's views and
principles. For instance, Satyacharya says that with the
exception of the specialities named by him the rest must be
interpreted as usual. Where a planet is in his own house,
his drekkana or his navamsa, he gives twice the term of
life granted by him. Suppose he occupies his own house,
his own drekkana and his own navamsa, then the term of
life granted by him ought not to be multiplied twice for
rasi, then twice for his navamsa. Whichever of these is
the stronger that planet only must be made to give twice

the period found out to his credit in the above formulated calculations. The same thing for Lagna Ayurdaya. No deductions should be made on account of the presence of other planets in the lagna when the Amsa Ayurdaya is made.

Saravali refers to Varahamihira and says that he alone, out of the many astrologers found out the truth in the method recommended by Satyacharya and approves his restrictions put upon multiplications.

Suppose a planet is retrograde and in exaltation. Then the term of life granted by him must be multiplied only thrice and not six times as the tenor of Maya and others suggest. When a planet gets multiplication twice and thrice then only multiply that term by 3 only. When division comes it must be similarly dealt with. Suppose a planet is in Neecha and Asta ; only subtract one term obtained by the greater of the two. When a planet is in the 11th and it also happens to be his unfriendly sign which should be first deducted ? The first deduction falls under the Chakrapatha and it is to be done first and then the term given by the planet in good or bad signs, etc.

From the quotation given from Gargi these matters are made very clear. First Chakrapatha should be done. Then the terms of loss must be ascertained and out of these the largest quantity obtained must be deducted. The multiplication sources must be found out and then the largest figure obtained must be multiplied.

Bhattotpala says that the author has given preference only to the Amsayurdaya which is not correct. Quoting Manitha and Saravali, Bhattotpala observes that when lagna is most powerful Amsayurdaya should be done.

When the Sun is most powerful, Pindayurdaya and if Chandra is most powerful Nisargayu should be consulted. Some others say that the term of life granted by the two methods Amsayurdaya and Grahadatta Pindayurdaya should be found out and whichever comes shortest in the two must be divided into Antardasas. If the last sub-period there, is owned by an unfriendly planet then death must be predicted. If it is ordinary the person passes through the danger, but if he is good then he escapes the danger and progresses well. Take an example.

Suppose by the Grahadatta Pindayurdaya a man gets 50 years while from the Amsayurdaya he gets only 40 years. Then take the lowest period, *i.e.*, 40 years granted by amsa. If at the end of the 40th year an unfriendly Antardasa happens the person dies at 40. But suppose the period of a good planet comes ; then the person will not be killed at 40 years but lives on.

गुरुशशिसहिते कुलीरलग्ने
शशितनये भृगुजे च केन्द्रयाते ।
भवरिपुसहजोपगैश्च शेषे-
रमितमिहायुरनुक्रमाद्विना स्यात् ॥ १४ ॥

Stanza 14.—If birth falls in Kataka and Guru and Chandra are in it, Budha and Sukra in the kendras, the rest in 3-6-11 the person lives very long and mathematical calculations for longevity do not apply to such a combination.

NOTES

The following is to illustrate the above stanza.   Lord
of 3 is in 4 in a friendly house.   Lord of 8 is in 11 in a
friendly house.   Lord of 2 is in 3 and lord of 7 in 11.

		Sani	
	RASI		Birth Guru Moon
Kuja		Sukra Budha	Ravi

Guru and Chandra must be in Kataka the birth
sign, Sukra and Budha may be in any of the kendras
with the rest of the evil planets Ravi, Sani and Kuja in
the 11th, 6th and 3rd either together or separately. That
is, these last three planets may be in any one or two or
three of these houses or each in one house. But anyhow
those three must be in these houses or in any one of them.
Under such combinations the person lives very long. The
author implies that longevity calculations do not apply to
such horoscopes. Bhattotpala touches a very fine point
which is quite worthy of the highest consideration. He
observes that the person for whom the period of longevity
has been found out cannot live longer, neither can he die
earlier than the terms granted by the planets under such
calculations. But the rules apply only to those who live
on definite principles of conduct, i.e., those who follow

good *Achara*. But he rightly says that such terms cannot be enjoyed by adulterers and vagabonds as the Dharma Sastras have distinctly laid down loss of terms of life for evil or sinful deeds in this life. But in the last yoga quoted as tending to give unlimited term of life this may be accomplished by taking such medical preparations as are recommended in the Ayurvedic principles. Thus all elements of uncertainty are here introduced which really and convincingly change the crooked theory of fatalism in astrology and introduces human efforts by adopting which they can either shorten or lengthen the periods of life granted by the planets as the results of previous Karmaic deeds. This is the key to the knowledge in astrology, and must be carefully remembered.

CHAPTER VIII

DASANTARDASA

दशान्तर्दशाध्याय:

उदयरविशशाङ्कप्राणिकेन्द्रादिसंस्था:
प्रथमवयसि मध्येऽन्त्ये च दद्यु: फलानि ।
न हि न फलविपाक: केन्द्रसंस्थाद्यभावे
भवति हि फलपक्ति: पूर्वमापोक्लिमेऽपि ॥ १ ॥

Stanza 1.—The most powerful among **Lagna, Surya** and **Chandra**, with planets in their kendras give results in the commencement, middle, and last periods of life respectively. If planets are not in kendras, etc., the results will flow in the commencement even from Apoklima planets.

NOTES

This stanza is very concisely put in and requires a great deal of explanation. After finding out the period of life for a man it becomes the duty of the astrologer next to deal out the good and evil terms which await him in his mortal career. The different *dasas* or periods of planets are given here to enable man to know when and how he will get his good and evil fortunes. The lagna represents body (physical), the Sun represents the atma (soul), and the Moon indicates manas (mind). Find out which of these three is the strongest in the horoscope and then ascribe the first dasa to it. Then the second dasa will be given by that planet which is the strongest in the kendras. If there are

two or more planets in the kendras they give the dasas consecutively one after the other according to the sources of
strength they possess.   After them comes the period of the
most powerful planet in the next houses to Kendras or
Panaparas.   After all these planets are finished then comes
the dasa of the strongest planet in the Apoklimas. Suppose
there are no planets in the kendras then the second dasa
begins with that planet which is the strongest in the Panaparas.   Suppose there are no planets in the kendras or
Panaparas, then all the planets will be in Apoklimas, and
the most powerful among them will give the second dasa,
and the third will be of him who is next to him in strength.
Kendras are 1-4-7-10, Panaparas 2-5-8-11, Apoklimas 3-6-9-
12. If the original stanza is carefully read, it reads very
ambiguous and smacks of a meaning quite inconsistent with
the clear explanations of Bhattotpala and the valuable quotations from Yavaneswara and the author's own *Swalpa Jataka,
Prathama Vayasi, Madhya Anthayacha*, etc. This refers to the
three periods of man's life, *viz.*, 1st, 2nd and 3rd part and
seems as if the *Phalam* (results) indicated happens in these
three divisions.

In other words it looks as if the kendra planets affect
the man in the first part of his life, the Panapara planets in
the second part and the Apoklima planets in the last period
of an individual's existence.   But this is not so.

आयुः कृतं येन हि यत्तदेव
कल्प्या दशा सा प्रबलस्य पूर्वम् ।
साम्ये बहूनां बहुवर्षदस्य
तेषां च साम्ये प्रथमोदितस्य ॥ २ ॥

Stanza 2.—The planet most powerful gives
the first dasa extending over that period of life
granted by him. If many planets are equally
powerful then the first dasa will belong to that
planet who gives the largest term of life. If some
planets give equal terms of life, then the first dasa
will be given by that planet who rises first.

NOTES

The extent of any planetary period will be that term,
which he gives after all the subtractions and multiplications,
are made about him.   First determine who is the strongest
among the Lagna, Surya and Chandra and give the first
dasa to the most powerful of these.   Then the 2nd dasa
will belong to him who is the strongest of the planets
occupying the kendras and if there are no planets in the
kendras then the strongest among the Panapara planets
gets the first dasa and if there are none there, then ascribe
the dasa to the most powerful among the Apoklima
planets. Suppose two planets are in exaltation and Vargottama.   Then both of them are equally strong. Who
should be preferred ? He who gets the Nisarga strength
(*See* St. 21, Ch. II).   Suppose Sani has 3 sources of
strength and Kuja has two sources. Then they both
become equal because Kuja has Nisargika as against Sani.
The Sthanabala, Digbala, Kalabala, Chestabala, and
Nisargikabala are the sources of strength as well as Shadvargas.   If careful calculations are made the strength of
each of the five planets can be measured and if in all
sources of strength two planets get equal strength then he
who gives the longest term will begin his dasa in preference

to the other. But if after all these sources of strength
are measured and two planets are found equal in strength,
then that planet out of these two, which rises from the Sun
first, will get preference. As many sources of strength are
recorded it would be almost difficult to say when any two
planets get equal strength from all those sources. The word
rising refers to the rising of the lagna as well as the rising
of a planet from the Sun. But the latter explanation is
supported distinctly by a fine quotation from Maharishi
Gargi.

एकर्क्षगोऽर्द्धमपहृत्य ददाति तु स्वं
न्यंशं त्रिकोणगृहगः स्मरगः स्वरांशम् ।
पादं फलस्य चतुरस्रगतः सहोरा-
स्त्वेवं परस्परगताः परिपाचयन्ति ॥ ३ ॥

Stanza 3.—The planet with the Dasanatha
gives half the term of that dasa with his results.
The planet who occupies the thrikona from him
gives one-third of that period with his results.
The planet in the 7th from him gives one-seventh
of his period. The planet who is in chaturasra
gives one-fourth of that term. In this manner
lagna and planets give their Dasas and Antardasas.

NOTES

This enables the student to find out the lords of the
sub-periods. The planet in conjunction with the dasa lord,
cuts half of the latter period and gives during that half his
own results. Lagna also gives its results as any planet does.

That is, if the lagna is with the lord of the dasa or in the
5th or 9th or 7th, or 4th or 8th from him it takes away the
proportionate periods named for the other planets and
introduces during those periods its own Phalam or results.

The first sub-period in a dasa must always be ascribed
to the lord of that dasa and then to others. If there are
many planets with the dasa lord then a sub-period must be
ascribed only to one planet who is the strongest of them.
This is implied by the singular noun the author has used
in the text.

This is ably supported by Bhattotpala with quotations
from Gargi, Yavaneswara, Satyacharya and Yama.

There are some writers who say that the sub-periods
will have to be distributed among all the planets in conjunction there, and some say, get the sub-period time for the
most powerful amongst them and then distribute the same
among all the planets in conjunction. But the commentator has shown his disapprobation of such hair-splittings.
Who is *Yama?* A quotation is made by Bhattotpala and
that is all we have here. He seems to have been a great
astrological writer to be quoted along with men of Gargi's
stamp and by a commentator like Bhattotpala.

स्थानान्यथैतानि सवर्णयित्वा
सर्वाण्यधश्छेदविवर्जितानि ।
दशाब्दपिण्डे गुणकाः यथांशं
छेदस्तदैक्येन दशाप्रभेदः ॥ ४ ॥

Stanza 4.—Bring all the fractions to a common figure, omit the denominators and multiply

severally the numerators by the dasa years and then divide the whole by the total of the numerators. By doing this you get the Antardasa periods.

NOTES

The term used in the original text is sthanam and means fractions. Bring these fractions to a common denominator. Omit the denominators. Take each of the numerators and then multiply each figure by the dasa number. Add all the numerators and then divide the total thus obtained by that figure. The quotient represents the sub-period in years, months, days, kalas, etc.

Take an example: The whole is worked out by fractions so that those who know mathematics can easily understand them. Kuja is the Dasanatha and he gives 3 years. Then we have $1/1 + 1/2 = 2/2 + 1/2$.

He now asks us to add the numerators and we get 3. The dasa has to be (1) multiplied by 2 and divided by the total 3; we get 2 years for the first lord. Then multiply the dasa 3 years by one and divide it by 3 and we get one year. Therefore the first lord gets 2 years of sub-period, while the 2nd lord or one who is with him takes one year or half of the first sub-period.

Take another example.

There is one planet with the lord of the dasa, another in the 5th, and another in the 7th. Then we have :—

$$1/1 + 1/2 + 1/3 + 1/7 = \frac{42 + 21 + 14 + 6}{42}$$

Suppose the lord of the dasa gives 16 years. Take the first numerator 42 and multiply it by 16, we have 672. By adding all the numerators we get 83. Thus we have to divide 672 by 83 to get years, etc.

$\frac{672}{83}$ years $= 8 - 1 - 4 \frac{58}{83}$ days.

Taking the second figure 21 and multiplying it by 16 we get 336. Divide this by 83 and we get 4 years, no months and $17\frac{29}{83}$ days. Taking the third figure 14 and multiplying it by 16 we get 224. This divided by $83 = \frac{224}{83} = 2$ years, 8 months, $11\frac{47}{83}$ days. Then take the last figure 6. Multiplying this by 16 we get $96 = \frac{96}{83} = 1$ year, 1 month and $26\frac{32}{83}$ days. The first figure, namely, 8 and odd years is the sub-period of the dasa lord. The second 4 and odd years are governed by the sub-lord who is with the dasa lord. The third figure two and odd years is governed by the sub-period of the planet who is in the 5th house from the dasa lord. The last one and odd years are governed by the planet who is in the 7th house from the dasa lord. Taking all these, *viz.*, the dasa lord, the planet in the 7th and the planet in the chaturasra (4 or 8th) we are able to get 32 varieties of antardasas. For six we get 4, for five we get 7, for four we get 9, for three we get 7, for two we get 4 and one nil. Therefore we have $1+4+7+9+7+4 = 32$ varieties in the sub-periods, when many will be guided by the order in which the dasa lords take precedence. But when a planet gets power to give a sub-period and does not possess power to give a dasa period then the sub-period for him should be entirely omitted.

Some say that the Antardasas are regulated in the following manner :

First, the Antardasa of the dasa lord ; 2nd, the sub-period of the planet with him ; 3rd, the planet in the tri-kona ; 4th, the planet in the 7th ; and 5th, the planets who are in trikona, 5th and 9th, or in chaturasra 4th and 8th ; then determine their relative strengths and ascribe the sub-period. But this is not recognised as correct by Maha-rishis, and Gargi clearly explains that the Antardasa should be distinctly regulated in accordance with the lords of the dasas. More examples in this connection seem to be quite unnecessary as the principles have been fully demonstrated.

सम्यग्बलिनः स्वतुङ्गभागे संपूर्णा बलवर्जितस्य रिक्ता ।
नीचांशगतस्य शत्रुभागे ज्ञेयानिष्टफला दशा प्रक्तौ ॥ ५ ॥

Stanza 5.—The Dasa (period) of a most powerful and exalted planet is called the *Poorna Dasa.* The dasa of a powerless planet is called the *Rikta.* The period of that planet which is in the navamsa of unfriendly amsa is called the *Aristaphala.*

NOTES

The *dasa* is the major period of a planet and its results will be as per names given to those. *Dasa Sampurna* means that which gives full or complete good and to get this name the planet must not only be deeply exalted but must also be possessed of all the sources of strength detailed in this work.

Suppose a planet gets all these sources of strength and is not exalted or it is exalted but without some sources of strength, then it cannot be called *Sampurna* or perfect. As

the author and the commentator have fixed the limits in
definite language, very few people get this *Sampurna Dasa*.
Bhattotpala says that during the time of such a *Poorna Dasa*
the person will have good health, wealth, and reputation
and they go on increasing daily. But if a planet is powerful
and occupies exaltation, then the dasa is called *Poorna*.
This gives health and wealth. *Rikta* means poor or devoid
of any power. During such times there will be bad health
and losses.

Arista means undesirable or miserable and all these
have been distinctly quoted by Bhattotpala from Bhagavan
Gargi.

उच्चस्य तुङ्गादवरोहिसंज्ञा
मध्या भवेत्सा सुहृदुच्चभागे ।
आरोहिणी निम्नपरिच्युतस्य
नीचारिभांशेष्वधमा भवेत्सा ॥ ६ ॥

Stanza 6.—The planet who has fallen from
exaltation gives Avarohi Dasa. If he joins friendly
or exalted navamsa, he constitutes Madhya Dasa.

The planet who is ascending from his debilitation gives *Arohani Dasa*. If such a planet
occupies debilitated or unfriendly navamsa, he
gives a worthless period.

NOTES

Avaroha means falling from a high to a low place or
state, and *Arohani* means rising from a low place to a high
place or state. As a planet falls from exaltation he must

give bad, but if he occupies exalted or friendly navamsa, then the results of his dasa will be ordinary. The names are indicative of the results they produce and Sanskrit is so sweet, pleasant, rich, constructive and expressive that for those who have intellects to use, the language includes the whole gist of what the planets give or do. The words waning and waxing may be conveniently used. Waning indicates evil and waxing good. Bhattotpala makes a slight difference between *Anista* and *Adhama*. The former means the worst, while the latter is not so bad. This is supported by quotations from Gargi.

नीचारिभांशे समवस्थितस्य
शस्ते गृहे मिश्रफला प्रदिष्टा ।
संज्ञानुरूपाणि फलान्यथैषां
दशासु वक्ष्यामि यथोपयोगम् ॥ ७ ॥

Stanza 7.—If a planet is in a good house and joins debilitated or unfriendly navamsa, it gives mixed results. The names are fixed for these indicative of their results. I shall give the results of the periods of the Sun, etc., later on.

NOTES

By good houses the author means planets in deep exaltation, Moola Thrikona, their own houses and the house of a friendly planet. By *Misraphala* or mixed results the author means wealth with disease, or health with poverty and so forth. The periods are—

(1) Sampurna=Perfect or excellent results.
(2) Poorna=Good results.

(3) Adhama = Ordinary good with miseries.
(4) Rikta = Poverty and misery.
(5) Anista = Bad in every way.
(6) Misra = Mixed results.

उभयेऽधममध्यपूजिता द्रेष्काणैश्वरभेषु चोत्क्रमात् ।
अशुभेष्टसमाः स्थिरे क्रमाद्द्वोरायाः परिकल्पिता दशा ॥ ८ ॥

Stanza 8.—If lagna rises in common sign, its drekkanas constitute *Adhama, Madhya* and *Pujita* respectively. If lagna is movable, the order must be reversed. If lagna is fixed, they constitute *Ashubha, Ista* and *Sama* respectively. Lagna Dasas are thus arranged.

NOTES

If the birth sign falls in the first drekkana of Dwiswabhava Rasi (common) it gives Adhama Dasa. If it falls in its 2nd Drekkana, it gives *Madhyama* or mixed and if it falls in its 3rd Drekkana it gives *Pujita* or good results. In movable or Chara Rasis the 1st Drekkana gives Pujita, the 2nd Madhyama and the 3rd Adhama results.

In fixed or Sthira Rasis, the 1st Drekkana gives bad results, the 2nd gives *Ista* or desirable and the 3rd *Sama* or mixed results.

Mesha, Kataka, Thula and Makara are movable signs.

Vrishabha, Simha, Vrischika and Kumbha—fixed.

Mithuna, Kanya, Dhanus and Meena—common or Dwiswabhava.

एकं द्वौ नव विंशतिर्द्ध्रतिकृती पञ्चाशदेषां क्रमा-
चन्द्रारेन्दुजशुक्रजीवादिनकृद्दैवाकरीणां समाः ।
स्वैः स्वैः पुष्टफला निसर्गजनितैः पंक्तिर्दशायाः क्रमा-
दन्ते लग्नदशा शुभेति यवना नेच्छन्ति केचित्तथा ॥ ९ ॥

Stanza 9.—Moon, Mars, Mercury, Venus, Jupiter, the Sun and Saturn give 1, 2, 9, 20, 18, 20, 50 years respectively of Nisargika Dasa. If in the previously stated dasa period of the planets, they get also this Nisargika dasa, they produce good results. Some of Yavanas say that the Lagna Dasa comes in the end and gives good. Some do not accept this view.

NOTES

The Moon gives one year of Nisargika Dasa from the time of birth. Mars gives 2 years of his period after the Moon. This makes the total 3 years. Mercury then gives 9 years. This makes 12 years. Venus gives 20 years after Mercury and this brings up the age to 32 years. Then comes the period of Jupiter for 18 years and this makes up a total of 50 years. Then comes the Sun with 20 years, making a total of 70 years. Then comes the long period of Saturn for 50 years and this brings up the total to 120 years. If they are powerful and occupy the upachayas (3—6—10—11 houses), they produce good. If the reverse they produce bad. The author says that he has great experience in these dasas and their results are highly encouraging. Without mentioning the years Yavaneswara thus attributes the

Nisarga planetary periods. Milk-drinking age for Chandra, teething season for Kuja, student's life to Budha, youthful and sensual life to Sukra, manhood to Guru. Ravi governs the next age or old age and Saturn completes the imbecility or the last stage. If, at any period of life, the Nisargika dasa and the dasa for the same planet as described in the Ayurdaya Bhaga run together much good will result. Take for instance the dasa of Sukra running from the 13th year to the 32nd year by the Nisargika system. If in these 20 years of Sukra, comes in the period of Sukra as ascertained by the Dasantardasa, then that period will be good. Suppose from the 24th to 29th, the Antardasa of Sukra comes according to planetary periods. This period will be very favourable as the man has both the Nisargika and ordinary dasa ruled by Sukra. From this it may be inferred that if the Nisargika is bad then his own period or sub-period in that time will also be bad and if that is good this will also be good.

But this view is negatived by direct quotations from Yavaneswara and Satyacharya who maintain that Nisargika Dasas are always good when the same planetary period joins them. According to old Yavanas (Purana Yavanas) the lagna and Nisargika Dasa comes after 120 years and it is good.

If it is asked why the Lagna Dasa comes after 120 years they say that as the 120 years are allotted to the various planets lagna has no opportunity to assert its power. Then it may be questioned as to whether there be any who live above 120 years. A combination is given which shows that lives even after 200 years are possible. Birth is in the end of Meena which is powerful. All the planets, some exalted

and others retrograde occupy the Meena navamsa. As
Meena is powerful it gives 24 years. The planets, each of
them being in Meena give 12 years. Excepting the Sun, the
other planets, some exalted and others retrograde give
thrice their terms or 36 years each. The Sun is in Mesha,
and in its last Navamsa Dhanus, so he gives 27 years.
Thus :—

Lagna	...	24 years
Ravi	...	27 „
Chandra	...	36 „
Kuja	...	36 „
Budha	...	36 „
Guru	...	36 „
Sukra	...	36 „
Sani	...	36 „
		267 years

The views of all writers agree in the fact that the
Lagna Dasa becomes good only when it is powerful and
not otherwise. The methods by which they approach the
question differ.

Shruta Kirti says that the dasa will be good or bad
according to the strength or weakness of the Lagna. Varahamihira has already stated that the Lagna Dasa should be
judged in the movable, fixed and common signs, by the
rising drekkanas at birth and Yavanas affirm that it is
good. Varahamihira does not agree with Shruta Kirti
because he advances an unsupported view of his own,
at variance with the declared opinions of the great
Maharishies.

पाकस्वामिनि लग्नगे सुहृदि वा वर्गेऽस्य सौम्येऽपि वा
प्रारब्धा शुभदा दशा त्रिदशषड्लाभेषु वा पाकपे ।
मित्रोच्चोपयस्त्रिकोणमदने पाकेश्वरस्य स्थित-
श्चन्द्रः सत्फलबोधनाति कुरुते पापानि चातोऽयथा ॥ १० ॥

Stanza. 10.—If the anthardasanatha is in
lagna, or if his friend is in lagna, or if lagna
falls in his friend's or in his varga, the dasa
beginning then, will be productive of good. Or
if he is in the 3rd, 6th, 10th or 11th houses it is
good. Or if the Moon occupies the exaltation
house of the Pakaswami or his friendly rasi, or
thrikona, or the 7th from him, it produces good.
If it is the reverse it produces bad.

NOTES

That planet whose sub-period commences is called the
Pakaswami or lord of the Antardasa. If this planet, the
lord of the Antardasa, is in birth or if his friends are in
birth, or if birth falls in the vargas of that planet, or if
a good planet happens to be in lagna at the commencement
of that sub-period, or if the sub-lord is in 3, 6, 10 or 11
from lagna, in all these cases the Antardasa produces good
results.

If this sub-period comes during the period of friends,
it becomes very good, but if it falls in that of unfriendly
or evil planets, it produces evil. Now the author tries to
answer a very important question. Under certain combinations sketched above, the planetary sub-period is said to be

good. But does good come all along that period or when
and how does it come? As the lord of the sub-period
moves on (*in gochara*) day after day in the zodiacal signs,
he falls into temporary friendly relations with the other
planets. Then, wherever the Moon occupies or moves
into such friendly planetary houses the person gets good
during such times or if the Moon occupies the exaltation
sign of the *Pakaswami* or if the Moon falls into *Upachaya*
houses from the lord of the sub-period or in the 5th, 7th
or 9th from him, these times must be considered as good.
By good what are we to understand and with reference to
what event in our life does it come. The Moon has been
given 3rd, 5th, 6th, 7th, 9th, 10th, 11th and the exaltation
house of the Pakaswami, for producing good results. Now,
find out which of the *bhavas* from birth Lagna are occupied
by the above signs and in which the Moon is moving and
predict good only for such events indicated by those
bhavas. Suppose Aries is the birth lagna and Mercury
is the Antardasadhipathi occupying the lagna. As the
Moon moves on, he occupies different positions from
Mercury. Suppose the Moon occupies the 5th or Leo,
then predict good for events signified by the 5th house
from lagna, *viz.*, children, father and intelligence. Suppose
the Moon is in Thula, 7th and Budha in Lagna, good comes
to the 7th bhava which controls wife and passions. When
the Moon occupies other houses than this, then he inflicts
bad results upon bhavas indicated by those houses. All
these statements are supported by Maharishi Gargi.

प्रारब्धा हिमगौ दशा स्वगृहगे मानार्थसाख्यावहा
कौजे दूषयति स्त्रियं बुधगृहे विद्यासुहृद्रित्तदा ।

17

दुर्गारण्यपथालये कृषिकरी सिंहे सितर्क्षेऽन्दा
कुस्त्रीदा मृगकुंभयोर्गुरुगृहे मानार्थसौख्यावहा ॥ ११ ॥

Stanza 11.—That dasa which begins when the Moon is in his own house is good and gives honour, wealth and happiness. That dasa which begins when the Moon is in Kuja's house makes his wife immoral; if that dasa begins when the Moon is in Budha's house it gives education, friends and wealth; if the dasa begins when the Moon is in Simha it gives work for him in forts, forests, roads, houses and agriculture; if it begins when the Moon is in Sukra's house he gives all desirable food; if it begins when the Moon is in Sani's house it gives mean woman; if it begins when the Moon is in Guru's house it gives reputation, wealth and happiness.

NOTES

The Dasa or Antardasa (period or sub-period) lord may happen to be any planet. The Moon seems to have very great influence in producing misery and happiness. It must be remembered that the Moon represents mind and controls it.

All happiness and misery affect the mind. Therefore the Moon's position at the time of the commencement of the dasa or its sub-period has great significance. Two sets of planetary movements are jumbled up here. At the time of birth the planets are fixed (with reference to Gochara) and also the birth sign. At birth they are there, but later on they go on moving continuously. Having made calculations we get the Dasas and Antardasas as per directions given in the earlier stanzas in this chapter and suppose the Antardasa of Guru begins on a particular day. Find out the position of the Moon (in Gochara) on that day and then apply the above principles enumerated. If, at the time of the beginning of Guru's Antardasa, the Moon is in Cancer he gives good. If the Moon were in Aries or Scorpio at that time his wife commits adultery. If Chandra is in Simha he will give work to the man in forests, fortifications, agriculture, roads and homes.

सौर्यं स्वनखदन्तचर्मकनकक्रौर्याध्वभूपाहवै-
स्तैक्ष्ण्यं धैर्यमजस्त्रमुद्यमरातिः ख्यातिः प्रतापोन्नतिः ।
भार्यापुत्रधनारिशस्त्रहुतभुग्भूपोद्भवा व्यापद-
स्त्यागी पापरातिः स्वभृत्यकलहो हृत्क्रोडपीडामयाः ॥ १२ ॥

Stanza 12.—The Sun gives wealth by Nakha, (nails or claws) teeth, skins, gold, cruelty, travel, kings and wars. He makes the man hot-temper-ed determined in doing work, in getting reputation and good by courage. He gets misery through wife, children, wealth, enemy, weapon, fire and king. The Sun gives liberty, fondness for sinful deeds, quarrels among his workmen or servants, complaints in chest, stomach and other diseases.

NOTES

The author has omitted the proper adjectives and
verbs. The Sun is stated to give the above results, but
when and under what circumstances, Varaha Mihira has not
stated. In the first half of the stanza the results are those
which the Sun gives when he is favourable and well
situated both in his Dasa and Antardasa. These results
ascribed to the Sun must always be subjected to the influences of other planets and the students should be
careful in venturing their future predictions. " *Nakha* "
means skins or claws. Teeth refers to elephant's tusks,
etc., skins to tiger's skins, etc. He gets wealth by cruelty
or tyranny or courage or in war or from kings. All these
good results happen when the Sun is favourable.

By Dhairya used in the text Bhattotpala explains it to
mean equanimity of temper maintained under good and
evil influences and events. When the Sun is unfavourable
miseries arise through a man's wife, his children, his
servants, his monetary transactions, his enemies, his
weapons, and through fire, and kingly displeasure. By
liberality or extravagance he gets into bad positions or
debts and difficulties. But when the Sun is good he is
liberal in the right direction. Varaha Mihira here gives
what good and bad results may be expected in the dasa of
Ravi, and how those results are brought about. Suppose
the Sun is exalted or is occupying favourable position,
then he gives the native money through gold, scents, claws,
ivory, skins or hides, travelling, kings and war. He may
get money through all these sources or through one or
more of them according to the strength of the Sun. He
may become a traveller and get money, become a king's

man or employee and thus secure wealth or he may trade
in ivory, scents, claws, hides and other such articles.

इन्दोः प्राप्य दशां फलानि लभते मन्त्रद्विजात्युद्भवा
नीक्षुक्षीररविकारवस्त्रकुसुमक्रीडातिलान्नश्रमैः ।
निद्रालस्यमृदुद्विजामररतिः स्त्रीजन्ममेधावित
कीर्त्यार्थोपचयक्षयौ च बलिमिर्वैरं स्वपक्षेण च ॥ १३ ॥

Stanza 13.—During the Moon's period the
person gets money or profits from mantras,
Brahmins, sugarcane, milk, clothes, flowers,
playing, oil seeds, food and fatigue or pain. He
will be fond of sleep, laziness, enduring pain,
Brahmins and Devatas, getting female issues,
possessed of good intelligence, reputation, earning
and spending, and he will pick quarrels with his
own men and those who are more powerful than
himself.

NOTES

Varaha Mihira gives general results and does not say
which results are produced by good Moon and which are
given by bad Moon. But a careful student can easily make a
selection from the results given by the Moon waning or
waxing. If the Moon is favourable the person may get
money through mantras. These may be the secrets of
Saiva or Vaishnava or other symbolic language, by practic-
ing which, man gets some cleverness, efficacy or reputation,
and thus be able to make that source an open door for

income.   He gets money through priestly or religious men.
He may deal in products of sugarcane, like jaggery or sugar,
etc., or milk and its products, curds, butter, milk, cheese
and ghee.   He may deal in varieties of clothes or deal in
flower sales or by arranging plays or taking part in them.
Oil seeds referred to, are sesamum seeds and the oil obtained
from them.   He sells food or arranges for their preparation
and distribution and gets money by the sweat of his brow in
getting these.   He will get many female children, and will be
equanimous in temperament. His intelligence will be brighten-
ed and reputation enhanced.   He will earn well and spend
well. He will respect Brahmins and Devatas. The last are the
purified beings higher in the scale of creation than the Brahmins.   Scientifically speaking the laws of continuity reveal to
us that man is not the climax of creation.   Beyond him rise
beings superior in moral and physical scale and endowed probably with far higher physical and mental potencies.   When
the Moon is good he gives income or profit through these
sources and when he is unfavourable he makes the man lazy
and quarrel with his own men and with those who are far
more powerful than himself.   This undoubtedly leads him
into the folds of great misery and poverty.   The unit of
man's bliss is shown below as compared to Brahmananda :

1. If Man's is 1 then.
2. Manushya Gandharva's—100.
3. Devagandharva's—100,00.
4. Pitrulokananda—1,000,000.
5. Smarta Devalokananda—100,000,000.
6. Karmadevananda—1,000,000,0000.
7. Devananda—1,000,000,000,000.
8. Indrananda—1,0000,0000,0000,00.

9. Brihaspatiananda—1,0000,0000,0000,0000.
10. Prajapathiananda—1,0000,0000,0000,0000,00.
11. Brahmananda—1,0000,0000,0000,0000,0000.
    As such Brahmananda is incomprehensible.

भौमस्यारिविमर्दभूपसहजक्षित्यविकाजैर्धनं
प्रद्वेषः सुतमित्रदारसहजैर्विद्वद्गुरुद्वेष्टृता ।
तृष्णासृग्ज्वरपित्तभंगजनिता रोगाः परस्त्रीकृताः
प्रीतिः पापरतैरधर्मनिरतिः पारुष्यतैक्ष्ण्यानि च ॥ १४ ॥

Stanza 14.—During the period of Mars
there will be destruction of enemies, gains from
rulers, lands, brothers, sheep and wool. He will
have hatred among his children, wife, friends,
brothers, learned men, and preceptors. He will
suffer from thirst, bloody diseases, fever, bile,
fractures. He will be fond of others' wives, sinful
men and uncharitable deeds. He will be harsh,
hot and evil tempered.

NOTES

Here again it is to be made out when Mars gives out all
these results. If Mars is good he destroys a man's enemies
and gives him wealth through kings, brothers, trading in
sheep and goats and in woollen stuffs. But when he is bad,
he subjects the man to family hatred and the displeasure of
his friends, educated men and his own preceptors.

The person suffers from all such complaints which arise
from corruption of blood or by passing of blood, piles, dis-
charging blood by nose or mouth, or through anus in stools.

Mars produces thirsty and bilious complaints. Fractures or broken limbs are under the direct control of this red planet. He will make the person adulterous, join the company of bad and sinful men and engage himself in unlawful or uncharitable deeds. In the text one reading is " *Para Stri Krita Pritthi* " meaning fondness for others' wives. Another reading is " *Rogaha* " meaning venereal diseases got from fondness for others' wives. Another reading is *Parastrishtatha* meaning one who is fond of others' wives. Both interpretations are acceptable.

वौध्यां दौत्यसुह्हुरुद्विजधनं विद्वत्प्रशंसा यशो-
युक्तिद्रव्यसुवर्णवेसरमहीसौभाग्यसौख्याप्तय: ।
हास्योपासनकौशलं मतिचयो धर्मक्रियासिद्धय:
पारुष्यं श्रमबन्धमानसशुच: पीडा च धातुत्रयात् ॥ १५ ॥

Stanza 15.—In the period of Mercury the person gets wealth by embassy, friends, preceptors and Brahmins. He will be praised by learned men and gets reputation thereby. He gets gold, mules, lands and personal charm, and happiness. He will be witty and humorous and will be clever in serving. He will have good mind, and charitable disposition. Harshness, fatigue, restraint or imprisonment, mental disease, and complaints from the three *Dhatus*, will result.

NOTES

Mercury is a beneficial planet but all planets may be good or bad as they own or occupy good or bad houses.

In Sanskrit he is called Soumya or Somaputra or the son
of the Moon. But Soumya also indicates a beneficial planet
and this is the sense in which the word is generally used.
When Mercury is good, the person can make wealth through embassy or diplomacy, through the good offices of his
friends and through the influences of his priests or preceptors. He gets reputation and men learned in sciences
praise him. He gets gold, mules and lands, and magnetism
by which his personality will be agreeable to and welcomed
by every one who knows or sees him. His wit and humour
will be cultivated and thus he gets a good name and attraction as a speaker or writer. His mind will be noble and
engages itself in doing charities. When Mercury is bad he
will be harsh and have to bear much fatigue. He may be
placed under bodily or mental restraints or may suffer imprisonment. His mind will be greatly affected, and he will
suffer from complicated diseases due to the elevation of the
three " Dhatus ". In Sanskrit Ayurveda (Medical Sci_
ence) three dhatus are mentioned, viz., (1) " Vata ", (2)
" Pitta " and (3) " Sleshma ". The first includes all windy
complaints or diseases which arise from accumulation of
bad gases and which lead to very serious complaints like
rheumatism, paralysis, burning sensation in the soles and
hands and nervous debility. Pitta indicates bile and heat
and complaints from these are many and various. Oozing
of blood from the various organs, overheat in the body and
burning sensation in the eyes and body, may happen. Most
fevers are based upon bile or heat, passing blood, constipa-
tion, piles and so forth.

Sleshma is the excess of lymph or fat and from these
various complications arise such as asthma, cough, dropsy,

dysentery, and accumulation of much fat. There is hardly
any disease in which these three *Dhatus* do not figure; but
what the author here means is that such diseases in which
these three *Dhatus* are equally prominent will trouble the
person when Mercury is bad.

नैर्ग्यां मान्गुणोदयो मतिचयः कान्तिप्रतापोऽति-
र्माहात्म्योद्यममन्त्रनीतिनृपतिस्वाध्यायमन्त्रैर्धनम् ।
हेमाश्वात्मजकुंजराम्बरचयः प्रीतिश्च सद्भूमिपैः
सूक्ष्म्योहागहनाश्रमः श्रवणरुग्वैरं विधर्मांश्रितैः ॥ १६ ॥

Stanza 16.—In his period Jupiter gives honour,
good character, good mind, personal charm,
courage, philanthropic disposition, determination
and devotion. He gets wealth through mantras,
kings, vedic recitation, counsel, skill in diplomacy.
He will have gold, houses, sons, elephants, clothes,
and friendship with good rulers. He gets troubled
by deep thinking, diseases in the ear and hatred
among lawless people.

NOTES

Jupiter is the most beneficial planet we have and when
he is well placed he gives honour, purity of mind, personal
charm or beauty, great courage, charitable disposition, devotion and determination in the execution of great or important
work. There are certain classes of men, among all nations,
whose chief occupation consists in repeating their sacred
books or prayers and who are remunerated either by ruling

monarchs or by public subscription and charities. Such
men are called in India, Ghanapaties, and whose sole
business consists in learning the Vedas by heart and repeating them in temples, large assemblies, and on marriage
and other sacred occasions. Personal charm means that
when a man is in the luck's way he gets an indescribable
beauty, which is attractive and which continues as long as
the good dasa lasts. There are many men who are fair
and well proportioned but who are somehow repulsive
and hateful in appearance. This indiscribable charm or
fascination comes with good dasas and disappears with
evil periods. Courage will be agreeable when it is shown
in a righteous cause, but not when a man goes on murdering
and committing dacoities and other unlawful deeds. When
the period of Guru is bad, troubles and anxieties arise
from all the good sources named above and from ear
disease and the enmity of lawless people. When he is
good, the person gets excellent horses, much gold, elephants,
varieties of rich clothes and much skill in carrying on
diplomatic relations. These will also be sources of income
for him and he will be honoured and made much of, in their
possession. Deep thinking, specially in unfortunate
circumstances produces harmful effects on the mind and
body and therefore becomes bad.

शौक्र्यां गीतरतिप्रमोदसुरभिद्रव्यान्नपानाम्बर-
क्षीरब्द्युतिमन्मथोपकरणज्ञानेष्टमित्रागमाः ।
कौशल्यं क्रयविक्रये कृषिनिधिप्राप्तिर्धनस्यागमो
वृन्दोर्विंशनिषादधर्मरहितैर्वैरं शुचः स्नेहतः ॥ १७ ॥

Stanza 17.—During the period of Venus (Sukra) the person will be fond of music, pleasure, fine scents, good meals and drinks, clothes, females, gems, personal charm, sensual pleasure, yogis, desirable personages, friends, skill in merchandise, agriculture, treasure-troves, wealth, hated by communities, kings, wild people, vagabonds and sorrow through friendship.

NOTES

For all wordly purposes Venus when auspicious, will give all desirable results and makes a man, what the general public call, materially happy. He gives him musical tastes and talents, taste in refined arts, enables him to procure all pleasures in the shape of food and sweet scents, fine clothes, luxurious meals, rich and delicious drinks, fine and costly gems, great personal charm and attractions, all sense pleasures, handsome females, desirable and agreeable people, and obliging friends, skill in buying and selling articles, successful agriculture, finding treasure-troves, and wealth by other pleasant means. He will come in contact with yogis and learn yoga to some extent. He will have high intelligence and great liking for dramatic compositions and performances, His horses, carriages, and cattle will be good and his houses will be handsome, well built, attractive and nicely and tastefully furnished. When Sukra is bad, the person will be hated by all communities, incur kingly displeasure, be on bad terms with wild and ferocious tribes and lawless gangs. He gets sorrow and misery through friends. This means that his former intimate friends will become his bitter enemies and this will certainly be a very good source for acute pain and worry, and the consequent unhappiness. When Sukra is powerfully situated and aspected by the benefic Guru, he will get lucky sons and daughters, but when he is unfavourable, daughters suffer and cause him misery.

सौरीं प्राप्य खरोष्ट्रपक्षिमहिषीवृद्धाङ्गनावाप्तयः
श्रेणीग्रामपुराधिकारजनिता पूजा कुधान्यागमः ।
श्लेष्मेर्ष्यानिलकोपमोहमलिनव्यापत्तितंद्राश्रमान्
भृत्यापत्यकलत्रभर्त्सनमपि प्राप्नोति च व्यङ्गताम् ॥ १८ ॥

Stanza 18.—During the period of Saturn the person gets donkeys, camels, birds, buffaloes, old women, leadership over communities, towns, or cities and inferior gains. He gets miseries or troubles through phlegm, jealousy, wind, anger, derangement, dirt, laziness and fatigue. He will be insulted and terrified by servants, children, and wife and will suffer the loss of a limb.

NOTES

Saturn is the worst planet to do good and the best to do evil. When he is good and auspicious, the man becomes a leader of a community, town or city. He gets wealth through inferior grains such as ragi, kumbu, maize, sesamum seeds, birds, buffaloes, iron, hides and salt. If Saturn is well situated or aspected by benefics, he will trade on a large scale in donkeys, camels, birds and buffaloes. He may be engaged in selling or buying these in large quantities, or in transacting work in which the products obtained from these objects may be sold or bargained. He will marry old women or have connection with such women. He may trade in iron, salt, claws, skins and feathers. He may become a leader or chief of his community or may be appointed as magistrate over them ; but if Saturn is debilitated or is otherwise disposed towards the native unfavourably then he gives a lot of misery, which can hardly be matched by any other miseries caused by other evil planets. As he represents blackness, and power for absorbing all beneficial rays, he will be able to inflict on the unfortunate man untold miseries. Various diseases of phlegm attack him, jealousy troubles him a great deal and causes much pain, and diseases from excess of wind in the body may also be predicted. He becomes easily excitable and the anger of himself and those with whom he comes in contact, will be a fruitful source of trouble and loss. His brain reels or derangement sets in, his surroundings will be dirty and he suffers from laziness and constant fatigue. His servants try to lord over him and his wife and children terrify him or offer insults. He may lose a limb or an operation might take away one of his limbs. He will lose his wealth, his lands and his previous agreeable surroundings, and will suffer severely in every way.

दशासु शस्तासु शुभानि कुर्व-
न्त्यनिष्टसंज्ञास्वशुभानि चैवम् ।
मिश्रासु मिश्राणि दशाफलानि
होराफलं लग्नपतेः समानम् ॥ १९ ॥

Stanza 19.—Good periods give happiness and bad periods produce misery. Mixed periods

produce mixed results, and the result of Lagna
Dasa will be similar in nature to its lord.

NOTES

In the course of the first fourteen verses Varaha
Mihira has elaborately discussed about the planetary
periods and sub-periods ; and when they would be good and
when they would be bad and what is meant by mixed dasas.
In all these cases, exaltations, Moola-trikonas, own and
friendly signs, beneficial conjunctions and aspects, and
occupations of good divisions, ownership and position, play
a great deal, and make the planet yield good results. By
good, we must understand that the man will be honoured,
healthy, influential, happy, educated, possessed of good
children, wife and relations, surrounded by pleasant and
agreeable friends, and respected and attractive. He will
command all appendages to happiness or enjoyment, such
as good houses, gardens, horses, carriages, clothes, gems
and valuable furniture. During the period of evil planets
the reverse happens. He loses wealth, houses, lands,
conveyances, character, becomes dull and careless of honour,
suffers from various complaints brought on by the three
dhatus : Vata-wind, Pitta-bile and Sleshma-phlegm. He
gets into all sorts of sorrow, becomes a drunkard or rake,
incurs the displeasue of rulers, the hatred of relations and
friends, and will get lawless, untruthful and vagabond
classes as companions. Wife, children, and close relations
begin to hate him and go where he will, there will be insult,
insubordination, and unpleasantness staring him in the face.
During the mixed periods there will be good and bad, often
following each other rapidly or coming together or partly

neutralising each other's results. Here it would be advantage-
ous to summarise Bhattotpala's commentaries on this stanza
as he throws considerable light on judging the good and bad
results.   Those planets who occupy *oopachayas* and who are
bright, give enjoyment.   Those planets who occupy *apa-
chyas*, who are struck by comets and meteors, who are dull
and contracted in size, give unfavourable results.   Planet in
swocha or kalabala, gives favourable results, or when he is
in moolatrikona or his own house.   Planet in a friendly
house gives mixed results.   Planet in debilitation, unfriendly houses or divisions, or defeated, or cut or assum-
ing different colour, or lustreless; or is unfriendly with
the lord of the birth, or owns sixth or eighth house, the
period of such a planet will be full of defects and miseries.
Quoting Satyacharya, Bhattotpala confirms what has been
already stated above.   The results of lagna dasa will be
similar to what its lord is able to give.   One born in Mesha
will have the dasa results similar to what Kuja is able to
give, and born in Vrishabha will have his results similar to
what Sukra would give, or the lagna may give good if it
rises in a good drekkana or bad if it occupies a bad
drekkana. Quoting Saravali, Bhattotpala says :—If a planet
is powerful at the time of the commencement of his period
or sub-period, has beneficial aspects and occupies good
divisions at the time of birth, he will not kill the person
although he may be armed with deadly powers.

If the lord of the sub-period is powerless, he will not
give any results, but he will not kill him although he may
make him sick or suffer from accident.   If the sub-lord is a
victor in the planetary war, and combines with the benefics
or if he occupies exaltation, he will not kill the man.

संज्ञाध्याये यस्य यद्द्रव्यमुक्तं
कर्माजीवो यश्च यथोपदिष्टः ।
भावस्थानालोकयोगोद्भवं च
तत्तत्सर्वं तस्य योज्यं दशायाम् ॥ २० ॥

Stanza 20.—In the period of each planet, the results will be based upon the materials or objects which have been detailed in the Saumgnyadhyaya, and the means of livelihood detailed in the Karma Jivadhyaya. Results of the planets will be determined by the aspects, occupation and other combinations given elsewhere.

NOTES

In the first two chapters planets have been given various characteristics, events, and objects. (See St. 12, Chap. II.)

The Sun gives in good dasa, copper and takes it away or causes loss to it in his bad dasa. In Chap. X means of livelihood are detailed and they will flow in good dasas and disappear in evil ones. In Chap. XX he gives the results of the planets occupying the various bhavas and they will be good when the planets are auspicious and bad when they are evil. In Chap. XIX he sketches the results of planetary aspects and they must be similarly explained. Excepting in Nabhasa yogas (Chap. XII) in all other yogas or conjunctions, the results good or bad will be prominent in the planetary periods which are the most powerful among them in causing that yoga. But in the

Nabhasa conjunctions, the planets which cause those yogas will be fruitful and will produce good results whenever their Dasas or Antardasas come, whether in themselves or in the periods of other planets.

छायां महाभूतकृतां च सर्वे
ऽभिव्यञ्जयन्ति स्वदशामवाप्य ।
कम्बुमिवायम्बरजान् गुणांश्च
नासास्यदक्तवक्छ्रवणानुमेयान् ॥ २१ ॥

Stanza 21.—The different planets give their lustre of the Mahabootas in their periods. This lustre or shade has to be identified by the nose, face, eyes, skin, and ear obtained by or through the earth, water, fire, air and space (*Akasa*).

NOTES

This is a difficult stanza and its real explanation will be the clue or key to the whole knowledge of the planetary periods and sub-periods. This stanza is supposed to enable a person to find out the planetary period and sub-period passing in the career of a man who has no horoscope or recollection of his time of birth. (*See* St. 6, Chap. II). Chaya is the word Varahamihira has used in the original. Chaya means the lustre or shade of the colour the person possesses. It is natural to say that a man has good or bad charm or fascination about his person. This represents Chaya. The planets give such colour or personal charm of the Mahaboota which they represent. When a person emits good or sweet smell he represents the earthly

characteristic of smell and therefore will be passing the
period of Budha. This can be learnt by the nose. The
watery characteristic is *Rasa* or taste and this has to be
known by the tongue. When he eats luxurious or good
meals, he will be passing the periods of Sukra or Chandra,
both of whom represent water. The Sun and Mars govern
fire and its characteristic is beauty, and this has to be
learnt by vision or eyes. When a man is handsome or
fascinating, then he must be passing the periods of Ravi
and Kuja. When air controls a man, the body will be
soft and this can be identified by the skin which is governed
by Saturn, and therefore known by the touch. When
Akasa controls him its characteristic of sound predominates,
and the period of Jupiter can be identified by the good
speech of the man by the ears. Varahamihira refers to
this Chaya elaborately in his Brihat Samhita in Chap.
LXVIII.

शुभफलद्दशायां ताद्गेवान्तरात्मा
बहु जनयति पुंसां सौख्यमर्थागमं च ।
कथितफलविपाकैस्तर्कयेद्वर्तमानां
परिणमति फलोक्तिः स्वप्नचिन्तास्वबीर्यैः ॥ २२ ॥

Stanza 22.—During the time of an auspicious planet the mind of the person (*innerman*)
will be good. It enables the man to get wealth
and secure happiness. The dasa may also be
known by the happiness or misery the man is
subjected to. The results produced by powerless
planets will be enjoyed in dreams and thoughts.

NOTES

Bhattotpala quotes from Brihat Samhita and remarks that with the exception of Vayuchaya, in all others there will be good or bad, but in the Vayu everything seems to be evil (*see* St. 93, Chap. 68). The *Vayuchaya* makes a man dirty, harsh or cruel, dark, stinking, die, imprisoned, unhealthy, unfortunate or lose property. Here we see all evil results and therefore this has been omitted or excepted. There are apparently several important methods of finding out the dasas and periods. The periods or sub-periods may be ascertained by regular calculations, by Chayas, by the innerman or mental peculiarities or by the results a man is enjoying as the product of dasa influences. When a good dasa comes, the mind or the inner consciousness will also be good, but when the period is bad, it will also be bad. In Varahamihira's Yatra work (or travelling) he thus observes : There is a light in man which is small and great, by which the past, present and the future may be known, and it is to this light that the name *Atma* is given. A person can certainly know by consulting his own *Atma* what prospects he will get in the course of his journey. There are many omens and evils and there are many encouraging signs but whatever they may be, it is the clearness of the *Manas* (mind) that enables a person to achieve success. A man enjoys or suffers in many ways. The periods of planets have been given peculiar characteristics and one therefore can easily identify the dasa by the man's surroundings. In the evil period of Saturn loss of limb is predicted but we see many persons under such Sani losing no limbs, and many under the auspicious dasa of Saturn losing limbs. Similarly many do not get *treasure troves* in good periods

of Venus and some get them in bad periods. With a view
to clear these doubts, Varahamihira says that many of the
results or events are enjoyed in thought regions or in dreams.
Such enjoyments or miseries will be the results of powerless or weak planets.   Here with reference to such remarks,
I may offer the following. In other works on astrology
enjoyment or misery may take various shapes and forms.
Say a man has good *Vahana Yoga* (conveyances).   He
keeps a coach or coaches, horses, bulls, etc., and enjoys
them. A friend of his who keeps none of these goes regularly on a drive or ride with him and he also has this *Vahana
Yoga* but in a powerful form. When they are driving they
see another friend of theirs and give him a lift for a certain
distance.   Then again his coachman and groom have
Vahana Yoga for they mount the carriage before and get
down the carriage after the master does so. Then any of
these may have constant thoughts about buying and keeping carriages while others may simply be dreaming of drives
and rides during their sleep. Provision is made in astrology about these differences in enjoyment and the causes
are traceable in the relative powers of the planets.

एकग्रहस्य सदृशे फलयोर्विरोधे
नाशं वदेच्चदधिकं परिपच्यते तत् ।
नान्यो ग्रहः सदृशमन्यफलं हिनस्ति
स्वां स्वां दशामुपगताः स्वफलप्रदाः स्युः ॥ १३ ॥

Stanza 23.—If one planet represents two
contrary results, the effect will be destruction to
those events.   But if one is stronger than the

other the stronger will prevail. If one planet represents one and another indicates a contrary result, there will be both the results. Planets give good or bad in their own periods.

NOTES

When a planet, by its dasa, gives gold, while by other combinations (Ashtaka Varga, etc.) it takes away the gold, then the result will be, the man gets no gold at all. But of these two sources o power, of giving and destroying whichever is stronger will prevail. When both are equal in a planet they produce nothing.

But suppose Jupiter gives gold and Mars takes it away at the same time, the person gets the gold and loses it again. When a planet gives by one source of power gold, and by another source silver, what would be the result ? Some say that according to the strength of sources it will give gold as well as silver while others maintain that whichever source is the strongest the result will be similar to that source.   If the silver source is stronger, then he gives silver and suppresses gold and if gold source is stronger he gives gold and suppresses silver. But I hold that when a planet has various sources of strength independently, it is reasonable to think that such sources produce results which are ascribed to them.

CHAPTER IX

ASHTAKA VARGA

अष्टकवर्गाध्यायः

स्वादर्कः प्रथमायबन्धुनिधनव्याज्ञातपोद्यूनगो
वक्रात्स्वादिव तद्देव रविजाच्छुक्रात् स्मरान्त्यारिषु ।
जीवाद्धर्मसुतायशत्रुषु दश्न्यायारिगः शीतगो-
रेष्वेवान्यतपःसुतेषु च बुबाह्यात् सबन्धवत्यगः ॥ १ ॥

Stanza 1.—The Sun is favourable from his position at the birth in 1, 11, 4, 8, 2, 10, 9 and 7. He is similar from Mars and Saturn. From Venus he is good in 7, 12 and 6. From Jupiter in 9, 5, 11 and 6. From Moon in 10, 3, 11 and 6. From Mercury in 3, 10, 11, 6, 12, 9 and 5. From lagna in 10, 3, 11, 6, 4 and 12 he is favourable.

NOTES

There are two sets of conjunctions to be considered. One set consists in fixing the planets correctly in their positions at the time of birth. But at any given time after birth, the planets by their incessant movements will be found in different situations both from the lagna as well as from their own fixed positions at the birth time. *Ashtaka Varga* means eight sources of energy for each planet including the lagna. Rahu and Kethu are omitted throughout this work, except for names and direction for Rahu. Say a horoscope contains the Sun in the 10th, which is

Kumbha. Vrishabha is birth and Ravi is in Kumbha, or
10th from it. But after 4 months Ravi will not be in
Kumbha, but by Gochara he will be in Mithuna. He is
now really in the 5th house from himself, and the 2nd
house from lagna. As he keeps on moving from day-to-day
he forms various angles from his original position not only
with reference to himself, but also with reference to all
the other planets. Take an example. At birth the combinations stood thus :—

	Chandra Rahu	Birth	Sani
Ravi Budha Guru	Mr. B.S.R.'s Horoscope Rasi.		
Sukra		Kuja Kethu	

But four months hence, where would all the planets
be, and where would each of the planets be with reference
to his own original position, as also with reference to
other planets fixed at the time of birth.

When understanding the principles laid down in this
chapter, the author enables the reader to know the good
and bad results which the everyday moving planets give,
when they form various angles from the original positions
occupied by them. He has already given the results of

Dasas and Antardasas but the commentator observes that results from these will be more certain in their influences on men. In this chapter the results sketched may be

Rabu	Sukra		Ravi Budha Sani
Guru	Four months later.		
Kuja		Sani	Kethu Chandra

marked by figures and ciphers. In the horoscope given we see the Sun in Kumbha. The following from Kumbha occupied by Ravi will produce good results, and in these houses put ciphers, and in the rest put the figure 1.

0	1	0	1
Ravi 0			1
1			0
0	0	0	0

Thus in this horoscope writing the ciphers and figures,
first from Kumbha is itself, the 2nd is Meena, the 4th is
Vrishabha, the 7th is Simha, the 8th is Kanya, the 9th
is Thula, the 10th is Vrischika and the 11th is Dhanus.

This means that whenever the Sun moves in these
houses where ciphers are placed, he forms such chemical
combinations, or takes such angular positions, that he is
able to produce good to the native. But when he moves
in houses in which the figure (1) is marked, he does not
give good results. The Sun gives good in similar positions
from Mars and Sani as have been sketched for himself
here.

1	0	0	0	0	0	1	Sani 0
1			0	0			0
0			0	0			1
1	0	Kuja 0	1	0	1	1	0

Take now the position of Sukra. He is in Dhanus at
the time of birth. The following positions taken by Ravi
from him are good.

That is when the Sun moves in Vrishabha, Mithuna
and Vrischika, he takes favourable angles from Sukra and
produces good. In other houses he shows evil with

reference to Sukra. From Guru, he is favourable in 9, 5, 11, 6. Referring to the horoscope above we find Guru in Kumbha.

1	1	0	0
1			1
1			1
Sukra 1	0	1	1

Thus when the Sun moves in Mithuna, Kataka, Thula and Dhanus, he is good, with reference to Guru and is unfavourable in other houses.

1	1	1	0
Guru 1			0
1			1
0	1	0	1

From Chandra in 10, 3, 11 and 6, Ravi is good.

1	Chandra 1	1	0
0			1
0			1
1	1	1	0

In the horoscope Chandra is in Mesha. When Ravi moves in Mithuna, Kanya, Makara and Kumbha he produces good and in the rest unfavourable results. From Budha in 10, 3, 11, 6, 12, 9 and 5, Ravi is good. We find Budha in Kumbha at birth. When Ravi moves in Mesha, Mithuna, Kataka, Thula, Vrischika, Dhanus and Makara, he forms favourable angles and produces good results. From Lagna Ravi is good in 10, 3, 11, 6, 4 and 12.

1	0	1	0	0	0	Lagna 1	1
Budha 1			0	0			0
0			1	1			0
0	0	0	1	1	1	0	1

When Ravi moves in Kataka, Simha, Thula, Kumbha, Meena and Mesha he produces good and in the rest unfavourable results. I have shown to each of the planets and lagna the favourable and unfavourable angles formed by Ravi in his gochara movements, and this is called *Suryashtaka Varga.*

000 11111	0000 1111	000 11111	000000 11
0000 1111			00000 111
0000 1111	Suryashtaka Varga		000 11111
0000 1111	0000 1111	00000 111	000 11111

The above shows that when the Sun moved in Mithuna, Kataka and Thula, he produced good results in Meena, Vrishabha, Simha and Kanya he produced unfavourable results and the rest Mesha, Vrischika, Dhanus, Makara and Kumbha, he was neutral, *i.e.*, neither good nor bad. So, the Sun was good for 3 months in the year, bad for 4 months and neutral for 5 months. The author gives such positions for all the planets and whenever in a house, we have more ciphers that indicates good. Ciphers and figures are technical. Ciphers are placed for good angular positions and figures for unfavourable positions.

लग्नात् षट्त्रिदशायगः सधनधीधर्मेषुचाराच्छशी
स्वात्सास्तादिषु साष्टसप्तसु रवेः षट्त्र्यायधीश्रो यमात् ।

धीत्र्यायाष्टमकण्टकेषु शशिजाज्जीवाद्ययायाष्टगः
केन्द्रस्थश्च सितात्तु धर्मसुखधीत्र्यायास्पदानङ्गः ॥ २ ॥

Stanza 2.—Chandrashtaka Varga:

Chandra in 6, 3, 10, 11 from Lagna.
  ,,   6, 3, 10, 11, 2, 5, 9 from Kuja.
  ,,   6, 3, 10, 11, 7, 1 from himself.
  ,,   6, 3, 10, 11, 8 and 7 from Ravi.
  ,,   6, 3, 11 and 5 from Sani.
  ,,   5, 3, 11, 8, 1, 4, 7 and 10 from
          Budha.
  ,,   12, 11, 8, 1, 4, 7 and 10 from
          Guru.
  ,,   9, 4, 5, 3, 11, 10 and 7 from
          Sukra produces good.

वक्रस्तूपचयोश्विनात्सतनयेष्वाद्यादिकेषूदया-
च्चन्द्रादिग्विफलेषु केन्द्रनिधनप्राप्संचार्थगः स्वाच्छुभः ।
धर्मायाष्टमकेन्द्रगौश्र्कतनयाज्ज्ञात् षट्त्रिधीलाभगः
शुक्रात् षड्व्ययलाभमृत्युषु गुरोः कर्मान्त्यलाभारिषु ॥ ३ ॥

Stanza 3.—Kujashtaka Varga:

Kuja in 3, 6, 10, 11 and 5 from Ravi.
  ,,   3, 6, 11, 10 and 1 from Lagna.
  ,,   3, 6 and 11 from Chandra.
  ,,   1, 4, 7, 10, 8, 11 and 2 from himself.

Kuja in 9, 11, 8, 1, 4, 7 and 10 from Sani.

  ,,   6, 3, 5 and 11 from Budha.

  ,,   6, 12, 11 and 8 from Sukra.

  ,,   10, 12, 11 and 6 from Guru producee good.

 व्याधायाष्टतपःसुखेषु भृगुजात् सत्र्यात्मजेष्विन्दुजः
साज्ञास्तेषु यमारयोर्व्ययरिपुप्राप्त्यष्टगो बाक्पतेः ।
धर्मायारिसुतत्र्ययेषु सवितुः स्वात् साधकर्मत्रिगः
षट्स्वायाष्टसुखास्पदेषु हिमगोः साधेषु लग्नाच्छुभः ॥ ४ ॥

Stanza 4.—Budhashtaka Varga :

Budha in 2, 1, 8, 11, 9, 4, 3 and 5 from Sukra.

  ,,   2, 1, 11, 8, 9, 4, 10 and 7 from Kuja and Sani.

  ,,   ·12, 6, 11 and 8 from Guru.

  ,,   9, 11, 6, 5 and 12 from Ravi.

  ,,   9, 11, 6, 5, 12, 1, 10 and 3 from his own position.

  ,,   6, 2, 11, 8, 4 and 10 from Chandra.

  ,,   6, 2, 8, 11, 4, 10 and 1 from Lagna will produce good results.

दिक्स्वबधाष्टमदायवन्धुषु कुजात्स्वात् सत्रिकेष्वज्ञिराः
सूर्यात् सत्रिबधेषु धीस्वनवदिग्लाभारिगो भार्गवात् ।

जायायार्थनबात्मजेषु हिमगोर्मन्दात् त्रिषड्धीव्यये
दिग्धीषट्स्वसुखायपूर्वनवगो ज्ञात् सस्मरश्रोदयात् ॥ ५ ॥

Stanza 5.—Guruashtaka Varga.

> Guru in 10, 2, 1, 8, 7, 11 and 4 from Kuja.
> ,,   10, 2, 1, 8, 7, 11, 4 and 3 from himself.
> ,,   10, 2, 1, 8, 7, 11, 4, 3 and 9 from Ravi.
> ,,   5, 2, 9, 10, 11 and 6 from Sukra.
> ,,   7, 11, 2, 9 and 5 from Chandra.
> ,,   3, 6, 5 and 12 from Sani.
> ,,   10, 5, 6, 2, 4, 11, 1 and 9 from Budha.
> ,,   10, 5, 6, 2, 4, 11, 1, 9 and 7 from Lagna produces good results.

लग्नादासुतलाभरन्ध्रनवगः सान्त्यः शशाङ्कात् सितः
स्वात् साझेषु सुखत्रिधीनवदशच्छिद्राखिगः सूर्यजात् ।
रन्ध्रायव्ययो रवेर्नवदशत्राप्तयष्टधीस्थो गुरो-
र्झिद्वीत्र्यायनवारिगत्रिनवषट्पुत्रायसान्त्यः कुजात् ॥ ६ ॥

Stanza 6.—Sukrashtaka Varga :

> Sukra in 1, 2, 3, 4, 5, 11, 8 and 9 from Lagna.
> ,,   1, 2, 3, 4, 5, 11, 8, 9 and 12 from Chandra.
> ,,   1, 2, 3, 4, 5, 11, 8, 9 and 10 from himself.
> ,,   4, 3, 5, 9, 10, 8 and 11 from Sani.

Sukra in 8, 11 and 12 from Ravi.

,,   9, 10, 11, 8 and 5 from Guru.

,,   5, 3, 11, 9 and 6 from Budha.

,,   3, 9, 6, 5, 11 and 12 from Kuja pro-
       duces favourable results.

मन्दः स्वात् त्रिमुतायशत्रुषु शुभः साझान्त्यगो भूमिजात्
केन्द्रायाष्टधनेश्विनादुपचयेष्वाधे सुखे चोदयात् ।
धर्मायारिदशान्त्यमृत्युषु बुधात् चन्द्रात् त्रिषड्लाभगः
पछायान्त्यगतः सितात् सुरगुरोः प्राप्तयन्त्यधीशत्रुषु ॥ ७ ॥

Stanza 7.—Saniashtaka Varga :

Sani in 3, 5, 11 and 6 from himself.

,,   3, 5, 11, 6, 10 and 12 from Kuja.

,,   1, 4, 7, 10, 11, 8 and 2 from Ravi.

,,   3, 6, 10, 11, 1 and 4 from Lagna.

,,   9, 11, 6, 10, 12 and 8 from Budha.

,,   3, 6 and 11 from Chandra.

,,   6, 11 and 12 from Sukra.

,,   11, 12, 5 and 6 from Guru produces
       good.

NOTES

Readers must be very careful as regards predictions.
They are based upon a large number of facts and events,
that when persons do not take into account all the sources
of strength and weakness relating to the positions, conjunctions and aspects the planets possess, along with the lagna,
they may not be successful.

19

इति निगदितमिष्टं नेष्टमन्यद्द्विशेषा-
दधिकफलविपाकं जन्मभाच्चत्र दद्युः ।
उपचयगृहमित्रस्वोच्चगैः पुष्टमिष्टं
त्वपचयगृहनीचारातिगैर्नेष्टमम्पत ॥ ८ ॥

Stanza 8.—The places mentioned above are
good and the rest are evil. The good or bad
results will be ascertained by the ciphers and
figures marked as stated above and the balances
show good. Planets in Upachaya, in friendly and
own houses and exaltations will give plenty of
good ; planets in Apachayas, in neecha or
unfriendly houses give no good.

NOTES

As the places mentioned above are good, ciphers have
to be put in there, and in the other houses not mentioned
put figure 1 in each. Here as the planets keep continuously
moving from house to house, it will be seen that they take
endless positions both with reference to themselves as well
as with reference to other planets and the birth sign. Light,
heat and other invisible agencies radiated and reflected by
the planets, will undergo endless varieties of changes and the
ancient Maha Rishies seem to have found out that when they
move in certain houses, they shed good influences and when
they move in other houses, they produce bad or neutralise
the good effects indicated. Therefore when these ciphers
and figures have been placed as per directions given above,

we get a certain number of ciphers and a certain number of figures. Deduct the figures from the ciphers in each sign and take the balance of ciphers. In each rasi if the balanced ciphers are eight then predict complete good, but when the ciphers are 6, then ¾ths of the original good only has to be expected. When there are only four ciphers, the good will be half and when there are only 2, the good anticipated will only be ¼th of the promised benefit. But when the rasi contains no cipher there will be only evil, *vide* the Suryashtaka Varga given above at the end of Stanza 1.

Referring to the horoscope given in Stanza 6 of Chapter VII, Bhattotpala gives the Ashtaka Varga for Kuja.

Applying the rules given in Kujashtaka Varga we get the following ciphers and figures :

Birth Sukra	Ravi	Moon Budha		11111 000	11111 000	11111 000	11111 000
	RASI		Guru	1111 0000	KUJASHTAKA VARGA		1111 0000
Kuja				111 00000			00000 111
		Sani		11111 000	1111111 0	111 00000	111111 00

In Mesha we have five figures and three ciphers. Deduct the ciphers, we have only two figures. Therefore whenever Kuja moves in Mesha he causes 2/8ths of bad to the man concerned.

In Vrishabha a similar result and in Mithuna the same. But in Kataka, figures and ciphers are equal and cancel each other. Therefore when Kuja moves in Kataka there is neither good nor bad. In Simha we have five ciphers and 3 figures. Therefore there is a balance of two ciphers and whenever Kuja moves in Simha he produces 2/8ths of the happiness. In Kanya we have 6 figures and two ciphers, subtracting we have four figures and therefore when Kuja moves in Kanya he will give 4/8ths of the evil. In Thula we have 3 figures and five ciphers and therefore there will be 2/8ths of good. In Vrischika we have seven figures and one cipher and deducting this from seven, we get 6 figures thereby indicating that when Kuja moves in Vrischika he produces 6/8ths of bad. Similarly it must be judged for all other signs. But when there are 4 ciphers and four figures as in Kumbha given above, then there will be no result. When there are eight ciphers, the best results must be expected, and when there are eight figures the result will be most unfavourable. This is supported by quotations from Badarayana. There are many astrological writers who say that the results predicted by the Gochara will be very general and cannot be depended upon, while the results predicted by the system of calculations based on Ashtaka Varga Shodhana are certain and could be depended upon.

Badarayana and Yavaneswara have given the results to each of the planets in Ashtaka Varga and say that the predictions based upon these will be certain. They further say that this Ashtaka Varga should be specially consulted in Yatra or travelling. If a planet gives good in Ashtaka Varga and occupies Oopachaya from Moon or birth, then that planet will give much good. Devakirthi clearly says that the

Oopachayas should be taken from birth as well as from the
Moon. If a planet becomes bad in Ashtaka Varga, and he also
occupies the Apachayas 1, 2, 4, 5, 7, 8, 9, 12 or unfriendly
or neecha houses then he gives immense bad. These
Oopachayas must be referred to birth time and not as per
Gochara. Yavaneswara and Devakirthi are quoted by
Bhattotpala to clear this point and Satyacharya supports this
view. All the planets will give good or bad only when they
are powerful except Chandra. Even when Chandra is
auspicious, if he is powerless he will give evil results.
Devakirthi supports this view. Summing up all, the learned
commentator says that these states of planets, *viz.*, exaltation, moolatrikona, own and friendly houses, debilitation and unfriendly houses have always reference only to the
time of birth and not to their Gochara movements. But the
favourable or unfavourable positions as ascertained by
Ashtaka Varga and Bindu (cipher) Shodhana (*examination*)
refer to the movements of the planets in their Gochara. (For
fuller treatment of *Ashtaka Varga* see " Hindu Predictive
Astrology" by B.V. Raman.)

CHAPTER X

KARMAJEEVA—PROFESSION

कर्मांजीवाध्यायः

अर्थाप्तिः पितृपितृपलिशत्रुमित्र-
भ्रातृस्त्रीभृतकजनादिवाकरचैः ।
होरेन्द्वोर्देशमगतैर्विकल्पनीया
मेन्द्रर्कांस्पदपतिगांशनाथबृत्या ॥ १ ॥

Stanza 1.—From the Sun, etc., the acquisition of wealth must be predicted through father, mother, enemy, friend, brother, woman and servant respectively, when he occupies the 10th house from birth or Moon, or through lord of the navamsa occupied by the lord of the 10th, from birth, the Moon or the Sun.

NOTES

This is a very important chapter inasmuch as this gives us all the ways and means by which a man earns his money and livelihood. The callings of men are as various, as interesting and as diversified, as the individual peculiarities they exhibit, and it becomes extremely important to learn the details given here as carefully as possible. Take the Lagna or the Moon at birth, and see who occupies the tenth house from it. If the Sun is in the 10th house the person inherits paternal property; if the Moon

is there, he gets money through the mother ; if Mars
occupies it, he procures wealth through his enemy ; if
Mercury joins the 10th, he gets money through friends ; if
Jupiter is found there, the person has wealth through
brothers ; if Venus is in the 10th, then money come through
women ; and if Saturn occupies it, servants fetch him
money. Some astrologers say that the most powerful
among the two must be found out and then the source of
wealth predicted from the planet who occupies the 10th
from it. Suppose there are two or more planets in the 10th
from Lagna or Chandra or from both, then money flows in
through those channels which are ascribed to the planets
in their Dasas and Antardasas. If there is no planet in
the 10th house from Lagna or Chandra, Varaha Mihira
thus proceeds to find out the source of income. Take the
lord of the navamsa occupied by the lord of the 10th from
Bha (Lagna), Indu (Moon) and Arka (Sun), and ascribe
the acquisition of wealth to such methods or processes
which are controlled by that planet. Bhagavan Gargi
supports the above views distinctly. As a man may get
money from various ways both at one time as well as at
different periods in his life, the view taken by Bhattotpala
and his quotations from Gargi seem to be the best in my
humble opinion. A man may be a lawyer, may have lands
yielding produce, may carry on ready money transactions,
may be a paid trustee or manager in some charitable institution or temple and may hold shares in banks, funds and
other speculations and be at the same time a Government
Pleader paid so much per month. His father and mother
may give him money, his wife may bring down dowry and
his brothers and friends may also help him. Therefore the

view advanced by some that the income should be ascribed
to the planet in the 10th either from the Moon or the birth,
whichever is the stronger, falls to the ground and does not
receive support from eminent writers like Gargi.

अर्कांशे तृणकनकोर्णमेषजादै-
श्चन्द्रांशे कृषिजलजाङ्गनाश्रयाच्च ।
धात्वग्निप्रहरणसाहसैः कुजांशे
सौम्यांशे लिपिगणितादिकाव्यशिल्पैः ॥ २ ॥

Stanza 2.—If the lord of the navamsa is the
Sun, the person gets wealth through scents, gold,
wool, medicines, etc. If the amsa lord is the Moon,
wealth flows through agriculture, watery products
and dependence upon women, etc. If the lord
of the navamsa is Mars, he gets money through
minerals, fire, weapons, adventures and physical
strength.

If the lord of the navamsa is Mercury
money is obtained by writing, mathematics,
poetry and fine arts.

NOTES

When there are no planets in the 10th house from the
Moon or the birth sign, then we have to take the lord of
the 10th house from the birth, Moon and the Sun and
then find out which navamsa is occupied by him. Then
take the lord of that navamsa and if he is the Sun, the
person makes money by scented articles, gold, wool and
medicines. He may be a medical man himself or may be

an attendant or nurse upon the patients. If he is the Moon, he gets money by dealing in corals, pearls, shells, agricultural products and dependence upon women. If Mars owns that navamsa, he will make money by minerals, ores, or compounds, by weapons of various kinds, by fire in being engaged in fireworks, kitchens, engine driving or wherever there is work connected with fire and by rash adventures or speculations and venturesome deeds or such actions, in which physical strength is utilised. If Mercury becomes the lord of that navamsa, the person becomes a writer, mechanic, painter, sculptor, engraver, poet, mathematician, architect or scent maker.

जीवांशे द्विचविबुधाकरादिधर्मैः
काव्यांशे मणिरजतादिगोमहिष्यैः ।
सौरांशे श्रमवधभारनीचशिल्पैः
कर्मेशाध्युषितनवांशकर्मसिद्धिः ॥ ३ ॥

Stanza 3.—If the lord of the navamsa is Jupiter, he gets money from Brahmins, priests, Gods, in mines or manufactures, and from charities. If that lord is Venus he makes money by gems, silver, cows, buffaloes, etc.

If he is Saturn he gets money from labour, by execution, carrying, and by low artisanship. The source of income may be such as that which is controlled by the lord of the navamsa, occupied by the lord of the 10th in Gochara.

NOTES

When Jupiter becomes the lord of the navamsa occupied by the lord of the 10th, the person gets money through Brahmins, priests, educated classes, temples and charities, mining operations and manufactures, sacrifices, discipleship, pilgrimage, and Khedda operations. When Sukra becomes the navamsa lord, he gets wealth by gems, metals, cows and buffaloes. When he is Saturn the man earns money by labour, such as travelling and carrying, by being an executioner or hangman, and such mean trades which are against the traditions of his family. All these refer to the planetary combinations at the time of birth. But now Varahamihira gives a clue to read the sources of income by the Gochara of the planets. Karmesa is the lord of the 10th. Find out in which navamsa he is at any given time by the Gochara movements. Then ascribe such means of income as are controlled by the lord of that navamsa. This is supported by quotations from Gargi. This Gochara method, says the learned commentator. applies only to those who have their birth horoscopes but not to others.

A practical example is given here to illustrate the points mentioned above. Note the positions of the planets in the following chart:

There no planets in the 10th house from lagna. So the lord of 10th is Sukra and he is in Meena in the nayamsa. So ascribe Jupiter's profession to some extent. Secondly from Moon, Budha is in the 10th and hence Budha's professions have to be taken. From Ravi, the lord of 10 is Budha and he is in Thula in the navamsa. So Sukra becomes its lord. Out of these three we have to find out, which is the most powerful. The planet who is

in the last navamsa of the house where he is situated becomes the Karaka or the most powerful.   Here the Moon
is in the 8th navamsa and becomes the most powerful.
Moreover he has Parivarthana yoga with Sani.   From Moon,
Budha lord of 9 is in 10 and the lord of 10 is in 9 and they

Kethu Chandra	RASI	Sani Birth Rahu
	Kuja	Budha	Ravi Sukra Guru

both have Parivarthana.   Hence the calling is by teaching
and writing and the native was in the Educational service
as a Gazetted Officer, as Budha gave the Karma Jeeva.
Budha dasa will also make him bring out some books and
enable him to live as a writer.

There are many who have no horoscopes and for whom
lost horoscopes (Nasta Jatakas) are prepared according to
the methods given at the end of this book by Varahamihira.
To such this system probably does not apply.

मित्रारिस्वगृहगतैर्ग्रहैस्ततोऽर्धां-
स्तुङ्गस्थे बलिनि च भास्करे स्ववीर्यात् ।
आयस्यैरुदयधनाश्रितैश्च सौम्यैः
संचिन्त्यं बलसहितैरनेकधा स्वम् ॥ ४ ॥

Stanza 4.—Planets give wealth similar to the houses they occupy. If the Sun is exalted and powerful the man gets wealth by self-acquisition. If powerful benefics are in lagna, 2nd or 11th, he gets money by many ways.

NOTES

Take those lords in the 10th either from Chandra or Lagna, and find out in what house he is. If the house he occupies is his own he gets money in his house. If it is his friend's then he gets money through friends. If he occupies unfriendly houses, then he makes money through his enemies. If he happens to be Sun, and is in his exaltation and is otherwise powerful the person acquires wealth by self-exertions. This is clearly explained by Gargi. By marking the Sun with this characteristic of self-acquisition it sounds as if other planets are not able to do such work. If all the benefics are powerful and occupy the lagna, 2nd and 11th houses, the person will make money by various ways. The commentator says that such a person will succeed in any business he undertakes, however divergent it may be from his original work. If there are no planets in the 10th house, find out where the lord of the 10th from Sun, or Moon or Lagna is situated in the navamsa and if he is in a friendly or inimical sign predict as above. To the above must be added the fact of the Sun being exalted, *i.e.*, in Aries, to make the man acquire wealth by self-exertion.

CHAPTER XI

RAJA YOGA

राजयोगाध्यायः

प्रहुर्यवनाः स्वतुङ्गैग क्रूरमतिर्महपितिः ।
क्रूरैस्तु न जीवशर्मणः पक्षे क्षित्यधिपः प्रजायते ॥ १ ॥

Stanza 1.—Yavanas say that three or more cruel planets in exaltation will produce a cruel-minded king. Jeevasarma and his school say that exalted cruel planets will not raise a man to kingly power.

NOTES

Three or more planets when exalted make a person king when born in a royal family, and five or more planets exalted make any person a king. The same may be said of planets in moolatrikonas. This is a well-known principle of astrology found in all works on the subject especially *Laghu Jataka*. Yavanas and Jeevasarma differ in this combination for a king. Yavanas (Yavanacharya, Yavaneswara and their followers) maintain that when 3 cruel planets, Sun, Mars and Saturn in Aries, Capricorn and Libra, are exalted they raise a man to a king's position and make him a cruel or tyrannical ruler. Jeevasarma says that three exalted cruel planets cannot make a man king, but will produce a rank almost equal to his; the person will be wealthy but cruel and evil-minded. Manithacharya supports Yavana's views and says, that if the three planets

exalted are cruel the king becomes cruel-minded, if they
are benefics he becomes a generous minded king and if
they are mixed (malefics and benefics) the temper of the
king would be mixed. Bhattotpala says that Varaha Mihira
supports the views of Yavanas.

वक्रार्कजार्कगुरुभिः सकलैस्त्रिमिश्र
स्वोच्चेषु षोडशनृपाः कथितैकलग्ने ।
द्वेकाश्रितेषु च तथैकतम विलग्ने
स्वक्षेत्रगे शशिनि षोडशभूमिपाः स्युः ॥ २ ॥

Stanza 2.—If Mars, Saturn, Sun and Jupiter
or any three of them are exalted and one of these
three occupies the lagna, 16 Raja yogas arise.
If the Moon is in his own house, and any two of
the above planets are in exaltation, with one of
them in the birth, or if any one of the above
named planets is in exaltation occupying the
Lagna, they produce 16 Raja yogas.

NOTES

If Mars, Saturn, Sun and Jupiter are exalted and one
of them occupies the birth sign, we naturally get four combinations for royalty. Take an example. Sun in Aries,
Jupiter in Cancer, Saturn in Libra and Mars in Capricorn,
with the other planets in any order produce (1) with the
Sun in birth in Aries, (2) with the birth in Cancer with
Jupiter in it, (3) with birth in Libra with Saturn in it, and
(4) with Capricorn as birth with Mars in it.   If three of

these planets are exalted, with one of them in birth, they
give rise to 12 Raja yogas. Thus take the Sun in Aries,
Jupiter in Cancer, and Saturn in Libra. With the other
planets in any order these produce 3 combinations for
royalty, i.e. (1) when Aries becomes Lagna, (2) when Cancer
becomes Lagna, and (3) when Libra becomes Lagna. Then
again take Ravi in Mesha, Guru in Kataka and Kuja in
Makara with other planets in any order. This gives rise to
3 combinations for royalty by the lagna being placed in
Mesha, Kataka or Makara respectively. Then place
Ravi in Mesha, Sani in Thula and Kuja in Makara
with the other planets in any order, we get 3 combinations
by the lagna being placed in Kataka, Thula or Makara
respectively. Thus we have 12 conjunctions for royalty
and adding the first four yogas (*combinations*) we get 16
Raja yogas. If the Moon is in his own house (*Kataka*)
with any two of the above four planets in exaltation and
with one of them in the lagna we get 12 Raja yogas. Thus
the Sun in Aries and Jupiter and the Moon in Cancer give
two combinations by the lagna being placed in Mesha or
Kataka. Take the Sun in Aries and Saturn in Libra with
Moon in Cancer. We get two combinations by the lagna
being posited (1) in Aries, and (2) in Libra. Similarly the
other ten conjunctions can easily be worked out. If any
one of the four planets Saturn, Mars, Jupiter and the Sun
is exalted, with that exalted planet in birth and with Moon
in his own house, we get four combinations for royalty.
Thus take Aries as lagna with the Sun there and the Moon
in Cancer : (1) take Cancer as lagna with Moon and
Jupiter there ; (2) take Libra with Saturn there and the Moon
in Cancer ; (3) and take Capricorn as lagna with Mars

there and the Moon in Cancer (4).   Thus we have 16 combinations for royalty sketched here.

In all the latter 16 cases there will be no yoga if Chandra is not in his own house.   I beg to offer a few observations here based upon an examination of thousands of horoscopes extending over a period of sixty years.   I have in my possession many horoscopes with Chandra and Guru in Kataka as the lagna and the men are in ordinary circumstances.   Then again there are many who have Ravi in Mesha as birth sign and Chandra in Kataka, who have no pretentions to royalty or even a high social life. Bhattotpala is mercilessly silent in this connection and I feel almost certain, that whatever may have been the strength of the planets in those good old days (Varaha Mihira lived nearly 20 centuries ago), to produce Raja yoga, when one of the four planets was in exaltation with birth there and Chandra in his own house, they have lost that good influence of making persons kings or even his equals, and consistent with those great authors' erudition and grasp of astrology, it may be said that the last combinations would raise a man to kingly or ruler's position only when he is born in a royal family but not otherwise.

वर्गोत्तमगते लग्ने चन्द्रे वा चन्द्रवर्जितैः ।
चतुराद्यैर्गृहैर्दृष्टे नृपा द्वाविंशतिः स्मृताः ॥ ३ ॥

Stanza 3.—If Lagna or Chandra occupies **Vargottama** and has the aspects of four or more planets (excepting Chandra) twenty-two Raja yogas are generated.

NOTES

By these combinations forty-four Raja yogas are arranged thus : Vargottama is the 1st, 5th and 9th navamsas of movable, fixed and common signs. (*See* St. 14, Ch. I.)

But for easy grasp it may be thus explained if the navamsa of any sign falls in it, it becomes Vargottama. Thus Mesha navamsa in Mesha, Vrishabha navamsa in Vrishabha, Mithuna navamsa in Mithuna, and Kataka navamsa in Kataka become Vargottama. If Lagna rises in Vargottama and is aspected by four or more planets twenty-two Raja yogas are arranged. Chandra is excepted. But if he aspects, the yoga is not disturbed. The aspecting planets must be four without Chandra. In a similar way if Chandra occupies Vargottama, and has the aspect of four or more planets, there arise twenty-two Raja yogas. If the Lagna or Chandra is aspected by four planets 15 Raja yogas arise.

Thus (1) Ravi, Kuja, Budha and Guru aspecting Lagna or Chandra.

(2) Ravi, Kuja, Budha and Sukra aspecting Lagna.

(3) Ravi, Kuja, Budha and Sani aspecting Lagna.

(4) Ravi, Kuja, Guru and Sukra.

(5) Ravi, Kuja, Guru and Sani.

(6) Ravi, Kuja, Sukra and Sani.

(7) Ravi, Budha, Guru and Sukra.

(8) Ravi, Budha, Guru and Sani.

(9) Ravi, Budha, Sukra and Sani.

(10) Ravi, Guru, Sukra and Sani.

(11) Kuja, Budha, Guru and Sukra.

(12) Kuja, Budha, Guru and Sani.

(13) Kuja, Budha, Sukra and Sani.

(14) Kuja, Guru, Sukra and Sani.

(15) Budha, Guru, Sukra and Sani.

If five planets aspect the lagna we shall get 6 combinations thus—

(1) Ravi, Kuja, Budha, Guru and Sukra.

(2) Ravi, Kuja, Budha, Guru and Sani.

(3) Ravi, Kuja, Budha, Sukra and Sani.

(4) Ravi, Kuja, Guru, Sukra and Sani.

(5) Ravi, Budha, Guru, Sukra and Sani.

(6) Kuja, Budha, Guru, Sukra and Sani.

If six planets aspect the lagna there will be one combination. Thus twenty-two combinations are produced.

In a similar way it must be calculated for Chandra. Properly speaking all these merge into two principal combinations. If the Lagna rises in Vargottama and 4 or more planets aspect it ; (1) if Chandra is Vargottama and four or more planets aspect it ; and (2) if the permutations and combinations are taken a little more minutely, *viz.*, taking Chandra in Vargottama in each of the 12 signs we get 264 yogas, and a similar number of yogas for Lagna Vargottama in each of the 12 signs. Thus a total of 528 combinations for royalty are obtained by these conjunctions and aspects of planets. Mandavya says that if powerful Lagna or Chandra occupies the Vargottama, aspected by four or more planets (excepting Chandra) the combinations produce mighty kings. (*Vide* ROYAL HOROSCOPES, Pp. 29.) The following horoscope illustrates to some extent the above combinations.

				Rahu Jupiter	Sun	Saturn
		Kethu				Mer.
	RASI			AMSA		
Rahu						
Birth Mars Jupiter Saturn	Mer.	Sun	Moon Venus	Birth Mars		Kethu	Moon Venus

Lagna, Mars, Moon, Venus are Vargottama, Jupiter, Saturn and Mars in Rasi Lagna and aspecting in navamsa.

यमे कुंमे ड्कें ड्जे गवि शशिनि तैरेव तनुगै-
नृयुक्सिंहालिस्थैः शशिजगुरुवक्रैर्नृपतयः ।
यमेन्दू तुझे ड्झे सवितृशशिजौ षष्ठभवने
तुलाजेन्दुक्षेत्रैः ससितकुजजीवैश्च नरपौ ॥ ४ ॥

Stanza 4.—If Sani is in Kumbha, Ravi in Mesha, Chandra in Vrishabha, and Lagna rises in one of these, and Budha, Guru and Kuja are in Mithuna, Simha and Vrischicka, there will be combinations for royalty.

If Sani and Chandra are in exaltation and lagna rises in one of these signs and if Ravi and Budha are in the 6th, and if Sukra, Kuja and

Guru are in Thula, Mesha and Kataka, they generate two Raja yogas.

	Ravi	Chandra	Budha
Sani Lagna	I	I	
	I	I	Guru
	Kuja		

	Kuja	Chandra Lagna	
	II	II	Guru
	II	II	
		Sani Sukra	*Ravi Budha

NOTES

Here five Raja yogas are sketched. Sani in Kumbha, Ravi in Mesha, Chandra in Vrishabha and lagna falls in one of these, and Budha, Guru and Kuja are in Mithuna, Simha and Vrischika respectively. We get three Raja yogas by lagna being placed (1) in Kumbha, (2) in Mesha, and (3) in Vrishabha. If lagna falls in Thula, or Vrishabha with Sani and Chandra in exaltation and if Budha and Ravi are in 6th (Kanya) and Sukra, Kuja and Guru are in Thula, Mesha and Kataka respectively, two Raja yogas arise. The expression " in the 6th " in this stanza is interpreted as the 6th from the lagna, but the quotation from Badarayana clearly explains the position of Ravi and Budha in *Kanya* as the 6th from Mesha. When Sukra is in Thula, Ravi and Budha cannot be in Meena.

---

* 6th from Vrishabha cannot be Kanya and so the 6th must mean Kanya (6th by nature from Mesha).

कुजे तुङ्गे ऽर्केन्द्रोर्धनुषि यमलग्ने च कुपतिः
पतिर्भूमेशान्यः क्षितिसुतविलग्ने सशशिनि ।
सचन्द्रे सौरे ऽस्ते सुरपतिगुरौ चापधरगे
स्वतुङ्गस्थे भानावुदयमुपयाते क्षितिपतिः ॥ ५ ॥

Stanza 5.—If Kuja is in Makara, Ravi and Chandra in Dhanus, and Lagna rising in Makara with Sani in it, the person becomes a king. If, in the above combination, the Moon joins Mars in birth, or if Saturn and the Moon are in the 7th, if Jupiter is in Dhanus, and Aries becomes lagna with the Sun there exalted the person becomes a king.

				Lagna Kuja		
Sani Kuja Lagna	I				II	
Ravi Chandra Guru				Guru		Sani Chandra

In the above the other planets have not been mentioned and the intelligent astrologer has to take the other five planets Ravi, Budha, Sukra, Rahu and Kethu and then predict Raja yogas.

NOTES

Three separate combinations of planets are given here for producing kings :

(1)   If Makara rises at birth with Sani and Kuja in it, and if Ravi and Chandra occupy the 12th from it, *viz.,* Dhanus.

(2)   If Makara rises with Kuja and Chandra in it and with Ravi in Dhanus.

(3)   If Mesha rises with Kuja and Chandra and Sani in Thula, and with Guru in Dhanus the person rises to royal power or becomes a king.   In the first part of the stanza, the author uses " *Yama Lagnay* " which means, according to some, the houses of Yama (Sani) or Makara and Kumbha, and according to others, it may be any lagna with Yama (Sani) in it.   This view is supported by Badarayana.   Bhattotpala prefers the first as meaning Makara alone, and such a view is clearly supported by Mandavya.

वृषे सेन्दौ ल॑ सवितृरूक्तीक्ष्णांशुतनयैः

सुहृज्जायाखस्थैर्भवति नियमान्मानवपतिः ।

मृगे मन्दे लग्ने सहजरिपुधर्मव्ययगतै

शशाङ्काद्यैः ख्यातः पृथुगुणयशाः पुंगलपतिः ॥ ६ ॥

Stanza 6.—If Taurus rises at birth with the Moon in it, and the Sun, Jupiter and Saturn are in the 4th, 7th and 10th respectively, the person certainly becomes a king.   If Capricorn is birth with Saturn in it, and 3, 6, 9 or 12 are occupied by the Moon, etc., the person becomes a famous, good natured, and prominent king.

NOTES

Two Raja yogas (combinations) are stated in this verse.

(1) If Vrishabha is Lagna with Chandra in it, Ravi in Simha, Guru in Vrischika and Sani in Kumbha, the person becomes certainly a king. (2) If Makara is Lagna with Sani in it, Chandra in Meena, Kuja in Mithuna, Budha in Kanya, Guru in Dhanus, and Sukra and Ravi in any houses, the person becomes a famous and mighty king with good and generous qualities. This is clearly explained by Mandavya.

	Kethu	Birth Moon		Chandra			Kuja
Sani	Sri Krishna's Horoscope				II Yoga		
			Ravi Sukra	Lagna Sani			
	Kuja	Rahu	Guru Budha	Guru		Sukra	Budha Ravi

हये सेन्दौ जीवे मृगमुखगते भूमितनये
स्वतुङ्गस्थौ लग्ने भृगुजशशिजावत्र नृपती ।
सुतस्थौ बर्कार्की गुरुशशिसिताश्वापि हिबुके ।
बुधे कन्यालग्ने भवति हि नृपोऽन्योऽपि गुणवान् ॥ ७ ॥

Stanza 7.—If Guru with Chandra is in Dhanus, Kuja in Makara, and Meena or Kanya

become lagna with Sukra or Budha respectively
two Raja yogas arise. If Kuja and Sani occupy
the 5th, Guru, Chandra and Sukra join the 4th,
if Kanya rises as Lagna with Budha in it, the
person becomes a king with good character.

NOTES

There are three combinations given here for royalty.

If Meena is Lagna with Budha in it, Sani and Kuja in
the 5th and Guru, Chandra and Sukra occupy 4th or
Dhanus, the person becomes a good king. Some of these
combinations found in navamsa kundali have also produced
kings of native states, *vide* ILLUSTRATIVE HOROSCOPES, Pp. 70.

झषे सेन्दौ लग्ने घटमृगमृगेन्द्रेषु सहितै-
र्यमारार्कैर्यों ऽभूत्स खलु मनुजः शास्ति वसुधाम् ।
अजे सारे मूर्तौ शशिगृहगते चामरगुरौ
सुरेज्ये वा लग्ने धरणिपतिरन्योऽपि गुणवान् ॥ ८ ॥

Stanza 8.—If Meena becomes Lagna with
Chandra in it, Sani, Kuja and Ravi, are in
Kumbha, Makara and Simha respectively the
person born will rule the earth.

If Mesha becomes Lagna with Kuja in it,
with Guru in Kataka.

or

If Kataka rises with Guru in it, with Kuja in
Mesha, a good king will be born.

NOTES

Three Raja yogas are sketched here.

Chan-dra Lagna			
Sani			
Kuja	RASI 1		Ravi

With other planets in any order.

or

	Lagna Kuja		
			Guru
	RASI 2		

With other planets in any order.

or

	Kuja		
			Lagna Guru
	RASI 3		

With other planets in any order.

In all these cases, peculiar powers seem to characterise the angular positions of the planets, which enable persons born under such combinations to become kings. Kings are of various descriptions and their nature, extent of their empire or Kingdom and their resources will be determined by the strength of the planets generating these royal combinations. Sri Rama's horoscope is an illustration.

कर्किणि लग्ने तत्स्थे जीवे चन्द्रसितज्ञै रायप्राप्तैः ।
मेषगतेऽर्के जातं विन्द्याद्विक्रमयुक्तं पृथ्वीनाथम् ॥ ९ ॥

Stanza 9.—If Cancer is birth with Jupiter in it and if the Moon, Venus and Mercury are in the 11th house, and the Sun is in Aries, a mighty king will be born.

NOTES

There is one Raja yoga here.

	Sun	Moon Venus Mer.	
			Birth Jupiter
	RASI		

With the other planets in any order.

This is a powerful combination and the prince becomes a great king.

मृगमुखेऽर्कतनयस्तनुसंस्थः
क्रियकुलीरहरयोऽधिपयुक्ताः ।
मिथुनतौलिसहितौ बुधशुक्रौ
यदि तदा पृथुयशाः पृथिवीशः ॥ १० ॥

Stanza 10.—If Capricorn is birth with Saturn in it and if Aries, Cancer and Leo are combined with their lords and if Gemini and Libra are occupied by Mercury and Venus the person becomes a renowned ruler.

NOTES

This is a good conjunction of planets and the king born must become famous.

	Mars		Mercury
			Moon
	RASI		
Birth Saturn			Sun
		Venus	

With Jupiter in any other house.

Reading the commentaries of Bhattotpala, I expected an explanation as regards the relative positions of the Sun and Mercury. Mercury never goes beyond 28° of the Sun either in the front or in the rear. Then again, in this combination Mercury is placed in Gemini while Venus is placed in Libra. This combination can never happen. It is explained thus. Now in any house Mercury can only be 28° distant from the Sun. Suppose the Sun is placed in the 10° of Leo. Then the most distant position that Mercury can attain would be the 28th° from him, *i.e.*, Mercury can go back as far as the 12th° of Cancer.

Venus never goes beyond 47° from the Sun and thus the extreme limit at which Venus can be placed from the Sun in front would be 47°, *i.e.*, Venus may be found in the 27th° of Virgo. Thus the greatest distance at which Mercury and

Venus may be imagined to be will be 28+47=75 degrees.
Thus if Mercury is in the 12th° of Cancer, Venus will be in
the 27th° of Virgo. This is clearly explained by Bhattotpala
in St. 6, Chap. VII (see notes to St. 6, Chap. VII).   But here
there are three clean rasis separating Venus and Mercury
and the mean distance must be more than 90 degrees which
appears absurd according to present movements of the
planets.   Then again Mercury is placed at a distance of
more than 30° from the Sun which is also absurd.   But
there are some places in this work where Varahamihira
gives conjunction of planets which are impossible under
present conditions but which probably might have been
possible under a different set of planetary movements with
velocities considerably differing from those of the present.

Varahamihira says in such places that as these yogas
were found recorded by the ancient Maharishis he has
placed them also in his works but which, he clearly says,
could not happen as being opposed to present mathematical
calculations relating to planetary bodies.   The present confusion in calculating the position of planets is mainly due
to there being no definite Ayanamsa calculated according to
any definite principle.   The Ayanamsa varies from 20° to
23° and no two almanacs agree even with regard to the
movements of the Sun on whom depends all calculations.
The predicative portion becomes very difficult and that is
why many of the predictions of the astrologers who depend
on their particular almanacs, which are all different, do not
tally nor happen.   We have to get a standard almanac.

स्वोच्चसंस्थे बुधे लग्ने भगौ मेषूरणाश्रिते ।
सजीवेऽस्ते निशानाथे राजा मन्दारयोः सुते ॥ ११ ॥

Stanza 11.—If exalted Budha occupies lagna, Sukra occupies the 10th, Chandra and Guru join in the 7th and Sani and Kuja occupy the 5th, the person becomes a Raja.

NOTES

One Raja yoga is sketched here and the Sun may be placed in any house. Very rarely can such a combination as Budha being in the fourth from Sukra may happen. Theoretically this may not be improbable as the distance

Guru Chandra	Kuja	Rahu	Sukra
		RASI	
Sani Kuja			
			Lagna Budha

may be within 75° from each other. Sukra may be in the 28th degree of Mithuna. Budha must be in the 15th degree of Kanya in order to be exalted and so the difference between Sukra and Budha would be 2+30+30+15 or 77 which is impossible.

अपि खलकुलजाता मानवा राज्यभाजः
किमुत नृपकुलोत्थाः प्रोक्तभूमालयोगैः ।
नृपतिकुलसमुत्थाः पार्थिवा वक्ष्यमाणे-
भवति नृपतितुल्यस्तेष्वभूपालपुत्रः ॥ १२ ॥

Stanza 12.—In the combinations for royalty sketched before, persons born in poverty will become kings; much more so persons born in royal families. The combinations to be given hereafter will make men kings who are born in royal families and others born in ordinary families will become equal to kings.

NOTES

In all the conjunctions of planets stated in the last eleven stanzas, even persons born in humble families become kings and therefore, remarks Varahamihira, there is no doubt whatever of persons becoming rulers who are born in royal families. The following horoscope illustrates how born poor, Hyder became a king.

			Rahu
		RASI	
Sukra			
Kethu	Sani Ravi Chandra Kuja Guru Budha	Birth	

Lord of birth is in 4 aspected by Sani, lords of 4 and 5. He had no motherly love. Lord of father is also lord of 12 and is in the 6th from Bhagya. Chandra is debilitated but with Kuja and Guru loses his debilitation. There is

Gurumangala yoga, Gajakesari yoga and the 2nd house
has 6 planets.   He was able to leave a cash of 80 crores
of rupees, many crores of rupees worth of jewellery and
gems, million well-trained troops, 300 strong forts, well
garrisoned and an empire from Krishna to Cape Comorin
yielding an annual revenue of 30 crores (at present about
600 crores) to his son Tippu who born rich, lost all.
Whatever may be the rationale of the political codes, and
the moral codes taking their stand upon politics there is
not the slightest doubt that even fools born in royal families
have greater chances of becoming rulers than the best of
men born in the humbler spheres of life. The starting
advantage possessed by royal family men is tremendous and
throws the best men in the humbler families far behind
them to achieve distinction.   Thus the fool of an emperor's
son is at once declared to succeed his father while the best
men in the empire will be simply asked to obey that fool
and be guided by him. Therefore Varahamihira realises this
inequality and ascribes royal powers to persons only when
the planetary combinations are very very powerful.   Thus
in all the previous Raja yogas, he says, that men will
become kings or rulers who are born in such combinations.
But in the combinations he is going to mention hereafter,
only those who are born in royal families become kings
while those who are born in poor families will rise up to
great eminence and will be similar to kings but will not
become actual kings.

उच्चस्वत्रिकोणगैर्बलस्थैस्त्रयाद्यैर्भूपतिवंशजा नरेन्द्राः ।
पञ्चादिभिरन्यवंशजाता हीनैर्वित्तयुता न भूमिपालाः ॥ १३ ॥

Stanza 13.—If there are three or more powerful exalted or Moolatrikona planets in a horoscope a person born in a royal family will become a king. If this number is five or more, then persons born in ordinary families will become rulers. If these planets are powerless the persons will not be kings but wealthy men.

NOTES

There must be three or more powerful planets in exaltation or Moolatrikona to make a man king when he is born in a royal family. If there are five or more similar planets in a horoscope, the man becomes a ruler wherever he may be born. But if the three or more planets in exaltation or Moolatrikona are not powerful (Kala, Nisargika, Chesta, Dik, etc.), then even a man born in a royal family will not become a king but will remain a wealthy man. All the planets need not be in exaltation or Moolatrikona. Suppose two are exalted and one is in Moolatrikona, does the person become a ruler? If born in a royal family he will become a king, but in other families he will become a wealthy man. If there are three planets in Moolatrikona and two planets in exaltation the person becomes a king wherever he may be born. If there are more planets, then certainly Raja yoga happens.

The following horoscope illustrates the above principle.

	Kethu	Saturn	
	RASI		Moon Mars Jupiter
Birth		Rahu Venus Sun	Mercury

Two planets Guru and Budha are exalted. Sukra is
in Moolatrikona, Ravi and Kuja though debilitated have
neechabhanga Raja yoga, which has made the native a
Dewan of 3 states and hold one of the most enviable
appointments.

लेखास्थे ज्ञें ज्ञेन्दौ लग्ने भौमे स्वोच्चे कुम्मे मन्दे ।
चापप्राप्ते जीवे राज्ञः पुत्रं विन्द्यात् पृथ्वीनाथम् ॥ १४ ॥

Stanza 14.—If Aries is lagna with the Sun
half-rising and Moon in it, Mars in Capricorn
and Jupiter in Sagittarius the person born in a
royal family becomes a king.

NOTES

Mesha must be the lagna with Chandra in it and Ravi
rising with his disc half visible in the horizon, Kuja in

Makara and Guru in Dhanus to constitute the above
combination. A person born in ordinary family in such a
time will become wealthy and influential. The word used
in the original is *lakha* which means the Sun half visible
in the eastern horizon. Some read it as *laya* which means
Leo or Simha. This is also acceptable as it forms
Moolatrikona for Ravi.

	Birth Chandra	
	RASI	
Kuja		Ravi
Guru	Sukra Sani	Budha

स्वर्क्षे शुक्रे पातालस्थे धर्मस्थानं प्राप्ते चन्द्रे ।
दुश्चिक्याङ्गप्राप्तिप्राप्तैः शेषैर्जातः स्वामी भूमेः ॥ १५ ॥

Stanza 15.—If Sukra occupies his house
which forms the 4th from Lagna, Chandra occupies the 9th and the rest are in the 3rd, 1st and
11th houses, the person becomes a king.

NOTES

This is possible for two lagnas. Kumbha as lagna
will have Sukra in the 4th in Vrishabha, or Kataka as lagna
will have Sukra in the 4th in Thula. In this combination a

person born in royal family will become a king and one
born in any other family will become wealthy.

Chandra		Sani	
			Lagna Guru
	RASI		
		Sukra	Ravi Budha Kuja

In Stanza 15, Kumbha Lagna will not be so good as
Kataka Lagna.

सौम्ये वीर्ययुते तनुयुक्ते वीर्याढ्ये च शुभे सुखयाते ।
धर्मार्थोपचयेष्ववशे पैर्धर्मात्मा नृपजः पृथिवीशः ॥ १६ ॥

Stanza 16.—If powerful Budha is in Lagna, a
powerful benefic in the 9th and the rest of the
planets in the 2nd, 9th, 3rd, 6th, 10th or 11th, the
person born in a royal family will become a
good and charitable king.

NOTES

The lagna must be combined with Budha while Guru
or Sukra or both must be in the 9th. The rest of the
planets must be in the 2nd, 3rd, 6th, 9th, 10th or 11th
house or in two or three of these houses in any order.
The idea seems to be that the remaining five planets must be
in any one or more of the houses named and not outside.

Some read sukha for subha and make the 4th house
occupied by a benefic. Under such a combination the
person will become a good natured king if born in a royal
family and a wealthy man in other families.

वृषोदये मूर्तिधनारिलाभगैः
शशाङ्कजीवार्कसुतापरैर्नृपः ।
सुखे गुरौ खे शशितीक्ष्णदीधिती
यमोदये लाभगतैर्नृपोऽपरैः ॥ १७ ॥

Stanza. 17.—If Vrishabha is lagna and
Chandra, Guru, Sani and other planets occupy
respectively (the 1st, 2nd, 6th and 11th), the person becomes a Raja. If Guru is in the 4th, Moon
and Ravi in the 10th and Sani in Lagna and other
planets in the 11th the person becomes a king.

NOTES

Two combinations are sketched here for Raja yoga. In
the first we have :

Sukra Ravi Kuja Budha		Lagna Chandra	Guru
	1st RASI		
		Sani	

There are three planets exalted here and the person becomes a king.

In the 2nd combination we have :

	Guru		
	2nd RASI		
Lagna Sani			
	Kuja Budha Sukra	Ravi Chandra	

Here the lagna is not given and I have simply put it in Makara. The lagna, therefore, may be placed in any house, only there should be Sani in it. Mesha lagna gives better results.

मेषूरणायतनुगाः शशिमन्दजीवाः
झारौ धने सितरवी हिबुके नरेन्द्रम् ।
वक्रासितौ शशिसुरेज्यसितार्कसौम्या
होरासुखास्तशुभखाक्षिगताः प्रजेशम् ॥ १८ ॥

Stanza 18.—If Chandra, Sani and Guru are in the 10th, 11th and 1st respectively, Budha and Kuja in the 2nd and Sukra and Ravi in the 4th, the person becomes a king. If Kuja and Sani

are in Lagna, Chandra, Guru, Sukra, Ravi and
Budha are in the 4th, 7th, 9th, 10th and 11th
houses respectively the person becomes a Raja.

NOTES

Two royal combinations are given here.

	Chandra	Sani	
			Lagna Guru
	1st RASI		Budha Kuja
		Sukra Ravi	

Here we notice the same objection of positing Budha
in the 3rd house from Ravi backwards and thus giving him
a minimum distance of more than 30 degrees which is not
possible now. It is curious that even a great scholar and
mathematician like Bhattotpala does not point out these
inconsistencies. The author makes no mention of it. But
as Bhattotpala clearly says that the greatest distance
between Ravi and Budha can only be 25 degrees, all
combinations in which this measurement is transgressed
must be taken to be those which the ancient Maha Rishis
have written down in their works and which have been
stated by Varahamihira in accordance with them.

(See commentaries of Bhattotpala on St. 6, Ch. VII
and my notes on that).

In the 2nd combination we have the following positions :

	Kuja Sani Lagna		
Budha			Chandra
	RASI 2nd		
Ravi			
Sukra		Guru	

In the first as well as in the second the lagna has been simply given by me by way of illustration. Any lagna may be taken provided the planets are given their allotted places. In all these combinations kingly power must be predicted only for those who are born in royal families but for others born in humbler surroundings great wealth and position may safely be predicted.

कर्मलग्रयुतपाकदशायां राज्यलब्धिरथवा प्रबलस्य ।
शत्रुनीचगृहयातदशायां छिद्रसंश्रयदशा परिकल्प्या ॥ १९ ॥

Stanza 19.—The person gets the royal power in the antardasa of the most powerful planet or of the planet who combines in the 10th or the 1st. He loses that power in the antardasa of the planet who is in unfriendly or neecha house because such period is called *Chidra dasa.* Then he must seek protection from a powerful king.

NOTES

By this stanza the author enables the astrologer to fix the period when a person may get kingly power and when he may expect to lose it or try to get over the misfortune. Take the planets in the 1st and 10th and whichever is the stronger, then predict the acquisition of power during his antardasa. But his antardasas may come several times and then the author says, that *antardasa* must be fixed as power-giving which appears as the most powerful with reference to Gochara movements. If there are no planets in the 1st and 10th then find out which of the whole lot of planets is the strongest and ascribe the power to him during his *antardasa*. Such kingly power or office will be lost when the antardasa of a planet which occupies an unfriendly or debilitated rasi intervenes.

The following horoscope illustrates the fall of the Czar of Russia, Nicholas II :

Chandra Guru	Kuja	Ravi Budha	Sukra			Sukra Budha	Kuja	Rahu
Kethu					Ravi			Lagna
	RASI		Lagna Rahu			AMSA		
	Sani				Chandra Kethu	Guru	Sani	

At birth he had Budha dasa for 16-3-15 and he lost his life and kingdom in Ravi dasa Sukra bhukthi. Note how the Sun is afflicted as birth lord with Saturn's aspect and how Sukra and Ravi are in 2nd and 12th and how Sani aspects lagna as well as the 10th from it.

This is called Chidra dasa which means accident or misfortune as well as a hole and therefore he gets into unfortunate position by losing his power. Then he must seek protection from a powerful king and thus try to get rid of his threatened misfortune. Bhagavan Gargi clearly speaks to a similar effect and the matter is also referred to by Varahamihira in his *Yatra* a book on travelling he has written.

गुरुसितबुधलग्ने सप्तमस्थे ऽर्केपुत्रे
वियति दिवसनाथे भोगिनां जन्म विन्द्यात् ।
शुभबलयुतकेन्द्रैः क्रूरभस्थैश्च पापै-
र्व्रजति शबरदस्युस्वामितामर्थभाक् च ॥ २० ॥

Stanza 20.—If Guru, Sukra or Budha is in Lagna, Sani in the 7th and Ravi in the 10th the person will enjoy his life well. If beneficial signs are powerful and fall in kendras and malefics occupy cruel signs, the person will be master of hunters, thieves and wealth.

NOTES

These are important combinations. The conversation of Alexander the Great and the robber may be remembered. There are some persons who enjoy their life very well although they may have no money and there are others who become masters or leaders of wild tribes, hunters and thieves or dacoits and become wealthy and very powerful. They

command hundreds or thousands of persons, live in wealth
and put on all the luxuries of rulers and kings. Guru or
Sukra or Budha must be in lagna, Sani must be in the 7th
and Ravi must occupy the 10th. Now, when Ravi is in 10,
Sukra and Budha can never be in the lagna as already
shown. Hence some say that the lagnas must be Leo,
Taurus, Libra, Gemini and Virgo. Even under Vajra yoga,
similar combinations are shown. Gargi also says that the
houses of Guru, Sukra and Budha should be strong and be
kendras to the birth lagna and evil planets should be in the
houses of Mars, Sun and Saturn, to produce a noted bandit
or dacoit leader. There seems to be some inconsistency. A
truant may be worse than a bandit chief and it is difficult to
say who can be called a constituted authority. Persons born
under such conjunctions of planets will enjoy their lives well
even when they are poor or quiet. In the latter part of the
stanza the beneficial signs namely Vrishabha, Thula, Dhanus
and Meena, must fall in the kendras, while the evil planets
must occupy evil signs. Then the person will lead dacoits,
or hunters, get money and live happily. There is also the
simple dictum that one should not examine a horoscope
which has neither Budha and Sukra in Lagna, Guru in
kendra, or Kuja in the 10th, as that horoscope is not going
to be useful to society. The science is meant to help really
deserving men whose rise is impeded by certain bad
influences which are capable of being neutralised and which
may then lead the man to power and wealth so that he may
help humanity at large.

CHAPTER XII

NABHASA YOGAS

नाभसयोगाध्यायः

नवदिग्नवसवस्त्रिकाग्निवेदै-
र्गुणिता द्वित्रिचतुर्बि कल्पजाः स्युः ।
यवनैस्त्रिगुणाहि षट्शती
सा कथिता विस्तरतोऽत्र तत्समाः स्युः ॥ १ ॥

Stanza 1.—By combinations of two, three and four the multiples of 9, 10, 8 by 3, 3 and 4 respectively will be the number of Nabhasa yogas obtained by this process. Yavanas have described 1800 varieties but I will describe them here briefly.

NOTES

Nabhasa yogas are of four varieties (1) Akruti, (2) Akruti, Sankhya, (3) Akruti, Sankhya, Asraya, (4) and Akruti, Sankhya, Asraya, and Dala. There are 20 of Akruti, 7 of Sankhya, 3 of Asraya and 2 of Dala, 9×3, 10×3 and $8 \times 4 =$ 27, 30 and 32. By taking combinations of two planets we get 27, by three 30 and by four 32. Thus Akruti is 20 and Sankhya is 7, the two together will give 27. Add to this Asraya yogas 3 we get 30. Add to this two Dalayogas we get 32. Old Yavanas have described these under 1800 varieties. Suchi-Dwaja declares that Nabhasa yogas are

countless.   Purana Yavanas give 23 Akruti yogas, Sankhya-
yogas at 127.   This is shown as below :—

1.	Ekavikalpaja Yogas	...	7
2.	Dvivikalpaja Yogas	...	21
3.	Trivikalpaja Yogas	...	35
4.	Chaturvikalpaja Yogas		35
5.	Pancha Vikalpaja Yogas		21
6.	Shadvikalpaja Yogas	...	7
7.	Saptavikalpaja Yoga	...	1

This Vikalpa cal-
culation is shown
more elaborately
in Sunapha and
Anapha yogas of
the Moon.

127

This 127 added to 23 Akriti yogas make 150.

As the lagna may fall in each of the 12 houses and as
these 150 yogas happen for each of the rasis they have
multiplied 150 × 12 = 1800 yogas.   Varahamihira says that
has made an abstract of all these yogas and given them as
32.   All the other yogas are incorporated in them and
therefore they can be easily grasped when the whole chapter
is carefully perused.

रज्जुमुशलं नलश्चरादेः सत्यश्चाश्रयजाङ्गगाद् योगान् ।
केन्द्रैः सदसद्युतैर्देलाख्यौ स्रक्सर्पौ कथितै पराशरेण ॥ २ ॥

Stanza 2.—If the planets are in Chara, etc.,
Rajju, Musala and Nala yogas are formed
respectively according to Satya.   These are
Asraya yogas.   Parasara mentions two yogas
as Dala under *sruk* and *sarpa* when the benefics and malefics are in kendras respectively.

NOTES

The stanza is very compressive and baffles easy
translation. There are three sets of houses, viz., Chara,
Sthira and Dwiswabhava, or movable, fixed and common
signs. This presupposes all the planets in kendras from
any lagna to form any of the three yogas mentioned by
Satyacharya. It is very rare to get such a horoscope.
According to Satyacharya it will be Rajju yoga when
all the planets occupy the movable houses; it is Musala
when all the planets are in fixed houses and when all the
planets occupy common signs it will be Nala. Planets in
these three cases need not be found in all the movable, fixed
or common signs. There are four movable signs Aries,
Cancer, Libra and Capricorn. All the planets may be in any
one or two or three or four of these houses in any order to
constitute *Rajju*. The word *Rajju* in Sanskrit means a rope,
Musala means pistol and *Nala* means grass. Satyacharya
gives the results of these different yogas which are of great
importance to be omitted here. Gargi lucidly explains these
in his inimitable yet homely style. One who is born in
Rajju will be unjust, resident in foreign countries and
wealthy. Musala produces men of self-respect and wealth.
Nala makes persons short of limbs or long limbed, skilful,
hoarders of treasure and enjoying life. If all the benefics
are in kendras the yoga is called *sruk*. If all the malefics
are in kendras it is called *sarpa*. Bhattotpala, with his vast
learning, gives the following summary, which otherwise
should have been very difficult to make out. He quotes
from Badarayana, Parasara, Gargi, Manitha and Satyacharya. All these are agreed on the points at issue and
hence Bhattotpala explains the latter half of this stanza in

simple language. If three quadrants are occupied by
Mercury, Jupiter and Venus without any malefic, either
with them or in the other kendra it constitutes *Sruk* yoga
which gives enjoyment in life and all that is pleasant. This
is not possible as Budha or Sukra can never be in two
different kendras and if they are in one kendra and Jupiter
in another then only two quadrants will be occupied.
Look at the I and II horoscopes :

Guru	Kethu Sani			Sani Chandra		Lagna Ravi Budha Rahu	Sukra
	I A promising horoscope				Kuja	II A Virgin widow	
Ku.a			Budha				Guru
Lagna Chandra		Rahu	Ravi Sukra		Kethu		

When the three malefics Saturn, Mars and the Sun
occupy the three kendras without any benefics with them
or in the 4th kendra, it is called Sarpa yoga and produces
a sorrowful and unpleasant life. The Sruk yoga is also
called a Mala (garland) yoga. Only three good and three
evil planets are mentioned and not the Moon. He is
both good and bad as he waxes or wanes and his presence
or absence makes no difference in the yoga.

Suppose the three malefics occupy the three kendras
and a Full Moon occupies the 4th kendra. He does not
disturb the Sarpa yoga. Suppose the three benefics occupy

the three quadrants and a waek Moon joins the 4th kendra
then the yoga is not also disturbed. In fact all the great
Maharishies quoted above have not taken any notice of
Chandra in this connection.

It is really not clear as to how the Moon (Manah-
karaka) governing the mind should have been omitted in
these yogas, as many of our miseries are more mental than
physical.

योगा व्रजन्त्याश्रयजाः समत्वं
यवाब्जवज्राण्डजगोलकाद्यैः ।
केन्द्रोपगैः प्रोक्तफलौ दलाख्या-
वित्याहुरन्ये न पृथक् फलौ तौ ॥ ३ ॥

Stanza 3.—Asraya yogas, according to some,
are really incorporated in the Yava, Abja, Vajra,
Andaja, Golaka, etc., to be stated hereafter.
Dala yogas have no separate significance, according to some, as the results of benefics and malefics occupying the kendras have already been
indicated.

NOTES

Some take objection for describing Dala yogas separately as it is well known that benefics in kendras produce
good while malefics there cause evil. Bhattotpala justifies
their enumeration here by Varahamihira in this way. All
Nabhasa yogas have permanent influences and their results
good or bad are manifested in all periods and sub-periods.

Dala yogas have a similar influence and therefore they have been included in this chapter by the author. Parasara declares that all *Nabhasa yogas* have a continuous effect as opposed to the influences of particular planetary periods and sub-periods.

आसन्नकेन्द्रभवनद्वयगैर्गदाव्य-
स्तन्वस्तगेषु शकटं विहगः खबन्ध्वोः ।
शृङ्गाटकं नवमपञ्चमलग्नसंस्थै-
र्लेयान्यगैर्हलमिति प्रवदन्ति तज्ज्ञाः ॥ ४ ॥

Stanza 4.—When two adjacent quadrants are combined with all the planets it goes under the name of Gada.

It will be called Sakata when all the planets occupy the 1st and the 7th houses. When all the planets occupy the 4th and the 10th it is called Vihaga. If all the planets occupy the 1st, 5th and 9th houses it is called Sringataka. If all the planets are in 5th and 9th it is called Hala. So say the learned in astrology.

NOTES

The readers should be careful in adjusting the results for all these *yogas*. In Sanskrit *yoga* is derived from *yuj*

22

to join or combine. Most of these yogas are mechanical
or chemical combinations and are produced by the inter-
changing of the various planetary rays whose junction is
designated as a yoga or combination. If a planet occupies
the 1st degree of Aries and another occupies the same
it must naturally be expected that some interchange takes
place there producing certain definite results. The positions of other planets have also great power to modify
these conjunctional results.   Varahamihira here sketches
many such combinations and indicates that their influences are permanent and effective. But the readers
have to be careful. Suppose Mesha is Lagna with
Ravi, Budha, Kuja and Sukra there and the rest of
the planets are in Kataka. Kindly consider the splendid
positions occupied here as against the same yoga appearing
in the second horoscope.

	Lagna Ravi Kuja Sukra Budha		
			Moon Gurn Sani
	1st RASI		

Guru Chandra Sani	2nd RASI		
		Lagna Ravi Sukra Budha Kuja	

In both these horoscopes the 1st and the 4th houses contain all the planets. But the relative strength, aspect and position of all the planets change considerably and although the yoga is Gada the same results must not be predicted.

In the 1st the Sun is exalted, Kuja is in Moolatrikona, Guru is exalted and Chandra occupies his own house ; that will be a splendid combination for anybody to have. But in the second Ravi is debilitated, Kuja occupies an unfriendly sign, Guru is debilitated, while Chandra is in a cruel sign and cruel associations. The results must differ and they do. In the I Rasi, Ravi is lord of 5' Chandra lord of 4, Budha lord of 3 and 6, Kuja lord of 1 and 8, Sukra lord of 2 and 7, and Guru lord of 9 and 12 occupies exaltation with lord of 10 and 11. Note the combinations of lords of 5 and 7, 9 and 10 and 1 and 5, forming Raja yogas. In the II, lords of 1, 2, 12, 11, 7 and 8 (except 2 and 7 Kuja) are all bad. The lord of 3 and 6 is with lord of 4 and 5 and lord of 10. Hence one has to

be careful in giving the results, though in both the horoscopes we have the *Gada* yoga. Take a practical illustration.
There is village magistrate who has nominal powers, there
is town magistrate who has a larger area and powers and
there is a district magistrate whose powers are still greater
and whose jurisdiction must embrace a wider area. All
go under the name of magistrates but there is a world of
difference in power, pay, personal respect and status in life.

Thus the result of Gada may be produced on a small
or large scale according as the planets are powerful or
weak. There are four Gada yogas : (1) when all the planets
are in the 1st and 4th, (2) when they are in 4th and 7th,
(3) when they are in the 7th and 10th, and (4) when they
are in the 10th and 1st. All these yogas are called *Akriti*
yogas. The names are indicative of the forms the planets
present when occupying the different signs. Gada means
a club. Sakata means a cart, Vihaga indicates a bird, Sringataka denotes a triangle, and Hala means a plough. If all
the planets are not in the houses named here then this combination is not formed and its results must not be predicted.

शकटाण्डजवच्छुभाशुभैर्वंजं तद्विपरीतगैर्यैवः ।
कमलं तु विमिश्रसंस्थितैर्वापी तद्यदि केन्द्रबाह्यतः ॥ ५ ॥

Stanza 5.—When benefics are in first and
seventh and malefics are in fourth and tenth it is
called Vajra. If the planets are reversed then it
is called Yava. If the planets are mixed it is
called Kamala. If the planets are outside kendras
it is called Vapi.

NOTES

In the Vajra the benefics must be in the 7th and 1st while the malefics are placed in the 4th and the 10th. In Yava the malefics, must be in the 1st and 7th while benefics must be in the 4th and 10th. If all the planets, benefics and malefics occupy all the four kendras in any order it is called Kamala. Benefics and malefics may join or be separate in the houses.

When all the planets occupy either *Panaparas* or *Apoklimas* it is called Vapi. In all these cases there must be no planet outside the specified houses. For Panaparas and Apoklimas (see St. 18, Ch. I.)

> 2, 5, 8, 11 are Panaparas
> 3, 6, 9, 12 are Apoklimas
> 3, 6, 10, 11 are Upachayas
> 6, 8, 12 are Dusthanas

Now 6 is an Apoklima, Upachaya and Dusthana, but how should it be considered. 11 also comes under two headings. In all these cases we have to take the strength of the planet in the shadvargas and give him the good points among these. Six comes under Upachaya and is not so bad as 8 and 12.

पूर्वशास्त्रानुसारेण मया वज्रादयः कृताः ।
चतुर्थभवने द्व्यार्ज्ञसितौ भवतः कथम् ॥ ६ ॥

Stanza 6.—I have given these Vajra yogas, etc., in accordance with older sciences, but how can Budha and Sukra be in the 4th from the Sun ?

NOTES

Vajra and Yava do not happen but Varahamihira
says he has recorded them under the sanction of the older
sciences. The author uses Adi after Vajra to show that
all such improbable or impossible combinations have been
mentioned by him, as he found them described by Maya,
Manitha, Yavana and Satyacharya. When the Sun is in a
house, Mercury can only be at a distance of 28 degrees
from him either in the East or in the West and therefore
either in the same sign or in the 2nd or 12th sign occupied
by the Sun. Venus has been shown already not to move
more than 47 degrees from the Sun, and therefore the
utmost distance he can be found from the Sun will be
either in the 3rd house or 11th from the Sun. A few points
may be advantageously discussed here with reference to
astronomy and astrology. Varahamihira was a great
mathematician and composed a work called Pancha
Siddhantika. This means that it gives the purport of five
Siddhantas which he has named in St. 3, Ch. II of *Brihat
Samhita.* They are (1) Poulasa, (2) Romaka, (3) Vasishta,
(4) Saura and (5) Paithamaha. Vasishta is venerable and
has written various learned works on astronomy and
astrology. Paithamaha or Brahma and Saura or Surya,
have also written Siddhantas. Combinations of planets
are given here which cannot be found under the present
velocities and movements of planets. The question therefore now arises as to whether Varahamihira blindly quotes
combinations which he found recorded in the older works
of Vasishta and Gargi, Badarayana and Parasara, or did he
seriously believe in their possibility in the earlier centuries
of the earth's creation. Where a thing is recorded which

looks quite absurd on its face whatever may be the reverence to the professor who recorded it, the duty of the later writers is to simply omit them as savouring of impossibility under the present mathematics. Another important question which crops up at this stage is whether Vasishta, Surya, Paithamaha, Vyasa, Parasara, Marichi, Kasyapa, Chandra and other eminent astronomers recorded facts, which happened during their time or whether they simply blindly recorded combinations of planets which they found in still older works of which we have not got now even bare references. These are really extremely difficult but very interesting questions which better men than myself may attempt to answer.

It strikes me from a careful perusal of the existing astronomical and astrological literature, that it would be unreasonable to apply one set of physical conditions, and their results to another set of similar conditions, after a long lapse of time in the womb of which may be marked an inexhaustible series of changes. In the Mahabharata, Vyasa deliberately says that *Budaprakaso Jagadaprakasaha,* i.e., when Mercury shines well—visible to the naked eye— the destruction of the world may be predicted. (See St. 1, Ch. VII, *Brihat Samhita.*) Kasyapa and Vriddha Gargi give similar opinions. See also Romasa. Vyasa is an astronomer and astrologer, a Maharishi, compiler of the Vedas, author of the Bhagavad Gita and the immortal Brahma Sutras in addition to his 18 voluminous Puranas. There must, therefore, be times during which Mercury may either gain greater velocity than he posseses now or may be separated from the Sun far beyond what we have been now accustomed to calculate mathematically as

possible.   There is no guarantee that the planetary movements, as now ascertained, were the movements many many
millions of years ago.   Geologists and astronomers are now
racking their brains to determine the physical development
of the earth from its earliest evolution.   800 millions of
years are reached by some of them while others say that
they are not sufficient to bring the earth to the present
condition in which we find it.   It would be unreasonable
therefore to determine that planets could not have assumed
certain angular positions, some billions of years ago which
they are able to do just now, or *vice versa.* The age of
the creation of the earth in its present form as given by
Hindu astronomers is 195 and odd crores of solar years,
and it would be absurd to maintain now what the conditions, physical and celestial were same 195 crores of years
ago. Without calling upon the present generation of
mathematicians either to support or to criticise me in my
views, it looks to me reasonable to suppose that there
were times when the planets were moving at far higher
rates, than they are doing now, and that combinations
such as those which have been mentioned by Vasishta and
Parasara, were combinations of planets actually seen by
them or considered quite reasonable and mathematical
during their times. The Sun attracts all other planets of
the solar system with the solar gravitation at a certain rate
now during the last some thousands of years ago but who
can dogmatically maintain unless he is a fool (who does
not care to take the changes wrought by the all powerful
hand of time) that these solar attractions and their rates
are stationary and that planets have been moving all along
at the present rates uniformly? The Sun constantly

changes his position in space, his position on his axis and his position with reference to other planets and so also other planets. This is clearly shown by the Sayana and Niryana systems. Attractions are guided by the quantity of heat and light and electricity and ether, which any planet exhibits towards other planets, and if there is any sense or truth in these statements, then we can easily imagine the conditions for the Sun and the attendant planets when their mutual attractions and repulsions were quite different from what they are now, and we can as reasonably predict that such attractions and repulsions which the present astronomico-mathematics give us, may not be found existing when the planets have made some more revolutions on their axis and the orbital lines fixed for them by the solar attractions. All these and many more facts show clearly that in the earlier centuries of the world, there were conjunctions of planets, in which Sukra and Budha could have taken angular positions from the Sun, and that there may be some occasions in the remote future when they may attain to such positions with reference to their master and lord the Sun.

कण्टकादिग्रहवृत्तैस्तु चतुर्गृहगतैग्रहैः ।
यूपेषुशाक्तिदण्डाख्या होराद्यैः कटकैः क्रमात् ॥ ७ ॥

Stanza 7.—If all the planets are within the first four houses of the 1st, 2nd, 3rd and 4th kendras Yupa, Ishu, Sakthi and Danda yogas are respectively formed.

NOTES

If all the planets are in the 1st, 2nd, 3rd and 4th houses from lagna it is Yupa, if they occupy the 4th, 5th, 6th and 7th then it is called Ishu.   If all the planets are in the 7th, 8th, 9th and 10th it goes under the name of Sakthi and if all these are in 10th, 11th, 12th and 1st, they constitute Danda yoga.

नौकूटच्छत्रचापानि तद्वत्सप्तर्क्षसंस्थितै ।
अर्द्धचन्द्रस्तु नावाधैः प्रोक्तस्त्वन्यर्क्षसंस्थितैः ॥ ८ ॥

Stanza 8.—If all the planets are in the first 7 houses from the 1st, 2nd, 3rd and 4th kendras they give rise to Nau, Kuta, Chatra and Chapa yogas respectively.   If these yogas are in other houses they are called Ardachandra.

NOTES

If all the planets are in 1, 2, 3, 4, 5, 6 and 7, it forms Nau Yoga. If they are in 4, 5, 6, 7, 8, 9 and 10, it is called Kuta. If all these occupy the 7, 8, 9, 10, 11, 12 and 1, it is called Chatra yoga. If all are placed in 10, 11, 12, 1, 2, 3 and 4, it goes under the name of Chapa.   In the other half of the stanza if all the planets are placed in Panaparas we get four yogas and if all be placed in Apoklimas, there will be four yogas.   These are styled Ardachandra. Thus if all the planets are found in 2, 3, 4, 5, 6, 7 and 8 : or in 5, 6, 7, 8, 9, 10 and 11 : or in 8, 9, 10, 11, 12, 1 and 2 ; or in 11, 12, 1, 2, 3, 4 and 5.   In all these four cases the yogas take their start from Panaparas (see Stanza 18, Chap. I). Now take the Apoklimas. If all the planets are in 3, 4, 5, 6, 7, 8 and 9 ; or in 6, 7, 8, 9, 10, 11 and 12 ; or in 9, 10, 11,

12, 1, 2 and 3 ; or in 12, 1, 2, 3, 4, 5 and 6. In all these
eight cases the yoga goes under the name of Ardachandra.

	Birth Ravi	Budha	Sukra
			Guru
	Nau Yoga		Kuja
		Moon	Sani

		Birth	
		Kuta Yoga	Ravi
Chandra			Budha
Guru	Kuja	Sani	Sukra

	Ravi	Budha	Sukra
			Guru
	Chatra Yoga		Kuja
		Birth Sani	Chandra

	Ravi	Budha	Sukra
			Lagna Guru
	Chapa Yoga		Kuja
		Sani	Moon

It is not possible to get such combinations now nor
have we been able to come across any horoscope having
these combinations. One factor should be noted, viz., the
absence of Rahu or Kethu in any of these combinations.

एकान्तरगतैरर्थात्समुद्रः षड्गृहाश्रितैे ।
विलभ्मादि स्थितैश्चक्रमित्याकृतिजसंग्रहः ॥ ९ ॥

Stanza 9.—If all the planets are in the alternate houses from the 2nd from lagna, it goes under the name of Samudra. If from lagna planets are similarly situated, it forms Chakra. This is the summary of Akriti yogas.

NOTES

If all the planets are in 2nd, 4th, 6th, 8th, 10th and 12th houses, it is called Samudra Yoga.

Guru		Lagna Chandra	
	CHAKRA		Sani
Kuja			
	Sukra		Ravi Budha

Guru	Lagna	Chandra	
	SAMUDRA YOGA		Sani
Kuja			
	Sukra		Ravi Budha

Varahamihira says that he has made a summary of the Akriti yogas mentioned by the previous writers on this science.

In any horoscope where planets are not in 2 and 12 or 6 and 8 mutually there the native will have very few cares or even if there be trouble, care a two pence for them. The late following horoscope illustrates this.

	Chandra Rahu	Lagna	Sani
Guru Ravi Budha	RASI Mr. B. S. Rao's Horoscope		
Sukra		Kuja Kethu	

Note that planets have not 2 and 12 or 8 and 6 places from each other. Hence he kept a jolly temperament till his end.

संख्या योगाः स्युः सप्तसभ्यर्क्षसंस्थै-
रेकापायाद्वल्लकीदामिनी च ।
पाशः केदारः शूलयोगो युगं च
गोलश्चान्यान् पूर्वमुक्तान्विहाय ॥ १० ॥

Stanza 10.—By all the planets occupying 7, 6, 5, 4, 3, 2 and 1 houses, they form seven yogas, *viz.*, Vallaki, Dama, Pasa, Kedara, Shula, Yuga and Gola, respectively. These are to be considered in the absence of the previously mentioned yogas.

NOTES

When all the planets are within seven houses they form
Vallaki. When they occupy 6 houses it goes under the
name of Dama, when they are in 5 houses they form
Pasa, when they are in 4 houses they compose Kedara,
when they are in 3 houses they form Shula, when they are
in 2 houses they compose Yuga, and when all the planets
are in one house they make the Gola yoga. In the previous stanzas the planets are required to be in all the
houses consecutively or alternately as stated. But in these
yogas, the planets may be in any order. If they occupy
a definite number of houses they form a special conjunction. Take an example. It may be questioned that when
there is Ardachandra yoga, there must necessarily be Vallaki
also. When both are present and satisfy the conditions mentioned by the author are we required to prescribe these two
yogas separately or take one yoga in preference to another
which is suppressed by its presence. The latter is the case.
When Ardhachandra and Vallaki are present Vallaki is suppressed and the results must be ascribed only to Ardhachandra

	Lagna Sukra	Ravi	Budha		Lagna	Sun	Mercury
							Venus
	VALLAKI				ARDACHANDRA		
			Kuja				Mars
Guru	Sani	Moon			Saturn	Jupiter	Moon

			Birth	Sani Budha	Ravi Moon	Sukra
Sukra		Chandra				Kuja
	DAMA	Sani		PASA		
Ravi	Budha Guru	Birth	Kuja			Guru

Birth			Guru	Chandra Ravi Budha	Sukra Sani Kuja	Guru
	KEDARA	Sani				
		Ravi Kuja Budha Sukra			SHULA	
	Moon			Birth		

The students should carefully mark all these conjunctions and then predict their results according to the strength and position of the planets, their aspects and associations.

Rahu and Kethu are entirely omitted in all these combinations and what are we to say if Rahu and Kethu encircle all these yogas in their ' Kalasarpa yoga '. It is not clear whether Varahamihira did not consider Kalasarpa yoga as one counteracting very strongly the good results of all these yogas. Bhattotpala is also silent. The Asrayadi yogas have to be given preference to the Sankhya yogas, *i.e.*, we have to give preference to the positions of planets in kendras and trikonas, to the positions of planets in 2, 3, 4, 5 and 6 houses. It is a point to be noted that while Kalidasa, a contemporary of Varahamihira has mentioned Rahu and Kethu in his Uttarakalamrita, Chapters IV and VI, Varahamihira has not taken the good and evil effects produced by these two planets in these yogas.

Ravi Budha Sukra Sani	Birth	Kuja Guru Moon			Ra. Ch. Sa. Ku. Gu. Su. Budha		Birth
	YUGA				GOLA		

ईर्ष्युर्विदेशनिरतो ऽध्वरुचिश्च रज्जवां
मानी धनी च मुसले बहुकृत्यसक्तः ।
व्यङ्गः स्थिराढ्यनिपुणो नलजः सगुत्थो
भोगान्वितो भुजगजो बहुदुःखभाक् स्यात् ॥ ११ ॥

Stanza 11.—Rajju produces envy, foreign residence and fondness for travelling. Musala makes one proud, wealthy, and capable of doing many works. Nala makes a person limbless, determined, rich and courageous. Srik makes him happy and Sarpa gives him great misery.

NOTES

The author has sketched the planetary combinations forming these yogas already and now proceeds to give the results of these planetary conjunctions. As the results are stated in simple and clear language, no further commentaries are, I believe, needed to explain them.

आश्रयोक्तास्तु विफला भवन्त्यन्यैर्विमिश्रिताः ।
मिश्रा यैस्ते फलं दद्युरमिश्राः स्वफलप्रदाः ॥ १२ ॥

Stanza 12.—Asraya yogas, when they join other yogas become fruitless. The yogas with which Asrayas join will give results. When Asrayas are free, they give their own results.

*Varahamihira observes that when Asraya yogas join with other yogas or are present with other combinations, they give no results, and they only produce results when these are not disturbed by the presence of other yogas. Yoga means a conjunction or combination of planets. When a movable sign rises at birth and all the planets are in fixed or common signs, or when a fixed sign rises at birth and all the planets are in movable or common signs or when the birth falls in a common sign with the other planets in movable or fixed houses, then these Asraya yogas do not combine with other combinations.

---

* For a more comprehensive account of these yogas see " Three Hundred Important Combinations " by B.V. Raman.

23

It must also be noted that in these yogas, the relative
strength of each planet should be noted to find out who is
influenced more than the other and are they sufficiently
strong to produce the yoga.   For example let us take two
examples here.

Sukra	Ravi Budha				Sani	
			Lagna Guru Moon			Kuja
Kuja	Chart I			Lagna Guru Moon	Chart II	
		Sani			Ravi Budha	Sukra

Except the difference in lagna, the positions of all the
planets are the same.   Sani in 4, Kuja in 7, Sukra in 9,
Ravi and Budha in 10, Guru and Chandra in 1, *i.e.*, all the
planets are in kendras and trikonas.   While 5 planets are
exalted in Chart I, these 5 are debilitated in Chart II.
Can we predict the same yogas mentioned in this chapter
for planetary combinations in kendras.

यज्ज्वार्थभाक् सततमर्थरुचिर्गदायां
तद्वृत्तिभुक्छकटजः सरुजः कुदारः ।
दूतो ऽटनः कलहकृद्विहगे प्रदिष्टः
शृङ्गाटके चिरसुखी कृषिकृद्धलाप्ये ॥ १३ ॥

Stanza 13.—Gada=fond of sacrifices, rich;
Sakata=lives by carriages, sickly, bad wife;
Vihaga=ambassador, traveller, quarrelsome;
Sringataka=happiness after a long age; Hala=
agriculturist.

NOTES

The combinations for all these yogas have already
been explained.

वज्रे ऽन्त्यपूर्वेसुखिनः सुभगो ऽतिशूरो
वीर्यान्वितो ऽप्यथ यवे सुखितो वयोन्तः ।
विख्यातकीर्यमितसौख्यगुणश्च पद्मे
वाप्यां तनुस्थिरसुखो निधिकृन्न दाता ॥ १४ ॥

Stanza 14.—Vajra=enjoys happiness in the
beginning and end of his life, popular, courageous;
Yava=warlike, happy in the end; Padma=well-
known reputation, great happiness, and good
character; Vapi=good health, accumulator of
money and miser.

NOTES

In Vajra the planets make a man enjoy life in the
commencement and end of life. This implies that he will
be unhappy during the middle period. There are many
peculiarities in the enjoyment. Some are born in the lap
of luxury, are brought up so for some years and then
become hopelessly miserable. Some are born on the lap of

poverty, endure their hard lot throughout the first period
of their life, then become prosperous and enjoy life, during
the rest of their days.   Some are born in misery, spend
two-thirds of their life in that stage, then mount the ladder
of fortune and die in plenty, some are poor in the middle
of their life and enjoy life well at the other two ends.

त्यागात्मवान् ऋतुवरैर्यजते ज यूपे
हिंस्रो ऽथ गुप्त्यधिकृतः शरकृच्छराख्ये ।
नीचोऽलमः सुखधनैर्वियुतश्च शक्तौ
दण्ड प्रियार्विरहित पुरुषोऽन्त्यवृत्तिः ॥ १५ ॥

Stanza 15.—Yupa = liberal, watchful, performs sacrifices ;   Sara = fond of killing, jailor,
maker of weapons ;   Sakti = mean, lazy, devoid
of wealth and happiness ;   Danda = servitude, rejected by or separated from those who are dear.

NOTES

Sacrifices are those which are done according to Hindu
Sastras, but this is a restricted sense.   It means any offerings which are made to their deities by men in different parts
of the world according to their religious and moral codes.

कीर्त्यायुतश्चलसुखः कृपणश्च नौजः
कूटेऽनृतप्लवनबन्धनपश्च जातः ।
छत्रोद्भवः स्वजनसौख्यकरो ऽन्त्यसौख्यः
शरश्च कार्मुकभवः प्रथमान्त्यसौख्यः ॥ १६ ॥

Stanza 16.—Nou=famous, unsteady **fortune**
and miserly; Kuta=liar, imprisonment; **Chatra**=
helping relations, enjoyment in old age; Chapa=
courageous enjoying life in the first and **last**
parts of his days.

अर्धेन्दुजः सुभगकान्तवपुः प्रधान-
स्तोयालये नरपतिप्रतिमस्तु भोगी ।
चक्रे नरेन्द्रमुकुटद्युतिरञ्जिताङ्घ्रि-
र्वीणोद्भवश्च निपुणः प्रियगीतनृत्यः ॥ १७ ॥

Stanza 17.—Ardhachandra=popular, **hand-**
some, leader; Samudra=equal to a ruler, **happy**;
Chakra=respected by sovereigns; Veena=intel-
ligent and skilful, clever in dancing and music.

NOTES

Veena is called by Varahamihira as Vallaki in St. 10.

दातान्यकार्यनिरतः पशुपश्च दाम्नि
पाशे धनार्जनविशीलसभृत्यबन्धुः ।
केदारजः कृषिकरः सुबहूपयोज्यः
शूरक्षतो धनहृचिर्विधनश्च शूले ॥ १८ ॥

Stanza 18.—Damini=liberal, philanthropic,
protector, many cattle; Pasa=possessing relations and servants who are clever in acquiring
wealth, and bad in behaviour; Kedara=agricul-

turist, helping many ; Shula=courageous, having wounds, fond of wealth but poor.

धनविरहितः पाखण्डी वा युगे त्वथ गोलके
विधनमलिनो ऽज्ञानोपेतः कुशिल्प्यलसो ऽटनः ।
इति निगदिता योगाः साद्धँ फलैरिह नाभसा
नियतफलादाश्रिन्त्या ह्येते समस्तदशास्वपि ॥ १९ ॥

Stanza 19.—Yuga=poor, unbeliever ; Gola= penniless, sinful, ignorant, skilful in mean arts, lazy, travelling.   These are Nabhasa yogas related by me, and they will always be productive of their own results.

NOTES

The *Nabhasa yogas* are continuously productive of results good or bad as the case may be. If they are really so, then there is some objection against some of these yogas in which Varahamihira has clearly stated that the person will have happiness in the first and last periods of a man's existence. The answer is simple. When the results of a combination of planets take a particular turn, then other rules or principles cannot be applied to them. For, it is the nature of such a combination to produce those results irrespective of general influences. What he means here is that the results delineated here as pertaining to conjunctions of planets under Nabhasa yogas will make themselves prominent in a man's career although now and then they may not be present so prominently on account of the presence of other yogas. If these results are per-

manently felt then some will have all good, while others
will have all evil. It is not so. Bhattotpala very clearly
remarks—rich men may have external objects for enjoyment,
but their minds may be greatly affected and they may feel
themselves miserable, through various other causes. Poor
men may have external marks of misery, but at heart they
may feel quite happy and contented. Happiness and
misery are relative terms and are made so by the bent of
the mind the man possesses and the view he takes of the
presence of evil and good about him.

Milton's famous lines may be remembered in this
connection :—

" The mind in itself and in its own place can make a
heaven of hell and a hell of heaven."

It depends upon the outlook one has about life and its
happiness. Some are entirely devoid of humour and to
them life is miserable. The Moon in Dusthanas or aspected
by Sani or Kuja or Sani and Kuja aspecting each other,
Sani being in the 4th from Kuja, make the man worry
himself unnecessarily. One should be sportive and laugh
at these things and reduce his burden of misery.

There are evil and good results which come to man as
the natural consequence of planetary periods and sub-periods.
Then there are the results which happen to him as the results of the planetary movements as ascertained by *Ashtaka
Varga.* Then again there are the results of the planetary
combinations or yogas on the man exercised by their peculiar angles and states. All these do not counteract each
other's influences but confer enjoyment during their respective periods and in a conjunctional or individual manner.
Dala yogas and Akriti yogas do not come together. Dala

and Asraya do not concurrently happen. Dalas and San-
khyas may come together and then Dalas will have preference. Akriti and Asraya may come together when Akriti
will produce its results. Akriti and Sankhya yogas may
come together when the influences of Akriti will prevail.
Asraya and Sankhya may come together when Asraya will
have preference. Asraya yogas always contain Sankhya
yogas but we may have Sankhya yogas separately and by
themselves. Therefore when Asraya and Sankhya yogas
are present preference should be given only to Asraya yogas.
For example, if all the planets are in one house, there is
Sankhya yoga but not Asraya. The old Yavanas have given
1,800 varieties of these Nabhasa yogas. Sankhya yogas are
127. There are 23 Akriti yogas. The two sets added
$127+23$ will give 150 yogas. But there are 12 different
zodiacal signs and if each of these signs has 150 yogas the
total number of Nabhasa yogas possible will be $150 \times 12 =$
1,800 yogas or planetary conjunctions. When the number
of planets taken is seven one yoga arises ; when six planets
are taken at a time there arise seven yogas ; when the
number of planets taken is five we get 21 yogas ; when that
number is four we get 35 ; when three planets are taken at a
time we get 35 ; when two planets are taken at a time we
get 21 ; and when we take one planet at a time we get seven.
Thus we get $1+7+21+35+35+21+7=127$ yogas. When
we add 23 Akriti yogas to these we get 150 yogas for each
lagna of the zodiac or 1,800 for the 12 signs.

CHAPTER XIII

CHANDRAYOGADHYAYA

चन्द्रयोगाध्यायः

Results from Lunar Positions and Conjunctions.

अधमसमवरिष्ठान्यर्ककेन्द्रादिसंस्थे
शशिनि विनयवित्तद्यानधीनैपुणानि ।
अहनि निशि च चन्द्रे स्वेऽधिमित्रांशके वा
सुरगुरुसितदृष्टे वित्तवान् स्यात् सुखी च ॥ १ ॥

Stanza 1.—By the Moon occupying kendras, etc., from the Sun, three yogas arise called *Adhama, Sama, Varishta* respectively, producing politeness, wealth, wisdom, intelligence and skill, accordingly. If the Moon is in his own or friendly navamsa during the day and night possessing the aspect of Jupiter and Venus respectively, the person will be wealthy and happy.

NOTES

The brevity and suggestiveness of Varahamihira's verses are admirable and cannot be done justice to in English translations like this. If the Moon is in a kendra from the Sun at the time of birth he will have very faint or no traces of politeness, wealth, wisdom, intelligence and skill. If the Moon is in Panaparas from the Sun, *i.e.,* in

2, 5, 8, 11, then he will have all these characteristics to a
moderate extent. But if the Moon is in Apoklimas from
the Sun, *viz.*, in 3, 6, 9 or 12, the person will have all those
qualities to the fullest extent possible. For those who are
born during the day, if the Moon occupies his own navamsa or that of the navamsa of his intimate friend aspected
by Jupiter, he will give wealth and happiness. The same
result must be predicted when the Moon is in any of those
above named navamsas and has the aspect of Venus. Some
say that the Moon in his own amsa during the day and in his
friendly navamsa during the night aspected by Jupiter and
Venus respectively, causes these results. But Bhagavan
Gargi clearly says as I have explained above and Bhattotpala quotes also Yavaneswara to the same effect.

Uttarakalamrita, Khanda IV, Stanza 8, says that if at
birth, the Moon with her digits full and endowed with
strength, be in her exaltation, swakshetra or a friend's
house, identical with 4, 7, 9 or 10, and be aspected by or
in conjunction with Jupiter or Venus, the person will be

		Guru		Budha	Kuja	Rahu	Ravi
Kethu Sani	RASI			Guru	AMSA		
			Sukra Rahu				Sukra
Kuja	Chandra	Lagna	Ravi Budha		Moon Kethu	Lagna Sani	

omniscient, endowed with all virtues, extolled by people and be a highly munificent and great personage. (See also Stanzas 25 and 26).

Note how Chandra in a friend's house, having Vargottamamsa and aspected by Jupiter and in Apoklima (3) from Sun in rasi and (6) in amsa, has made the above horoscope a very wealthy personage and one who has the honour of being the guest of Viceroys and travelled widely, but the position of the Moon (debilitated) has made him a bit unhappy.

सौम्यैः स्मरा

रिनिधनेष्वधियोग इन्दो-
स्तस्मिश्चभूपसचिवक्षितिपालजन्म ।
संपन्नसौख्यविभवाहतशत्रवश्च
दीर्घायुषो विगतरोगभयाश्च जाताः ॥ २ ॥

Stanza 2.—When benefics occupy the 6th, 7th and 8th from the Moon, they cause Adhi yoga and the result is the birth of a commander, a minister, or a king. Persons born in this conjunction (Adhi yoga) will be gentlemanly, happy, surrounded with luxury, foeless, long lived and rejected by the diseases.

NOTES

In this *Adhi yoga* all the benefics, *viz.*, Mercury, Jupiter and Venus must be in one of these houses. All of them may be in the 6th, 7th and 8th, or in 6th or 7th or 8th, or in the 6th and 7th or 6th and 8th, or in the 7th and 8th. Thus

seven varieties of Adhi yogas have been named here. If all
these benefics are completely powerful, the person will
become a great king, if they possess ordinary (medium
power) then he will become a minister, and when all these
are powerless, the man becomes a commander.

Vide Stanza 26 of Khanda IV of Uttarakalamrita of
Kalidasa for this Adhi yoga.

Srutakirti observes that if in these places there are evil
planets from the Moon then they will produce the same
results, but the person will be evil minded and tyrranical.
If mixed planets are found there, the results will be mixed,
and when the benefics are there the results will be good.
But the quotations from Badarayana, Mandavya and
Saravali, clearly indicate the presence of benefics in those
houses and Srutakirti does not seem to have been supported
by them in his inference of making Papadhi yoga by putting
evil planets in those houses. But as their quotations are
not full we cannot draw any conclusions definitely.
Mandavya and Saravali declare that this *Adhi yoga belongs
to Raja yoga* and produces kings and emperors, when the
planets are powerful. It is not always possible to say why
a certain combination produces a certain result, but it is
easy to say from study and experience that a special
combination of planets produces special and definite results.
It will be seen in this world that there are many varieties of
power developed by the planetary conjunctions, each of
which has its own value and power and several of which
may be combined in one and the same individual. As
objects drawn together under special physical and mental
conditions exhibit different moods in their behaviour so also

men produced by different planetary conjunctions exhibit a wonderful variety of phenomena, which requires long and tedious study to understand its nature and complications. Some have wonderful talking power while others have special walking capacity. Some are excellent hunters while others are splendid fighters. We have refined writers and magnificent poets. Some are eminent in art while others are great in religious faith. Some are great tyrants while others are honourable philanthropists. Some have special theiving propensity while others distinguish themselves in giving to others what they have. Some think deeply while others see far into the future. Some have easy reproductive capacity while others are characterised by stern barrenness. All these and many more are due ot planetary influences as moulded into definite forms by the energy which results from good and bad karma. The astrologer will be a great naturalist. His capacity must be great and his observation keen and piercing. It is a most interesting and intricate science and has been most profoundly dealt with by the ancient masters in this field of sublime knowledge.

हित्वार्कं सुनफानफादुरुधराः स्वान्त्योभयस्थैर्ग्रहैः
शीतांशोः कथितोऽन्यथा तु बहुभिः केमद्रमोऽन्यैस्तवसौ ।
केन्द्रे शीतकरेऽथवा ग्रहयुते केमद्रमो नेष्यते
केचित्केन्द्रनवांशकेषु च वदन्त्युक्तिः प्रसिद्धा न ते ॥ ३ ॥

Stanza 3.—With the exception of the Sun other planets in the 2nd house from the Moon,

in the 12th from him and in the 2nd and 12th
from the Moon cause Sunapha, Anapha and
Dhuradhura yogas respectively. If these are
not so, many say it is Kemadruma. If planets
are in kendra from birth or the Moon or if the
Moon is combined with planets there is no
Kemadruma. Some say these yogas arise from
kendras and navamsas, but their doctrine has
not been accepted.

NOTES

This is a very important stanza and explains some of
the most prominent permanent yogas (conjunctions) which
affect the careers of individuals. Several systems are
brought out and the most acceptable among them have
been clearly indicated. After fixing correctly the planetary
positions in a horoscope, take the position of the Moon.
If in the second house from the Moon there are planets a
special yoga called Sunapha is generated. When there
are planets in the 12th house from the Moon the yoga goes
under the name of Anapha. When planets are found both
in the 2nd and 12th houses from the Moon, the yoga is
called Dhuradhura. If there are no planets on both sides
of the Moon, i.e., 2nd and 12th houses, then the yoga is
called Kemadruma. Many have said so and they are
quoted by Bhattotpala. If in the kendras from birth or the
Moon, planets are found, or if the Moon joins with any
other planet, there will be no Kemadruma. Look at these
two horoscopes.

In both there are no planets in the 2nd and 12th from the Moon unless we take Rahu and Kethu as planets, but both have planets in the kendra from the Moon.

	Rahu Moon	Lagna	Sani				
Ravi Guru Budha				Kethu			Sani
	A				B		Lagna Rahu
				Chandra			
Sukra		Kuja Kethu			Kuja	Budha	Ravi Guru Sukra

The presence or absence of the Sun does not interrupt these yogas. That is, if there is Sun in the 2nd house from the Moon he does not cause Sunapha unless there is some other planet with him. If there are one or more planets in the 2nd house from the Moon and also the Sun with them he does not disturb the Sunapha yoga. Some say that the word *Kendrasitakarey* should be interpreted as n kendras, from Chandra but this is against the spirit of quotations from Gargi and Saravali. Some Acharyas represent these conjunctions from the kendras of the Moon. Srutakirti observes: " When planets are in the 4th house from the Moon it is Sunapha, when they are in the 10th from the Moon it is Anapha, when they are both in the 4th and 10th from the Moon it is Dhuradhura, but when they are not there, there will be Kemadruma " Jivasarma declares on the strength of some Acharyas that planets in the 2nd house from the Moon in the navamsa create Sunapha, if they are in the 12th from him it is Anapha, when they are in the 2nd and 12th frem him it is Dhuradhura, and if there are no planets in these houses it is Kemadruma. But these explanations are not consistent with the view of eminent ancient writers and therefore says Varahamihira, are not acceptable. Perusing these remarks of eminent astrologers, carefully, I beg to venture here a few observations. Readers of my translation may draw their own conclusions after a special study of these important yogas. When planets are not in certain *Bhavas* (houses) signifying events then writers on astrology direct the students to go to those bhavas in the navamsa and find out the planets and predict the results ascribed to them. Varahamihira has done so in many places in this work (see St. 23, Chap. V and St. 1 in Chap. X). In Chapter VII he also recommends the Amsayurdaya propounded by Satyacharya and now the question will be simply this. When planets produce certain results in the rasi, they will also produce the same in the navamsa.

This is an interesting problem which has been tackled to some extent in the columns of THE ASTROLOGICAL MAGAZINE as to how far, the results in the rasi bhavas have to be modified in the navamsa. Can we say that when planets in certain positions in the rasi, producing certain results, will produce the same results when they are in the navamsa ? In that case we have to say that every blessed planet has to be in the Vargottama, so that the same combinations hold good.

Then again we have on good astrological authority
to consult planetary conjunctions from the Lagna or
Chandra whichever is stronger.   In this case, if planets are
in the 4th and 10th houses from Chandra there are good
yogas and the results will be favourable. The same holds
good when they are in kendras from lagna. If planets can
produce Sunapha, Anapha and Dhuradhura, when they are
in the 2nd or 12th, or 2nd and 12th from Chandra in the
Rasi I can see hardly any material objection to the generation of those same yogas when the same planets occupy
similar positions from the Moon in the navamsa. Suppose
a man has no planet in the 7th from Lagna or Chandra
in the Rasi but there are planets from Chandra in the navamsa, do we not indicate the colour, features, dispositions
and position of the wife by looking at the planet or planets
in the 7th house from Chandra in the navamsa ? But what
probably Varahamihira and his illustrious commentator
mean here, seems to be that the positions of the planets
in the navamsa or in the kendras from Chandra, may not
successfully create these special yogas as the older and the
most famous writers of India did not countenance such a
view. I am sure there will be yogas as per slokas quoted
by Bhattotpala from Srutakirti and Jivasarma, but they may
not be identical with these special combinations detailed
here as Sunapha, Anapha, Dhuradhura and Kemadruma.

निशत्सरूपाः सुनफानफाख्याः
षष्टित्रयं दौरुधरे प्रमेदाः ।
इच्छाविकल्पैः क्रमाशोऽभिनीय
नीते निवृत्तिः पुनरयनीतिः ॥ ४ ॥

24

Stanza 4.—There are 30 varieties of Sunapha and Anapha conjunctions. There are three-sixties of varieties (180) in Dhuradhura. The intended varieties can be found out by placing planets in regular order and dropping the first in proceeding to the last and repeating this.

NOTES

The yogas can be found out by permutations and combinations of planets in the signs. $60 \times 3 = 180$ varieties of Dhuradhura are named. The principles of mathematics involved here are easily explained by Bhattotpala. He says, take the number of planets and the varieties they produce.

Thus—

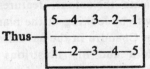

$$\frac{5-4-3-2-1}{1-2-3-4-5}$$

A little knowledge of permutations and combinations will enable one to easily understand these.

If five planets are in the 2nd there will be one yoga; if four planets are there five varieties are produced ; if in the 2nd three planets are taken at a time we have ten varieties ; if two planets are taken at a time ten varieties; and if one planet is taken at a time five varieties. Thus there are 30 varieties for Sunapha and an equal number for Anapha. The commentator asks the student to put five planets taken at a time in the reverse order under the first set of figures.

Thus—

$$\frac{5-4-3-2-1}{1-2-3-4-5}$$

Take the first figure five and divide it by the lower figure 1—we get 5 varieties of one planet taken at a time in the 2nd house from the Moon.   Take the product 5 and multiply it with the next figure 4—we get 20, divide this by the figure 2, which represents two planets taken at a time— we get 10 varieties.   Multiply this product 10 by the next figure 3 we get 30, divide this by the lower figure 3 and we have 10 varieties of 3 planets taken at a time.   Multiply this 10 by the next figure 2 and we get 20.   Divide this by the lower figure four and we get five varieties of four planets taken at a time.   Then multiply this 5 by the next figure 1 and divide it by the lower figure 5, we get 1.   Thus the total will be $5+10+10+5+1=31$ yogas.

The total is 31 and not 30 as stated though the original clearly says Trimsat Swarupaha, *i.e.*, 30.

There are 180 varieties of Dhuradhura for which the author, as well the commentator, gives a hint to call in the skill of the student to find out the number.   They are thus formed :

    (1)   Mars and Mercury
    (2)   Mercury and Mars
    (3)   Mars and Jupiter
    (4)   Jupiter and Mars
    (5)   Mars and Venus
    (6)   Venus and Mars
    (7)   Mars and Saturn
    (8)   Saturn and Mars
    (9)   Mercury and Jupiter
  (10)   Jupiter and Mercury
  (11)   Mercury and Venus

(12)   Venus and Mercury
(13)   Mercury and Saturn
(14)   Saturn and Mercury
(15)   Jupiter and Venus
(16)   Venus and Jupiter
(17)   Jupiter and Saturn
(18)   Saturn and Jupiter
(19)   Venus and Saturn
(20)   Saturn and Venus
(21)   Mars—Mercury and Jupiter
(22)   Mars—Mercury and Venus
(22)   Mars—Mercury and Saturn
(24)   Mars—Jupiter and Venus
(25)   Mars—Jupiter and Saturn
(26)   Mars—Venus and Saturn
(27)   Mercury—Mars and Jupiter
(28)   Mercury—Mars and Venus
(29)   Mercury—Mars and Saturn
(30)   Mercury—Jupiter and Venus
(31)   Mercury—Venus and Saturn

Similarly if we go on counting the different combinations of planets, we get the large number of 180 varieties for Dhuradhura.

स्वयमधिगतवित्तः पार्थिवस्तत्समो बा
भवेति हि सुनफायां धीधनरव्यातिमांश्च ।
प्रभुरगदशरीरः शीलवान् ख्यातकीर्ति-
विषयसुखसुवेषो निर्वृतश्चानफायाम् ॥ ५ ॥

Stanza 5.—A person born in Sunapha will be king or his equal with self-acquired wealth, intelligent, wealthy and reputed. A person born under Anapha will be a ruler, healthy, moral, renowned, enjoying good pleasures, fond of decorations and free from mental sorrow.

NOTES

Varahamihira now gives the results of Sunapha and other yogas he has given in Stanza 3. A person will be a king or his equal only when the planets causing this (yoga) Sunapha are exalted and powerful. But when they are weak and debilitated they give the persons some position, which may be important in small localities. Suppose Moon is in Pisces and Saturn is in Aries. There is Sunapha so also when the Moon is in Virgo and Saturn is in Libra. The student in these two cases ought not to predict the same results and position as Saturn is exalted in Libra and debilitated in Aries. These general sources of strength and weakness play their role all through human experience, and astrologers must be very careful and cautious in making predictions.

In the Anapha yoga the word Vishaya Sukha, sense pleasures or enjoyments is purposely used and Bhattotpala clearly explains by saying that this combination does not give that grand pleasure which the Yogis are said to enjoy as the result of their deep contemplation on Parabrahma. The pleasure will be from the satisfaction of sense craving, but not in immoral ways. For instance if a man has a good wife and enjoys her company or has good horses and drives

or rides on them, has nice houses and furniture, excellent
food and clothing, he may be said to gratify his sense
cravings but in the approved methods. Sense pleasures are
short-lived. There will not be the mental happiness or
glow. They give pleasure while enjoying them, but after
enjoyment, they weaken the man and sometimes exhaust
him. In Yogic pleasure, the body becomes stronger, there
is mental peace and spiritual force generated.

उत्पन्नभोगसुखभुग्धनवाहनाढ्य-
स्त्यागान्वितो दुरुधराप्रभवः सुभृत्येः ।
केमद्रुमे मलिनदुः खितनीचनिःस्वाः
प्रेष्याः खलाश्च नृपतेरपि वंशजाताः ॥ ६ ॥

Stanza 6.—One born under Dhuradhura
enjoys all pleasures, has wealth and conveyances,
will be liberal and possessed of good servants.
The person born under Kemadruma, although he
may take his birth in a royal family, will be dirty,
sorrowful, doing work against his caste, poor,
dependent and roguish.

NOTES

Enjoying all pleasures may mean, that the person will
be fortunate enough to get objects from different parts of the
world which are likely to give him pleasure or will have
pleasure from products grown in the places where he
happens to live. There is a slight difference in reading
Su Britya and *Sa Britya*. The first means good servants,

while the second means with servants. The first is preferred
as Bhattotpala supports it. *Kemadruma* seems to be a
dreaded yoga as evils are predicted for it. Varahamihira
adds emphasis by saying that men born even in royal families
suffer these evils predicted by Kemadruma, and therefore
those who are born in ordinary families will surely have
much more of them. *Malina* is interpreted as having dirty
unwashed clothes and person. Sorrow refers to physical as
well as mental sorrows. *Nicha* used here means that the
person will do such acts as are prohibited by his religious
and social codes and therefore degrades himself in the
estimation of his fellow-subjects. *Khala* means all roguish
and desperate acts which unprincipled men are apt to do.

उत्साहशौर्यधनसाहसवान्महीजः
सौम्यः पटुः सुवचनो निपुणः कलासु ।
जीवोऽर्थधर्मसुखभाङ् नृपपूजितश्च
कामी भृगुर्बहुधनो विषयोपभोक्ता ॥ ७ ॥

Stanza 7.—If Mars causes these yogas, the
person will be energetic, wealthy, warlike and
adventurous. If Mercury causes the yogas, the
person will be skilful, have sweet speech and he
learned in arts. If Jupiter causes the yogas, the
person will be rich, charitable, happy and respected by rulers. If Venus, he will be fond of
women, very wealthy and will enjoy sensual
pleasures.

NOTES

The stanzas are given with a view to find out the particular results from the special planetary positions in causing these yogas, viz., Sunapha, Anapha and Dhuradhura. These results do not apply to Kemadruma as there will be no planets on either side of the Moon. If one planet is in the 2nd, the result may be given in their entirety if he is strong, but when two or more planets are in one house, the results will have to be predicted for all of them according to their strength and position. Suppose Mars and Jupiter are in the second. They are friends and augment each other's strength. But suppose the Sun and Saturn are in the second from the Moon. The results are greatly neutralised as they are inimical and counteract each other's influences.

परविभवपरिच्छदोपभोक्ता
रवितनयो बहुकार्यकृद्द्रणेशः ।
अशुभकृदुडुपो द्वि दृश्यमूर्ति-
र्गलिततनुश्च शुभो न्यथाऽन्यदूहम् ॥ ८ ॥

Stanza 8.—If Sani causes these yogas, the man will enjoy other's wealth and articles, will be engaged in various works, and be a leader of an assembly. The Moon, if visible in the day, does mischief but when he is invisible, he will be auspicious. Otherwise the results will be different.

NOTES

When Saturn causes these yogas, the person will enjoy
life at the cost of others.   He will be engaged in a variety
of work, and will also be elected as the leader of men or
assemblies.   This will give him great influence and
probably he will support himself at their cost.   The word
used for the visibility and invisibility of the Moon is
Drisya and Adrisya.   Bhattotpala explains it as Drisya
Chakram.   In Stanza 22, Chapter V of this work, I have
explained these words and what they mean and refer the
readers to it.   When the Moon is in Drisya Chakra
during the day, he will produce evil and when he is in
Adrisya Chakra, he will be auspicious.   This will be
reversed in the night.   When the Moon is in Drisya
Chakra in the night, he is auspicious; when he occupies
the Adrisya Chakra during the night, he becomes inauspicious.

लभ्रादतीव वसुमान्वसुमाञ्छशाङ्क्रात्
सौम्यग्रहैरुपचयोपगतैः समस्तैः ।
द्वाभ्यां समोऽल्पवसुमांश्च तदूनताया-
मन्येष्वसत्स्वपि फलेष्विदमुत्कटेन ॥ ९ ॥

Stanza 9.—When all benefics are in Upachayas from lagna, the person will be extremely
wealthy.   When all benefics are in Upachayas
from the Moon, he will be wealthy.   When two
benefics are in Upachayas, there will be moderate
wealth.   Less than that will produce little wealth.

The results from these will predominate over others.

This is shortly and sweetly expressed in the original. The three benefics are Jupiter, Venus and Mercury. The Upachayas are the 3rd, 6th, 10th and 11th houses from the Lagna or the Moon. (See Stanza 10, Ch. I and St. 5, Ch. II.) When these three benefics are situated in the Upachayas from lagna, the person will be very rich but when they are so from the Moon, he will be rich. When two of the benefics are in Upachayas from Lagna or Chandra the person will be moderately rich. When one of them is so, he will be little wealthy, but when there are no benefics, there will be poverty. In the following diagram, we can easily see that even when Chandra is not

Birth			Moon
			Sun
			Jupiter Venus Mercury

in Lagna, the benefics may be in Upachayas from both. Birth is Pisces and the three benefics Jupiter, Mercury and Venus are in the 6th Upachaya. The Moon is in Gemini and they are in the 3rd house from him, also an Upachaya.

In such cases, when the three benefics are in Upachayas both from the birth and from the Moon, it is hardly necessary to say that the person wi!l be immensely rich or what will be called a millionaire.

The following horoscope illustrates the truth of this. The native is a rich coffee planter who was on the brink of bankruptcy but the sudden rise in the price of coffee enabled him to liquidate his debts and become a sufficiently rich man worth about 10 to 15 lakhs at present.

From Lagna, Guru, Sukra and Budha are in Upachayas and from the Moon, Sukra is in Upachaya. This makes him a wealthy man.

		Rahu	Sukra
Guru	RASI		Ravi Kuja Budha
Moon			
	Kethu		Lagna

CHAPTER XIV

DWIGRAHAYOGADHYAYA

द्विग्रहयोगाध्यायः

(Results from the conjunction of two Planets)

तिग्मांशुर्जैनयत्युपेशसहितो यन्त्राश्मकारं नरं
भौमेनाघरतं बुधेन निपुणं धीकीर्तिसौख्यान्वितम् ।
क्रूरं वाक्पतिनान्यकार्यनिरतं शुक्रेण रङ्गायुधै-
र्लब्धस्वं रविजेन धातुकुशलं भाण्डप्रकारेषु वा ॥ १ ॥

Stanza 1.—If the Sun conjoins with the Moon, the person will be skilled in machinery and masonry; if with Mars, fond of sinful deeds; if with Mercury, skilful, intelligent, renowned and happy; if with Jupiter, he will be cruel and always doing other's work; if with Venus, he will make money on stage and by weapons; and if with Saturn, he will be skilful in working ores or earthenware.

NOTES

Here Varahamihira is very short and suggestive and the students will have to explain a great deal from their experience and the experience of their instructors. The Sun and the Moon in conjunction produce men skilled in making, handling or dealing with all machinery and under this head we may bring in mechanics, engineers, chemists, and other workmen.

Here it is desirable to point out that in many of the horoscopes, the combination of Ravi and Budha has also produced engineers more than the combination of Ravi and Chandra. Ravi and Chandra join on Amavasya day or a day previous or later and as such the Moon is weak or Kshina.

Ravi Moon Sukra Kethu	Budha			Kuja Sani		Lagna Rahu Moon	Ravi Budha
Kuja	Late Chief Engineer of a State Chart I RASI				Engineer in Military Service Chart II RASI		Sukra
			Lagna				Guru
	Guru	Rahu	Sani		Kethu		

In the Chart I Ravi and Chandra are combined and in the Chart II Ravi and Budha are combined. The Chart I has better combination and carried the man to a Chief Engineer's place on Rs. 2,500 while the Chart II is drawing only a few hundreds—about 5 or 6. The combinations indicate Engineering profession.

Asma means large flat-stones used in building houses and the man may be a mason, a seller of these stones and examiner of them or cutter and fitter. When the Sun joins Mars, the person will be fond of sin and vice. In all these cases the position of the man has nothing to do with his character.   Prince and statesman, priest and poets, philosophers and literates have been known to be guilty of the most abominable vices, while poor and ignorant men have been known to be strictly moral and religious. The tendencies of men are shown herewith and they pursue their courses suitable to their rank.   If the Sun joins an exalted Saturn, the person may not become a regular potter but may be in charge of earthenware depot or if he is in some high political life he may prepare rich pottery and take delight in such manufactures.

कूटस्त्रचायासथायासवकुंभपण्यमशिवं मातुः सवक्रः शशी
सङ्गः प्रश्रितवाक्यमर्थनिपुणं सौभाग्यकीर्त्यान्वितम् ।
विक्रान्तं कुलमुख्यमस्थिरमतिं विचेश्वरं साङ्गिरा
वक्त्राणां ससितः क्रियादिकुशलं सार्किः पुनर्भूसुतम् ॥२॥

Stanza 2.—The Moon in conjunction with Mars makes a man a counterfeit, a seller of women, wives and pots and doing mischief to mother ; the Moon with Mercury makes a person polite in speech, clever in interpretation, popular and renowned ; the Moon with Jupiter makes a person successful against enemies, chief of that sect or family, capricious and wealthy ; the Moon with Venus makes a man skilful in weaving ; and the Moon with Saturn makes a person the son of a second marriage.

NOTES

The commentator gives various *panyams* or saleable articles. Kutapanyam, Streepanyam, Asnapanyam and Kumbhapanyam. When the Moon joins with Mars he will make the native counterfeit all sorts of saleable articles, sell women, wines and pots. In fact, in all these expressions, the various relations which a man can have with such articles are indicated. The seller of toddy, the preparer of that, the superintendent of those shops and the forgerer or imitator of such articles come under this heading according to the strength of the conjoined planets.

A man may sell his daughter, his wife, his mother, or get other women and pimp them to adulterous people. In all these cases, he makes some gain and this is due to planetary conjunctions. The son of a second marriage is called punarbhusuta " born again." Bhattotpala quotes an authority and describes punarbhu as follows. When a woman marries and voluntarily neglects her husband, marries again a man of her choice from her own sect and thus stands both polluted and pure she is called a punarbhu.

The son of a second marriage should not be understood to mean, the son of a second wife, but that the woman having her husband living, leaves him and gets a son by some one else than her first married husband. The birth of the Pandavas comes under this category as Kunti while Pandu was living, got children by other husbands who married her according to *Gandharva* rites. Kunti is not classed as polluted.

मूलादिस्नेहकूटैर्व्यवहरति वणिग्बाहुयोद्धा ससौम्ये
पुर्यध्यक्षः सजीवे भवति नरपतिः प्राप्तवित्तो द्विजो वा ।
गोपो मल्लोऽथ दक्षः परयुवतिरतो द्यूतकृत्सासुरेज्ये
दुःखार्त्तोऽसत्यसंधः ससवितृतनये भूमिजे निन्दितश्च ॥ ३ ॥

Stanza 3.—When Mars joins Mercury the
person will be a dealer in roots, etc., oils,
imitation articles and versed in boxing. Mars
with Jupiter produces a ruler of a city or Raja or
a rich Brahmin. Mars with Venus produces cow-
herds, wrestler, skilful, fond of other women and
gambler. Mars with Saturn makes the man
sorrowful, untruthful, and disgraced or blamed.

NOTES

By the word Mooladi in the original, it is meant to
denote bulbs, roots, flowers, fibres, cloths and fruits. Mercury and Mars in conjunction make a man dealer in the
above articles, oils of all descriptions, preparation and
selling of imitation stuffs and also a good boxer.

Jupiter with Mars (called Guru Mangala Yoga) will
make a man a chief officer or leader or protector or magistrate in a city or a king or a learned or wealthy Brahmin as
we take the reading " Prapta vitta or Prapta vidya."

Venus in conjunction with Mars makes a good wrestler,
a cowherd, a gambler, skilful and fond of other women. It
may be noted in this connection that in thousands of horoscopes I have had occasion to examine, I invariably found the
morals of the individual with this combination very loose
and himself or herself suffering from venereal complaints.

(2) The following horoscopes of persons well known to me illustrate the truth.

	Chandra	Kethu		Sani		
Guru			Lagna	Chandra		Kethu
	Male Horoscope				Female Horoscope	
Sani				Guru Rahu		
	Ravi Budha Rahu	Kuja Sukra		Lagna		Ravi Budha Kuja Sukra

Both suffered from serious venereal diseases, though the male horoscope was worse in that respect.

The conjunction of Mars with Saturn culminates in producing misery, falsehood and disgrace in the person.

सौम्ये रङ्गचरो बृहस्पतियुते गीतप्रियो नृत्यविद्
वाग्मी भूगणपः सितेन मृदुना मायापटुर्लैङ्कः ।
सद्विद्यो धनदारवान्बहुगुणः शुक्रेण युक्ते गुरौ
ज्ञेयः श्मश्रुकरोऽसितेन घटकुज्जातोऽन्नकारोऽपि वा ॥ ४ ॥

Stanza 4.—When Mercury and Jupiter join, they produce a man who figures constantly on the stage, when Mercury joins Venus the man will be fond of music, dancing, eloquence and protection of lands and assemblies. Mercury with Saturn makes a man a cheat and disobedient. Jupiter

25

with Venus produces good education, wife, wealth
and men of many virtues. Jupiter with Saturn
produces barber, potter or cook.

NOTES

The stanza is easy and requires few notes. Those who
appear on the stage may do so under various capacities and
forms and all these varieties have to be made out by the
relative strength and position of these planets.

असितसितसमागमेऽल्पचक्षु-
युवतिसमाश्रयसंप्रवृद्धवित्तः ।
भवति च लिखिपुस्तकचित्रवेत्ता
कथितफलैः परतो विकल्पनीयाः ॥ ५ ॥

Stanza 5.—Venus with Saturn gives a man
small eyes, wealth from depending upon some
females, artistic capacity, ordinary writing and
painting. Similarly results of combinations of
more than two planets must be made out.

NOTES

The last part requires some further explanation.
Varahamihira true to his motto of writing little and sug-
gesting much, asks the readers to make out results similarly
for larger combinations. Suppose the Sun, Moon and Mars
are in one house. Then we have to take out the results of
the conjunction of (1) the Sun with the Moon, (2)
the Sun with Mars, and (3) the Moon with Mars. Suppose there are two planets in one house and three planets

in another house. Then all the results mentioned here must be traced out according to their relative strength. Suppose there are 4 planets in one house, *viz.*, the Sun, Moon, Mars and Mercury. As above suggested, conjunctional results for all these must be made out.

The readers should do well to work out their own horoscopes. The following horoscopes illustrate this:

				Guru	Rahu		
Kethu	CHART I		Sani		CHART II		Moon Sukra
Moon			Lagna Rahu				
	Kuja	Budha	Guru Ravi Sukra			Ravi Budha Kethu Lagna	Sani

Chart I gives Ravi and Guru, Ravi and Sukra and Guru and Sukra (three combinations). Ravi and Guru— cruel and doing other's work; Ravi and Sukra—makes money on stage and by weapons; Guru and Sukra—good education, wife, children and wealth, and man of many virtues.

Chart II is the horoscope of a great Matadhipathi (ruler of a Mutt) and a man of rare devotion and Tapobala. Note here Ravi and Budha and Chandra and Sukra forming combinations. He is renowned, intelligent and a great scholar. Study the Chart II to understand the next chapter about Sanyasa yoga or Pravrajya yoga.

CHAPTER XV

Pravrajya Yoga

प्रव्रज्यायोगाध्यायः

(Renunciation of the world or Sanyasa)

एकस्थैश्चतुरादिभिर्बलयुतैर्जाताः पृथग्वीर्यगैः
शाक्याजीविकमिक्षुवृद्धचरका निर्ग्रन्थवन्याशनाः ।
माहेयज्ञगुरुक्षपाकरसितप्राभाकरीनैः क्रमात्
प्रव्रज्या बलिभिः समाः परजितैस्तत्स्वामिभिः प्रच्युतिः ॥१॥

Stanza 1.—When there are four or more powerful planets in one house, the persons born will become Sakya, Aajivika, Bikshu, Vriddha, Chakra, Nirgrantha and Vanyasana, when Mahaya, Gnya, Guru, Kshapakara, Sita, Prabhakari and Ina are powerful respectively. The Pravrajya yogas are determined by the most powerful planets. When these planets have suffered a defeat, the person will renounce the Pravrajya afterwards.

NOTES

To the Hindu, the spiritual has as much attraction—if not more—as the material comforts and taken from such a standard the combinations sketched out here are really very valuable as the person can make out, when and what kind of Sanyasa he will become and what would be his spiritual progress after renouncing the worldly pleasures. There must be four or more planets in a house for this yoga.

Seven planets four at each time would give us many permutations but what is meant is that there should be at least four planets in a house and according to the most powerful among the seven, the Moon, etc., seven kinds of Sanyasa yogas are formed. *Laghu Jataka* also says that if more than one planet is powerful, the different kinds of Sanyasis will be taken up one after the other and if no planet is powerful, there will be no yoga of Sanyasa.

The following two horoscopes of two great Sanyasis are given to illustrate a few combinations. The I is Adi Shankaracharya's and the II of the late Sringeri Jagadguru Abhinava Narasimha Bharati Swami who died in 1912.

	Ravi Budha	Lagna Sukra	Rahu
			Chandra
Kuja	Adi Shankaracharya Chart I		
Kethu	Guru	Sani	

Sukra	Guru		
Ravi Budha Rahu	Abhinava Narasimha Bharati Swami Chart II		Sani
Chandra			Kethu
	Kuja	Lagna	

In Chart I, Ravi, Kuja and Sani are exalted, Sukra and Chandra in their own houses.

The following strong planets in this conjunction will produce the undermentioned varieties of Pravrajya yoga :—

1.   Powerful Mars : Sakya—those Sanyasis who wear red clothes.

2.   Mercury : Aajivika—a Sanyasi bearing Ekadanda or single staff.

3.   Jupiter : Bikshu—ordinary Sanyasis who have yellowish rose-coloured clothes.

4.   The Moon : Vriddha—Kapalika or one who moves about with a skull in his hand.

5.   Venus : Chakra—one who carries a chakra or ring or circle.

6.   Saturn : Nirgrantha—moving about in nude forms.

7.   The Sun : Vanyasana—those who live on roots and bulbs in a forest. Bhattotpala quotes for the first time from "Vankalakacharya" and elaborates verses in pure Prakrit and in excellent style. Who this great astrologer was and where he lived would be a very interesting research to make. The language unmistakably shows his remote antiquity and it would be quite a gain to astrological literature if we could throw some light upon this ancient astrological writer and his works. He apparently seems to have been the author of a Samhita. Vriddha stands for Vriddhasravaka and is beautifully explained by Vankalakacharya. These Sanyasis stand for devotion to Eswara while Aajivikas are those who are devoted to Vishnu.

When two planets are powerful among the lot, the order of Sanyasi will be determined first by the most powerful among them, and then the person may embrace the second   It is only when a planet is very strong that he

makes the man a Sanyasi for a long time. If the planet
is weak, then he will only make the person long after it but
will not induce him to take it up. When the most powerful planet is defeated in the planetary fight the person will
take up Sanyasa and after some time renounce it. If the
last powerful planet is not defeated, then the person will
die in that yoga which is ruled by that planet. If two of
them are powerful and suffer no defeat then, when the first
planet's sub-period comes he embraces the first and when
the sub-period of the second planet comes he will renounce
the first and take up the second and keep it on. If only one
planet is powerful and has not suffered defeat then he takes
the order indicated by him and keeps it on uninterruptedly.

रविलुप्तकरैरदीक्षिता बलिभिस्तद्व्रतभक्तयो नराः ।
अभियाचितमात्रदीक्षिता निहितैरन्यनिरीक्षितैरपि ॥ २ ॥

Stanza 2.—If the powerful Pravrajya causing planets are in combust with the Sun then the
persons born will not take up Sanyasa but will
greatly worship those who have embraced Sanyasa. If the Yogakaraka and defeated planets
are aspected by other planets the person would be
making application for Diksha.

NOTES

Pravrajya arises only when there are four or more
planets in a house. Of the most powerful of these which
cause this yoga, the combusted planets produce no Diksha
or Sanyasa but produce admiration or regard for those who
have taken Sanyasa similar to that which the planet governs.

Regarding combustion or Asta, Bhattotpala says that simply because a planet is in the same house with the Sun, it must not be presumed that he is in combustion, neither should it be presumed that the planet who is in the 2nd house from the Sun is not in combustion. The fact of combustion or not must be ascertained by regular mathematical calculations. If the powerful Yogakaraka planets are defeated and aspected by other planets, then the man will simply make application to be admitted but they would not become Sanyasis. In the first stanza it was alleged that powerful planets defeated in planetary fight would give Sanyasa and then would make him renounce it afterwards. But now he clears this by saying that the man would take up Sanyasa only when the planet is not aspected by other planets. But when others aspect the planet then the man will only be applying for it without taking or getting. The planet will give Sanyasa during his sub-period, when in the gochara movements, he obtains the greatest strength.

जन्मेशोऽन्यैर्यथ्यघदृष्टोऽर्कपुत्रं
पश्यत्यार्किंजन्मपं वा बलोनम् ।
दीक्षां प्रमोत्यार्किंद्रकाणसंस्थे
भौमार्क्येशे सौरदृष्टे च जन्द्रे ॥ ३ ॥

Stanza 3.—When *Janmesa* is not aspected by other planets, but aspects Saturn, or when Saturn aspects the weak *Janmesa* or if the Moon is in Saturn's drekkana and occupies the amsa of Saturn or Mars and has saturnine aspect, the person will have *Diksha*.

NOTES

Now he gives three sets of combinations, when the Diksha or the ordinance of a Sanyasi may take place even when there are not planetary conjunctions of four or more in one house. Bhattotpala explains *Janmesa* as the lord of the house occupied by the Moon at the time of birth.

Generally *Janmesa* means the lord of birth, but here it is to be understood as the lord of the house in which the Moon is situated. Take the horoscope No. II given under Stanza 1. The lord of the house where the Moon is situated is Saturn and he is aspecting his own house. So also in Sankaracharya's horoscope, the Moon in his own house is aspected by Saturn.

(*a*) If this lord is not aspected by any other planets but aspects Saturn, then there will be a Pravrajya yoga. The Sanyasa then will take that form which is ruled by Saturn as mentioned in the first stanza. This comes in during the sub-period of the most powerful among these two, *viz.*, Janmesa and Saturn.

(*b*) When Saturn is powerful and aspects the weak lord of the house occupied by the Moon, then the saturnine form of Pravrajya will be obtained.

(*c*) If the Moon occupies a Saturnine drekkana in any sign and also occupies the navamsa of Mars or Saturn, and is not aspected by any other planet than Saturn, then the man will assume the Sanyasa peculiar to Saturn.

Here the commentator insists on the necessity for also applying the conditions laid down in the first two stanzas, that is we must take into consideration the planetary combustions and defeats.

सुरगुरुशशिहोरास्वार्किदृष्टासु धर्में
गुरुरथ नृपतिनां योगजस्तीर्थकृत् सयात् ।
नवमभवनसंस्थे मन्दगेऽन्यैरदृष्टे
भवति नरपयोगे दीक्षितः पार्थिवेन्द्रः ॥ ४ ॥

Stanza 4.—If Jupiter, the Moon and birth are
aspected by Saturn, and if Jupiter is in the 9th,
the person born would be a Raja who would write
on shastras or sciences. If 9th is occupied by
Saturn unaspected by any planet, the person will
become a Dikshita when he is born in Raja yoga.

NOTES

Here Varahamihira gives two combinations peculiar to
kings.

(*a*) If Saturn aspects the Moon, birth and Jupiter, with
Jupiter in the ninth (9th) house, then, a king in whose horoscope such conjunction rises, becomes a writer on sciences.
Bhattotpala here gives instances of persons, who, although
born as rulers and princes, become great as scientists and
philosophers. This is a strange fact brought to light by him.

He quotes Kanada, Buddha, Panchasikha, Varahamihira and Brahmagupta. Kanada was the first great
writer on Tarka or Sanskrit logic and his system even today
goes under the name of Kanada matham. From what
Bhattotpala says, Kanada must have been a royal personage,
who devoted himself to sciences and who became a great
authority on Hindu logic or Tarka.

Buddha is too well-known a royal personage, who
renounced the regal pleasures when young and enunciated

one of the most profound systems of religious faith and
philosophy. Panchasikha must have been a well-known
Prince and writer on science before Bhattotpala's time. Who
he was and what he has written are now not known. From
this statement of Bhattotpala, Varahamihira appears to have
been a petty Raja or chief and whose scientific works are
now so well known to the educated public. Brahmagupta
was a great astronomer and probably, he belonged to a
royal family and was a high personage in Kashmir. Some
explain the first part of this stanza as referring to the two
houses of Jupiter and the sign of the Moon, viz., Sagittarius,
Pisces and Cancer. But this is contradicted by the clear
quotation from Maharishi Mandavya. If there is a Raja yoga
coupled with the above named yoga, then the person will
not be a king but only will be a scientist. If the person has
two Raja yogas, along with this yoga, then he will become
a ruling king and also a great writer on sciences. Instances
of Jina, Kasiraja and Sphujidhwaja and Janaka are quoted
in support of this principle. Jina was probably the great
reviver of Jainism and must have been of a high royal
family. Kasiraja was the King of Banares who taught the
great Medical Science of Ayurveda to Susruta, Oupadhenava,
Vytharana, Ourabhra, Poushkalavatha, Karavirya and
Gopurarashita and claims to have received his knowledge
from heavenly Gurus. Janaka was the King of Mithila and
was a great yogi and father of Sitadevi, wife of Sri Rama.
But if a person has no Raja yoga but has this combination,
then he will become a Sanyasi.

Then Chart I given at the end of Chapter XIV can be
studied with advantage. Sani aspects Jupiter and the Moon
and Jupiter is in the 9th from the Moon. The native has an
inclination to spiritual matters and is orthodox.

CHAPTER XVI

RIKSHASILADHYAYA

ऋक्षशीलाध्यायः

(Influences of Constellations)

प्रियभूषणः सुरूपः सुभगो दक्षोऽश्विनीषु मतिमांश्च ।
कृतनिश्चयसत्यारुग्दक्षः सुखितश्च भरणीषु ॥ १ ॥

Stanza 1.—The person born in Aswini will be fond of decoration, handsome, popular, skilful and intelligent. One born in Bharani will be determined, truthful, healthy, skilful and happy.

बहुभुक् परदाररतस्तेजस्वी कृत्तिकासु विख्यातः ।
रोहिण्यां सत्यशुचिः प्रियंवदः स्थिरमतिः सुरूपश्च ॥ २ ॥

Stanza 2.—The person born in Krittika will be a voracious eater, fond of other's wives, attractive and renowned. Rohini makes a man truthful, clean, following religious and moral principles, sweet in speech, fixed mind and handsome.

चपलश्चतुरो भीरुः पटुरुत्साही धनी मृगे भोगी ।
शठगर्वितः कृतघ्नो हिंस्रः पापश्च रौद्रर्क्षे ॥ ३ ॥

Stanza 3.—Mrigasira—Capricious, skilful, cowardly, good speaker, hopeful, rich and enjoying. Aridra—Dissimulating in self-interest, proud, ungrateful, cruel and sinful.

दान्तः सुखी सुशीलो दुर्मेधा रोगभाक् पिपासुश्च ।
अल्पेन च संतुष्टः पुनर्वसौ जायते मनुजः ॥ ४ ॥

Stanza 4.—Punarvasu—Religious endurance, happy, good, dull, sickly, thirsty and pleased with small gifts.

शान्तात्मा सुभगः पण्डितो धनी धर्मसंस्तुतः पुष्ये ।
शठसर्वभक्षपापः कृतघ्नधूर्त्तश्च भौजङ्गे ॥ ५ ॥

Stanza 5.—Pushya—Control over passions, popular, learned, rich and charitable. Aslesha—Dissimulator, clever in selfishness, sinful, ungrateful and a cheat.

बहुभृत्यधनो भोगी सुरपितृभक्तो महोद्यमः पित्र्ये-
प्रियवाग्दाता द्युतिमानटनो नृपसेवको भाग्ये ॥ ६ ॥

Stanza 6.—Makha—Many servants and great wealth, enjoying, respector of elders and gods and very enterprising.   Pubba—Sweet speech, liberal, handsome, fond of travelling and royal servant.

सुभगो विद्याऽधनो भोगी सुखभाग्द्वितीयफाल्गुन्याम् ।
उत्साही धृष्टः पानपोऽद्घृणी तस्करो हस्ते ॥ ७ ॥

Stanza 7.—Uttara—Popular, self-acquired property, enjoying and happy. Hasta—Enterprising, intelligent or (shameless), drunkard, cruel and thievish.

चित्राम्बरमाल्यधरः सुलोचनाङ्गश्च भवति चित्रायाम् ।
दान्तो वणिक् कृपालुः प्रियवाग्घर्मासहितः स्वातौ ॥ ८ ॥

Stanza 8.—Chitta—Using various clothes and
garlands, good looks and limbs. Swati—Polite,
merchant, kind hearted, not able to endure
thirst, sweet tongued and generous.

ईर्ष्युर्लुब्धो द्युतिमान्वचनपटुः कलहकृद्द्विशाखासु ।
आढ्यो विदेशवासी क्षुधालुरटनोऽनुराधासु ॥ ९ ॥

Stanza 9.—Visakha–Jealous, avaricious, handsome, clever speaker and quarrelsome, or maker
of money. Anuradha—Master or chief, living
in foreign countries, not able to bear hunger
and fond of travelling.

ज्येष्ठासु न बहुमित्रः संतुष्टो धर्मकृत्प्रचुरकोपः ।
मूले मानी धनवान् सुखी न हिंस्रः स्थिरो भोगी ॥ १० ॥

Stanza 10.—Jyeshta—Few friends, contented,
charitable, very irritable. Moola—Proud, rich,
happy, good, steady and enjoying.

इष्टानन्दकलत्रो मानी दृढसौहृदश्च जलदैवे ।
वैश्वे विनीतधार्मिकबहुमित्रकृतज्ञसुभगश्च ॥ ११ ॥

Stanza 11.—Purvashada—Good and pleasant
wife, proud and a steady friend. Uttarashada—

Polite, knowing, virtuous, many friends, grateful
and popular.

श्रीमाञ्छ्रवणे श्रुतवानुदारदारो धनान्वितः ख्यातः ।
दाता चाढ्यः शूरो गतिप्रियो धनिष्ठासु धनलुब्धः ॥ १२ ॥

Stanza   12.--Sravana—Rich   surroundings,
learned, good and liberal or liberal to wife,
wealthy and renowned. Dhanishta—Liberal, rich,
courageous, fond of music and money.

रफुटवाग्व्यसनी रिपुहा साहसिकः शतमिषजि दुर्ग्राह्यः ।
माद्रपदाद्वद्विप्रः स्त्रीजितधनीपट्टुरदाता च ॥ १३ ॥

Stanza   13.—Satabhisha—Plain and truthful,
striken frόm sorrow through females, etc., killer
of enemies,   adventurous and   irreconcilable.
Poorvabhadra—Sorrowful, loss of money through
females, skilful and miserly.

वक्ता सुखी प्रजावान् जितशत्रुर्धार्मिको द्वितीयासु ।
संपूर्णाङ्गः सुभगः शूरः शुचिरर्थवान् पौष्णे ॥ १४ ॥

Stanza   14.—Uttarabhadra—Good and witty
speaker in society and meetings, happy, many
children and grandchildren, successful over
enemies and charitable. Revati—Well-developed
organs, popular, courageous, clean and wealthy.

NOTES

Riksha has been explained by Varahamihira to mean (1) constellations, and (2) zodiacal signs (see St. 4, Ch. I). Here both of these are explained.

In St. 8 of this there are two readings :
1. Kripalu=generous.
2. Thrishalu=thirsty.

In St. 9 of this there are two readings :
1. Vachanapatuhu=clever speaker.
2. Arthapatuhu=clever in earning money.

In Stanza 13 two different interpretations are given : (1) Strijitaha=conquered by females, and Dhani=wealthy and patuhu=clever. Or Strijithadhani—one whose wealth has been acquired through females. These results must be predicted according to the strength of the Moon. If he is weak in a constellation then there will be very faint traces of the characteristics. If he is strong, then these qualities will be possessed to a larger extent.

Readers are requested to refer to the book ' Nakshatra Chudamani ' where detailed characteristics for each quarter of a constellation are given. For example Krittika covers two rasis and the characteristics cannot be the same.

CHAPTER XVII

राशिशीलाध्यायः

RASISILADHYAYA OR THE LUNAR EFFECTS
IN THE VARIOUS SIGNS

वृत्तातात्रद्गुष्णशाकलघुभुक् क्षिप्रप्रसादोष्टनः
कामी दुर्बलजानुरस्थिरधनः शूरोऽङ्गनावल्लभः ।
सेवाङ्गः कुनखी व्रणाङ्कितशिरा मानी सहोत्थाग्रजः
शक्त्या पाणितलेऽङ्कितोऽतिचपलस्तोये च भीरुः क्रिये ॥१॥

Stanza 1.—Moon in Aries.—Round and
red eyes, eating hot and light food, fond of grains,
easily calmed, traveller, passionate, fleshless knees,
changeable wealth, courageous, liked by females,
good servant, bad nails, cut or scar in the head,
proud, chief among brothers, has Saktirekha (line)
in the palm, capricious and dreading water.
Another version is Ati Bhiru—one who is afraid
very much. The stanza says Thoyecha Bhiru.

(Many lines on the palm of the hand are
given different names in the science of palmistry.
Readers may refer to ' Hasta Samudrika ' and the
articles appearing in THE ASTROLOGICAL MAGA-
ZINE.)

26

कान्तः खेलगतिः पृथूरुवदनः पृष्ठास्यपार्श्वाङ्कित-
स्त्यागी क्लेशसहः प्रभुः ककुदवान् कन्याप्रजः श्लेष्मलः ।
पूर्वैबन्धुघनात्मजैर्विरहितः सौभाग्ययुक्तः क्षमी
दीक्षाग्निः प्रमदाप्रियः स्थिरसुहृन्मध्यान्त्यसौख्यो गवि ॥२॥

Stanza   2.—Moon in Taurus.—Handsome,
playful walk, long thighs and face, back sides and
face contain some marks, liberal, bearing fatigue,
possessing paraphernalia, begetting girls—phlegmatic, separated from elders, relations, family,
wealth and children ; popular, patient, strong
digestion, loved by females, firm friendship and
happy in the middle and end of his life.

स्त्रीलोलः सुरतोपचारकुशलस्ताम्रेक्षणः शास्त्रवित्
दूतः कुञ्चितमूर्द्धजः पटुमतिर्हास्येङ्गितद्यूतवित् ।
चार्वङ्गः प्रियवाक् प्रभक्षणरुचिर्गीतप्रियो नृत्यवित्
क्लीबैर्यातिरतिं समुन्नतनसश्चन्द्रे तृतीयर्क्षगे ॥ ३ ॥

Stanza 3.—Moon in Gemini.–Fond of women,
skilled in sexual sciences, red eyes, scientist,
ambassador, curled hairs, clever knowledge in
wit and human nature and gambling, handsome
organs, sweet speech, good eater, fond of music,
skilled in dancing, playing with impotents, high
nose.

आवक्रद्रुतगः समुन्नतकटिः स्त्रीनिर्जितः सत्सुहृद्
दैवज्ञः प्रचुरालयः क्षयधनैः संयुज्यते चन्द्रवत् ।
ह्रस्वः पीनगलः समेति च वशं साम्नासुहृद्वत्सलः
तायोद्यानरतः स्ववेश्मसहिते जातः शशाङ्के नरः ॥ ४ ॥

Stanza 4.—Moon in Cancer.—Walking in
curves quickly, high buttocks, submissive to
women, good friends, astrologer, many houses,
waxing and waning wealth like the Moon, short,
stout neck, amenable to kind words, fond of
friends, water and gardens.

तीक्ष्णः स्थूलहनुर्विशालवदनः पिङ्गेक्षणोऽल्पात्मजः
स्त्रीद्वेषी प्रियमांसकाननगः कुप्यत्यकार्ये चिरम् ।
क्षुत्तृष्णोदरदन्तमानसरुजा संपीडितस्त्यागवान्
विक्रान्तः स्थिरधीः सुगर्वितमना मातुर्विधेयोऽर्केमे ॥ ५ ॥

Stanza 5.—Moon in Leo.—Angry, high or
broad cheeks, coloured eyes, few children, hater of
women, fond of flesh, wilderness and mountains,
long displeasure, suffering from complaints
arising out of hunger, thirst, stomach, teeth and
mind ; liberal, courageous fixed, proud mind and
obedient to mother.

व्रीडामन्थरचारुवीक्षणगतिः स्रस्तांसबाहुः सुखी
श्लक्ष्णः सत्यरतः कलासु निपुणः शास्त्रार्थविद्धार्मिकः ।

मेधावी सुरतप्रियः परगृहैर्त्तित्तैश्च संयुज्यते
कन्यायां परदेशगः प्रियवचाः कन्याप्रजोऽल्पात्मजः ॥ ६ ॥

Stanza 6.—Moon in Virgo.—Walk and sight
will be characterised by modesty, bent shoulders
and hands, happy, sweet speaker, truthful,
charitable, skilled in arts, learned in sastras,
intelligent, passionate, possessed of other's wealth
and houses, foreign residence, calm speech, female
children and few issues.

देवब्राह्मणसाधुपूजनरतः प्राज्ञः शुचिः स्त्रीजितः
प्रांशुश्चोन्नतनासिकः कृशचलद्गात्रोऽष्टनोर्थान्वितः ।
हीनाङ्गः क्रयविक्रयेषु कुशलो देवद्विनामा सरुक्
बन्धूनामुपकारकृद्भिरुषितस्त्यक्तस्तुतैः सप्तमे ॥ ७ ॥

Stanza 7.—Moon in Libra.—Fond of worship-
ping Gods, Brahmins, pious people, intelligent,
clean, submissive to women, tall, long nose, weak
and disjointed organs, traveller, rich, ill-developed
organs, clever in merchandise, having the second
name pertaining to God (meaning that he
will not have the names of Gods as Rama,
Krishna but that which denotes the names of
Gods as Shanmuga—six faced—Gangadhara,
etc.), sickly, helping relations, and coerced and
rejected by relations. (Another version is

Penangaha having well-developed organs, but
this will be inconsistent with what has already
been stated).

पृथुलनयनवक्षा वृत्तजंघोरुजानु-
र्जनकगुरुवियुक्तः शैशवे व्याधितश्च ।
नरपतिकुलपूज्यः पिङ्गलः क्रूरचेष्टो
झषकुलिशखगाङ्कच्छन्नपापोऽडलिजातः ॥ ८ ॥

Stanza 8.—Moon in Scorpio.—Broad eyes
and chest, round knees, buttocks and thighs,
separated from parents and Guru, sickly in
infancy, respected by royal members, honey-color,
cruel, has marks of fish, vajrayudha, and bird,
secret sinner.

व्यादीर्घास्यशिरोधरः पितृधनस्त्यागी कविर्वीर्यवान्
वक्ता स्थूलरश्रा धरनसः कर्मोद्यतः शिल्पवित् ।
कुब्जांसः कुनखी समांसलभुजः प्रागल्भ्यबान्धर्मवि-
द्धन्धुद्विट् न बलात्समेति च वशं साम्रैकसाध्योऽश्वजः ॥ ९ ॥

Stanza 9.—Moon in Sagittarius.—Long face
and neck, paternal wealth, liberal, poet, strong,
clever speaker, thick teeth, ears, tips and
nose; active worker, fine arts, bent shoulders,
bad nails, strong arms, highly intelligent, skilled
in righteous knowledge, hater of relations and
won over by fair means and kind words.

नित्यं लालयति स्वदारतनयान्धर्मध्वजोऽघः कृशः
स्वक्षः क्षामकटिर्गृहीतवचनः सौभाग्ययुक्तोऽलसः ।
शीतालुर्मनुजोऽटनश्च मकरे सत्वाधिकः काव्यकृ-
ल्लुब्धोऽगम्यजराङ्गनासु निरतः सन्त्यक्तलज्जोऽघृणः ॥१०॥

Stanza 10.—Moon in Capricorn.—Pleaser of
wife and children, pretending charity, lean in
the lower half, good eyes, lean buttocks, grasping
intelligence, popular, idle, not able to bear cold,
traveller, strong or liberal, poet, learned, miserly,
incestuous and low intercourse, shameless and
merciless.

करभगलः शिरालुः खरलोमशदीर्घतनुः
पृथुचरणोरुपृष्ठजघनास्यकटिर्जरठः
परवतितार्थपापनिरतः क्षयवृद्धियुतः
प्रियकुसुमानुलेपनसुहृद्घटजोऽध्वसहः ॥ ११ ॥

Stanza 11.—Moon in Aquarius.—Long neck
like a camel, bulging veins and arteries, rough
and closely haired, and long body, big legs,
thighs, buttocks, back, waist, face, stubborn,
fond of other's wealth and women, and sinful,
changeable fortune, surrounded by good flowers,
scents and friends, bearing fatigue on the way.

जलपरधनभोक्ता दारावासोऽनुरक्तः
समरुचिरशरीरस्तुङ्गनासो बृहत्कः ।
अभिभवति सपत्नान् स्त्रीजितश्चारुदृष्टिः
द्युतिनिधिधनभोगी पण्डितश्चान्त्यराशौ ॥ १२ ॥

Stanza 12.–Moon in Pisces.—Enjoying other's
wealth and aquatic articles, fond of wife and
clothes, well proportioned and handsome body,
prominent nose, big head, conquering enemies,
submissive to women, charming eyes, enjoying
treasure trove, lustrous articles, wealthy and
learned.

बलवति राशौ तदधिपतौ च
स्वबलयुतः स्थाद्यदि तुहिनांशुः ।
कथितफलानामविकलदाता
शशिवदतो न्येत्कनुपरिचिन्त्याः ॥ १३ ॥

Stanza 13.—When the Moon, the sign in
which he is, and its lord are powerful, the results
indicated above will be fully verified. The other
planetary results must be similarly suggested.

NOTES

The Moon at the time of birth occupies a zodiacal sign
and this is technically called the Janmarasi. The Moon is

identified with the rising constellation at the time and will be moving there. If the Moon is strong as well as the house he occupies, and its lord, the results predicted will be completely visible. But when two of them are powerful, they will be partly visible. When one is powerful there will be traces of these characteristics. But when all of them are weak, then there will be no traces even of the qualities named in the respective places. The author is now going to relate the results from the occupation of other planets in the various houses of the zodiac and desires the readers to judge of them on the lines of argument suggested here. As the results of the occupation of the Moon in the 12 zodiacal signs are clearly given in simple language, I do not think any further notes in this connection are wanted.

CHAPTER XVIII

Rasisiladhyaya

राशिशीलाध्यायः

(The Results of Planets in various Rasis)

प्रथितश्चतुरोऽटनोऽल्पवित्तः क्रियगे त्वायुधभृद्वितुङ्गभागे ।
गवि वस्त्रसुगन्धपण्यजीबी वनिताद्विट् कुशलश्च गेयवाद्ये ॥१॥

Stanza 1.—When the Sun is not in his deep
exaltation in Aries, the person will become
famous, clever, traveller, possessed of little wealth
and bearer of arms. When the Sun is in Taurus,
the person will sell scents and clothes, hate
females and be clever in drumming and music.

NOTES

Aries extends over 30 degrees of the zodiac and in its
10th degree the Sun is in Swatunga or deep exaltation. But
in the first 9 degrees and from the 11th to the 30th degree
inclusive, he is said to be in exaltation in Aries. When he
is in deep exaltation, the Sun will make the man very
famous, clever, wealthy, and commander of men bearing
arms. So much is not in the original, but Bhattotpala
rightly adds in his commentaries the results above sketched,
getting his information from other valuable sources. The
original work has not treated this under a separate chapter,
but continues it as a continuation of the previous chapter.

Even the previous chapter Rikshasiladhyaya was not treated as a separate chapter.

Ravi in his deep exaltation, *i.e.*, in 10th degree will not make the person have little wealth, travel and bear arms, but make him very rich, guarded by armed men and become famous.

विद्याज्योतिषवित्तवान् मिथुनगे भानौ कुलीरे स्थिते
तीक्ष्णोऽस्वः परकार्यकृच्छ्रमपथक्लेशैश्च संयुज्यते ।
सिंहस्थे वनशैलगोकुलरतिर्वीर्यान्वितो ज्ञः पुमान्
कन्यास्थे लिपिलेख्यकाव्यगणितज्ञानान्वितः स्त्रीवपुः ॥ २ ॥

Stanza 2.—When the Sun is in Gemini, the native becomes educated, astrologer and wealthy. In Cancer, he makes the native angry, poor, doing other's work, and suffer from fatigue by travelling and other cares.   In Leo, the Sun makes one love the forests, mountains and cattle, courageous and dull.   When the Sun is in Virgo, the person becomes skilful in writing, painting, poetry, philosophy and mathematics, and possess a feminine body.

जातस्तौलिनि शौण्डिकोऽध्वनिरतो हैरण्यको नीचकृत्
क्रूरः साहसिको विपार्जितधनः शस्त्रान्तगोऽलिस्थिते ।
सत्पूज्यो धनवान्धनुर्धरगते तीक्ष्णो भिषकास्कृको
नीचोऽञ्झः कुवणिङ् मृगेऽल्पधवा लुब्धोऽन्यभाग्यै रतः ॥ ३ ॥

Stanza 3.—When the Sun occupies Libra, he makes the man a toddy-seller, drunkard, traveller, goldsmith and mean. When the Sun is in Scorpio, he makes the man cruel, adventurous and rash, making profits by sales of poisonous substances, losing wealth by robbers, and skilled in military weapons, and destroyer. When the Sun is in Sagittarius, the person will be respected, rich, angry, doctor and artisan. When the Sun is in Capricorn, the person will be mean, ignorant, seller of low articles, little wealth, covetuous and enjoying at other's cost.

नीचो घटे तनयभाग्यपरिच्युतोऽस्वः
तोयोत्थपण्यविभवो वनिताद्दतोऽन्त्ये ।
नक्षत्रमानवतनुप्रतिमे विभागे
लक्ष्मादिशेतुहिनराश्मिदिनेशयुक्ते ॥ ४ ॥

Stanza 4.—The Sun in Aquarius makes a man mean, separated from children and wealth, and poor. The Sun in Pisces causes wealth through articles found in water and fondled by women. When the Sun and the Moon are combined in a rasi, marks or moles in the organ which is governed by Kalapurusha, are found.

NOTES

The stanzas are easy enough. As per author's previous
suggestions, the results indicated by the Sun in the twelve
zodiacal signs will be full, when the Sun as well as the house
he occupies and its lord are strong. In St. 4, Chap. I of this
work, I have clearly explained the different organs governed
by Kalapurusha. Thus if the Sun and the Moon are in
Aries, the person will have a mole or mark on the head. If
they are in Scorpio, the mark will be on the sexual organ.
The author now proceeds to give the results of the other
planets in different rasis. Two rasis are combined and
results are given as for one only, *viz.*, the houses of the
planets. It comes to mean, Mars in his own house, in
Sukra's house, in Budha's house, in Chandra's house, in
Ravi's house and in the houses of Jupiter and Saturn.

Here it may be asked how Mars in Mesha as the lord
of 4 and 11 for Makara Lagna gives the very same result as
he would give in Scorpio for Simha Lagna, when he becomes the lord of 4 and 9. For Simha he is a Rajayoga
karaka but not for Makara. Hence readers should be very
careful.

नरपतिसत्कृतोऽटनश्चमूवणिक्कृसधनाः
क्षततनुश्रौरभूरिविषयांश्च कुजः स्वगृहे ।
युवतिजितान् सुहृत्सुविषमान् परदाररतान्
कुहकसुवेषभीरुषान् सितभे जनयेत् ॥ ५ ॥

Stanza 5.—Mars in Aries and Scorpio.--Res-
pected by kings, traveller, commander, merchant,

rich, cut or scarred body, thief, running through various sense pleasures or objects.

Mars in Taurus and Libra.—Submissive to women, ungrateful friend, fond of other's wives, cheat, fop, timid and unsocial.

बौधेऽसहस्तनयवान् विसहृत्कृतज्ञो
गान्धर्वयुद्धकुशलः कृपणोऽभयोऽर्थीं ।
चान्द्रेऽर्थवान् सलिलयानसमर्जितस्वः
प्राज्ञश्च भूमितनये विकलः खलश्च ॥ ६ ॥

Stanza 6.—Mars in Gemini and Virgo.—Jealous, sons, friendless, grateful, clever in music and martial work, miserly, undaunted and mendicant.

Mars in Cancer.—Rich, wealth procured through ships or through travelling, intelligent, wanting in organs and cruel.

निःस्वः क्लेशसहो वनान्तरचरः सिंहेऽल्पदारात्मजो
जैवे नैकरिपुर्नरेन्द्रसचिवः ख्यातोऽभयोऽल्पात्मजः ।
दुःखार्तो विधनोऽटनोऽनृतरतस्तीक्ष्णश्च कुंभस्थिते
भौमे भूरिधनात्मजो मृगगते भूपोऽथवा तत्समः ॥ ७ ॥

Stanza 7.—Mars in Leo.—Poor, enduring, travelling in forests, few children and wife.

Mars in Sagittarius and Pisces.—Many enemies, minister, renowned, courageous and few children.

Mars in Aquarius.—Sorrowful, poor, traveller, untruthful and irritable.

Mars in Capricorn.—Much wealth and many children, and king or his equal.

द्यूतर्णपानरतनास्तिकचौरनिःस्वाः
कुस्त्रीककूटकृदसत्यरताः कुजक्ष ।
आचार्यभूरिसुतदारधनार्जनेष्टाः
शौक्रे वदान्यगुरुभक्तिरताश्च सौम्ये ॥ ८ ॥

Stanza 8.—Mercury in Aries and Scorpio.— Fond of gambling, borrowing and drinking, atheist, thief, poor, bad wife, cheating and untruthful.

विकत्थनः शास्त्रकलाविदग्धः प्रियंवदः सौख्यरतस्तृतीये ।
जलार्जितस्वः स्वजनस्य शत्रुः शशांकजे शितकरर्क्षयुक्ते ॥ ९ ॥

Stanza 9.—Mercury in Taurus and Libra.— Fond of getting instructors, children, wives and wealth, liberal, and respectful to elders. Mercury in Gemini.—Liar, skilled in arts and sciences, polite speeches, and fond of happiness. Mercury in Cancer.—Wealth through water, and hateful to his relations.

स्त्रीद्वेष्यो विधनसुखात्मजोऽटनोऽज्ञः
स्त्रीलोलः स्वपरिभवोऽर्कराशिगे ज्ञे ।
त्यागी ज्ञः मन्चुरगुणः सुखी क्षमावान्
युक्तज्ञो विगतभयश्च षष्ठराशौ ॥ १० ॥

Stanza 10.—Mercury in Leo.—Hateful to women, without wealth, happiness and children, traveller, stupid, fond of women, and disgraced by his own community.

Mercury in Virgo.—Liberal, learned, many noble qualities happy, patient, expedient or resourceful and intrepid.

परकर्मकृदस्वशिल्पबुद्धी
ऋणवान् विष्टिकरो बुधेऽर्कजर्क्षे ।
नृपसत्कृतपण्डितात्मवाक्यो
नवमोऽन्त्ये जितसेवकोऽन्त्याशिल्पः ॥ ११ ॥

Stanza 11.—Mercury in Capricorn and Aquarius.—Engaged in other's work, poor, not fond of arts, debtor, carrying out others orders.

Mercury in Sagittarius.—Respected by king, learned, timely speech.

Mercury in Pisces.—Winning over servants to his side, and mean artist.

सेननीर्बहुवित्तदारतनयो दाता सुभृत्यः क्षमी
तेजोदारगुणान्वितः सुरगुरौ ख्यातः पुमान् कौजभे ।
कल्पाङ्गः सधनार्थमित्रतनयस्त्यागी प्रियः शौक्रमे
बौघे भूरिपरिच्छदात्मजसुहृत्साचिव्ययुक्तः सुखी ॥ १२ ॥

Stanza 12.—Jupiter in Aries and Scorpio.—
Commander, possessed of large family, children
and wealth, liberal and good servants, forgiving,
handsome, good wife and famous.

Jupiter in Taurus and Libra.—Healthy,
possessed of happiness, friends, wealth and
children, liberal and popular.

Jupiter in Gemini and Virgo.—Surrounded
by worldly paraphernalia or titles, children and
friends, minister, consul and happy.

चन्द्रे रत्नसुतस्वदारविदारविभवप्रज्ञासुखैरन्वितः
सिंहे स्याद्बलनायकः सुरगुरौ प्रोक्त च यच्चन्द्रमे ।
स्वर्क्षे माण्डलिको नरेन्द्रसचिवः संग्नापतिर्वा धनी
कुम्मे कर्कटवत्फलानि मकरे नीचोऽल्पवित्तोऽसुखी ॥१३॥

Stanza 13.—Jupiter in Cancer.—Possessed of
great wealth and gems, children, wife, enjoyment,
intelligence and happiness.

Jupiter in Leo.—Commander and all the
results indicated above in Cancer.

Jupiter in Sagittarius and Pisces.—King or minister or commander or wealthy.

Jupiter in Kumbha or Aquarius will produce the results ascribed to him in Cancer. Jupiter in Capricorn.—Mean, poor and unhappy.

परयुवतिरतस्तदर्थवादै-
हृतविभवः कुलपांसनः कुजर्क्षे ।
स्वबलमतिधनो नरेन्द्रपूज्यः
स्वजनविभुः प्रथितोऽभयः सिते स्वे ॥ १४ ॥

Stanza 14.—Venus in Aries and Scorpio.— Fond of other women, losing money through their flattery and hater of his race.

Venus in Taurus and Libra.—Self-acquired property, respected by rulers, leader of his men, renowned and courageous.

नृपकृत्यकरोऽर्थवान् कलावि-
निमिथुने पष्ठगतेऽतिनीचकर्मा ।
रविजर्क्षंगतेऽमरारिपूज्ये
सुभगः स्त्रीविजितो रतः कुनार्याम् ॥ १५ ॥

Stanza 15.—Venus in Gemini.—Doing ruler's work or service, wealthy and learned.

Venus in Virgo.—Doing very mean acts. Venus in Capricorn and Aquarius.—Popular, slave to women, and intercourse with bad women.

27

द्विभार्योऽर्थी भीरुः प्रबलमदःशोकश्च शशिमे
हरौ योषासार्थैः प्रवरयुवतिर्मन्दतनयः ।
गुणैः पूज्यः सस्वस्तुरगसहिते दानवगुरौ
झषे विद्वानाढ्यो नृपजनितपूजोऽतिसुभगः ॥ १६ ॥

Stanza 16.—Venus in Cancer.—Gives two wives, mendicant, timid, full of sexual passion and sorrow through it.

Venus in Leo.—Getting wealth through a woman, handsome wife and few children.

Venus in Sagittarius.—Adorned with many good qualities and rich.

Venus in Pisces.—Learned, wealthy, respected by rulers and very popular.

मूर्खोंऽष्टनः कपटवान्विसुहृद्यमेऽज्जे
कीटे तु बन्धवधभाक् चपलोऽघृणश्च ।
निर्हींसुखार्थतनयः स्खलितश्च लेख्ये
रक्षापतिर्भवति मुख्यपतिश्च बौधे ॥ १७ ॥

Stanza 17.—Saturn in Aries.—Ignorant, itinerant, cheat and friendless.

Saturn in Scorpio.—Imprisonment, whipping, capricious and merciless.

Saturn in Gemini and Virgo.—Childless, poor, shameless, unhappy, not knowing painting,

protective officer and chief man. (One reading
is skilled in painting. Another reading says he
will be Rakshasapathi or lord of Rakshasas or
evil genii).

बर्ज्यस्त्रीष्टो न बहुविभवो भूरिभार्यो वृषस्थे
ख्यातः स्वोच्चे गणपुरबलग्रामपूज्योऽर्थवांश्च ।
कर्किण्यस्वो विकलदशनो मातृहीनोऽसुतोऽज्ञः
सिंहेऽनार्यो विसुखतनयो विष्टिकृत्सूर्यपुत्रे ॥ १८ ॥

Stanza 18.—Saturn in Taurus.—Connections
with prohibited and low caste women, ordinary
wealth and many wives.

Saturn in Libra.—Famous, respected by
communities, towns, army and village, wealthy.

Saturn in Cancer.—Poor, loose teeth, mother-
less, childless and ignorant.

Saturn in Leo.—Bad, childless and unhappy,
carrying loads.

स्वन्तः प्रत्ययितो नरेन्द्रभवने सत्पुत्रजायाधनो
जीवक्षेत्रगतेऽर्कजे पुरबलग्रामाग्रनेताऽथवा ।
अन्यस्त्रीधनसंवृतः पुरबलग्रामाग्रणीर्मन्ददृक्
स्वक्षेत्रे मलिनः स्थिरार्थविभवो भोक्ता च जातः पुमान् ॥ १९ ॥

Stanza 19.—Saturn in Sagittarius and Pisces.—Good death or happy in the end, confident with princes or rulers, good children, wife and wealth, commander of towns, armies and villages.

Saturn in Capricorn and Aquarius.—Getting other's women, wealth and other's houses, chief of towns, villages and army, short-sighted, dirty, permanent wealth, general prosperity and enjoying.

NOTES

In the results sketched above they must be predicted in full, when the house is strong, as also its lord and the planet which occupies it. If two of these are strong, the results will be moderate, if one of them is strong there will be some of these characteristics; but if none of these is strong, then there will be traces of these results. For the sake of brevity, I have not added many notes to these stanzas and I don't think they are needed as the translation itself is given in the simplest language possible. These results given by Varahamihira must be carefully predicted. As in medical drugs so also in planets individually each may have its more prominent characteristics but its results are influenced by time, place and other menial conditions, habits and nature and the greatest skill of the doctor and the astrologer is wanted in discriminating the right result. Readings differ and sometimes they give radically opposite meanings. It is extremely difficult to say which is correct and as these planetary rays of light are mixed up with the different rays

of light of the zodiac it is possible to imagine results of
quite a different nature from what we may expect from
ordinary conjunctions. In St. 17 under " Saturn in Gemini
and Virgo" one reading is " Kusalascha Lakhay"
meaning one well skilled in painting. The other reading
is " Skhalitascha Lakhay" meaning one who is discomfited
in his attempts at painting. These two are radically
different in purport. One reading is Rakshapathi or he
who protects people and another reading is Rakshasapathi
or lord of evil genii or Rakshasas or giants mentioned in
many of the Puranic works. This must be taken as referring
to one who commands evil natured or bad men.

शिशिरकरसमागमेक्षणानां
सदृशफलं प्रवदन्ति लग्नजातम् ।
फलमधिकमिदं यदत्र भावाद्
भवनभनाथगुणैर्विचिन्तनीयाः ॥ २० ॥

Stanza 20.—The results which have been
stated for the presence of the Moon in each rasi,
and the results of aspects on Moon by other planets in the different signs will have to be applied
for lagna. The prosperity and adversity of each
bhava must be predicted by the strength of the
bhava and its lord.

NOTES

What the author means by this is that all those results
which are attributed to the Moon in each sign will also
apply to each of the signs or lagnas. A man born in Aries

will have the results predicted similar to those attributed to the Moon when he is in Aries. (See St. 1, Ch. XVII.)

Maharishis have said that the results of the lagna as well as of the Moon are similar, and bear no difference, because they are similar in nature. (See notes on St. 8, Ch. VII). Satyacharya, the great authority, on whom Varahamihira relies for support, thus gives the results of the various lagnas.

Aries as Lagna.—Bad nails, irritable, creating quarrels, stammering, bilious and windy temperament, miser, suffering much from diseases, losing parents at an early age, few children, helping relations and brothers, perilous, going to foreign countries, doing unremunerative work, getting as a wife a woman who is already married or who is base in character or a tale-bearer, or who has lost a limb, friendly, windy or bilious complaints, death by poison, or by the treachery of his own men or by fire, or rain or by falling from fort walls.

Taurus as Lagna.—Thick lips, nose, cheeks, big forehead, windy and phlegmatic, liberal, spending in various ways, female children, few sons, doing much evil to parents, active, engaged in immoral work, wealthy, fond of wife, destruction by weapon, doing always bad to relations, will die in a foreign country by weapons, chains or ropes, beasts, fatigue, water, cross or by force, travelling or quadrupeds.

Gemini as Birth sign.—Defective or abnormal organs, polite, specially skilful in work, mixed temperament, two mothers, ordinary intelligence, and body, respected by holy men and parents, few brothers, suppressor of enemies, virtuous, fond of many works, charitable, making remedies for illegal sources of wealth, many wives, gets over many diseases, death by rutted elephants, wild beasts, poison, animals or water.

Cancer as Lagna.—Capricious, diseased sexual organ, timid, mole or mark on the chest, windy and phlegmatic temperament, quick comprehension, sinful, troubled by enemies, misappropriating other's monies, rejected by relations, having miscarriages, doing hard work in foreign countries, leader of other people, unrivalled wife, suffering defeats, respected by large communities, death by neck disease, ropes, phlegm, breaking of bones, separation of limbs by cuts or dropsy.

Leo as Lagna.—Fond of flesh, bilious, suffering big losses, undertaking many enterprises, big family, misery, loved by good people, famous, causing trouble to brothers, destruction to relations, warlike, sorrowless, accomplishing work by various devices, uncharitable, many wives from different castes, suffering pain from back knees and teeth, death by weapons and poisons, sticks, phlegmatic diseases aquatic animals or thefts.

Virgo as Birth sign.—Polite speech, handsome, long arms and legs, mixed temperament, good, sores, wealthy miser, having many daughters, quarrels among brothers, virtuous, satisfied with small profits, clever in work, death by quadrupeds of various kinds, weapons, bilious complaints, sorrow, burning sensation from diseases or ropes.

Libra as Birth.—Deformed organs, crooked temper, windy and phlegmatic constitution, capricious, short neck, grateful, reputation by large deeds, fond of serving parents and instructors, respected by father, brothers, and other people, traveller, charitable, ruin by family troubles, widower, quarrelsome, suffering various sorrows, death by a leader, relations, quadrupeds, sorrows from separation, fasting or travelling.

Scorpio as Birth.—Large nose, belly and face, cruel, bilious, golden eyes, soft and quick walk, leader, of foreigners, big family and relations, extravagant, many issues, cruel, unhappy, having many enemies, many bulls, unrighteous, disgust through wife, victorious over enemies, not inclined to give many charities, has enemies in his own family, many diseases, death by fever, cutting of limbs, capture by enemies, ropes, beating, sinful diseases or fire.

Sagittarius as Lagna.—Thick lips, nose and teeth, windy and phlegmatic, large sexual organ, big arms and thighs, bad nails, active, warlike, company with bad and base men, loss of wealth through thefts, fire and fines from rulers, highly intelligent, greatly respected, fond of murdering brothers and going to foreign countries, getting wealth from rulers, not much inclined to charity, quarrelling with wife, facial diseases, death by quadrupeds, serpents, imprisonment.

Capricorn as Lagna.—Small nose, long face, arms and legs, windy, deer-faced, timid, capricious, imprisonment, bad wife, little wealth, miserly, daughters, deaths among relations, many brothers, earning wealth through strength, kings or forest, fasting, getting a base woman as wife, quarrelsome, short hairs, weak knees, sickly, death by children, wind, weapon, ruler, poison, falling, elephant, bile, indigestion, or loss of way.

Aquarius as Birth.—Idle, cruel, chief in family, windy and bilious disposition, good nose, spending earnings, many servants, becoming poor through various expenditure, enemy to parents, clan or race, people, friends and relations, sinful, acquiring profits to his desires, looking generous and charitable and religious, quarrelsome wife, phlegmatic or lung complaints, death by stomach diseases, vomitting or feminine schemes.

Pisces as Birth.—Thick lips, fishy eyes, long nose, windy and phlegmatic temperament, dignified, cutaneous eruption, capricious mind and unsteady work, good earning and spending money, servants, respected by his relations and women, chief among his brothers, engaged in righteous work, brought up by father, base but handsome wife, many enemies, danger through nasty blood diseases, lions, elephants, death by base disease in sexual organ, medicine, fast or travelling.

When the lagna and its lord are strong, there will be good health, when the second and its lord are powerful, he will be rich. When the third and its lord are strong, courage and brother's prosper. Similarly for all the twelve different significations or bhavas the results should be ascertained. But these results should be reverted in the 6th, 8th and 12th houses. When the 6th and its lord are weak, then the results indicated by that house would be destroyed. The following hints may be carefully noted. The lagna must be strong as also its lord. The lord of the house occupied by the lord of Lagna or Chandra must also be strong. They must have good conjunctions and aspects and they should not be placed betwixt evil planets. The vargas occupied should be beneficial and they must have also clear and brilliant rays. The rays of exalted planets are certainly different from the rays of debilitated planets, planets in unfriendly signs will have weaker influences than those who are in friendly mansions.

CHAPTER XIX

DRISTI PHALADHYAYA

दृष्टिफलाध्यायः

(Results of Planetary Aspects)

चन्द्रे भूपबुधौ नृपोपमगुणी स्तेनोऽधनश्चाजगे
निःस्वः स्तेननृमान्यभूपधनिनः प्रेष्यः कुजाद्यैर्गवि ।
नृस्येऽद्योव्यवहारिपार्थिववबुधाभीस्तन्तुवायोऽधनो
स्वर्क्षे योद्धृकविज्ञभूमिपतयोऽयोजीविविद्ग्रोगिणौ ॥ ९ ॥

Stanza 1.—When the Moon is in Aries aspected by Mars, etc., the person becomes a king, philosopher, equal to a ruler, virtuous, thief and poor, respectively.

When the Moon is in Taurus aspected by Mars, etc., the person becomes poor, thief, respected by people, ruler, wealthy and servant respectively.

When the Moon is in Gemini aspected by Mars, etc., the person will be a seller of weapons, ruler, learned, courageous, weak and poor respectively.

When the Moon is in Cancer aspected by Mars, etc., the person will be a warrior, poet, learned, ruler, living by weapons and have eye complaints respectively.

NOTES

True to his motto Varahamihira is very brief and suggestive in these stanzas. One or two explanations offered here will be quite sufficient to make his meaning clear.

When the Moon occupies Aries aspected by Mars the person becomes a ruler, aspected by Mercury he becomes learned or philosopher, aspected by Jupiter he becomes a statesman or some other personage equal to a king or ruler, aspected by Venus the person becomes virtuous or full of good qualities, some read here Vanik instead of Guni and make it mean a merchant, aspected by Saturn he becomes a thief, and aspected by the Sun the man becomes poor.

In the case of Saturn, Jupiter and Mars, there will be powerful aspects in the 3rd and 10th, 5th and 9th and 4th and 8th houses respectively as well as in the 7th from all other planets. Thus when the Moon is in Aries with Saturn in Cancer, Jupiter in Leo and Mars in Virgo, we shall have the aspect of Saturn in the 10th, of Jupiter in the 9th, and of Mars in the 8th. When the Moon is in Aries and Saturn is in Libra there is saturnine aspect and the person will become a thief but as Saturn is exalted in Libra the rank of the person may be good among the thiefs. He becomes their leader. If the Sun is in Libra he aspects the Moon in Aries and makes the person poor as he has his fall in that house. The concensus of astrological opinion seems to say that the most powerful aspect will be in the 7th house although special sights have been enumerated both in *Brihat Jataka* and other eminent works. When the Moon is in Taurus aspected by Mars the person becomes poor, aspected by Mercury thief, aspected by Jupiter res-

pected by people, some read *Nripadhya* instead of *Nrimanya*
and explain by saying that he will be a ruler, aspected by
Venus king, aspected by Saturn wealthy, and aspected by
the Sun the person becomes a servant. Similarly explain
regularly for other signs and aspects.

These results will also hold good for lagna or birth
sign when aspected by Mars, etc. That is if birth is Aries
aspected by Mars the person becomes a king, aspected by
Mercury learned, by Jupiter equal to a ruler, by Venus
virtuous, by Saturn thief, and by the Sun poor.

ज्योतिर्ज्ञाद्यनरेन्द्रनापितनृपक्षमेशाबुधार्यैर्हरौ
तद्द्रूपचमूपनैपुणयुताः षट्छेऽशुभैः स्त्र्याश्रयः ।
जूके भूपसुवर्णकारवणिजः शेषेक्षिते नैकृती
कीटे युग्मपितनतश्च रजको व्यङ्गोऽधनो भूपतिः ॥ २ ॥

Stanza 2.—If the Moon is in Leo aspected
by Mercury, etc., the person will become learned
in astrology, chief or lord, Raja, barber, ruler and
thief respectively.

If the Moon is in Virgo aspected by Mercury,
etc., the man becomes a ruler, commander, dex-
terous and aspected by malefics the person lives
as a dependent upon women respectively.

If the Moon is in Libra aspected by Mercury,
etc., he becomes a ruler, goldsmith, merchant
and by the evil planets killer of animals respectively.

When the Moon is in Scorpio aspected by Mars, etc., the person becomes father of twins, polite, washerman, defective in organs, poor and ruler respectively.

NOTES

Here he has commenced from Mercury, etc., with a view to shorten the stanza and make it more suggestive. The planets are always to be taken in their usual order of the Sun, Moon, Mars, Mercury, Jupiter, Venus and Saturn. Suppose we commence with Mercury then the order will be Mercury, Jupiter, Venus, Saturn, the Sun and Mars as we are treating of the aspects of these planets upon the Moon. Here to cut short the language and give greater suggestion the last three planets are malefics, *viz.*, Saturn, the Sun and Mars and hence he gives one result for all these malefics.

If the Moon is in Leo aspected by Mercury the person becomes learned in astrology. This term astrology in Sanskrit includes both 'Siddhanta (Astronomical Mathematics) and Phalabhaga or predictive or Judicial astrology. If the Moon is in Leo aspected by Jupiter the person becomes a lord, if aspected by Venus ruler, aspected by Saturn barber, aspected by the Sun king, aspected by Mars a ruler. Similarly for other signs. The word Yugmapitha is used, which means father of twins. Aspected by Mercury applies to a person who is the father of twins. In the last case it is to be explained as a man being born to one father and then if his mother marries another man and he gets another father. This is very frequently met with among the Western nations. The first Yugmapitha suits well grammatically as representing the father of twins, but the second interpretation seems to be strained from a grammatical point of view.

ज्ञात्युर्वीशजनाश्रयश्च तुरगे पापैः सदंभः शठ-
श्चात्युर्वीशनरेन्द्रपण्डितधनी द्रव्योनभूपो मृगे ।
भूपो भूपसमोऽन्यदारनिरतः शेषैश्च कुंभस्थिते
हास्यज्ञो नृपतिर्बुधश्च झषगे पापश्च पापेक्षिते ॥ ३ ॥

Stanza 3.—If the Moon [is in Sagittarius aspected by Mercury, etc., the person will protect relations, be a king, master of many, aspected by malefics the person will be showy or dissimulator, inattentive to other's interests respectively.

If the Moon is in Capricorn aspected by Mercury, etc., the person becomes king of kings, Raja, pandit, wealthy, and poor respectively.

If the Moon is in Aquarius aspected by Mercury, etc., he becomes a Raja, equal to a ruler, fond of other's wives and aspected by other planets he will be fond of other's wives respectively.

If the Moon is in Pisces aspected by Mercury, etc., the person will be a jester, Raja, pandit and aspected by malefics becomes sinful.

NOTES

Here he has not given the results of the aspects of the Moon upon lagna. Bhattotpala thus reconciles or explains

this omission. (See Ch. I, Stanza 19.) The lagna becomes
powerful when aspected or joined by its lord, by Jupiter or
Mercury.   Therefore when Cancer becomes lagna and the
Moon aspects it, it becomes powerful and good results must
be predicted. When other signs become lagna (ascendant)
and the Moon aspects them, they do not become powerful
and therefore no good results would follow.

होरेशर्क्षदलाश्रितेः शुभकरो दृष्टः शशी तद्द्रत-
स्त्यंशे तत्पतिभिः सुहृद्द्वनगैर्वा वीक्षितः शस्यते ।
यत्प्रोक्तं प्रतिराशिवीक्षणफलं तद्वादशांशे स्मृतं
स्यर्याद्यैरवलोकितेऽपि शशिनि ज्ञेयं नवांशेष्वतः ॥ ४ ॥

Stanza 4.—If the other planets occupy the
same horas as the Moon and aspect him the results
will be beneficial. When the lord of the
drekkana occupied by the Moon aspects him the
results are favourable. If the Moon is aspected
by planets in friendly houses, it is good. The
results which have been stated above for each of
the houses of the zodiac by the occupation of the
Moon and the aspecting of other planets will
also be similar when the Moon occupies the
Dwadasamsa of those planets. Hereafter the
aspects of the Sun, etc., in the navamsas, and the
Moon in the navamsas will be detailed.

NOTES

Hora means half of a sign (see Sts. 9 and 11, Ch. I).
The Moon necessarily occupies some hora of a sign at the

time of birth.   Suppose he occupies the solar hora in
Aries.   Then if he has the aspects of planets in solar horas
in any other sign or signs the results will be favourable.
But if they occupy lunar horas and aspect such Moon the
results will be malefic.   Suppose the Moon is in the lunar
hora in Virgo ; then if he has the aspects of planets
occupying lunar horas in any other house the results will
be favourable, but if they occupy solar horas and aspect
the Moon in a lunar hora, the results are evil.   Lagna must
similarly be explained.   Coming to the drekkana (one-
third part of a sign) suppose the Moon occupies the third
drekkana in Aries.   The lord of this drekkana will be
Jupiter.   If Jupiter aspects the Moon the results are good.

The word used is *Tatpathibhi*, *i.e.*, lord of those houses.   By
this Varahamihira includes the aspects in *navamsas,
dwadasamsas and trimsamsas*.   When the lords of thes
divisions (aspecting the Moon) are benefics the results
are very good, but when they are malefics, the results are
moderate.   In support of this view Bhattotpala quotes from
Varahamihira's *Laghu Jataka*.   Planets in friendly or own
houses will produce good when they aspect the Moon,
thereby implying that planets in unfriendly houses will
produce bad.   Similarly for lagna.   The results now explained in *re.* the position of the Moon in the various signs
of the zodiac and the aspects of the other planets upon him
will hold good in his dwadasamsas.

आराक्षिको वधरुचिः कुशलो नियुद्धे
भूपोऽर्थवान् कलहकृत् क्षितिजांशसंस्थे ।

मूर्खोंऽन्यदारनिरतः सुकविः सितांशे
सत्काव्यकृत्सुखपरोऽन्यकलत्रगश्च ॥ ५ ॥

Stanza 5.—When the Moon is in the navamsas
of Aries or Scorpio aspected by the Sun, etc., the
person will be a ruler or chief of a town, fond of
killing, clever in wrestling, king, wealthy and
quarrelsome, respectively.   When the Moon is in
the navamsa of Taurus or Libra aspected by the
Sun, etc., he will be obstinate, fond of other's
wives, good poet and happy respectively.

NOTES

When the Moon occupies the navamsas of Mars, *viz.*,
Aries or Scorpio and has the aspect of the Sun the man will
be protector or magistrate of a town or city, aspected by
Mars he will be fond of killing living objects, aspected by
Mercury he becomes a good wrestler or clever in hand to
hand fight, aspected by Jupiter he becomes a ruler or a king,
aspected by Venus the person gets wealth and aspected by
Saturn the man becomes quarrelsome.   When the Moon is
in the navamsas of Venus—Taurus and Libra—aspected by
the Sun the man becomes stubborn and obstinate, aspected
by Mars or Saturn the person becomes fond of other's
wives, aspected by Mercury or Jupiter the man becomes a
good poet and aspected by Venus fond of happiness.   In
the case of the aspects of Mercury and Jupiter Bhattotpala
seems to make a slight difference.   When Mercury aspects
the Moon, the person will be versed in poetry and will also

be a good poet. When Jupiter aspects he will be able to compose pleasant poetry.

बौधे हि रङ्गचरचौरकवीन्द्रमन्त्री
गेयज्ञशिल्पनिपुणः शशिनि स्थितेंशे ।
स्वांशोऽल्पगात्रधनलुब्धतपस्विमुख्यः
स्त्रीपोष्यकृत्यनिरतश्च निरीक्ष्यमाणे ॥ ६ ॥

Stanza 6.—Moon occupying the navamsa of Gemini and Virgo, aspected by the Sun, etc., makes the man a stage wrestler, thief, poet, minister, musician and skilful in painting and arts respectively, when the Moon is in his navamsa aspected by the Sun, etc., the person will be lean, miserly or poor, saint, chief, brought up by females and fond of work respectively.

NOTES

When the Moon occupies Gemini or Virgo, aspected by the Sun he becomes a stage wrestler, aspected by Mars a thief, by Mercury a poet, by Jupiter a minister, by Venus a musician and by Saturn skilful in painting and arts. When the Moon occupies his own navamsa, *viz.*, Cancer aspected by the Sun the person will be lean, by Mars miser or poor, by Mercury a saint, by Jupiter a minister, by Venus brought up by females, by Saturn fond of work. Here it will be seen that for each aspect the author gives only one result. The degrees of poverty or proficiency must depend upon the associations and dispositions the planets have in the navamsa.

सक्रोधो नरपतिसंमतो निधीशः
सिंहांशे प्रभुरसुतोऽतिहिंसकर्मा ।
जीवांशे प्रथितबलो रणोपदेष्टा
हास्याङ्गः सचिवविकामबद्धशीलः ॥ ७ ॥

Stanza 7.—Moon in the navamsa of Leo,
aspected by the Sun, etc., makes a man angry,
protege of a king, get treasure trove, brooking no
opposition in command, childless and fond of
cruel deeds respectively. If the Moon is in the
navamsas of Sagittarius or Pisces, aspected by
the Sun, etc., the person becomes well known for
strength, clever in arranging armies in a battle,
jester or humourist, minister, impotent and righteous respectively.

अल्पापत्यो दुःखितः सत्यपि स्वे
मानासक्तः कर्मणि स्वेऽनुरक्तः ।
दुष्टस्त्रीष्टः कृपणश्चार्किभागे
चन्द्रे भानौ तद्वदिन्द्वादिदृष्टे ॥ ८ ॥

Stanza 8.—If the Moon occupies the navamsa
of Capricorn or Aquarius aspected by the Sun,
etc., the person has few issues, miserly while
wealthy, pride, fondness for his own sectarian
deeds, fondness for bad women and miserly habits

respectively and when the Sun is aspected by the Moon, etc., similar results must be predicted.

NOTES

Lagna navamsa must similarly be explained when the lagna falls in Karaka navamsa aspected by the Moon, the results are good but when it falls in any other house having the lunar aspects the results must be predicted as un-favourable. In the navamsas the aspects of Taragrahas, *viz.*, Mars, Mercury, Jupiter, Venus and Saturn upon Moon and the Sun produce similar results. The results predicted by the aspect of the Sun upon Moon will also be the results when the Moon aspects the Sun.

If the Sun in Aries and Scorpio is aspected by the Moon, the person will be a ruler, if he is in Taurus and Libra aspected by the Moon, he will be obstinate, if he is in Gemini and Virgo navamsas aspected by the Moon, he will be a stage wrestler, if he occupies his own navamsa of Leo aspected by the Moon he will be irritable, if he is in Sagittarius and Pisces aspected by the Moon, he will be a reputed athlete, if he occupies the navamsas of Capricorn and Aquarius he will have a few issues, if he is in Cancer aspected by the Moon, he will be a lean man.

वर्गोत्तमस्वपरगेषु शुभं यदुत्कं
तत्तुष्टमध्यलघुताशुभमुत्क्रमेण ।
वीर्यान्वितोंऽशकपतिर्निरुणद्धि पूर्बं
राशिक्षणस्य फलमंशफलं ददाति ॥ ९ ॥

Stanza 9.—The results which have now been detailed above for the Moon will be full, moderate and meagre as Chandra is in Vargottama, his own house or other houses. If the results are bad the above should be reversed. If the lord of the Amsa is powerful he will give his Amsaphala in preference to any phala which may be indicated by aspects in the rasi diagram.

NOTES

There are two sets of results by the aspects of planets upon Moon in the navamsa—good or bad. Take one example. When the Moon is in the navamsa of Aries aspected by the Sun the result will be good on the man as he will become a protector or chief magistrate in a town but when the Moon is aspected by Mars the result is bad as the person becomes fond of killing. Therefore when the Moon is in Vargottama, good results indicated by planetary aspects will be completely given. When the Moon is in his own amsa good indicated by planetary aspects will be moderate. When the Moon is in other navamsas then the good results indicated by planetary aspects will be small with reference to evil results. The process must be reversed then—when the Moon is in other navamsas the evil results indicated by planetary aspects will be competely given; when the Moon is in his own navamsa, the evil results will be moderately given, but when the Moon is in his Vargottama navamsa the evil results indicated by the planetary aspects will be less or nominal. Similarly the results must be explained for lagna and Ravi in the navamsa.

Bhattotpala explains by saying that the results of planetary conjunctions, of mutual exchanges of places, in rasis and amsas, and of their aspects, etc., are as immeasurable as are the waters of the mighty ocean and quotes a beautiful stanza in support of his view from Yavaneswara. The lord of the navamsa occupied by the Moon or Lagna at the time of birth, if powerful, will give the amsa aspect results in preference to rasi aspect results. By this Bhattotpala infers and rightly too, that the results of aspects, etc., in the hora, drekkana and dwadasamsa, are not affected by the strength of the amsa lord. But when this amsa lord is not powerful both the results of the rasi and amsa aspects must be predicted. This refers to the Moon and Lagna and not to the Sun.

CHAPTER XX
BHAVADHYAYA

भावाध्यायः

(Planets in Houses)

शूरः स्तब्घो विकलनयनो निर्घृणोऽर्के तनुस्थे
मेषे सखस्तिमिरनयनः सिंहसंस्थे निशान्घः
नीचेऽन्घोऽस्वः शशिगृहगते बुद्घदाक्षः पतङ्गे
भूरिद्रव्यो नृपहृतधनो वक्ररोगी द्वितीये ॥ १ ॥

Stanza 1.—When the Sun is in birth the person will be courageous, slow, short or defective in sight, and cruel. In Aries the Sun makes a man rich and diseased in eyes, in Leo the Sun makes a man night blind. In his neecha sign the Sun makes a man blind and poor. In Cancer the Sun gives defective sight. When the Sun is in the 2nd house the person will be very rich, pays heavy sums to rulers and has a diseased face.

NOTES

This is called the *Bhavadhyaya*. Bhava means the exact house which controls certain events of the man's life. Take a person born in the first degree of Aries. Then the next 30 degrees form the first bhava and those planets

which are within 30 degrees from it are supposed to remain
in the first bhava and affect it according to their powers.
The importance of mathematical astronomy in determining
the different bhavas, the correct positions of the planets,
their conjunctions, aspects, exaltations, retrogrades,
combustions, etc., cannot be sufficiently urged. Every
student of astrology who approaches this science without
mathematical ability to determine the various planetary
positions would be going to draw water in a well which
is dry or adorning a body which is forsaken by the
soul. They must know the preliminary calculations.
Rasis are different from bhavas and positions in a house
are different from real conjunctions. When the Sun
is exalted in Aries and it happens to be the birth the person
will be rich. But when the birth falls in Libra and the
Sun is there (debilitated) the person will be poor. When
the Sun is in the 2nd house from lagna, he will give great
wealth, but it will be confiscated or taken away in fines and
penalties by the rulers under some pretext or the other.
The person will also have some diseased face. This means
that the face will not have a healthy appearance and
probably there will be cutaneous eruptions, sores, or boils
or other skin diseases.

मतिविक्रमवांस्तृतीयगेऽर्के
विसुखः पीडितमानसश्चतुर्थे ।
असुतो धनवर्जितस्त्रिकोणे
बलवाञ्छत्रुजितश्च शत्रुयाते ॥ २ ॥

Stanza 2.—The Sun in the third produces
intelligence and valour. In the fourth he makes

a man unhappy and worried in mind. In the
fifth the Sun makes a man issueless and poor.
In the sixth house he produces strength, defeat
by enemies.

NOTES

About the results of the Sun and other evil planets in
the 6th house, there seems to be some divergence of
opinion. But on a careful examination there is apparently
no cause for any contest. Satyacharya lays down a general
principle in the following words—all houses or bhavas
(significations) occupied by benefics prosper while the same
will be destroyed when malefics occupy them. Take the
2nd house—denoting wealth. If Jupiter, Full Moon,
Venus or good Mercury occupies it, the person will have
much cash, but if malefics, like Saturn, Mars, or the Sun
occupies it, the person must lose wealth or be in poor
circumstances. The sixth house donotes debts, diseases,
enemies and sorrows. What would the good planets do
there as opposed to malefics is a question the solution of
which is most interesting for astrological students. Bhattotpala with his usual keen perception of these difficulties
comes to our relief and quotes from eminent authors to
throw light upon this vexed question. Satyacharya says
that if the Sun is in the 6th house he will destroy enemies,
disease and sorrow. But Varahamihira in this instance
seems to rely more upon the doctrine of Yavaneswara, who
says that evil planets, in the 6th increase enemies, disease
and sorrows. Quoting from Sphujidhwaja, Bhattotpala
observes : When the Sun is in the 6th house he makes the

person suffer from poison, weapons, burning, hunger, and
enemies. He also makes him to lose his teeth by fall or by
sticks, makes him travel and gives danger or wounds from
wild beasts. If Mars is in the 6th house he causes wounds
in the bodily organs, eye diseases, rejected by many. If
Saturn is in the 6th the man has danger from the falling of
stones or thunderbolt, windy complaint and blows from
fists. Varahamihira says later on that the results of malefic
conjunctions in the 6th will be similar to those produced
by the Sun. Hence there seems to be agreement in his
doctrine and that which is propounded by Sphujidhwaja.
(See notes on St. 10 of this Chap.)

स्त्रीभिर्गतः परिभवं मदगे पतङ्गे
स्वल्पात्मजो निधनगे विकलेक्षणश्च ।
धर्मे सुतार्थसुखभाक् सुखशौर्यभाक् खे
लाभे प्रभूतधनवान् पतितस्तु रिःफे ॥ ३ ॥

Stanza 3.—The Sun in the 7th—disgrace from
women. The Sun in the 8th—fine children,
defective sight. The Sun in the 9th—possessed of
children, wealth and happiness. The Sun in the
10th—happiness and courage. The Sun in the
11th—very wealthy. The Sun in the 12th—irreli-
gious.

NOTES

About the results of the Sun in the 9th house
Varahamihira differs from his leader Satyacharya. The
latter gives the following results:

When the Sun is in the 9th the person will act against recognised moral rules, suffer from disease and be a humble mendicant. Experience has shown that Satyacharya seems to be nearer the mark than Varahamihira, as persons born with the Sun in the 9th are more prone to suffer than to enjoy.

मूकोन्मराजडान्धहीनबधिरः प्रेष्याः शशाङ्कोदये
स्वर्क्षांजोषगते धनी बहुसुतः सस्वः कुटुम्बी धने ।
हिंस्रो आलृगते सुखे सतनये तत्मोक्तभावान्वितो
नैकारिर्मृदुकायवाहिमदनस्तीक्ष्णोऽलसश्चारिगे ॥ ४ ॥

Stanza 4.—The Moon in birth makes a man dumb, deranged, stubborn, blind, base, deaf or servant. If that birth falls in Cancer, Aries or Taurus he gets wealth, many children or rich respectively. In the 2nd house the Moon produces a big family. In the 3rd he makes a man cruel, or an executioner. In the 4th or 5th he will increase those significations. In the 6th house he gives many enemies, tender body, weak digestion, weak sexual inclination, cruel mind and laziness.

NOTES

The Moon is specially detested in the 6th, 8th and 12th houses as he produces great misery. When he is full or powerfully aspected by benefics these evil results must be greatly modified. When he is weak and has powerful evil aspects he produces much unpleasantness.   Weak sexuality may mean that the person may have little inclination to indulge in sexual correspondence or that the seminal discharge takes place very quickly.

ईर्ष्युस्तीव्रमदो मदे बहुमतिर्व्याध्यर्दितश्चाष्टमे
सौभाग्यात्मजमित्रबन्धुधनभाग् धर्मस्थिते शीतगौ ।
निष्पत्तिं समुपैति धर्मधनधीशौर्यैर्युतः कर्मगे
ख्यातो भाग्यगुणान्वितो भवगते क्षुद्रोऽङ्गहीनो व्यये ॥ ५ ॥

Stanza 5.—Moon in the 7th makes a man envious and passionately fond of women. In the 8th Moon produces capriciousness and suffering constantly from physical ailments. In the 9th popularity, children, wealth, relations and friends. In the 10th house Moon gives success in all undertakings, charitable, rich, intelligent and courageous.   In the 11th house Moon produces fame, gains and all those items indicated by that house. In the 12th he makes the person troublesome and defective in bodily organs.

NOTES

In all these cases the general principles of astrology, *viz.*, the sources of strength and weakness affecting these planets must not be forgotten in making predictions and attributing these characteristics in full or in part or as the case may be their absence altogether. Suppose Gemini is lagna and Moon is in Taurus. Here he is exalted and

good. But suppose he is in Scorpio debilitated and the
lagna is Sagittarius. In both these cases Moon is in the
12th from birth and the student must make a difference in
predicting results suitable to these places. In Taurus he
gives less evil than in Scorpio.

लग्ने कुजे क्षततनुर्धनगे कद्नो
धर्मेऽघवान्दिनकरप्रतिमोऽन्यसंस्थः ।
विद्वान् धनी प्रखलपण्डितमन्त्र्यशत्रु-
धर्मज्ञविश्रुतगुणः परतोर्ककवज्झे ॥ ६ ॥

Stanza 6.—Mars in Lagna—wounds or cuts in
the body. Mars in the 2nd—dirty meals. Mars
in the 9th—sinful. In other houses (bhavas) from
lagna Mars produces results similar to the Sun.

Mercury in the first eight houses, produces
learning, wealth, baseness, wisdom, minister,
foeless, versed in philosophy, and endowed with
good character respectively and in others he is
similar to the Sun in results.

NOTES

Varahamihira is short and suggestive. In the 3rd, 4th,
5th, 6th, 7th, 8th, 10th, 11th and 12th houses Mars is
declared to give similar results as the Sun does there. For
instance when the Sun is in the 3rd from birth he produces
intelligence and courage or valour. When Mars is in the
3rd from birth, he gives also intelligence and prowess.

Mercury produces the following characteristics in the man when he occupies the birth and the next seven houses respectively. In counting in these matters it should begin from birth itself as one. Thus if Aries is birth and Mars is in Leo we have to count from Aries as one, Taurus two, Gemini three, Cancer four and Leo five. Therefore Mars is in the fifth house from birth and results named for the Sun in the fifth must be applied to Mars also. Mercury in birth produces learning, in the second wealth, in the third baseness, in the fourth wisdom, in the fifth a minister, in the sixth no enemies, in the seventh a philosopher and in the 8th a man famous for his character, and in the 9th, 10th, 11th and 12th houses Mercury gives results similar to the Sun.

विद्वान् सुवाक्यः कृपणः सुखी च
धीमानशत्रुः पितृतोऽधिकश्च ।
नीचस्तपस्वी सधनः सलाभः
खलश्च जीवे क्रमशो विलग्नात् ॥ ७ ॥

Stanza 7.—Jupiter gives the following results in the 12 bhavas—from birth thus—learned, good speech, miser, happy, intelligent, foeless, eclipsing father, debased, pious, wealthy, profitable work and unscrupulous respectively.

NOTES

When Jupiter is in the first or birth house, the person becomes learned, in the second Jupiter gives good speech, in the third miserliness, in the fourth happiness, in the fifth intelligence, in the sixth no enemies, in the seventh

Jupiter makes the person greater than his father in good-
ness, in the eighth the person becomes mean or debased,
in the ninth pious, in the tenth wealthy, in the eleventh
profitable engagements, and in the twelfth unscrupulous
character.

स्मरनिपुणः सुखितश्च विलग्ने
प्रियकलहोऽस्तगते सुरतेप्सुः ।
तनयगतेऽसुखितो भृगुपुत्रे
गुरुवदतोऽन्यगृहे सघनोऽन्त्ये ॥ ८ ॥

Stanza 8.—Venus in Lagna gives skill in
sexual indulgence and happiness. In the 7th he
makes the native fond of quarrelling and sexual
intercourse. In the 5th he gives happiness and
in other houses the result will be similar to Jupiter and in the 12th Venus gives wealth.

NOTES

The word used for the 12th is Antya, end or last
house. Bhattotpala explains this as Pisces or Meena and
wherever this may fall in, the person becomes wealthy.
A patanthara or another reading runs thus—*Jhasha Droni-
encesyath* which means that Venus in Meena wherever it
might fall, gives wealth while the other reading is—*Antya
Griha Sadhanontya* which means that Venus in the 12th
gives wealth. The *Antya* here must be construed as Pisces
as per commentator. I am inclined to differ slightly from
him and to say that Venus produces good results in the 12th
house wherever that may fall in. If Aries is birth then 12th

is Pisces and Venus is good. So also if Cancer is birth and Venus is in Gemini, he will give good general sources of strength affecting planets alike. Venus in the 2nd, 3rd, 4th, 6th, 8th, 9th, 10th, 11th and 12th houses will produce *phalam* or results similar to Jupiter. Thus Venus in the 2nd gives good speech, in the 3rd miserliness, in the 4th happiness, in the 6th non-enmity, in the 8th baseness, in the 9th piety, in the 10th wealth, in the 11th gains, and in the 12th unscrupulousness.

अदृष्टार्थो रोगी मदनवशगोऽत्यन्तमलिनः
शिशुत्वे पीडार्त्तः सवितृसुतलग्नेऽत्यलसवाक् ।
गुरुस्वर्क्षोच्चस्थे नृपतिसदृशो ग्रामपुरपः
सुविद्रां श्वार्बङ्गी दिनकरसमोऽन्यत्र कथितः ॥ ९ ॥

Stanza 9.—Saturn in the first gives daily poverty, disease, cupidity, uncleanliness, sickness in early life, and indistinct speech. If Saturn occupies exaltation or houses of Jupiter or his own house, which happens to be lagna, he makes the person equal to a king, protector of villages or towns, learned, and handsome organs. In other houses he will give results similar to those given by the Sun.

NOTES

There are two readings. One goes on thus: *Guru-swarkshochhasthey* which means that when Saturn occupies his own house or the houses of Guru or his exaltation and the other reading runs: *Suhrutswarkshochhasthey* which

means when Saturn is in his own houses or exaltation or
his friend's houses.   Bhattotpala condemns this reading by
a quotation from *Saravali* which says *Swochay swajeva bhava-
nay.*   In the second Saturn gives good wealth, fines or
penalties from Government and facial disease.   In the third
intelligence and prowess.   In the fourth unhappiness and
mental worry.   (See Sts. 1, 2 and 3 of this chapter) and in
other houses results similar to those given by the Sun.

सुहृद्रिपरकीयस्वर्क्षतुङ्गस्थितानां
फलमनुपरिचिन्त्यं लन्नदेहादिभावैः ।
समुपचयविपत्ती सौम्यपापेषु सत्यः
कथयति विपरीतं रिःफषष्ठाष्टमेषु ॥ १० ॥

Stanza 10.—Take the birth sign, and the
body, etc., and predict results by the planets
occupying friendly, inimical, neutral, own, and
exalted houses.   Satyacharya declares that benefics and malefics in the houses produce good and
bad results in them respectively.   And the results
are reversed in the 6th, 8th and 12th houses.

NOTES

The notes given by Bhattotpala are clear and
exhaustive.   Take birth, 2nd, 3rd, etc., upto and including
the 12th and assign to them the proper events already
enumerated by Varahamihira and other astrological
writers.   Thus the birth indicates body, the second family,
the third brothers and so forth.   Here Varahamihira uses

the word lagna distinctly and asks the readers to count
from lagna. This looks like repetition. (See St. 15, Ch. I.)
As Yavaneswara has laid down the principle that the
bhavas may be begun by hora (birth) or *Sasibham*, the
house occupied by the Moon, *i.e.*, from the Moon, Varahamihira also supports this view in some instances. But here
with a view to avoid any reference to the Moon as a lagna
(Chandra Lagna) he specially mentions *lagna* only. The
prosperity or adversity to the various bhavas (significations)
must be judged by the conjunction of planets in those
houses. Bhavadhipathi (lord of the house indicating any
event) gives such results as are indicated by the terms
under which he occupies a house. *Suhrut* means a friend ;
Ari means an enemy ; *Parakiya* means a neutral ; *Swa*
means his own house ; and *Thunga* means exaltation. When
the lord of a particular bhava is in a friendly house he
gives prosperity to events indicated by that bhava. Take
the birth. It indicates body, personal characteristics, etc.
If its lord is in a friendly house he gives a good and healthy
body and desirable attributes. If he is in an unfriendly
house he introduces sickness, deformity, etc. Benefics or
malefics in unfriendly or debilitated houses produce evil to
events indicated by that *bhava*. If they are neutral houses
their results will be indifferent. If they are in exaltation,
Moolatrikona, their own houses or friendly houses they
give prosperity and success to events indicated by that
bhava. Bhagavan Gargi is quoted to support this view.
(*Vide* also ' *Bhavartha Ratnakara* ' and ' *How to Judge a
Horoscope* ' both by B. V. Raman.)

     According to Satya when benefics are in the 6th, 8th and
12th they destroy the evils indicated by those bhavas and

if evil planets are there they increase the evils. Bhattotpala quotes Satya here in conformity with the above view. In the previous part of this work all planets (*benefics and malefics*) have been declared to be productive of favourable results if they are in Upachayas of which 6th is said to be one. Now it is stated that malefics increase evils in the 6th house. When two distinct statements are made by Varahamihira, each contradicting the other the meaning should be thus explained. Among the Upachaya houses (3, 6, 10, 11) evil planets in the 6th must be declared to be inauspicious and not producing good results attributed to Upachayas. The commentator quotes from *Laghu Jataka* which says that benefics increase the bhavas they occupy excepting in the 6th where they destroy the events indicated by that bhava. This seems to be more correct than the other view, especially with regard to the 6th bhava, as malefics increase the evil results of the 6th house. The following horoscope illustrates this aspect. The lord of 6 is in 8 aspected by an evil planet. Six is occupied by an evil planet aspected by Rahu and lord of 3. Though

	Rahu Moon	Lagna	Sani
Guru Budha Ravi			
	RASI		
Sukra		Kuja Kethu	

the native earned lacs of rupees, he was always in debt and never free from it, till the end of his days.

Malefics destroy the bhavas they occupy. It is undesirable to have any planets in the 8th and 12th houses. Here Varahamihira contradicts himself. In the 6th according to the above quotations evil planets destroy the evils, while according to the present stanza evil planets in the 6th increase the evils. But Bhattotpala very clearly reconciles these apparent contradictions, by stating that Varahamihira who studied the several *Matas* (*systems or methods*) of the ancient Maharishis explains one system in *Brihat Jataka* and another in *Laghu Jataka* and this he further supports by a quotation from Varahamihira himself from his immortal Samhita, where Varahamihira thus explains his views with reference to various contradictions which he must have noticed in the course of his extensive and wonderful studies. Varahamihira observes—"Jyotisha is a Veda ; contradictions in it cannot be criticised by us, for it has been compiled by the great Munis who were blessed with *thrikala dristi* and therefore I simply give here the many systems propounded by the ancients". (See St. 7, Ch. IX, *Brihat Samhita.*) Here it will be seen that both the learned Varahamihira and his illustrious commentator Bhattotpala, deal a deathblow to such egotists, who in their narrow and self-elated views, think they are competent to express their own views as against the opinions expressed by the ancient Maharishis. Some of the braggadocio Western astrologers whose knowledge in astrology is comparable to the knowledge of the tortoise in a small well, think foolishly that they can cure the defects in astrology by their ill-digested views. These may

safely refer to the noble remarks of two of the most
eminent astrologers, and think seriously whether they are
not under the malevolent influences of an afflicted Luna,
when they boast of their learning, which is not even a
grain in the sands of the vast ocean.

Varahamihira clearly points out the different contradictory systems when they are ably and properly
supported by equal authorities. Bhattotpala here mentions
some other works of Varahamihira which have not been
before the public in any printed form. Varahamihira is
undoubtedly declared to have written (1) Brihatyatra,
(2) Laghuyatra, (3) Brihat Vivaha Patalam, and (4) Laghu
Vivaha Patalam and in these works he is stated to have
given various kundalis or planetary combinations (in horoscopes) to enunciate his principles and the different
doctrines he has compiled. When I was in Cochin, a few
carpenters of great skill and Sanskrit ability quoted verses
from Varahamihira's *Granthasamuchchaya*, which deals with
mechanics and carpentry and house-building. If the books
containing the horoscopes can be found they will be very
interesting factors.

उच्चत्रिकोणस्वसुहृच्छत्रुनीचगृहार्कगैः ।
शुभं संपूर्णपादोनदलपादाल्पनिष्फलम् ॥ ११ ॥

Stanza 11.—Planets in exaltation, in Moolatrikona, in own, friendly, inimical, debilitated
houses, and in combust with the Sun give good
in full, three-fourths, half, quarter, little and nil
results respectively.

NOTES

In planetary conjunctions two sorts of results are named (1) good, and (2) evil. When planets are inclined to give good they give full when they are in exaltation, three-fourths when they are in Moolatrikona, half when they are in their own houses, one-fourth in friendly houses, less than that in unfriendly houses, and no good result in debilitation and combust places. As regards the evil results the order must be reversed. If the combusted neecha planet is inclined to give evil he will give it in full, three-fourths in unfriendly houses, one-fourth in its own houses, in Moolatrikona less than one-fourth, and none in exalta-tion. A planet will give full good or bad only when he is powerful and this must be carefully applied to periods and sub-periods and Astakavarga, etc. Bhattotpala quotes an ancient authority which runs thus: "A planet when inclined to give good or bad will give it in full, etc., only when he is powerful". The sources of strength here indicated are detailed in Ch. II. As compared to other works, the results mentioned in Bhavadhyaya by Varahamihira are very short and vague. In *Rama Nadi* it is a bit more explanatory and *Sarvartha Chinthamani* is more exhaustive. *Brihat Jataka* along with Uttarakalamrita will enable an astrologer to give out fairly good results. Sanketa Nidhi also has something to say on these. As one proceeds one feels that so many conflicting ideas have to be analysed and to fix exactly the relative strength of a planet is no ordinary work and requires intuition, deep study and blessings of the Guru who teaches the science.

CHAPTER XXI

ASRAYA YOGADHYAYA

आश्रययोगाध्यायः

(Certain Special Combinations)

कुलसमकुलमुख्यबन्धुपूज्या
धनिसुखिभोगिनृपाः स्वभैकवृद्धया ।
परविभवसुहृत्स्वबन्धुपोष्या
गणपबलेशनृपाश्च मित्रमेषु ॥ १ ॥

Stanza 1.—When one and more planets are
in their own houses the man becomes equal to his
relations, chief of his family, respected by relations,
wealthy, equal to a ruler, happy, and king respectively. If one and more planets are in friendly
houses the person will be brought up by others,
by friends, by cousins, by brothers, chief of a
community, commander and king respectively.

NOTES

When one planet is in his own house the person becomes an equal to his relations which means that he will
attain to ordinary positions attained by his family members,
when two are in their own houses he becomes a chief of the
family, when three planets are in their own houses he
will be respected by his relations, when four planets are in
their own houses he will command wealth, when five planets
are in their own houses he will be happy, when six planets

are in their own houses he will be equal to a ruler, and when seven planets are placed in their own houses the person becomes a king. When one planet is in his friendly house he will be dependent and be brought up by others, when two planets are so he will be brought up by friends, when three planets are so he will be brought up by cousins, when four planets are so his brothers bring him up, when five are so he becomes the chief of a community or society, when six are so he becomes a commander or general, and when seven planets are in their friendly houses he becomes a king.

The following diagram illustrates the possibility :

	Mars				Kuja	Guru	
Saturn	In their own houses I		Moon	Sukra	In friend's houses II		
			Sun	Budha			Moon
Jupiter		Venus	Mercury	Ravi		Sani	

In I and II Lagna and Rahu and Kethu may be any-where.

जनयति नृपमेकोऽप्युच्चगो मित्रदृष्टः ।
प्रचुरधनसमेतं मित्रयोगाच्च सिद्धम् ।
विधनविसुखमूढव्याधितो बन्धतप्तो
वधदुरितसमेतः शत्रुनीचर्क्षगेषु ॥ २ ॥

Stanza 2.—If there is one exalted planet aspected by a friendly planet, the person becomes a king. When such a planet is conjoined by a friendly planet, he becomes very wealthy, and commands universal respect. If one and more planets are in unfriendly or debilitated houses, they produce poverty, misery, dullness, disease, imprisonment, sorrow and hanging respectively.

NOTES

In this it will seen that at least one planet must be in exaltation having a friendly aspect to produce a king. If a planet is exalted having the conjunction of a friendly planet he will get as much money as he wants and will be respected wherever he moves. If there is one planet in an unfriendly house or debilitation, the person becomes poor, when two planets are so he will be unhappy, when three planets are so he becomes ignorant or dull, when four planets are so he will be constantly suffering from disease, when five planets are in debilitation or unfriendly houses, he gets imprisonment, when six planets are so he will be drowned in sorrow and when seven are so the person commits acts which would take him to the gallows or he will be hanged.

No results have been stated here for exaltation of seven planets but in this stanza, *phalam* has been stated for seven planets in debilitation. Under the present astronomical conditions, calculations and movements of planets such a combination as the debilitation of seven planets seems to be an impossibility. For if the Sun be exalted in Aries, we can easily imagine the exaltation of Venus in Pisces but Mercury can never be in exaltation. For according to Bhattotpala's commentaries and present astronomical calculations Mercury can never be longer than 29° on either side of the Sun. The exaltation of Mercury is in Virgo and in the 15th degree. The Sun is exalted in the 10th degree of Aries. But if both of them are to be exalted at the same time there must be an elongation of Mercury from the Sun ranging over 155° which is absurd. When exaltations do not happen, debilitations, as a matter of fact, become also impossible. Bhattotpala says that Varahamihira gives these combinations in accordance with the principles contained in ancient sciences propounded by Gargi, Parasara and Vasishta. This shows that there must have been tremendous changes in the different epochs of the terrestrial and celestial phenomena and that the sciences in India seem to have attained to the greatest perfections long before the dawn of present European civilisation. The ancient works quote the following verse :

" Ekagrahoccha Jatasya
Sarvarishta Vinasanam
Dwigrahocchathu Samantha
Trigrahoccha Mahipathihi
Chaturgrahoccha Samratsyat
Panchoche Lokanayakaha."

If one planet is exalted, all evils will be removed, if two are exalted he becomes a petty king, if three a big ruler, if four an emperor, and if five ruler of the universe. The only horoscope, so far known is Sri Rama's where five planets are exalted. It is possible for six to be exalted except Mercury. (*Vide* Stanza 2 of Chapter XXII.)

न कुंभलग्नं शुभमाह सत्यो
न भागभेदाद्यवना वदन्ति ।
कस्यांशभेदो न तथास्ति राशे-
रतिप्रसङ्गस्त्विति विष्णुगुप्तः ॥ ३ ॥

Stanza 3.—Satya declares Kumbha Lagna
as bad. Yavanas observe Kumbha dwadasamsa
as evil. Vishnugupta asserts that Yavanas are
erroneous as Kumbha dwadasamsa occurs in
every lagna.

NOTES

Kumbha (Aquarius) as birth sign is condemned by
Satya for whom Varahamihira seems to have great regard
and admiration and whom he follows often closely. Bhattotpala quotes Satya here: " The Moon is bad in the 6th, 8th and
Lagna at the time of birth, and all biped signs are good
except Kumbha " (see notes on Ch. I, St. 19.) The biped
signs are, Gemini, Virgo, Libra, the first half of Sagittarius
and Aquarius. Continuing Satya's quotation :—The person
born in Aquarius will be sorrowful and miserable. Yavanas
maintain that Aquarius as birth is not bad, but the Dwadasamsa of Aquarius in each sign is bad. Bhattotpala who
was not able to secure the *Puranayavana* works (ancient
Yavana writing) but who possessed the Yavana literature
on astrology of later date quotes Srutakirti a follower
of the Yavana doctrine thus :—Birth may fall in any
house (rasi) but if its dwadasamsa falls in Kumbha
the person then born will be unhappy and bred on others

cost. Vishnugupta (the famous Chanikya who established
Chandragupta on the throne of Magadha in place of the
Nava Nandas in B.C. 322 or a few years after the invasion
of India by Alexander of Macedon (see Pp. 30 of my History
of Vijayanagar, Part I) observes with great force that the
Yavanas were impertinent or erroneous, for if the dwadasamsa of Aquarius is bad in every lagna then good results
predicted for all the signs, will be nullified and that there
can be no lagna or (zodiacal) sign without containing a Kumbha dwadasamsa which is bad and which is opposed to the
spirit of astrology and the best written works on the subject.
It is only the sign Kumbha as birth which stands condemned
by the great writers. Here one important question arises,
viz., why should of all signs, Aquarius be the worst ?
Neither the author Varahamihira nor his commentator has
thrown any light on the cause or causes for Kumbha being
inauspicious as a lagna. Wading through the whole of the
valuable commentaries and examining even the question of
Satya, Srutakirti and Chanikya we find no reasons are
advanced for Kumbha being the worst among the 12 signs.
I may however venture to suggest the following facts for
the consideration of the readers. Kumbha is owned by
the worst of the planets, *viz.*, Saturn. Besides, its lord
also happens to be the lord of the 12th house from it and
the 12th sign is called Nasa, Ripha and Vyaya. Therefore
when the lord of lagna also owns the 12th house he becomes evil and indicates in himself self-destruction. This
kind of combination occurs for Kumbha and not for any
other rasi or planet. Also Kumbha is called Hrit (heart)
and Roga (disease) (see St. 21, Chap. II and St. 8,
Chap. I.)

यातेष्वसत्स्वसममेषु दिनेशहोरां
ख्यातो महोद्यमबलार्थयुतोऽतितेजाः ।
चान्द्री शुभेषु युजि मार्दवकान्तिसौख्य-
सौभाग्यधीमधुरवाक्ययुतः प्रजातः ॥ ४ ॥

Stanza 4.—If malefics join the solar hora in
odd signs, the person becomes famous, undertakes
great works, possesses strength, wealth and great
personal attractions. If benefics join the lunar
hora in even signs, the person becomes tender-
hearted, handsome, happy, popular, intelligent
and polite speaker.

NOTES

Hora means one half of a rasi or sign and extends for
15°. Odd signs are Aries, Gemini, Leo, Libra, Sagittarius
and Aquarius. In all these the first 15 degrees are under
the solar control and hence the Sun is called the *Prathama
Horadhipathi* in these signs. If evil planets are in these
horas of the Sun, then the person becomes famous, etc.
In the even signs, *viz.*, Taurus, Cancer, Virgo, Scorpio,
Capricorn and Pisces, the first hora or half is ruled by
the Moon, and if benefics are in such hora the native
becomes kind-hearted, handsome, etc.

तास्वेव होरास्वपरर्क्षगेषु
ज्ञेया नराः पूर्वगुणेषु मध्याः ।
व्यत्यस्तहोराभवनस्थितेषु
मर्त्या भवन्त्युक्तगुणैर्विहीनाः ॥ ५ ॥

Stanza 5.—If the planets in the same horas are found in other rasis (signs) the person born then will have the results moderately.   If the planets are reversed in horas and rasis, the persons born will not have the above characteristics.

NOTES

The motto of Varahamihira to say briefly is terribly fulfilled here. He is splendidly helped by the flexible and highly developed Sanskrit language and the same brevity and suggestiveness can never be brought out in the poor English language. If evil planets are in solar horas in even signs the results named above will be moderately enjoyed. If benefics are in lunar hora in odd signs the results are moderate. But if evil planets are in Chandra hora in even signs there will be no *phalam* sketched above. If benefics occupy the solar hora in odd signs there will be no *phalam*. When there are two or more planets in similar position the intensity of good or evil must be proportionately considered. (See St. 11, Ch. I.) Here we see that odd signs are considered as cruel, masculine, etc., and even signs as mild, feminine, etc. The solar hora must be cruel as compared with the lunar, which is milder. Therefore cruel planets in cruel houses, in cruel horas give good results. If there are some in one and some in the other the results will be neutralised. If all the planets are topsy-turvy then these good results will not be present.

कल्याणरूपगुणमात्मसुहृद्द्रकाणे
चन्द्रोऽन्यगस्तदधिनाथगुणं करोति ।

व्यालोद्यतायुधचतुश्चरणाण्डजेषु
तीक्ष्णोऽतिहिंसगुरुतल्परतोऽटनश्च ॥ ६ ॥

Stanza 6.—If the Moon is in his own or
friendly drekkana the person will be handsome
and virtuous. If the Moon is in other drekkanas
the person will get the characteristics of the lord of
the drekkana. If the Moon is in Vyala, Udyathayudha, Chatuscharana and Andaja drekkanas, the
person born will be vindictive, very cruel, fouling
Guru's wife and traveller respectively.

NOTES

When the rasi (sign) is divided into 3 equal parts each
is called a drekkana, or each division gets 10 degrees. The
lords of these 3 drekkanas are the lords of the 1st, of the 5th
and of the 9th divisions respectively of that rasi. When the
Moon is in his own or friendly drekkanas he gives beauty
and virtue. But when he is in other drekkanas then the
characteristics will be decided by the lord of that drekkana.
If the lord of that drekkana where the Moon is, becomes
his temporary friend, then beauty and virtue will be full,
and when he is a neutral, they will be moderate, but when
he is a foe then they will be absent. *Vyala* means in Sanskrit serpent ; *Udyathayudha* means armed with weapons ;
Chatuscharana means four-footed or quadrupeds; and *Andaja*
means born of an egg or bird. If the Moon is in serpent
Drekkana the person will be vindictive or highly excitable.
The following are Vyala drekkanas : 2nd and 3rd
of Cancer, 1st and 2nd of Scorpio and 3rd of Pisces, if

the Moon is in *Udyathayudha* the person will be fond of killing or murdering. The following are armed Drekkanas : 1st and 3rd of Aries, 2nd and 3rd of Gemini, 2nd and 3rd of Leo, 2nd of Virgo, 3rd of Libra, 1st and 3rd of Sagittarius and 3rd of Capricorn.

If the Moon is in quadruped Drekkanas the person will commit adultery with his instructor's wife. The following are quadruped Drekkanas : 2nd of Aries, 2nd and 3rd of Leo, 3rd of Libra, 3rd of Scorpio, 1st of Sagittarius and the 1st of Capricorn.

If the Moon is in bird Drekkana the person will be a traveller. The bird Drekkanas are the following : 2nd of Gemini, 1st of Leo, 2nd of Libra and 1st of Aquarius. If now the Moon is in the 1st drekkana of Cancer, he will be both in his own drekkana and that of a quadruped also. The results will have to be predicted by reference to both. Suppose the Moon occupies the 2nd or 3rd drekkana of Leo. He occupies a friendly drekkana, an armed drekkana and a quadruped drekkana. What results should be predicted ? Bhattotpala says summarise the three sources of results and predict them. (See Chap. XXVII.)

(There seems to be some difference in the nature of the drekkanas mentioned in the original and in the English translation. In the quadruped Drekkanas, 2 of Taurus, 1 of Cancer and 1 of Leo are not mentioned by Mr. Rao ; and in bird Drekkanas, 3rd of Gemini is also included. The rest of the drekkanas naturally belong to the lords of those houses and those characteristics must be mentioned.)

स्तेनो भोक्ता पण्डिताढ्यो नरेन्द्रः
क्लीबः शूरो विष्टिकृद्दासवृत्तिः
पापो हिंस्रोऽमिश्र वर्गोत्तमांशे-
ष्वेषामीशा राशिवद्वादशांशैः ॥ ७ ॥

Stanza 7.—A person born in the Navamsas
of Aries, etc., will become a thief, an enjoyer,
learned, wealthy, ruler, impotent, warlike, carrier,
servant, sinful, cruel and intrepid. If these navamsas fall in Vargottamas, the person born then
will become master or chief of the above. The
results for the Dwadasamsas will be similar to
rasis.

NOTES

If any other sign than Aries is lagna and the navamsa
falls in Aries the person will become a thief, excepting the
sign Taurus, if the Navamsa Taurus rises in any sign the person enjoys well the comforts of this life, if the Gemini
navamsa rises in any other sign than Gemini the person becomes learned. And so for other signs. But suppose
Aries is the ascendant and that navamsa rises at birth. As
that navamsa falls in Vargottama, the person becomes a
leader or chief of thieves or robbers. Taurus Navamsa is the
Vargottama for Taurus sign and one born when Taurus is
ascendant as well as the navamsa, will be pre-eminent or
chief among those who enjoy the goods of life. When
Gemini is both the Rasi and Navamsa Lagna, the person
will be the chief or leader among the learned. (See St. 14,

Ch. I). The results mentioned for the Moon in the twelve
signs will be the results for the Dwadasamsa Lagnas from
Aries, etc. (See Ch. XVII). There are two readings
quoted by Bhattotpala for a petson born in Meenamsa :
(1) *Abhischa* which means fearless, and (2) *Adhischa* which
means without sense. The latter cannot be accepted as
Varahamihira distinctly says *Abhaya* in *Laghu Jataka*, in
this connection, and therefore Abhischa alone is *Sadhu* or
acceptable.

जायान्विंतो बलविभूषणसत्वयुक्त-
स्तेजोऽतिसाहसयुतश्च कुजे स्वभागे ।
रोगी मृतस्वयुवतिर्विषमोऽन्यदारो
दुःखी परिच्छदयुतो मलिनोऽर्कपुत्रे ॥ ८ ॥

Stanza 8.—When Mars is in his own Trimsamsa, the person will have wife, strength, ornaments, generosity, personal attraction, and
enterprising spirit. When Saturn is in his own
Trimsamsa, the person becomes sickly, loses his
wife, possesses double heart, enjoys others wives,
sorrowful, possessed of houses, cloths, servants,
etc., and will be uncleanly.

NOTES

In this stanza, Varahamihira uses the word Bhaga
which means Amsa, but when he gives the results of Venus
in the third, he distinctly says Trimsamsa, and hence
Bhattotpála rightly interprets Bhaga, here as Trimsamsa.

Besides the results of Amsas have already been stated.   In
odd signs the lords of the Trimsamsas are—

Mars	Saturn	Guru	Budha	Sukra
5	5	8	7	5

=30°.   In even signs the order should be reversed thus—

Venus	Budha	Guru	Saturn	Mars
5	7	8	5	5

=30.   (See St. 7, Ch. I.)

स्वांशे गुरौ धनयशःसुखबुद्धियुक्ताः
तेजस्विपूज्यनिरुगुधमभोगवन्तः ।
मेधाकलाकपटकाव्यविवादशिल्प-
शास्त्रार्थसाहसयुताः शशिजेऽतिमान्याः ॥ ९ ॥

Stanza 9.—When Jupiter is in his own
Trimsamsa, the person will have wealth, reputation, happiness, intelligence, attraction, respect,
health, hope and enjoyment.   When Mercury
occupies his own Trimsamsa, he gives the man
intelligence, education, show, poetical ability,
eloquence, skill in arts, philosophic acumen,
enterprise and much respect.

NOTES

The stanza is clear and needs no explanation.

स्वे त्रिंशांशे बहुसुतसुखारोग्यभाग्यार्थरूपः
शुक्रे तीक्ष्णः सुललिनबपुः सुप्रकीर्णेन्द्रियश्च ।

शूरस्तब्धौ विषमवधकौ सद्गुणाढ्यौ सुखिड्ज़ौ
चार्वड्ज़िष्टौ रविशशियुतेष्वारपूर्वांशकेषु ॥ १० ॥

Stanza 10.—When Venus occupies his own
Trimsamsa, the man will be blessed with many
sons, much happiness, health, popularity, wealth,
beauty, vindictiveness, handsome body and enjoyment with many women. When the Sun and the
Moon are in the Trimsamsa of Mars, etc., the
person will be warlike and slothful, cruel and
killing, virtuous and wealthy, happy and learned,
handsome and popular respectively.

NOTES

There are two readings with reference to Venus:
(1) Bhagya which means popularity, and (2) Bhogya which
means wife. Both are admissible. If the Sun and the
Moon are in the Trimsamsa of Mars, the person will be
warlike and slothful. In Saturn's Trimsamsa, the person
will be cruel and murderous. In Jupiter's Trimsamsa, he
will be virtuous and wealthy. In Mercury's Trimsamsa,
he will be happy and learned. In Venus Trimsamsa, he
will be handsome and popular.

CHAPTER XXII

PRAKIRNAKADHYAYA

प्रकीर्णाध्यायः

(*Mixed Results*)

स्वर्क्षतुङ्गमूलत्रिकोणगाः कण्टकेषु यावन्त आश्रिताः ।
सर्व एव तेऽन्योन्यकारकाः कर्मगस्तु तेषां विशेषतः ॥ १ ॥

Stanza 1.—Planets in kendras when they happen to be in their own houses, in exaltations or in Moolatrikonas are mutually termed *karakas*. Of these, the planet in the 10th will be the best karaka.

NOTES

Mixed results or enumeration of various matters goes under the name of *Prakirna*. If there is any planet in a kendra from birth, which is his own house or exaltation or Moolatrikona and there is another planet in a similar state in another kendra, these two planets are said to be the karakas mutually or to one another. Of these karakas the most powerful is the one who occupies the 10th. This requires a little more explanation.

Budha is in Lagna Kendra and in his own house and he becomes a Karaka. Guru is in the 10th house and being in his own house he becomes a Karaka. Guru is in the 10th from the Karaka Budha and becomes thus the most powerful karaka.   Another version about these karakas is given here for comparison.

For the Sun,   Guru in   9th is the Karaka.
  ,,   Moon,   Sani in   11th ,,   ,,
  ,,   Mars,   Sani in   11th ,,   ,,
  ,,   Mercury, Venus in   5th ,,   ,,
  ,,   Jupiter, Moon in   7th ,,   ,,
  ,,   Venus,   Guru in   12th ,,   ,,
  ,,   Sani,   Guru in   6th ,,   ,,

Guru			Birth Budha
	RASI		

कर्कटोदयगते यथोडुपे
स्वोच्चगाः कुजयमार्कसूरयः ।
कारका निगदिताः परस्परं
लग्नगस्य सकलोऽम्बराम्बुगः ॥ २ ॥

Stanza 2.—If birth falls in Cancer with Moon in it and Mars, Saturn, Sun and Jupiter are in exaltations they become mutual karakas. For the planet in Lagna, the planets in the *Ambara* and *Ambu* become karakas.

NOTES

Bhattotpala gives a kundali or zodiacal diagram which belongs to Sri Rama, the national hero of India. His horoscope as explained by Valmiki in Balkanda is thus given in the Ramayana.

In this stanza Varahamihira clearly refers to Rama's horoscope. This proves the great antiquity of Ramayana.

Such a combination of planets is of rare occurrence and in this five planets are exalted and the Moon is in his own house. Here the planets are not only in kendras but also in their exaltations and they become karakas to each other, the results of which will be explained later on.

Venus	Sun	Mer.	Kethu
	Rama's horoscope Rasi diagram		Birth Moon Jupiter
Mars			
Rahu		Saturn	

Ambara means the 10th house and *Ambu* means the 4th house. When there is a planet in birth and there are planets in the 4th and 10th, those planets which are in the last two houses become karakas of the former, *i.e.*, the planet in the ascendant. Except for Aries, Cancer, Libra and Capricorn, for no other lagnas could the planets be in these kendras as also exalted.

	Ravi		
			Guru Lagna
Kuja	I		
		Sani	

	Ravi		
			Guru
Kuja	II		
		Sani Lagna	

	Ravi		
Kuja Lagna	III		Guru
	Sani		

and Mesha as Lagna.

स्वत्रिकोणोच्चगो हेतुरन्योन्यं यदि कर्मगः ।
सुहृत्तद्गुणसंपन्नः कारकश्चापि स स्मृतः ॥ ३ ॥

Stanza 3.—If the planet in the 10th house from the planet who occupies his own house or Moola-thrikona or exaltation, happens to be a Nisarga friend and also Tatkalika, he becomes a karaka.

NOTES

He gives here a separate case altogether unconnected with kendra planets. If a planet is not in Lagna Kendra but occupies any other house and another planet occupies the 10th house from such a planet and this 10th house happens to be its own house or Moolatrikona or exaltation then this planet becomes a karaka provided he is an intimate friend to the other planet. Here Bhattotpala seems to make some difference in *karakas*. The planet in the 10th house does not become a karaka to the planet from whom he is in the 10th.

Take Sani in Meena, Budha is in his own house· Sani now becomes a karaka, but not a karaka to Budha. Sani is a temporary as well as a permanent friend of Budha and is located in the 10th house from Budha.

Sani		Ravi Kethu	Sukra Kuja Budha
	RASI		Lagna
	Rahu		Guru Moon

The use of these *karakas* is elaborately given in Varahamihira's Yatra. During the dasas of karakas the person will do well to go to some ruler, win his favour and serve under him, so that his difficulties may be warded off. Rikta dasa (defeated planet's dasa), the dasas of the lords of birth and Chandra and during the sub-periods of their enemies, the results will be bad and hence the recommendation to go and serve under some monarchs (see notes on Ch. XI, St. 19).

शुभं वर्गोत्तमे जन्म वेशिस्थाने च सद्ग्रहे ।
अशून्येषु च केन्द्रेषु कारकाख्यग्रहेषु च ॥ ४ ॥

Stanza 4.—If the lagna falls in Vargottama, if good planets are in the Vesi, if the kendras are not unoccupied, if there are karaka planets, then the person will be happy.

NOTES

Vargottama Navamsa will be the 1st navamsa of the movable, the 5th navamsa of the fixed and the 9th navamsa of the *double bodied* signs and when examined will be found to fall in the same houses. Thus the Vargottama of Aries will be Aries in the navamsa, that of Taurus will be Taurus and Gemini will fall in Gemini. This also applies to the Moon. *Vesi* means the 2nd house from where the Sun is located for the time being. *Vide* ' Satayogamanjari ' by Mr. B. S. Rao, Pp. 17 and 18. This must be occupied by benefics. There are four quadrants from lagna and one of them at least must be occupied by planets. Here if evil planets are found, the good will be moderate but if benefics are there, the results will be eminently satisfactory. Bhattotpala quotes a verse from Varahamihira's Yatra, which says that in travelling or in any business or in birth there must at least be a benefic in one of the kendras. If all the factors enumerated above are present then the happiness will be unlimited, but when less, the results will also be proportionately less. When there are karakas in a

Mer.	Venus Mars	Saturn Rahu	
Sun	NAVAMSA		Jupiter
Moon			
	Lagna Kethu		

horoscope it is good.   (See Ch. I, Sts. 14 & 20).   No horoscope can be considered good unless planets are in kendras
from each other or aspect each other.   If every bhava
is aspected by its lord the planets must be in kendras (7th)
to that bhava.   The following horoscope illustrates this :
Lagna is aspected by its lord, 2nd lord, 3rd and 4th lord ;
4th house is aspected by its lord, 5th by its lord,   6th has
its own lord, 7th and 8th are not aspected, 9th, 10th, 11th
and 12th are aspected by its lords, respectively.   Seven
houses are aspected by their lords and it is a powerful
yoga horoscope.

मध्ये वयसः सुखप्रदाः केन्द्रस्था गुरुजन्मलग्नपाः ।
पृष्ठोभयकोदयर्क्षगास्त्वन्तेऽन्तः प्रथमेषु पाकदाः ॥ ५ ॥

Stanza 5.—If Guru, Janmadhipathi   or
Lagnadhipathi occupies a kendra, the person will
have happiness in the middle of life.   Planets in
Prushtodaya, Ubhayodaya and Sirshodaya give
results in the end, middle and beginning of the
man's life respectively.

NOTES

Janmadhipathi means the lord of the house where the
Moon stays at the time of birth.   Lagnadhipathi is the lord
of the birth or ascendant.   If any one of these or Guru
occupies a kendra, the person gets happiness in the middle
life.   If the lord of the dasa happens to be in Aries, Taurus,
Sagittarius or Capricorn at the time of commencement of
his period, he will give results at the end of his dasa.   If

the planet occupies Pisces, then the results will be given in
the middle, and if the planet is in Gemini, Leo, Virgo,
Libra, Scorpio or Aquarius the results will be produced in
the commencement. These results may be good or bad
and they will be given by the Dasanatha at the time
indicated. Thus we have here to refer to their Gochara
movements to find out where they are and when they begin
the dasas. Gargi is quoted by the commentator to support
this explanation as the original is short and silent. This is
an important point to be remembered while making predictions. The astrologer is expected to know the position of
planets in their Gochara movement. For example, the
position of planets would be Sani in Cancer, Guru in
Vrischika till February 1948 and then in Dhanus, Rahu in
Vrishabha till the end of November 1947 and Mars in
Cancer and Leo. The rest would be moving once a month
from house to house and could be known from any almanac.
Find out where the planet is at the time of the commencement of his dasa. Then if he is in—

(1) Mithuna, Simha, Kanya, Thula,   ... Results will be
    Vrischika or Kumbha (Sirshodaya)   seen in the
                                           beginning.
(2) Pisces (Meena) Ubhayodaya   ... In the middle.
(3) Mesha, Vrishabha, Dhanus,   ... In the end.
    Makara, Kataka-Prushtodaya.

दिनकररुधिरौ प्रवेशकाले
गुरुभृगुजौ भवनस्य मध्ययातौ ।
रविसुतशशिनौ विनिर्गमस्थौ
शशितनयः फलदस्तु सर्वकालम् ॥ ६ ॥

Stanza 6.—The Sun and Mars give results when they enter a house, Jupiter and Venus in the middle and Saturn and the Moon in the end and Mercury always.

NOTES

Here the results are indicated with reference to the Ashtakavarga already explained in Ch. IX. Take the Sun. He gets certain power according to Ashtakavarga calculations and thereby becomes powerful to give good or evil results. Divide the rasi into 3 equal divisions. The Sun and Mars give their results when then enter a rasi, and before they leave the 1st division, Jupiter and Venus do so in the 2nd division and Saturn and Moon in the 3rd division. But Mercury continues to give his results all through the house he occupies. This must be taken into account in predicting future events.

CHAPTER XXIII

ANISHTADHYAYA OR MISFORTUNES

अनिष्टाध्यायः

लग्नात्पुत्रकलत्रमे शुभपतिप्राप्तेऽथवालोकिते
चन्द्राद्वा यदि सम्पदस्ति हि तयोर्डेंयोऽन्यथा संभवः ।
पाथोनोदयगे रवौ रविसुतो मीनस्थितो दारहा
पुत्रस्थानगतश्च पुत्रमरणं पुत्रोऽवनेर्येच्छति ॥ १ ॥

Stanza 1.—If the 5th and 7th houses from Lagna or Chandra be occupied or aspected by benefics or their lords, then these bhavas will prosper; if not they will suffer.

If Kanya falls as birth with Ravi in it and Sani in Meena, the wife will be lost. If in this conjunction the 5th house is occupied by Kuja, he causes loss to children.

NOTES

This Chapter is called Anishta or Arishta and means that which treats of misfortunes. When a horoscope is given to an astrologer he will be able to say from what misfortunes the person is suffering from and this is very important for men to know. If the 5th house from Lagna or Moon is occupied or aspected by benefics or its lord, the person will be blessed with children. If the 5th house

from Lagna or Chandra is not so occupied the person will
be childless.   There are 12 kinds of children mentioned in
the sastras and combinations for all these varieties are
quoted from Saravali by Bhattotpala.

The twelve kinds of children are :—
(1) Aurasa—born to lawful wife.
(2) Kshetraja—born to one's wife with the consent of
    husband.
(3) Datta—given in adoption.
(4) Kritrima—nursing any one as one's own child.
(5) Adhama Prabhavan—one born to a wife without
    the husband's knowledge by a low caste man.
(6) Ghudhothpanna—one born to wife similarly but
    for men of equal caste. Ghuda means in secret,
    one born secretly to the wife without the hus-
    band's knowledge.
(7) Apaviddha—one neglected after birth.
(8) Pounarbhava—a child born to a second husband
    after the woman renounces the first.
(9) Kanina—born to an unmarried girl.
(10) Sahodha—born to second wife.
(11) Kritaka—a child purchased while the first is living
(12) Dasiprabhava—born of illegitimate connection.

Saravali thus explains these varieties of children. If
the 5th house in a horoscope belongs to a benefic or has
its conjunction or aspect the person will have children.

If the 5th house falls in any one of the 6 divisions of
Guru, or falls in a beneficial sign the person will get
legitimate children, that is in Dhanus or Meena in Rasi,
Hora, Drekkana, Navamsa, Trimsamsa and Dwadasamsa.

Compare this with Chapter IV where the legitimacy or otherwise of the child is discussed at full length. Unless Guru aspects Lagna, Chandra or Surya either in rasi or in amsa, the legitimacy of the child has to be suspected.

If the 5th house from Lagna or Chandra, whichever is more powerful, has beneficial aspects the person will have lawful children. If the navamsa of the 5th house fall in a beneficial sign the number of children will be determined by that navamsa. If a benefic aspects it the number will be doubled. If this falls in a malefic amsa the number of losses will be determined by that navamsa. If the 5th falls in one of Sani's houses aspected by Budha, the child will resemble Sani. If Guru, Kuja and Ravi aspect the same, the child will be blind.

If the 5th house belongs to Budha aspected by Sani, Kshetraja will be born. Pandavas are said to be Kshetrajas since Kunti got the three sons, Dharma Raja from Yama, Bhima from Vayu (God of wind) and Indra giving her Arjuna while the 2nd wife Madri got Nakula and Sahadeva from Aswini Devatas (celestial physicians) with the consent of her husband Pandu as he was under a curse not to approach his wife. If the 5th house belongs to Sani with Sani there aspected by Chandra, the son will be adopted. If the 5th house belongs to Budha with Budha there aspected by Chandra, the child will be purchased.

If the 5th house joins Kuja's Saptamsa with Sani there unaspected by other planets, the child will be Kritrima. If the 5th house falls in Sani's varga with Ravi there aspected by Kuja, the child will be *Adhama Prabhava*. If the 5th joins Kuja's amsa with Chandra there, aspected by Sani, unaspected by other planets, the child will be Gudhotpanna.

31

If the 5th joins Sani's varga with Kuja there aspected by Ravi, Apaviddha will be born as per Charaka Muni.

If the 5th falls in Sani's varga with Sani and Chandra there aspected by Sukra and Ravi, the child will be Punarbhava.

If the 5th falls in Cancer conjoined or aspected by the Sun, the child will be Kanina. Kanina means one who is born to an unmarried girl as Karna to Kunti before she was wedded to Pandu.

If the 5th falls in Ravi's or Chandra's divisions with Ravi or Chandra in it aspected by Sukra, the child will be Sahodha.

If the 5th falls into malefic signs aspected by powerful malefics, unaspected by benefics, the person will have no children. If the 5th house falls in Sukra's navamsas, aspected by Sukra, the children will be from concubines.

If the 5th falls in Chandra Navamsa with his aspect, similar results must be predicted. If the 5th falls in Sukra or Chandra vargas and conjoined or aspected by them there will probably be daughters or the child's nature will partake of that rasi. Similarly if the 7th house from Lagna or Chandra is combined or aspected by benefics or its lord is there, there will be prosperity to wife. If there is no conjunction or aspect for the 7th then there will be no wife. Here the author has quoted two bhavas, the 5th and 7th as examples and thereby shows the readers that these principles may be extended to all other bhavas. Bhattotpala quotes Yavaneswara who says that the events of life may be judged either from birth or the Moon. There seems to be some contradiction in the views of the learned commenta-

tor. In Ch. XX, St. 10 in his valuable notes he says that
the different bhavas must be taken from Lagna and not
from Chandra and that is the reason why his author Varahamihira repeats, *Lagna Dehadi Bhavyhi.* See notes. If
Venus, Jupiter, Moon or Mercury or all of them occupy or
aspect the 7th or if the 7th falls in the house of any one of
these or their divisions then the nature of the wife will be
according to the lord of the varga or the nature of the sign.
If the 7th from birth or Moon, whichever is powerful—
is combined or aspected by malefics there will be loss or
destruction to wife. If the 7th house is occupied by Saturn
and Moon his wife will marry separately while he is living.
The number of wives will have to be determined by the
number of navamsas the lord of the 7th has gained or by the
number of planets who aspect the lord of the 7th. If the
7th falls in the amsas of Ravi, Kuja, Guru or Budha, there
will be one wife. If the 7th is powerful and occupied by
Chandra and Sukra or aspected by them, probably he will
have many wives. If Sukra occupies or aspects the 7th
there will be many wives. If Guru and Sukra occupy the
7th the wife comes from his own caste. If Ravi, Kuja,
Chandra and Sani occupy or aspect the 7th the girl will be
from a lower caste. If Sukra occupies or aspects 7th,
the wife probably will behave like a dancing woman or
prostitute. If Kanya is birth with the Sun there and Saturn
is in Pisces, his wife will die before him. If in this connection Mars occupies the 5th, Capricorn, the person loses
all his children during his life. Kuja is exalted in Makara
and still he will kill the issues. The 7th and 5th houses
are allied to each other closely since if he should have
children, he must have a wife, while if he has a wife, he may

or may not have children, but can adopt and thus have
children. Unless there is a wife, the question of children,
of whatever denomination they may be does not arise.
Hence both the bhavas are discussed in detail here.

उग्रग्रहैः सितचतुरस्रसंस्थितै-
र्मध्यस्थिते भृगुतनयेऽथवोग्रयोः ।
सौम्यग्रहैरसहितसंनिरीक्षिते
जायावधो दहननिपातपाशजः ॥ २ ॥

Stanza 2.—If cruel planets are in the 4th and
the 8th from Venus or if Venus is between malefics or if Venus is not combined or not aspected
by benefics, the wife will be killed by fire, fall or
ropes.

NOTES

In these combinations the fact to be remembered is the
death of the wife when the person is living. The cruel
planets are the Sun, Mars and Saturn and if these in any
order occupy the 4th and the 8th the person will lose his
wife by fire or burning. If Venus has evil planets in the
2nd and the 12th houses from him the wife will die by fall
from an elevated place. In this case if Venus is in the same
house with malefics, but is placed between two evil planets
in ten degrees the same results must be predicted with
greater force. If Venus does not join with or is not aspected
by any benefic, the wife will die by being tied with ropes.
Some misinterpret this verse but Bhattotpala supports the
above explanation by quoting Bhagavan Gargi, who is very
clear on this point.

लग्नाद्व्ययारिगतयोः शशितिग्मरश्म्योः
पत्न्या सहैकनयनस्य वदन्ति जन्म ।
घूनस्थयोर्नवमपञ्चमसंस्थयोर्वा
शुक्रार्कयोर्विकलदारसुशन्ति जातम् ॥ ३ ॥

Stanza 3.—If the 6th and 12th houses from
lagna are occupied by the Sun and the Moon, the
husband and wife will have each one eye. If
Venus and the Sun occupy the 7th, 9th or 5th,
the wife will be defective.

NOTES

In the first half of the verse the 12th and the 6th must
be occupied by the Sun and the Moon in any way to
produce defective vision in both the couple. The second
half of the stanza requires that the Sun and the Venus must
be together in the 5th and 9th or the 7th house to produce
defect in any particular organ of the wife.

कोणोदये भृगुतनयेऽस्तचक्रसन्धौ
वन्ध्यापतिर्यदि न सुतर्क्षमिष्टयुक्तम् ।
पापग्रहैर्व्ययमदलग्नराशिसंस्थैः
क्षीणे शशिन्यसुतकलत्रजन्म धीस्थे ॥ ४ ॥

Stanza 4.—If Saturn occupies birth, Venus
in the 7th when it is in gandantha and if the 5th
is unoccupied by benefics the person will become
husband of a barren woman. If malefics occupy
12th, 7th and birth with weak Moon in the 5th,
the person will have no wife or son.

NOTES

The last navamsas of Kataka, Vrischika and Meena
are called technically *Chakra sandhies* or important junctions. When these navamsas happen to become the 7th
house with Sukra there, with Yama (Saturn) in the lagna
and when there are no benefics in the 5th, the person's wife
will be a barren woman. This combination can arise only
in Makara, Vrishabha and Kanya. The author uses the
expression *Vandhyapathi*. This means that even if he
marries two or three wives he will get no children because
his wife or wives will be barren women. All the malefics
may be in 12th, 7th or birth or in any two or three of them,
weak Moon must be in the 5th. Under such circumstances
he will have no wife or children. (See notes on St. 5,
Ch. II for Kshina Chandra).

असितकुजयोर्विर्गेंऽस्तस्थे सिते तदवेक्षिते
परयुवतिगस्तौ चेत्सन्द् स्त्रिया सह पुंश्चलः ।
भृगुजशशिनोरस्तेऽभार्यो नरो विसुतोऽपि वा
परिणततनु नृक्षयोर्दृष्टौ शुभैः प्रमदापती ॥ ५ ॥

Stanza 5.—If Sukra occupies the 7th, which
happens to be the varga of Sani or Kuja and
aspected by them the person becomes fond of
other women. If Sani and Kuja join Chandra in
the 7th and have the aspect of Sukra the person
and his wife both become adulterous. If Sukra
and Chandra have Sani and Kuja in the 7th the

person becomes wifeless or issueless. If female
and male planets have Sani and Kuja in the 7th
aspected by benefics the couple would be married
when old.

NOTES

If Sukra occupies any one of the vargas of Sani or Kuja
and is located in the 7th and is aspected by any one of them
the person becomes adulterous.

The following I horoscope of a late ruling prince
illustrates this :—

The II is that of a woman noted for her incestuous
intercourse :—

Sukra	Moon	Kethu Kuja			Guru	Ravi Budha Sukra	
Ravi				Lagna			Rahu
Budha	I			Kethu	II		Moon Kuja
	Rahu	Guru	Birth Sani		Sani		

Look at the 7th house and 4th house in both. In I,
Sukra in 7th is aspected by Sani and 4th is aspected by Kuja.
In II, the 7th house has Kuja and Chandra, aspected by
Sani in Kuja's house and Sukra is aspected by Sani and 4th
has Ravi, Sukra and Budha and Kuja aspects Sani. She had
a reckless character.

If Chandra, Kuja and Sani are in conjunction in the 7th house and aspected by Sukra who is found in any of the vargas of Sani or Kuja, then the person goes in search of other women and his wife seeks other men. Both become adulterous. If Sukra and Chandra join in any sign having Sani and Kuja in the 7th house from them, the person will have no wife or children. Varahamihira uses *va* indicating *or* and meaning having no wife *or* children. But the learned commentator asks the readers to interpret the passage as conjunctional for *va* and gives a hint to interpret as having no wife and children.

If there are two planets in a house one female and the other a male and the 7th from them is occupied by Sani and Kuja and the latter have beneficial aspects, the person when old will marry an old woman.

The following horoscope of a rich zamindarini illustrates this. Sun is male, Budha is female and 7th from them is occupied by Sani and Guru aspects Sani. Kuja aspects the 7th from lagna. She lost a husband and after a few years married a second time. She is now dead.

	Sun Budha	Sukra	Kuja Guru
Rahu			Chan-dra Lagna
	RASI		Kethu
		Sani	

वंशच्छेत्ता खमदसुखगैश्चन्द्रदैत्येज्यपापैः
शिल्पी त्र्यंशे शशिसुतयुते केन्द्रसंस्थार्किदृष्टे ।
दास्यां जातो दितिसुतगुरौ रिफःगे सौरभागे
नीचोर्कें्द्रोर्मदनगतयोर्दृष्टयोः सूर्यजेन ॥ ६ ॥

Stanza 6.—If the 10th, 7th and 4th are occupied by Chandra, Sukra and malefics respectively, the person destroys his family. If Sani in kendra aspects the house indicated by the Drekkana joined by Budha, the person becomes a *silpi.* If Sukra occupies the 12th, joining the navamsa of Sani, the person becomes the son of a menial servant woman. If Ravi and Chandra occupy the 7th aspected by Sani, the person does degrading acts.

NOTES

The Moon must be in the 10th, Venus in the 7th, and malefics—Sun, Mars and Saturn in the 4th, to make the person's family extinct. There are some persons who represent the last of their families and with whose death, the family name ceases. This is considered to be a great misfortune as he will cause the termination of his family. Bhattotpala quotes Duryodhana the eldest son of Kurus as an example. All of them died and their family ceased to exist. Budha occupies some Drekkana. The house indicated by that Drekkana must be aspected by Sani who must be in a kendra, to produce a *silpi.* This term is made to indicate persons living by painting, engraving, etc., hence we may call these as artists or skilled men. Some authors interpret this part as indicating the aspect of Budha by Sani in the rasi. But as the author clearly uses *Thriamsay* it means Drekkana. Suppose Budha is in Mesha and in the 3rd Drekkana. This will be Dhanus. If, in the rasi, Sani occupies a kendra from lagna and aspects Dhanus then the person becomes an artist. Here it will be seen that if Budha is in the 3rd Drekkana, then it represents Dhanus and Sani is in the 10th from birth and therefore in a kendra. He aspects the 7th house Dhanus and such a combination produces *silpi*. But suppose Sani is in Thula.

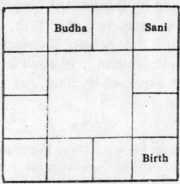

Even then he aspects Dhanus in the 3rd house, but as Thula is the 2nd house from lagna and not a kendra, there will be no yoga for producing a *silpi*. If Sukra is in the 12th from lagna and is located in the navamsa of Sani then the child will be born of a woman who is a menial servant in any capacity. If the Sun and the Moon are in the 7th house from lagna and aspected by Sani, the person does disgraceful and degrading acts, quite beneath the dignity of his family traditions. This can only happen on

2¼ days when the Sun and the Moon are joined together in a rasi in every month.

पापालोकितयोः सिताबनिजयोरस्तस्थयोर्वाध्यरुक्
चन्द्रे कर्कटवृश्चिकांशकगते पापैर्युते गुह्यरुक् ।
थ्रिग्रि रिःफधनस्थयोरशुभयोश्चन्द्रोदयेऽस्ते रवौ
चन्द्रे खेऽविनिजेऽस्तगे च विकलो यद्यर्कजो विशिगः ॥ ७ ॥

Stanza 7.—If Venus and Mars join the 7th house aspected by malefics, there will be serious danger from dysentery. If the Moon joins the navamsa of Cancer or Scorpio and is in conjunction with malefics, the person will have diseases in the secret places. If the Moon joins lagna, Sun in the 7th and two malefics in the 12th and 2nd, the person will be attacked by a serious form of leprosy. If the Moon occupies the 10th, Mars in the 7th and Saturn in the 2nd house from the Sun, the person will be defective in limbs.

NOTES

If Kuja and Sukra are in the 7th and evil planets aspect them, the person will suffer from *Vriddhiruk* or dysentery. There is a second reading which runs as *Ardha Deik* meaning that the man will have half sight. But this is not supported by the commentator. Among the European nations dysentery is dreaded like a great epidemic and sometimes it proves fatal. The Moon may be in any sign. If he joins the navamsas of Kataka or Vrischika and is in conjunction with a malefic, the person will have diseases

in private parts like sexual organ, testes, anus, etc.
Where should the Moon join the malefic, in rasi or
navamsa? The original seems to countenance both. In
many places where navamsas are stated the conjunctions
often refer to the rasi. The Moon should not only join
Kataka or Vrischika navamsas but must also join there
with malefics.   But suppose the Moon is in Kataka or
Vrischika navamsa and an evil planet joins him in the
rasi. I should attribute disease in private parts even in
this combination.

Chandra should be in Lagna, Ravi should be in the
7th and two evil planets Kuja and Sani should be in the
2nd and 12th to produce white leprosy. This is one form
of a hideous disease, and there are other forms such as
black, red and blue leprosy. The word in the original is
Ashubhas or evil planets and Bhattotpala interprets this as
referring to Sani and Kuja. When the Sun and the Moon
are in the 7th house from each other, the days must be
Full Moon days. The 2nd house from the Sun at the time
of birth is called Vesi. Saturn should be in the 2nd house
from the Sun, the Moon must be in the 10th house, and Mars
must be in the 7th house from lagna to produce defect in
the limbs. This means that either the man will have limbs
cut off by various weapons or he will be born without suitable limbs and become what we call defective or deformed.

अन्तः शशिन्यशुभयोर्मृगगे पतङ्गे
श्वासक्षयग्रिहकविद्रधिगुल्मभाजः ।
शोषी परस्परगृहांशगयो रवीन्द्रोः
क्षेत्रेऽथवा युगपदेकगयोः कुगो वा ॥ ८ ॥

Stanza 8.—When the Sun is in Makara, and
the Moon is between two malefics, the person
gets asthma, consumption, enlargement of spleen,
carbuncle or abdominal tumours. If the Sun
and the Moon mutually exchange their places in
Rasi or Amsa, the person gets pthisis. If these
two join together in any one of their houses, he
may become consumptive or emaciated.

NOTES

The Sun must be in Capricorn, and the Moon must be
between two evil planets, Saturn and Mars to produce
asthma, consumption, spleen enlargement, carbuncle (vidra-
dhi) or abdominal tumours. If the Sun is in Cancer and
the Moon is in Leo either in the rasi or in the navamsa
the person gets consumption. Some are of opinion that
the Sun must be both in the rasi and the navamsa of
Cancer while the Moon must be similarly situated in Leo
to produce this result. But Bhattotpala quotes from Gargi,
who plainly supports the first interpretation. If the Sun
and the Moon are (1) in Cancer or (2) in Leo, they produce
consumption or weakness in the body or emaciation or
undesirable leanness and debility. There are some people
who are not particularly sick but who are extremely weak.

चन्द्रेऽधिमध्यझषकर्किंमृगाजभागे
कुष्ठी समन्दरुधिरे तदवेक्षिते वा ।
यातैस्त्रिकोणमलिकर्किंवृषैर्मृंगे च
कुष्ठी च पापसहितैरवलोकितैर्वा ॥ ९ ॥

Stanza 9.—If the Moon occupies the 5th
amsa of Sagittarius or the amsas of Pisces,
Cancer, Capricorn or Aries, and aspected by or
is in conjunction with Saturn or Mars, the person
will suffer from leprosy.

If Scorpio, Cancer, Taurus or Capricorn
becomes one of the thrikonas aspected by or in
conjunction with evil planets, the person suffers
from leprosy.

NOTES

If the Moon joins the 5th navamsa of Dhanus, *viz.*,
Simha or the navamsa of Meena, Kataka, Makara or Mesha
having the aspects or conjunction of Kuja or Sani the man
suffers from leprosy. Bhattotpala explains that in such
conjunctions, suppose there is beneficial aspect the man
suffers from cutaneous eruptions or irritation, verging on
leprosy. This view of the commentator is supported by a
quotation from Yavaneswara which is clear on this point.
If Vrischika, Kataka, Vrishabha or Makara happens to be
the 5th or 9th from any lagna having an aspect or conjunction of a malefic, the person suffers from leprosy.

निधनारिधनव्ययस्थिता रविचन्द्रारयमा यथा तथा ।
बलवद्भृद्दोषकारणैर्मनुजानां जनयन्त्यनेत्रताम् ॥ १० ॥

Stanza 10.—If Ravi, Chandra, Kuja aud
Sani occupy 8th, 6th, 2nd and 12th in any way,
the person loses his sight by the elevation of that
Dhatu which is indicated by the most powerful
of these planets.

NOTES

Four planets are indicated here, *viz.*, Sun, Moon, Mars and Saturn and four houses, *viz.*, 2nd, 6th, 8th and 12th. Any of these planets may be located in any of the houses and the author requires no particular order or method. The *Dhatus* referred to are (1) Vata (wind), (2) Pitha (bile) and Sleshma (phlegm). Find out which of these four planets is the strongest and attribute that Dhatu, which is indicated by him. (See notes on Ch. II. Sts. 8-9-10-11). The sight will be lost or the blindness will be caused by the increase of such complaints, which are caused by the excess of these Dhatus.

नवमायवृतीयधीयुता न च सौम्यैरशुभा निरीक्षिताः ।
नियमाञ्छ्रवणोपघातदा रदवैकृत्यकारश्च सप्तमे ॥ ११ ॥

Stanza 11.—If malefics occupy 9th, 11th, 3rd and 5th houses unaspected by benefics, the person will suffer from deafness. If these evil planets are in the 7th house, there will be decomposition of the teeth.

NOTES

By malefics we are to understand here Ravi, Chandra (must be Kshina Chandra to be a malefic) Kuja and Sani. All these planets must be found in the 9th, 11th, 5th and 3rd. They may be in one or two or more houses or one in each of the houses. Then hard hearing or deafness will result. The deafness will be caused by the elevation of that Dhatu, which is governed by the most powerful among these planets. If all these planets are in the

7th house without beneficial aspect, the person suffers from bad or ugly teeth.   These results must be predicted during the periods and sub-periods of planets causing such combinations.   (See notes on St. 20, Ch. VIII).

उदयत्युडुपे सुरास्यगे सपिशाचोऽशुभयोत्त्रिकोणयोः ।
सोपप्लवमण्डले रवावुदयस्थे नयनापवर्जितः ॥ १२ ॥

Stanza 12.—If the Moon eclipsed by Rahu occupies birth and evil planets are found in trines, the person suffers from devils.

If the Sun is eclipsed and occupies the birth, the person becomes blind.

NOTES

When the Moon is eclipsed by Rahu and occupies the birth with evil planets in the 5th and 9th houses, the person suffers from spirits, devils, hobgoblins, etc. The belief in devils is still strong though many scientists may laugh at this statement. I have seen with my own eyes certain of these and I have in my humble experience witnessed a few cases of unnatural phenonena of my brother-in-law's wife said to be possessed of a devil, able to lift up a stone of about 100 lb. easily in her right hand, carry it to the river at Closepet and throw it into the water and then saying she would jump to the tree and fall down senseless. She lived a year later but could not remember anything personally though I have tried my best. I could not see devils *as they are*, but have seen men possessed of them.

If Ravi is eclipsed by Rahu, Kuja and Sani are found in the 5th and 9th houses the person becomes blind. In the original the occupation of konas by malefics is left out but it is to be supplied as in the first half.

संस्पृष्टः पवनेन मन्दगयुते द्यूने विलग्ने गुरौ
सोन्मादोऽवनिजे स्थितेऽस्तभवने जीवे विलग्नाश्रिते ।
तद्वत्स्वर्यसुतोद्येऽवनिसुते धर्मात्मजधननगे
जातो वा ससहस्ररश्मितनये क्षीणे व्यये शीतगौ ॥ १३ ॥

Stanza 13.—If Jupiter occupies birth and
Saturn is in the 7th, the person suffers from windy
complaints. If Jupiter occupies Lagna with Mars
in the 7th, the person suffers from insanity or
madness. If Saturn occupies Lagna and Mars
is found in 9, 7 or 5, the person suffers from
insanity. If weak Moon with Saturn joins the
12th house, the same insanity must be predicted.

NOTES

Asitirvataja Rogas or the principal complaints arising from
the excess of wind are 80 in number, and these take various forms in various constitutions. (*Vide* Charaka and Susruta Eng. Translation). When Guru is in Lagna and Sani
occupies the 7th house (from lagna and therefore from Guru
also) there will be suffering from windy complaints. If in
the same conjunction Kuja occupies the 7th instead of Sani,
the person suffers from insanity. If Saturn occupies Lagna
with Mars in 5, 7 or 9 the person suffers from insanity. If
Kshina Chandra joins Sani and occupies the 12th from
lagna the man suffers from insanity. Bhattotpala is not
explanatory in this connection. In the horoscope of Sri
Rama, birth is Kataka with Guru there and Kuja is in the

32

7th. Rama was not insane and nobody could ever attribute such a state to him. Here Sani is not in lagna, though Kuja is in the 7th and Kshina Chandra does not join Sani. Probably Bhattotpala means that Sani must be in Lagna and Kuja in 5, 7 or 9. At any rate Kuja and Sani aspecting each other cause a little idiosyncracy. Here as well as other horoscopes within my observation insanity must be predicted only when the planets are powerless and not in conjunction with others.

Sukra	Ravi	Budha	Kethu
			Birth Guru Moon
	Sri Rama's Horoscope		
Kuja			
Rahu		Sani	

राश्यंशपोष्णकरग्रीतकरामरेज्यै-
नीचाधिपांशकगतैररिभागगर्बा ।
एभ्योऽल्पमध्यबहुभिः क्रमशः प्रह्वताः
ज्ञेयाः स्वुरभ्युपगमक्रयगर्भदासाः ॥ १४ ॥

Stanza 14.—If the lord of the Rasyamsa, Sun, Moon and Jupiter join neecha or unfriendly amsa they produce self-slavery, slavery by purchase or hereditary slavery when one or two or more of the above planets occupy such positions.

NOTES

Rasyamsa is the navamsa occupied by the Moon. If its lord, Sun, Moon and Jupiter are found located in their neecha or unfriendly navamsas, they produce slavery. If one of them is so the person will go in as a slave by self-will ; if two are so occupied then he will be sold as a slave ; and if three or more are so located he will be descended from a hereditary family of slaves.

विकृतदशनः पापैर्दृष्टे वृषाजहयोद्ये
खलतिरशुभक्षेत्रे लग्ने हये वृषमेऽपि वा ।
नवमसुतगे पापैर्दृष्टे रवावदृढेक्षणो
दिनकरसुते नैकव्याधिः कुजे विकलः पुमान् ॥ १५ ॥

Stanza 15.—If birth happens to be Vrisha-bha, Mesha or Dhanus, aspected by malefics the person will have ugly teeth.   If birth falls in malevolent signs or Dhanus or Vrishabha and is aspected by evil planets the person becomes bald-headed.   If the Sun is in the 5th or 9th aspected by malefics the person will have weak eyes.   If Saturn is so situated he suffers from many complaints. If Mars is so situated there will be defect in organs.

NOTES

Ugly teeth, bald-headedness, short or weak visions, suffering from many diseases and possessing defective organs are also classified as misfortunes and no doubt they are so.

When the lagna falls in Vrishabha, Mesha or Dhanus aspected by malefics, the man will have ugly or ill-set teeth. When the birth falls in malefic signs like Mesha, Simha, Vrischika, Makara or Kumbha and also Dhanus or Vrishabha aspected by malefic planets, the person will have a bald head. If the Sun is in the 5th or 9th sign from lagna aspected by malefics, the person will have weak eyes. If Saturn is in the 5th or 9th from lagna aspected by malefics, there will be complaints of many varieties and if Kuja occupies the 5th or 9th aspected by evil planets, there will be some defect in the organs.

व्ययसुतधनधर्मगैरसौम्यै-
भवनसमाननिबन्धनं विकल्प्यम् ।
भुजगनिगडपाशभृद्दृकाणे-
बलवदसौम्यनिरीक्षितैश्च तद्वत् ॥ १६ ॥

Stanza 16.—If evil planets occupy 12th, 5th, 2nd or 9th, the person will be imprisoned according to the nature of that house. If lagna falls in Bhujaga or Nigada Drekkana, aspected by powerful malefics, the person will be similarly confined.

NOTES

If all the evil planets are in any one or more of these houses—*viz*., 2nd, 5th, 9th or 12th, the person will suffer bondage or imprisonment according to the nature of the houses they occupy. If the planets are in Aries, Taurus and Sagittarius the person will be tied by ropes, chains, etc.

If these evil planets are in Gemini, Virgo, Libra and
Aquarius, the person will be shakled or fettered. If these
evil planets are in Cancer, Capricorn and Pisces, the person
will be confined in *Durgas* or forts. If these are in Scorpio
their confinement will be in underground cells. If birth
falls in Bhujaga or Nigada Drekkana and if the rasi represented by this Drekkana is aspected by powerful evil
planets, the person's confinement will be similar to that Rasi.

Bhujaga Drekkanas are the 2nd and 3rd of Cancer, the
1st and 2nd of Scorpio and the last of Pisces. Nigada
Drekkana is the 1st of Makara. Bhujaga is the same as
serpent as mentioned already and Nigada is quadruped.
According to the original it would appear as if the author
has given a 3rd Drekkana called the Pasabhrit. But in
the enumeration of the 36 Drekkanas in Ch. XXVII no
mention is made of Pasabhrit as a separate one. Hence
Bhattotpala asks the readers to refer this as an adjective to
the Bhujaga and Nigada Drekkanas.

परुषवचनोऽपस्मारार्तः क्षयी च निशापतौ
सरवितनये वक्रलोकं गते परिवेषगे ।
रवियमकुजैः सौम्याद्दृष्टैर्नभस्थलमाश्रितै-
भृतकमनुजः पूर्वोदिष्टैर्वराधममध्यमाः ॥ १७ ॥

Stanza 17.—If the Moon with the ring or
halo around him joins Saturn and is aspected by
Mars, the person will be harsh, suffer from
hysteria and consumption. If the Sun, Saturn
and Mars are in the 10th house unaspected by

benefics, the person will become a servant. If three or two or one of them occupy the 10th, the man becomes inferior, ordinary and superior servant respectively.

NOTES

Sometimes we see haloes or ring-like appearances round the Sun as well as the Moon. In ordinary parlance they denote rain or wet weather. When there is a ring (Parivesha) round the Moon, Saturn joins him and Mars aspects such a Moon the person will suffer from the above complaints. Here three different states for Moon are indicated (1) halo round his disc, (2) conjunction with Saturn, and (3) aspect of Mars. There are also three complaints mentioned by the author, *viz.*, (1) harshness in speech, (2) hysteria, and (3) consumption. Bhattotpala therefore observes that if the Moon is possessed of one of these states the person will have one of these complaints, if two the person will suffer from two complaints, and if all three states are found the person suffers from the three complaints named. Then the author gives a special combination for servantship. If the Sun, Mars and Saturn unaspected by any benefic occupy the 10th, the person becomes a menial or servant. If there are two of these planets in the 10th, then he becomes a higher menial. If there is only one planet in the 10th, then he becomes the leader of menials or head-servant.

CHAPTER XXIV

STRIJATAKADHYAYA

स्त्रीजाताकाध्यायः

यद्यत्फलं नरभवे क्षममङ्गनानां
तत्तद्वदेत्पतिषु वा सकलं विधेयम् ।
तासां तु भर्तृमरणं निधने वपुस्तु
लग्नेन्दुगं सुभगतास्तमये पतिश्च ॥ १ ॥

Stanza 1.—Such of those results as the females could not possess or enjoy must be attributed to their husbands. From the 8th house in a female's horoscope the death of her husband, from the birth sign and the Moon her (female's) own physical beauty and from the 7th house her husband and his love to her must be predicted.

NOTES

From the commencement of this work, the author has been detailing results for males and now he specially devotes a chapter to the females with a view to point out certain physical and mental peculiarities which do not happen to males but which are confined only to females. Delivery, conception, attainment of age, appearance of menses, etc., are peculiar to females. But suppose a planet indicates health or sickness, a female can have it as well as a male. There are three kinds of results which must be

differentiated.   First, there are some events which must be
predicted only for females.   Second, there are some which
must be predicted for their husbands and third there are
others which can be shared in both by the females as well
as by their husbands.   The results   indicated   in   St. 1,
Ch. XIII are applicable to females.   Rajayogas, etc., must
be referred to their husbands as also to them.   The results
such as produced by Sunapha, Anapha, etc.,   must be
applied to both females and their husbands. We have
heard of several eminent queens and empresses who have
managed their estates and kingdoms with great credit and
ability.   The nature of the husband, his love to her and
qualifications must be predicted from the 7th house in a
female's horoscope, as the nature of the wife, her love and
her features must be predicted with reference to the 7th
house in a man's horoscope.

युग्मेषु लग्नशशिनोः प्रकृतिस्थिता स्त्री
सच्छीलभूषणयुता शुभदृष्टयोश्च ।
ओजस्थयोश्च मनुजाकृतिशीलयुक्ता
पापा च पापयुतवीक्षितयोर्गुणोना ॥ २ ॥

Stanza 2.—If the birth and Moon fall in
even signs, the female will be modest, if they are
aspected by benefics she will be virtuous, if the
birth and Moon fall in odd signs, she will have
masculine temperament and form, and if these
two are aspected or are in conjunction with
malefics, she will be sinful and characterless.

NOTES

If Chandra and Lagna both fall in even signs such as Kataka, Vrishabha, etc., she will be natural and possess feminine grace and temperament. If Lagna and Chandra are aspected by good planets, she will be virtuous, modest and full of feminine grace. If these two—birth and Moon— are in odd signs, such as Mesha, Mithuna, etc., she will become masculine and if aspected by or are in conjunction with evil planets, she will become sinful, cruel and masculine in form and temperament. Her thoughts, deeds and behaviour, will be devoid of feminine grace. If birth falls in an even sign and Chandra is in an odd or *vice versa*, she will be possessed of common temperament. If one of them is aspected by a benefic and another by a malefic, the character, etc., will be middling, *i.e.*, she will be in some acts feminine and others masculine.

कन्यैव दुष्टा व्रजतीह दास्यं
साध्वी समाया कुचरित्रयुक्ता ।
भूम्यात्मजर्क्षे क्रमगोंशकेषु
वक्रार्किजीवेन्दुजभार्गवानाम् ॥ ६ ॥

Stanza 3.—If the birth or Moon falls in the house of Mars and occupies the Trimsamsa of Mars, Saturn, Jupiter, Mercury or Venus, the girl will be immoral before puberty, dancing woman, virtuous, double hearted, or sinful respectively.

NOTES

Trimsamsas have been explained by me under notes to St. 7, Ch. I. If the birth or Moon occupies Aries or

Scorpio and falls in the Trimsamsa of Mars, she becomes
adulterous even before she attains her age. The expression
also means that she has connection before marriage. If the
Trimsamsa falls under Saturn, she becomes a dancing girl
before her puberty ; if the Trimsamsa falls under Guru, she
will be] virtuous ; if the Trimsamsa falls under Mercury,
she, becomes deceitful or double hearted ; and if Venus
governs that Trimsamsa, she will be sinful or immoral.
In this Chapter, the results are indicated with reference to
Trimsamsa and Bhattotpala advises his readers to examine
them carefully. The *Amsa* used in the original refers to
Trimsamsa as will be clearly explained later on by the
author. The world used is *Kanya* and it means a girl who
has not attained her puberty. Kanya also means a girl who
is not yet married. There cannot be any immorality before
puberty or attaining her age as there can be no sex-
connection. No doubt a boy of 10 and a girl of 10 may
hug each other or try to imitate the sex act, but it can
never be construed an immoral act. The text says *Kannaiva*
meaning before marriage. Kanya means only a girl and it
is not stated as one who has not attained her age. The text
says before marriage and seems alright.

दुष्टा पुनर्भूः सगुणा कलाज्ञा
ख्याता गुणैश्चासुरपूजितर्क्षे ।
स्यात्कापटी क्लीबसमा सती च
बौधे गुणाढ्या प्रविकीर्णकामा ॥ ४ ॥

Stanza 4.—If birth or Chandra falls in
Vrishabha or Thula rasi and occupies the

Trimsamsas of the above planets, she becomes sinful, marrying a second husband, virtuous, skilful in arts and reputed respectively. If birth or Chandra falls in Mithuna or Kanya and occupies the above planetary Trimsamsa, the woman becomes deceitful, impotent, virtuous, good and adulterous respectively.

NOTES

If birth or Chandra falls in Vrishabha or Thula and occupies the Trimsamsa of Kuja, she becomes immoral ; in Sani, she marries a second husband while the first is living (Punarbhu). In Guru she will be virtuous; in Budha she will be skilled in fine arts like painting, music, etc., and in Sukra she will be famous for her good qualities. If birth or Chandra falls in Mithuna or Kanya and occupies the Trimsamsa of Kuja, she becomes deceitful, in Sani's Trimsamsa she will be impotent, in Guru's she becomes virtuous, in Budha's she will be blessed with good qualities, in Sukra's she will become adulterous promiscuously, i.e., she does not care who the man is so long as he satisfies her lust.

स्वच्छन्दा पतिघातिनी बहुगुणा शिल्पिन्यसाध्वीन्दुमे
त्राचारा कुलटार्कमे नृपवधूः पुंचोषिता गम्यगा ।
जैवे नैकगुणाल्परत्यतिगुणा विज्ञानयुक्ता सती
दासी नीचरतार्किमे पतिरता दुष्टाऽप्रजास्वांशकैः ॥ ५ ॥

Stanza 5.—If Chandra or birth falls in Kataka and occupies the Trimsamsa of the

planets already named, she does what she likes,
causes death to husband, blessed with good
qualities, skilled in arts and immoral respectively.
If birth or Chandra falls in Simha and occupies
the Trimsamsas of the planets already named,
she will become masculine, adulterous, queen,
manly, and commit incestuous intercourse
respectively.   If birth or Chandra falls in Meena
or Dhanus and occupies the above named
Trimsamsas, the woman will be good, have little
sexual desire, virtuous, skilled in arts and
adulterous respectively.   If birth or Moon falls
in Capricorn or Aquarius and occupies the
above Trimsamsas, the woman becomes servant,
fond of low men, virtuous, sinful and childless
respectively.

NOTES

The Trimsamsas are running in the following order:
Kuja, Ravi, Guru, Budha and Sukra and the results must
be attributed to them respectively. If birth or Chandra
occupies Kataka and is in Trimsamsa of—

Kuja = self-willed and doing as she likes.
Sani = causes death to her husband. This may be
by herself or by prompting others and abetting his murder.
Guru = blessed with many admirable qualities.
Budha = skilled in refined arts.
Sukra = evil tempered or sinful.

If birth or Chandra falls in Simha and is found in the T. Amsa of Kuja=masculine in temperament. Here some read the original as *Vachata* instead of *Nrachare* and explain it as meaning very talkative and impertinent.

> Sani=adulterous.
>
> Guru=wife of a king or a ruler.
>
> Budha=masculine.

Sukra=committing adultery among prohibited relations or among forbidden castes and communities. The word used is *Agamyya*, that is going to a person with whom she ought never to have any connection.

If birth or Chandra occupies Meena or Dhanus and falls in T. Amsa of—

> Kuja=blessed with good qualities.
>
> Sani=easily satisfied in sexual intercourse or possessed of weak sexual desire. There are some men and women who are not passionate while there are others who are very lustful.
>
> Guru=blessed with all good qualities.
>
> Budha=skilled in fine arts.
>
> Sukra=immoral.

If birth falls in Makara or Kumbha and occupies the T. Amsa of—

> Kuja=servant.
>
> Sani=fond of low or worthless men.
>
> Guru=virtuous.
>
> Budha=bad or sinful.
>
> Sukra=barren or issueless.

I have explained these at considerable length because
the students may in a hurry misapply the words or expressions and thus fall into errors. *T. Amsa* stands for Trimsamsa. Each lagna contains 30 bhagas or degrees and
the Trimsamsas, are distributed among the five planets
Kuja, Sani, Guru, Budha and Sukra.

शशिलग्नसमायुक्तैः फलं त्रिंशशकैरिदम् ।
बलाबलविकल्पेन तयोरुक्तं विचिन्तयेत् ॥ ६ ॥

Stanza 6.—The results have now been
described for Lagna or Chandra in the various
T. Amsas, and the results must be ascertained
with reference to the strength or weakness of birth
and Chandra.

NOTES

Lagna as well as Chandra must necessarily occupy some
Trimsamsa, and this word is now distinctly used by
Varahamihira in this stanza. If both of them occupy the
same T. Amsa then the results indicated will be powerful
whether good or bad. But if one of them occupies a good
and another a bad T. Amsa then the results will have to be
modified according to their sources of strength. If one of
them is stronger than the other, then the results must be
given for the stronger of the two and not for the weaker.
In all these cases there should be no haste. For, to find
out the character of a man or woman, there are so many
other planetary conjunctions, whose influences should also
be taken into consideration.

दृक्संस्थावसितसितौ परस्परांशे
शौक्रे वा यदि घटराशिसंभवोंऽशः ।
स्त्रीभिः स्त्रीमदनविषानलप्रदीप्तैः
संशान्तिं नयति नराकृतिस्थितामिः ॥ ७ ॥

Stanza 7.—If Sani and Sukra are in each
other's navamsas, aspecting mutually, or if the
birth falls in Vrishabha or Thula, with the
navamsa rising in Kumbha the woman will get
sexual satisfaction from females dressed in male
attire.

NOTES

Here Sani must be in Sukra's and Sukra must be in
Sani's navamas with mutual aspects or the lagna must fall
in one of the houses of Sukra, *viz.*, Vrishabha or Thula,
with the rising navamsa of Kumbha to produce these
results. There are some women whose strong passions are
not satisfied by men and who resort to women for gratifica-
tion, with male leather organs attached to their waists. In
the History of the world many abominable practices have
been recorded from time immemorial and human nature is
a most puzzling problem for the philosophers to solve.
(*Vide* Dr. Mehta's ' Sexual Abnormalities ').

शून्ये कापुरुषोऽबलेऽस्तभवने सौम्यग्रहावीक्षिते
क्लीबोऽस्ते बुधमन्दयोश्वरगृहे नित्यं प्रवासान्वितः ।
उत्सृष्टा रविणा कुजेन विधवा बाल्येऽस्तराशिस्थिते
कन्यैवाशुभवीक्षितेर्कतनये शून्ये जरां गच्छति ॥ ८ ॥

Stanza 8.—If the 7th house is powerless, unoccupied and unaspected by benefics, the husband will be mean. If Mercury and Saturn are in the 7th house, the husband will be impotent. If the 7th is a movable sign, the husband will be constantly travelling. If the 7th is occupied by the Sun, aspected by malefics, she will be rejected by her husband. If there is Mars in the 7th aspected by evil planets, she becomes a widow early. If Saturn is in the 7th aspected by malefics, she will become old without marriage.

NOTES

These combinations must be taken both for Lagna and also for Chandra. If the 7th is occupied by Saturn and Mercury, the husband will be a eunuch or one who has no male organ. Bhattotpala rightly expands the idea suggested by the author about the movable nature of the 7th house. If the 7th house is fixed then the husband will always reside with the wife, but when it is a common sign the husband will be half travelling and half residing at home. Find out whether Chandra or Lagna is powerful and judge of the results from the stronger of the two. A question may be raised as to why these results must be predicted with reference to Lagna or Chandra, since the author makes no mention of Chandra in the original. Bhattotpala rightly suggests that as the results are named for all the planets in the 7th except for Chandra, the author implies clearly that the results must be predicted with reference to both.

आग्नेयैर्विंधवास्तराशिसहितैर्मिश्रैः षुनर्भूर्भवेत्
कूरे हीनबलेऽस्तगे स्वपतिना सौम्येक्षिते प्रोज्झिता ।
अन्योन्यांशगयोः सितावनिजयोरन्यप्रसक्ताञ्जना
द्यूने वा यदि शीतरश्मिसहितौ भर्तुस्तदानुज्ञया ॥ ९ ॥

Stanza 9.—If there are several malefics in the 7th she becomes a widow. If there are evil and good planets there, she will marry a second husband in the same caste. If there is a powerless evil planet in the 7th aspected by a benefic, she will be rejected by her husband. If Venus and Mars exchange their navamsas, she will be adulterous. If the Moon joins Venus and Mars in the 7th, she becomes adulterous with her husband's connivance.

NOTES

If there are several evil planets in the 7th, the girl is sure to become a widow. If the Sun or Saturn or Mars joins the 7th perfectly powerless and possess the aspect of a benefic, the girl will be rejected by her husband. Venus must be in the navamsa (Aries or Scorpio) of Mars and Mars must be in the navamsa (Taurus or Libra) of Venus, to produce an immoral woman. If Venus and Mars are in the 7th with the Moon then the woman commits adultery with the consent or connivance of her husband. Truth is stranger than fiction. Often we see woman encouraged to do evil acts by her friends, relations, parents and husbands for various considerations. In royalties and official classes these practices are more rampant on account of the temporal advantages, which the men fancy will flow to them by prostituting their wives and daughters. The following horoscopes illustrate the truth of the above.

In I, the 7th is aspected by two evil planets and Guru as lord of 1 and 10 is bad in 7th. Hence became a widow.

In II, Sukra (Bhartrukaraka) is aspected by Sani and 7th house is aspected by Sani. Kuja and Sani have joined.

In III, the woman had a reckless character and incestuous intercourse. (See Sukra and Kuja enchanging their navamsa.)

In IV, the Moon and Kuja are in 7 and she is separated from her husband and leading a loose life.

Kuja Sani Birth		Rahu		Rahu		Guru	x
Moon	I Became a widow early				II Deserted by her husband		
Sukra	Ravi Ketbu	Budha	Guru	Lagna	Sukra	Budha	Ravi Moon Kuja Sani Kethu

Ravi	Sukra	Kuja	Kethu		Moon Kuja	Kethu	
	Navamsa III Kundali		Guru		IV		
Sani			Budha				
Rahu		Lagna	Moon	Ravi Budha Sukra	Rahu	Lagna Guru	Sani

सौरार्क्षे लग्रगे सेन्दुशुक्रे
मात्रा सार्द्धं बन्धकी पापदृष्टे।
कौजेऽस्तांशे सौरिणा व्याधियोनि-
श्वारुश्रोणी वल्लभा सद्ग्रहांशे ॥ १० ॥

Stanza 10.—If the house of Mars or Saturn becomes Lagna with the Moon, and Venus there is aspected by malefics the girl becomes adulterous along with her mother. If the 7th navamsa from the Amsa Lagna falls in a house of Mars, aspected by Saturn, the woman's sexual organ will be diseased. If the 7th navamsa falls in a beneficial house, the woman will be handsome and loved by her husband.

NOTES

If Lagna falls in Aries, Scorpio, Capricorn or Aquarius joined by the Moon and Venus and aspected by malefics, the girl as well as her mother become immoral. There are numberless families in which when mothers are immoral girls also get into such nasty habits. When the 7th navamsa falls in Aries or Scorpio and is aspected by Saturn, the sexual organ will be rotten or diseased. This can happen only when the navamsa of the lagna falls in Taurus or Libra. The woman may keep a general healthy appearance or even possess fairly good health but she will have her private parts diseased. If the 7th navamsa falls in a beneficial sign her sexual organ will be healthy and she will be loved by her husband. Subhaga and Durbhaga may also mean handsome or repulsive, much depends upon the selection of the couple and the attraction and repulsion of their personal electrical currents. These currents are generally of two kinds, external and internal. First, a man and a woman may be attracted by external currents and may like each other. But when they join sexually, there will be further discharges of magnetic currents, which if not agreeable make the couple repulsive and miserable. The marriage relations must be carefully coupled with reference to astrological principles as otherwise they become failures and cause great misery to the combining parties. That is why there are so many divorce cases owing to sexual inadaptability.

वृद्धो मूर्खः सूर्यजर्क्षेंऽशके वा
स्त्रीलोलः स्यात् क्रोधनश्चावनेये ।
शौक्रे कान्तोऽतीव सौभाग्ययुक्तो
विद्वान् भर्ता नैपुञश्च बौधे ॥ ११ ॥

Stanza 11.—If the 7th from lagna or navamas falls in the house of Saturn, the husband will be old and stubborn; if the 7th from lagna or navamsa falls in the house of Mars, the husband will be fond of other women and cruel; if the 7th falls in the house of Venus, the husband will be handsome and loving; and if the 7th falls in the house of Mercury, the husband will be learned and intelligent.

NOTES

Now the author gives results of the 7th house when it is unoccupied by any planet. The 7th house may be taken from the lagna or its navamsa. Take an illustration. This is the horoscope of a woman (now widowed) born on the 10th September 1895 at about sunrise. Here it will be

		Moon			Mer. Rahu		
Rahu			Jupiter	Mars Venus Saturn		NAVAMSA	
	RASI		Sun Birth Kethu				
		Sani	Mars Mer. Venus	Moon	Birth Sun	Jup. Kethu	

seen that there are no planets in the 7th house both in the rasi and also in the navamsa. Therefore the 7th from lagna or its navamsa must be taken. As the 7th from Lagna is Aquarius, one of the houses of Saturn the husband will be aged or old and also will be stubborn.

मदनवशगतो मृदुश्च चान्द्रे
त्रिदशगुरौ गुणवान् जितेन्द्रियश्च ।
अतिमृदुरतिकर्मकृच्चसौर्ये
भवति गृहेऽस्तमयस्थितेऽशके वा ॥ १२ ॥

Stanza 12.—If the 7th falls in Cancer, the husband will be passionate and mild. If the 7th

falls in Sagittarius or Pisces, the husband will be
good and control his passions. If the 7th falls
in Leo, the husband will be mild and hard
working.

NOTES

If the 7th house falls in Cancer or its amsa (Cancer)
the husband will be passionate and mild. He will be very
fond of sexual intercourse but his nature will be mild.
The other combinations are easily understood. In the last
portion the Sanskrit expression is *Atimriduratikarmakrit*,
which may be divided into (1) Atimriduhu = very mild, and
(2) Atikarmakrit = very hard working; when taken as a
compound word, the meaning is very mild and passionate.
Another version is *Ratikarmakrit* one fond of sexual union.
As given under St. 11 if the 7th house in rasi differs from
the 7th house in the amsa, then the more powerful of the
two houses must be taken and attributes referred to it
must be predicted.

ईर्ष्यान्विता सुखपरा शशिशुक्रलग्ने
ऽन्दोः कलासु निपुणा सुखिता गुणाढ्या ।
शुक्रज्ञयोस्तु रुचिरा सुभगा कलाज्ञा
त्रिष्वप्यनेकवसुसौख्यगुणा शुभेषु ॥ १३ ॥

Stanza 13.—If the Moon and Venus are in
lagna, the woman will be jealous and fond of
happiness. If the Moon and Mercury occupy the
birth, she will be skilled in arts, happy and
blessed with good character. If Venus and

Mercury join the birth, she will be handsome, beloved and skilled in fine arts. If three benefics are in birth, the woman will have much wealth, great happiness and fine character.

NOTES

There are five combinations here contemplated although the original refers only to four. The word *Api* (even that or that too) used indicates the combination of Mercury, Venus and Jupiter. Thus there may be in Lagna (1) Moon and Mercury, (2) Moon and Venus, (3) Venus and Mercury, (4) Moon, Venus and Mercury, and (5) Venus, Jupiter and Mercury. The meaning is plain enough to require further notes.

कूरेऽष्टमे विधवता निघनेश्वरोंशे
यस्य स्थितो वयसि तस्य समे प्रदिष्टा ।
सत्स्वर्थगेषु मरणं स्वयमेव तस्याः
कन्यालिगोहरिषु चाल्पसुतत्वमिन्दौ ॥ १४ ॥

Stanza 14.—The widowhood comes at that age which is indicated by the lord of the amsa occupied by the lord of the 8th house, when there is an evil planet in the 8th house. If benefics occupy the 2nd, she dies before her husband. If the Moon is in Virgo, Scorpio, Taurus or Leo, she will have few children.

NOTES

That woman becomes a widow whose 8th house from lagna is occupied by a cruel planet. When does she get it

is the question which the author tries here to solve. The
lord of the 8th house must be in some navamsa. Find the
lord of this navamsa and ascertain his age. The girl
becomes a widow at a time similar to that age. But this
idea does not recommend itself to Bhattotpala and his
arguments are summarised for ready reference. Some are
of opinion the ages of planets must be taken as detailed in
St. 9, Chapter VIII. The following are the ages given for
the planets :—

Chandra	...	1 year
Kuja	...	2 years
Budha	...	9 ,,
Sukra	...	20 ,,
Guru	...	18 ,,
Ravi	...	20 ,,
Sani	...	50 ,,
Total	...	120

The word used in the text is *Vayas* and it is to be interpreted as referring to periods and sub-periods and not to the
ages of the planets. Because, if the lord of the 8th is in
Moon's or Mars navamsa then the age indicated will be
one or two years. It is absurd to think that the girls would
be married at one or two years of their age, and therefore
they cannot become widows. Therefore the right interpretation will be to find out the period or the sub-period
of the lord of the navamsa occupied by the lord of the
8th and predict the widowhood during such times *after the
marriage*. In the original text, the words used are *Vayasi—
thasya—samay* and the author clearly says at that age,
which is equal to the age of the planet, who is the lord of
the navamsa occupied by the lord of the 8th house.

Bhattotpala clearly introduces, on his own authority, the words—after the marriage—in the commentaries.   If this holds good then the interpretation he condemns is as faulty as his own offered solution.   For, if the idea after the marriage is introduced then the girl becomes a widow after one or two or nine years as indicated by the lord of the navamsa, after her marriage and not when she is one or two years old.   If we take the Dasantardasas the same objection rules good unless we take the expression ‘ after the marriage ’.   For suppose the girl gets the Dasa or the Antardasa of the lord of the navamsa occupied by the lord of the 8th when she is an infant of one or two years, then the objection raised by Bhattotpala will have to be returned back to him in his own coin and the same absurdity of widowhood at one or two years has to be pointed out.   He may have charged other writers with dropping the expression ‘ after the marriage ’ but he has probably overlooked the word *samay* in the text and this is very important.   If there is a malefic in the 8th and benefics in the 2nd she will die before her husband.   In the text *benefics* is used while Bhattotpala says that even a single benefic in the second will kill her before her husband.   When the Moon occupies Taurus, Virgo, Scorpio or Leo, she will have few children.

सौरे मध्यबले बलेन रहितैः शीतांशुशुक्रेन्दुजैः
शेषैर्वीर्यसमन्वितैः पुरुषिणी यद्योजराश्युद्गमः ।
जीवारास्फुजिदिन्दवेषु बलिषु प्राग्लग्नराशौ समे
विख्यातगखिलशास्त्रयुक्तिकुशला स्त्री ब्रह्मवादिन्यपि ॥ १५ ॥

Stanza 15.—If Saturn is moderately power-ful, if Venus, Mercury and Moon are powerless

and the rest are powerful and if the birth falls in
an odd sign the woman will be adulterous.   If
lagna falls in an even sign and Guru, Kuja, Sukra
and Budha are powerful, she will become famous,
learned in many sciences, and a vedantini.

NOTES

Two combinations are given here. Sani must be neither
powerful nor powerless, Chandra, Sukra and Budha must
be entirely powerless and the rest, *viz.*, Surya, Kuja and
Guru must be powerful with the lagna in an odd sign like
Mesha, Mithuna, Simha, etc., then the woman will have
many lovers. No. IV horoscope given under stanza 9 of
this Chapter, illustrates this clearly. Lagna is odd (Thula),
Sani is in 12, not very powerful, Chandra is with Kuja and
Budha and Sukra in an enemy's house with Ravi are
powerless while Ravi in 3, Guru in Lagna and Kuja in his
own house are very powerful, thus making the woman very
loose in her character. Guru, Kuja, Sukra and Budha must
be powerful and may be found in any house and when the
lagna falls in an even sign, the woman will become famous,
versed in many sciences and a vedantini or one who seeks
Para Brahma.

पापेऽस्ते नवमगतग्रहस्य तुल्यां
प्रब्रज्यां युवतिरूपैत्यसंशयेन ।
उद्वाहे वरणविधौ मदानकाले
चिन्तायामपि सकलं विधयमेतत् ॥ १६ ॥

Stanza 16.—If an evil planet occupies the
7th, she will embrace that Sanyasa, which is
represented by the planet occupying the 9th

house.   These results may be foretold during the
wedding, during the search for the girl or during
the query.

NOTES

The author now introduces a new phase. The results
foretold when there are evil planets in the 7th, will only be
verified when there are no planets in the 9th house. By
this it is clear that when there are planets in the 9th house
the former results cannot be predicted. The woman will
take to that kind of *Pravrajya*, which is represented by the
planet in the 9th house. (See St. 1, Ch. XV).

These results detailed in this Chapter must be applied
only to the horoscopes of females and to none else. The
results will have to be predicted at the times at which we
have shown them to happen.

Varahamihira has written a work called *Vivahapatalam*
or marriage combinations. We have not seen this work
but Bhattotpala refers to two works one *Brihat* and the
other *Laghu*. When there is any difference between the
combinations sketched here during the marriage time and
those explained in Vivahapatalam, the latter must be given
credit. Varahamihira was really a great genius and seems
to have traversed all the departments of astrology in
a most masterly way. " Stri Jataka ", gives much information about female horoscopes and readers would do
well to go through that book dealing exclusively with all
aspects of a woman's life. " Sarvartha Chintamani "
chapter on 7th house is very exhaustive in dealing with
women's breasts, private parts, character, sex-pleasures,
dry or wet organs, and such other details.

CHAPTER XXV

NIRYANADHYAYA

नैर्याणिकाध्यायः

(Death)

मृत्युर्मृत्युगृहेक्षणेन बलिमिस्तद्धातुकोपोद्भव-
स्तत्संयुक्तभगात्रजो बहुभवो वीर्यान्विवतैर्भूरिभिः ।
अग्न्यम्बवायुधजोज्वरामयकृतस्तट्रक्षुत्कृतश्चाष्टमे
स्व्याँदैर्निधने चरादिषु परस्वाध्वप्रदेशेष्विति ॥ १ ॥

Stanza 1.—The man dies from such disease
as is indicated by the nature of the planet which
aspects the 8th house and in that organ or part
of the body which is represented by the 8th house
in the division under Kalapurusha. If many
planets aspect the 8th house there will be many
diseases before death. If the Sun, etc., occupy
the 8th house, the person dies from fire, water,
weapon, fever, disease, thirst and hunger respectively. If the 8th house is movable, etc., the death
will happen in foreign country, own land and
during travelling respectively.

NOTES

This is an important verse showing the nature and
place of death. As represented on several occasions the

results shown by the planetary conjunctions may be partly
or completely averted by the development of will-power
in the right direction. Hence consultation and previous
knowledge becomes of paramount importance. First, the
author takes the causes for death by the indications of the
aspecting planets. Planets have been given various *Dhatus*
as detailed in Sts. 8, 9, 10 and 11 in Ch. II. The meaning
is that if the Sun aspects the 8th house, the disease will be
developed by bile or heat. If the Moon aspects the 8th
house, the disease will be raked up by wind and phlegm ; if
Mars aspects it, by bile or heat ; if Mercury aspects the 8th,
the disease will be developed by a mixture of vata, pitha
and sleshma ; if Jupiter aspects the 8th, by phlegm ; if
Venus aspects the 8th, by phlegm and wind ; and if Saturn
aspects it, by wind. The disease will take a serious form
or appear in that organ of the human body which is governed by Kalapurusha. Take a horoscope. Here the 8th
house from Lagna is Thula and it is occupied by Guru
and aspected by Sani and Budha and also by Kuja in the
4th. But Thula falls among the organs of Kalapurusha
in the abdomen. According to Bhattotpala when there
are no planets in the 8th, aspects must be considered but
when there are planets in the 8th, aspects should not be
taken into notice. Thus we find Guru in the 8th and it
represents abdominal regions. Guru represents disease of
a complicated nature difficult to diagnose, and the man
should die from abdominal disorders. If Jupiter is powerful here then the result will result from good work or
Subhakarma and if he is powerless, from evil acts or
Papakarma. Among the Medical works, in this land of the
Vedas, diseases may result from good as well as bad work
or deeds. Diseases from good work can be remedied while

diseases from evil works are difficult to cure. Suppose the
horoscope stands thus :

	Kuja	
Sukra Kethu	RASI	
Ravi Guru Budha		Sani Rahu
Chandra	Birth	

Here there are no planets in the 8th house, but it is
aspected by the Moon, who is given very much of wind
and phlegm. The 8th house is Taurus which represents
the face of Kalapurusha. Accordingly when this man
dies, there will be some disorder in the face causing death.
Suppose there are no planets in the 8th house and it is
unaspected, the mode of dealth is detailed further by the
author in St. 11 of this Chapter. After finding out the
kind of disease, the author also proceeds to give the place
of death. If there is Sun in the 8th from lagna, death will
be caused by fire, if the Moon by water, if Mars by weapons,
if Mercury by fever, if Jupiter by complicated disease, if
Venus by thirst, and if Saturn by hunger. If the 8th is
movable, death occurs in a foreign country. If it is fixed,
in his own country and if it falls in a common sign it occurs
while travelling.

शैलाग्रामिहतस्य द्र्येकुजयोर्मृत्युः खबन्धुस्थयोः
कूपे मन्दशशाङ्कभूमितनयैर्बन्धवस्तकर्मस्थितैः ।
कन्यायां स्वजनाद्धिमोष्णकरयोः प्रापग्रहैर्दृष्टयोः
स्यातां यद्युभयोदयेऽर्कशशिनौ तोये तदा मज्जितः ॥ २ ॥

Stanza 2.—If the Sun and Mars occupy the
4th or 10th, death will be caused by stones. If
Saturn, Moon and Mars are in 4th, 7th and 10th
respectively, death will be caused by falling into
a well. If the Sun and the Moon are in Virgo
aspected by malefics, he will be killed by his own
people. If the birth falls in a common sign with
the Sun and the Moon in it, the person will be
drowned.

NOTES

Other modes of death are indicated here. If the Sun
and Mars join together and occupy the 4th or the 10th,
death results from blows from stones or rocks. When
Saturn is in 4, Moon in 7 and Mars in 10, the person falls
into a well and dies. When Virgo (Kanya) is occupied by
the Sun and [the Moon aspected by Mars or Saturn, the
person will be killed by his own men or relations. If birth
falls in common signs like Gemini, Virgo, Sagittarius or
Pisces and conjoined by the Sun and the Moon, death will
be caused by drowning. The Sun and the Moon join
together in a month for only 2¼ days and then only these
combinations are possible

मन्दे ककटगे जलोदरकृतो मृत्युंमृगाङ्क मृगे
शस्त्राग्निप्रभवः शशिन्यशुभयोर्मध्ये कुजर्क्षे स्थिते ।
कन्यायां रुधिरोत्थशोषजनितस्तद्वत्स्थिते शीतगौ
सौरर्क्षे यदि तद्वदेव हिमगौ रज्जवग्निपातैः कृतः ॥ ३ ॥

Stanza 3.–If Saturn is in Cancer and the Moon
occupies Makara the person dies from jalodara.
If the Moon occupies the house of Mars and is
betwixt evil planets the person dies from weapons
or fire. If the Moon occupies Virgo between malefics, death comes from corrupt blood or consumption. If the Moon occupies one of the
houses of Saturn between malefics the person dies
by ropes, fire or fall.

NOTES

When the Moon is in Capricorn and Saturn is in Cancer,
they will be not only occupying watery signs but will also
have mutual aspects and they cause a disease jalodora or a
particular kind of dropsy. It may be called ascites. (See
Sts. 23 and 24, Udara Nidhana in Madhava Nidhana.) If
the Moon is in Aries or Scorpio, between any two evil
planets Saturn, Mars and Sun, death will result from fire
or weapons. Take a horoscope.

Saturn	Sun Moon Mercury	Mars	Venns Rahu
			Birth Jupiter
	RASI No. I		
Kethu			

Here the Moon is situated between two malefics and the child died from watery complaint.

Take another.

Kuja	Sukra	Ravi	Budha Chandra Rahu
Guru			Lagna
	No. II		
Kethu		Sani	

Here the Moon is in Mithuna with Rahu and Budha and the Sun in the 12th. As regards the words betwixt or *Madhyagata*, it is enough even if the Moon is in the same house between two evil planets. Thus if the Sun occupies the 3rd degree of Aries, the Moon occupies the 10th degree and Mars occupies the 15th degree. the Moon must be con-

3.

sidered as being betwixt two malefics, although they are all in
the same sign. The Moon is in 12 hemmed in between Rahu
and Ravi, aspected by Kuja and the boy died in Guru dasa,
Guru bhukthi in his 5th year by slipping and dislocation of
hip joint.   If the Moon is found in Makara or Kumbha between two evil planets, death comes by ropes, fire or fall.
He may be bandaged or tied by ropes or may die from fire,
which takes so many forms or by falling from elevated
places.

बन्धाद्धीनवमस्थयोरशुभयोः सौम्यग्रहाद्दष्टयोः
द्रेकाणैश्च सपाशसर्पनिगडैरिच्छद्रस्थितैर्बन्धतः ।
कन्यायामशुभान्विते ऽस्तमयगे चन्द्रे सिते मेषगे
सूर्ये लग्नगते च विद्धि मरणं स्त्रीहेतुकं मन्दिरे ॥ ४ ॥

Stanza 4.— If the 5th and 9th houses are
occupied by malefics unaspected by benefics death
comes from bandage. If the Drekkana rising in
the 8th house falls in *Sarpa* or *Nigada* then
similar death occurs. If the Sun is in birth, Virgo
falls in the 7th with Moon in conjunction with a
malefic and Venus in Aries the person suffers
death from female agency in his house.

NOTES

If malefics are found in the 5th and 9th houses without
beneficial aspects, the person dies from being tied by ropes
or chains. If the 8th house rises in a Serpent or Nigada
(shackles) Drekkana, the person dies a similar death. The
2nd and 3rd in Kataka, the 1st and 2nd in Vrischika and

the 3rd in Meena are called Serpent Drekkanas. The Nigada Drekkana is the first of Makara. If the birth falls in Meena, with Ravi there, Chandra and a malefic in Kanya or the 7th, and Sukra is in Mesha or the 2nd, death will result from female intrigue in the house.

This combination is possible for only persons born in Meena. By female agency or intrigue the death of the person will be brought about. When the 7th is occupied

Birth Ravi	Sukra		
			Chandra Sani

by evil planets with an evil planet in lagna and with Sukra in the 2nd house Mesha, there will be much room for suspicion about the character of the wife and other females and they bring about his death.

शूलोद्विन्नतनुः सुखेऽवनिसुते स्वर्येंऽपि वा खे यमे
सप्रक्षीणहिमांशुमिश्र युगपत्पापैस्त्रिकोणाद्यगैः ।
बन्धुस्थे च रवौ वियत्यवनिजे क्षीणेन्दुसंवीक्षिते
काष्ठेनाभिहतः प्रयाति मरणं सूर्यात्मजेनेक्षिते ॥ ५ ॥

Stanza   5.—If the 4th is occupied by Mars and the Sun and the 10th by Saturn, the man will be crucified.   If malefics and Kshina Chandra occupy birth,   5th and 9th the same result happens.   If the Sun occupies the 4th, and Mars is in the 10th aspected by weak Moon, there will be crucifixion.   If Saturn aspects the above conjunction, death results from beating.

NOTES

There are three combinations for crucifixion here named.   First, there must be Mars and Sun in the 4th and Saturn in the 10th.   In this case all the malefics have mutual aspects and give the man *shula*.   In the second case the Sun, Mars, Saturn and powerless Moon must occupy birth, 5th or 9th to produce death from *shula*.   In this combination all these four planets may be in birth or 5th or 9th or in any two of them or in the three houses. They must not be outside those houses.   The word *shula* means any sharp pointed iron or wooden pike on which the intended victim would be mounted and torn to pieces. This is a kind of punishment probably now prevalent in semi-civilized countries.   Hanging in various ways now prevalent may be safely substituted for these forms of death. The Sun must be in the 4th and Mars in the 10th aspected by powerless Moon, for the person to be hanged.   If the Sun occupies the 4th and 10th is joined by Mars aspected by Saturn, he will be beaten to death by sticks.   Here the aspects named by Varahamihira must be carefully consider- ed.   (See Ch. II, St. 13).   If Saturn has to aspect Mars in the 10th then he must be in the 4th with the Sun or in the

8th house from lagna or he must be in the lagna.   All these
positions for Saturn are evil.

रन्ध्रास्पदाङ्घ्रिहिबुकैर्लगुडाहताङ्गः
अक्षीणचन्द्ररुधिरार्किदिनेशयुक्तैः ।
तैरेव कर्मनवमोदयपुत्रसंस्थे-
धूमाग्निबन्धनशरीरनिकुट्टनान्तः ॥ ६ ॥

Stanza 6.—If powerless Moon, Mars, Saturn
and the Sun occupy 8th, 10th, birth and the 4th
respectively, the death results from blows from
rods or clods of earth. If the same planets occupy
10th, 9th, 1st and 5th respectively, death comes
by smoke, fire, bandage or blows on the body.

NOTES

Powerless Moon in the 8th, Mars in the 10th, Saturn
in Lagna and the Sun in the 4th, cause death by blows from
iron rods or clods of earth. If powerless Moon occupies
10th, Mars 9th, Saturn 1st and the Sun 5th death may
result from excessive smoke, fire or bandage or blows on
the body by sticks, etc.

	Birth Sani				Birth Sani	
		Ravi				
	No. I Combination				No. II Combination	
Kuja				Chandra		Ravi
	Chandra			Kuja		

बन्ध्वस्तकर्मसहितैः कुजब्ध्र्यमन्दै-
निर्याणमायुधशिखिक्षितिपालकोपात् ।
सौरेन्दुभूमितनयैः स्वसुखास्पदस्थै-
र्ज्ञेयः क्षतक्रिमिकृतश्च शरीरधातः ॥ ७ ॥

Stanza 7.—If Kuja, Ravi and Sani occupy
4th, 7th and 10th respectively death results from
weapons, fire or the anger of the rulers. If Sani,
Chandra and Kuja occupy 2nd, 4th and 10th
respectively the person dies by worms génerated
in sores or wounds.

NOTES

Kuja must be in the 4th, Ravi in the 7th and Sani in
the 10th to produce death related in the first half of the
stanza. If the 2nd is occupied by Sani, 4th by Chandra and
10th by Kuja, the person will get wounds or sores and dies
from the increase of worms in them.

खस्थेऽर्केऽवनिजे रसातलगते यानप्रपाताद्घो
यन्त्रोत्पीडनजः कुजेऽस्तमयगे सोरेन्दिनाभ्युद्रमे ।
विण्मध्ये रुधिरार्किशीताकरणैर्ज्ञूकाजसौरर्क्षगै-
र्यांतैर्बां गलितेन्दुसूर्यरुधिरैर्व्योमास्तबन्धवाह्वयान् ॥ ८ ॥

Stanza 8.—If the Sun occupies the 10th and
Kuja is in the 4th, death comes by fall from conveyances. If Sani, Chandra and Ravi occupy the
Lagna with Kuja in the 7th, death comes by
machinery or rocks. If Kuja, Sani and Chandra

are in Thula, Mesha and a house of Saturn respectively, or if powerless Chandra, Ravi and Kuja are in the 10th, 7th and 4th respectively the person falls in night-soil and dies.

NOTES

If Ravi occupies 10th and Kuja is in the 4th, death comes by fall from vahanas or carriages. These may include all sorts of animals and vehicles used by man for his comforts. When the Sun is in the 10th and Mars is found in the 4th, they will be subjected to mutual aspects. Men are killed often by infernal machinery invented by the diabolical genius of man for the destruction and torture of his fellow creatures. Kuja must be in the 7th, with Chandra, Sani and Ravi in the Lagna for producing the above result. When the Sun is with the Moon, the latter is not powerless. There is a difference in the text. *Saurandvina* is substituted for *Kshinandvina*. But when the Moon is with the Sun, Kshina or powerless, will become a superfluous adjective. If Kuja occupies Thula, Sani is in Mesha, and Chandra in Makara or Kumbha, the person dies by falling in dirt or night-soil. If powerless Moon is in the 10th, Sun in the 7th and Mars is in the 4th the person dies by falling into dirty pits. There is much difference in saying Kshina Chandra and powerless Moon as when powerless Moon is in 10th and Ravi is in 7th, Moon will not be Kshina, since there will be a difference of more than 6 or 7 days for Moon to go four houses beyond the Sun and 5 days after Amavasya (New Moon), Chandra cannot be called Kshina. It is not clear how the Moon is not powerless when he is with the Sun. It has to be understood that Moon with the Sun when he becomes a lord of a quadrant, may be construed as powerful, as he is evil and so gets power.

वीर्यान्वितवक्रवीक्षिते क्षीणेन्दौ निधनस्थितेऽर्कजे ।
गुह्योद्भवरोगपीडया मृत्युः स्यात् कृमिशस्त्रदाहजः ॥ ९ ॥

Stanza 9.—If powerful Mars aspects powerless Moon with Saturn in the 8th the person dies from worms or fire or instruments in treating of disease in secret parts.

NOTES

Kshina Chandra must be aspected by the powerful Kuja, and Sani must occupy the 8th house from lagna. Then the man gets serious disease in the private parts. He may die by worms generating there or by treatment of those parts by fire or instruments.

अस्ते रवौ सरुधिरे निधनेऽर्कपुत्रे
क्षीणे रसातलगते हिमगौ खगान्तः ।
लग्नात्भजाष्टमतपःस्विनभौममन्द-
चन्द्रैस्तु शैलशिखराशनिकुड्यपातैः ॥ १० ॥

Stanza 10.—If Ravi occupies the 7th with Kuja and Sani joins the 8th and powerless Chandra is in the 4th death comes by birds. If Ravi, Kuja, Sani and Chandra are in the 1st, 5th, 8th and 9th respectively the person dies by falling from the tops of a mountain or by the fall of lightning or wall.

NOTES

Ravi and Kuja must be in the 7th, **Sani in the 8th**, with powerless Chandra in the 4th to produce the first form of death.

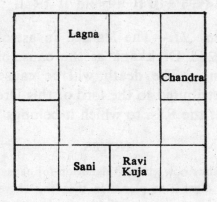

In the latter half of the stanza, Ravi must be in the Lagna, Kuja in the 5th, Sani in the 8th and Chandra in the 9th to produce the danger indicated there.

Death from birds may mean that he may be killed by birds, or his body after death may be eaten by birds for want of a burial or cremation. Bhattotpala however confines the meaning to the latter explanation. This may not stand the test of reason as all Parsees put their dead bodies on a Tower and allow the birds to prey on them. If so, then every horoscope of that community must have this combination. The idea would be far-fetched. It is only people who die on the way in forests that are eaten by birds and beasts.

द्वाविंशः कथितस्तु कारणं
द्रेष्काणो निधनस्य द्वारिमिः ।
तस्याधिपतिर्भवोऽपि वा
निर्याणं स्वगुणैः प्रयच्छति ॥ ११ ॥

Stanza 11.—The learned in astrology indicate the 22nd Drekkana as the cause of death to
the person.   The death will be caused by the
manner attributed to the lord of this Drekkana or
the lord of the Rasi to which it belongs.

NOTES

The author now gives explanation for cause of death in
cases where there is no planet in the 8th, where the 8th is
not aspected by planets and where none of the combinations, named already is present for causing death.   The 8th
house or bhava literally begins with the 22nd Drekkana.
There are three Drekkanas for each house and 7 houses
from lagna at 3 for each house will give 21 Drekkanas. Therefore the learned in astrology consider the 22nd Drekkana
as that of death or Mrithyu.   The 8th house begins with
the 22nd Drekkana.   The lord of that Drekkana kills the
person by that disease which is attributed to him in the first
stanza of this Chapter.   If not, the lord of the 8th house
to which the 22nd Drekkana belongs will cause death as
per his nature.   Bhattotpala points out that the stronger of
the two planets, *viz.*, lord of the 22nd Drekkana and the
lord of the 8th house will give death by such diseases as he
can cause.

होरानवांशकपयुक्तसमानभूमौ
योगेक्षणादिभिरतः परिकल्प्यमेतत् ।
मोहस्तु मृत्युसमयेऽनुदितांशतुल्यः
स्वेशेक्षिते द्विगुणितस्त्रिगुणः शुभैश्च ॥ १२ ॥

Stanza 12.—Death will take place in places
similar to the rasi occupied by the lord of the
navamsa, in which birth falls. Further details or
specialities must be described by conjunctions and
planetary aspects. The time of death has to be
identified by the unrisen number of navamsas in
the birth. If the birth lord aspects it, the time
must be doubled ; aspected by benefics the time
will be trebled.

NOTES

The birth falls in some navamsa, and the lord of this
navamsa occupies some rasi necessarily.   The place of
death resembles localities governed by that rasi. In the
horoscope given below, the lord of navamsa lagna, Ravi is
in Kanya and death in or near a well is indicated but it has
to be modified according to so many aspects, *viz.*, Sani's
aspect, association with Guru and Sukra and occupation
of Kataka in amsa. The four points enumerated for consideration by Bhattotpala may be applied in the horoscope
and it will be seen that Sani and Guru influence the house
and the place of death can be predicted near a well or watery

place in a house. If that rasi is Mesha the place of death will be frequented by goats, etc. If Vrishabha, grazing ground ; if Mithuna, in a house; if Kataka, a well ; if Simha, a wilderness ; if Kanya, a well ; if Thula, death will be in a place of merchandise; if Vrischika, low places; if Dhanus, places frequented by horses ; if Makara, marshy places ; if Kumbha, a house ; and if Meena, swamps. Bhattotpala cleverly raises a difficulty and solves it. In the Anishtadhyaya or Chapter on misfortunes, various modes of death have already been detailed. Then how is the reader to be guided when these combinations are present in a horoscope.

RASI

Kethu	RASI		Sani
Chandra			Lagna Rahu
	Kuja	Budha	Ravi Sukra Guru

NAVAMSA

Sukra			Ravi Sani Rahu
	NAVAMSA		Guru Lagna Chandra
Kethu			
		Kuja Budha	

He assures the students that when such uufortunate combinations exist, death must be predicted as per those *yogas*, but when they are not present, the present principles must guide the readers. It is not enough if we look into the nature of rasi. The conjunctions and aspects of that rasi must also be taken into consideration. The word *Adi* used in the original, further gives scope in extending the meaning, to the nature of navamsa sign occupied by the lord of the navamsa of the lagna which rises at the birth time. He has thus enumerated four points for consideration :

1. The nature of the rasi occupied by the lord of the navamsa rising in the lagna.

2. The nature of the navamsa rasi occupied by the lord of the navamsa of the lagna.

3. Planets in conjunction with the rasi occupied by the lord of the navamsa rising in the lagna, and

4. The planets who aspect that rasi occupied by the lord of the rising navamsa in lagna.

When all these are present in a horoscope or when two or more are there, then the nature of the locality of death must be determined by the strongest among these four. The nature of the ground for planets will be the nature of the zodiacal sign which they own. But when a planet owns two houses, then the nature of the house where he has his moolatrikona, must be represented. Thus Ravi has Simha, Chandra has Vrishabha, Kuja has Mesha, Budha has Kanya, Guru has Dhanus, Sukra has Thula, and Sani has Kumbha. Some also say that the places will be those governed by the planets in Chap. II, St. 12. But Bhattotpala does not approve of this.

Lagna rises in some navamsa and there may be other navamsas yet to rise. Take the total time of the unrisen navamsas and predict that the time of death will be equal to their total. If the lagna is aspected by its lord then this total time must be doubled. If a benefic conjoins lagna, it must be trebled. If lagna is both aspected by its lord and also has a beneficial conjunction, the period must be multiplied sixfold. Take a horoscope. Birth is Vrishabha and falls in the fourth navamsa at its end. Then there are five navamsas yet to rise. Vrishabha extends over 4½ ghatis. Thus 2 ghatis in Vrishabha have passed leaving a balance of 2¼

ghatis. The navamsa of birth consequently falls in Mesha.
The lord of Mesha is Kuja. He occupies Thula and the
nature of the locality where this man dies, should be such
as is represented by Thula.

	Chandra Rahu	Birth	Sani	Birth Guru	Rahu	
Ravi Budha Guru	RASI			NAVAMSA		
Sukra		Kuja Kethu		Budha	Kethu	Ravi Sani Sukra Kuja	Chandra

[The lord of the rising navamsa in birth, *viz.*, Kuja
occupies Thula Navamsa and therefore is in Vargottama,
but Thula is aspected in the rasi diagram by Guru and
Chandra. There are three points now to be considered,
viz., the nature of Thula, the nature of Guru and the nature
of Chandra. The place of death will be such as is represented by the strongest of these three, *viz.*, Thula, Guru
and Chandra. Thula as the place where lord of Navamsa
Lagna falls is aspected by Guru and Chandra. Chandra is
not very powerful, but Guru is very powerful and hence
the gentleman died in his own house near the gate. The
time of death for this particular horoscope was about 1 p.m.
on Magha Bahula Amavasya (12th March 1937). Lagna is
not aspected by its lord or by any benefic and therefore the
time of death will be 2½ ghatis. But here is a difficulty. If
we simply say 2½ ghatis without saying after sunrise or

sunset, or with reference to some definite time, how is the
reader to be guided? Bhattotpala is also silent on this
point. In Chap. IV, St. 21, hints as to the time of the birth
of children are clearly given. The same may be conveniently
applied here. If the lagna falls in day sign the time must
be taken as referring to day and if it falls in nocturnal sign
the time must be referred to night. The details regarding
these particulars are shown under notes in St. 10, Chap. I.
Probably the lagna referred to should be the Navamsa
Lagna and as it is the 5th navamsa and falls in a day sign
Mesha and as each sign has to be calculated at $2\frac{1}{2}$ ghatis
(Total $12 \times 2\frac{1}{2} = 30$) for day and $2\frac{1}{2}$ for night and as 5
navamsas have passed, it is $12\frac{1}{2}$ ghatis in the day, when
the native should have become unconscious prior to death.
His death was observed by about 12-30 or 1 p.m. Vrishabha
falls in 5th and being Mesha, the person died at 12-30 ghs.]

दहनजलविमिश्रैर्भस्मसंक्षेदशोषै-
निधनभवनसंस्थैर्व्यालवर्गेविडम्बः ।
इति शवपरिणाममश्चिन्तनीयो यथोक्तः
पृथुविरचितशास्त्राद्द्रत्यनूकादि चिन्त्यम् ॥ १३ ॥

Stanza 13.—The dead body as per the Drekkana in the 8th house, *viz*., *Dahana*, *Jala* and
Misra, will be reduced to ashes by fire or atoms
by water and putrefaction by atmosphere respectively. If the 8th house Drekkana is Vyala the
body will be disgraced. The disposal of the dead
body must be explained in this manner, and as
regards the past and future births, the reader
must consult elaborate works on the subject.

NOTES

Here we have rules to guide us in determining the disposal of the dead body. Man seems to have a great desire to have his dead body disposed of according to the most approved methods in vogue in his country. These disposals are of various forms. Sometimes the dead bodies are subjected to great indignities, as if their departed spirits watch them and feel such degrading cruelties. There are various methods; cremation, burial, drowning, and exposure to atmosphere. The rising Drekkana in the 8th house will be the 22nd from the birth, and if it falls in *Dahana Drekkana*, the body will be cremated and turned to ashes. Dahana Drekkanas are the divisions of evil planets. If the 22nd Drekkana happens to be a *Jala* (watery), the dead body will be thrown into watery places and there allowed to dissolve. The beneficial drekkanas are termed Jala Drekkanas. If the 22nd is *Misra* Drekkana, then the dead body will neither be burned nor thrown into water and probably this refers to all sorts of burials, where the atmospherical forces dissolve the body. If the beneficial drekkanas are joined by malefics, or if the malefic drekkanas are conjoined by benefics, they are counted as *Misra* (mixed) Drekkanas. If the rising drekkana in the 8th house is *Vyala* (serpent) the dead body will be exposed to birds and beasts or otherwise disgraced. Men somehow do not like that their dead bodies should be so dealt with. (*Vide* notes on Stanza 10). Serpent Drekkanas are the 1st and 2nd of Kataka and Vrischika, and the 3rd of Meena. Bhattotpala quotes in support of these views, from some ancient work which he does not name. The word *Adi* used in the text, gives a clue to important information concerning the place from which man has come to this birth, his status in his previous birth, and the place to which he would go after death in this life. He asks the readers to consult on these important points among elaborate treatises on astrology written by great Maharishis and promises to give a short abstract of it in the next verse.

गुरुखुपतिशुक्रौ सूर्यभौमौ यमज्ञौ
विबुधपितृतिर्श्चो नारकीयांश्च कुर्युः ।
दिनकरशशिवीर्यांधिष्ठितत्र्यंशनाथाः
प्रवरसमनिकृष्टास्तुझहासादनूके ॥ १४ ॥

Stanza 14.—Guru, Chandra and Sukra, Ravi and Kuja, and Sani and Budha bring people from Devaloka, Pitruloka, Tiryagloka and Narakaloka respectively. According to the position of the lord of the drekkana occupied by the most powerful of the Sun or the Moon, we have to predict the high, middle or low state of the man in his previous birth.

NOTES

In the first portion of this verse, the meaning is no clear. Find out who is the stronger of the two in a horoscope, *viz.*, the Sun or the Moon and ascertain in which drekkana the stronger of these two is conjoined. Then the man has come from that loka or existence which is represented by the lord of this drekkana. The following horoscope

35

will illustrate this point clearly. The Rasi and the Drekkana diagrams are given :

				Kuja		Guru Ravi	Kethu
Kethu	RASI		Sani		DREKKANA		Sani
Chandra			Birth Rahu				
	Kuja	Budha	Guru Ravi Sukra	Rahu Lagna		Budha	Chandra Sukra

Here it is clear that the Moon is more powerful than the Sun, having Parivartana yoga and being a benefic. He is in Budha Drekkana. Hence the person comes from Narakaloka where he must have occupied a high position, as Budha has Vargottamamsa and in a friendly sign.

If this Drekkana belongs to Guru predict that he has come from Devaloka.

If the Drekkana belongs to Chandra or Sukra he has come from Pitruloka.

If the Drekkana is governed by Ravi or Kuja, he comes from Tiryagloka.

If the Drekkana belongs to Budha or Sani, he has come from Narakaloka. To find out in what state he was in the previous birth or existence in that *loka*, the author throws out some hints which are interesting. If the lord of the above said Drekkana is exalted, then he occupied a high status or position in the previous loka, if he is ordinary tnen the position was middling, and if the planet is debilitated, he occupied a mean or degraded state. Devaloka represents a higher world where superior men are supposed to go after death. Here Devas or exalted order of beings are alleged to live enjoying greater privileges and higher prosperity than men.

Pitruloka indicates that order of existence which is inferior to Devaloka, where the spirits of the dead are supposed to live.

Tiryagloka represents an inferior order of existence where men, in the course of evil careers out-balancing their good actions, are supposed to live.

Narakaloka indicates that order of existence where men with evil deeds far in excess of their good actions have to take their turns of cosmic evolution.

गतिरपि रिपुरन्ध्रत्र्यंशपोऽस्तस्थितो वा
गुरुरथ रिपुकेन्द्रच्छिद्रगः स्वोच्चसंस्थः ।
उदयति भवनेऽन्त्ये सौम्यभागे च मोक्षो
भवति यदि बलेन प्रोज्झितास्तत्र शेषाः ॥ १५ ॥

Stanza 15.—The lord of the drekkana of the 6th or 8th, or the planet who occupies the 7th house indicates the state of man's future existence after death. If Guru in exaltation occupies 6th, 8th or any kendra, if Meena is Lagna occupying beneficial navamsa and other planets than Guru are powerless the person attains moksha.

NOTES

Here we have suggestions for finding out the state of existence to which a person goes after his death. If there are no planets in the 6th, 7th and 8th, then find out the lord of the drekkana rising in the 6th and 8th and ascertain which of these two is stronger and then attribute that *loka* to him which is denoted by that planet. In the above example, in Drekkana Kundali, the 6th and 8th are occupied by Guru, Ravi and Sani and the lords of these are Sukra and Chandra. Hence the man after his death will propably go to Pitruloka, which is said to be higher in status than our world. If there is a planet in the 6th, 7th or 8th house, then the man goes to that *loka* which is indicated by that planet. But if there are two or more in these houses then the strongest of the lot determines the loka to which the person proceeds. In the text, only the words *Asta* (7th) *Sthithova* (standing) are used. These preclude the idea of planets being taken in the 6th and 8th houses. Bhattotpala whose reading seems to be most comprehensive, explains *va* as standing for *cha* (and), and supports this view from quotations from *Laghu Jataka* of Varahamihira where the idea is fully expanded.

If Guru occupies 1, 4, 7, 8 or 10 from Lagna and is in Kataka (his exaltation) or if Meena rises at the time of birth and occupies a beneficial navamsa and if Guru is powerful and other planets are powerless, the person gets moksha or final emancipation from all gross forms of existence. These results of future states of existence may also be predicted from the conjunction of planets at the time of a man's death. This idea is supported by a quotation from *Laghu Jataka.*

CHAPTER XXVI

NASTA JATAKA

नष्टजातकाध्यायः

(Unknown Horoscopes)

आधानजन्मापरिबोधकाले
संपृच्छतो जन्म वदेद्विलग्नात् ।
पूर्वापरार्द्धे भवनस्य विन्ध्या-
द्वानाबुदक्षिणगे प्रह्वतिम् ॥ १ ॥

Stanza 1.—When a person has no record of
his birth time or the time of conception, the birth
must be predicted according to the lagna rising
at the time of question. The birth must be predicted in Uttarayana or Dakshinayana as the
first or the second hora in the lagna rises.

NOTES

Here the author wishes to help those persons with the
construction of a horoscope, who have no recollection of
their birth or conception time. It is quite unreasonable to
expect a man to know anything about the time of his conception by his mother and in fact, very few persons know
or care to know about the details of conception. Even the
woman who conceives sometimes does not know of the fact.
But generally the birth time is known to many interested in
the family. When a person goes to an astrologer and asks

him to prepare a lost horoscope or a new one he does so at
a definite time.   The astrologer should find out the proper
lagna which rises at the time and if the first hora prevails he
must say that the man was born in Uttarayana when the
Sun was in the 6 signs from Makara to Kataka.   But if the
second half of the lagna rises then the man must have been
born in Dakshinayana when the Sun was in the 6 months
from Kataka to Makara.   Thus Uttarayana comprises the
months of Makara, Kumbha, Meena, Mesha, Vrishabha
and Mithuna and Dakshinayana comprises Kataka, Simha,
Kanya, Thula, Vrischika and Dhanus.   If one knows the
time of conception but not the time of birth rules have
already been laid down for finding the birth from conception.
(See St. 21, Chap. IV).

लग्नत्रिकोणेषु गुरुस्त्रिभागै
विकल्प्य वर्षाणि वयोनुमानात् ।
ग्रीष्मोर्ककलग्ने कथितास्तु शेषै-
रन्यायनर्तोर्ऋतुर्कचारात् ॥ २ ॥

Stanza 2.—By the rising drekkana in the
lagna, Guru's position in 1, 5 or 9 must be
ascertained according to the appearance of the
querist.   If Ravi is in Lagna, the birth takes place
in Grishma and so on for other planets as stated
before.   If the *Rithu* falls in a wrong Ayana then
it must be corrected by the position of the Sun.

NOTES

Here the author enables the astrologer to find out the
year and the *Rithu* (season).   If the 1st Drekkana in Lagna

rises at the time of query then predict Guru as being in
Birth Lagna ; if the 2nd Drekkana in Lagna rises then
Guru must be placed in the 5th house ; and if the 3rd
Drekkana rises he will be in the 9th. As other places than
1, 5, 9 are not named here Bhattotpala gives hints to find
the correct house of Jupiter. Take the rising Dwadasamsa
in the query lagna. If the first Dwadasamsa rises Guru
will be in Lagna, if the second rises he will be in the 2nd
and if the 10th rises Guru will be found in the 10th
house from the Birth Lagna. Some astrologers explain the
meaning quite separately. They say that if the 1st Drekkana
rises in the question lagna, then find out the number of the
houses, Guru has travelled up to the question time and
predict that the person was born in a similar number of
years before. If the 2nd Drekkana rises then count from
the 5th house of the question lagna to the position of Guru
in the present period and predict that the man was born a
similar number of years before. If the 3rd Drekkana rises
at the question time, then count from the 9th house of the
query lagna to the present position of Guru in the zodiac
and predict birth before so many years. It would be better
understood by an illustration. Take the question time as
11-30 a.m. on 11th September, Friday 1908 (Salivahana
Saka 1830). Vrischika Lagna rises at about 11 ghatis
after sunrise. 11-30 a.m. converted gives about 14 ghatis
after sunrise. Therefore 3 ghatis out of $5\frac{1}{2}$ ghatis (the
extent of Vrischika) have passed and the 2nd Drekkana for
Vrischika will be Meena. On this date Guru is found in
Simha. We have to count therefore from Meena to Simha
and we get 6 years. Say that the child was born 6 years
ago or 18 years or 30 years or 42 years or 54 or 66 years

according as you find the querist's person. This interpretation is not approved by Bhattotpala who quotes Yavaneswara to support the first exposition. As Jupiter goes round
the whole zodiac in 12 years the age of the person must
be ascertained by the querist's physical appearance and
probable age. When there is a doubt or difficulty in
determining these cycles of 12 years or the difference of
that period, then ascertain the age of the party according
to the Purusha Lakshana explained in *Brihat Samhita.*
(See Chap. 70, Sts. 24-5-6). The astrologer may ask the
querist to touch any organ of his body or the organs of
Kalapurusha which he can keep in the form of a picture.
If the person touches the feet and the ankles then Guru
will be in the 2nd house ; if he touches the thighs,
sexual organ or testicles in the 3rd ; if naval or loins the
4th ; if belly the 5th ; if chest or breast the 6th ; if shoulders
the 7th ; if neck or lips the 8th ; if eyes or brows 9th ; if
forehead or head the 10th. As only 10 organs have been
named and we have 12 years before a complete circle of the
zodiac by Guru we have to divide these 12 years by 10,
and account by such counting, the position of Jupiter.
Thus for each organ, we get 1 year, 2 months and 12
days. Thus if a person touched the 7th organ then Guru
must be predicted in the 9th house, as we have $6 \times 1\frac{2}{5}$
years $= \frac{7 \times 6}{5} = 8$ years and $\frac{2}{5} \times 12 = \frac{24}{5} = 4$ months a n d
$\frac{4}{5} \times 30$ days $= 24$ days.

By this process stated in *Brihat Jataka* the time gained
would be that of Jupiter whose *Mana* is different from the
soura or solar sidereal years. The jovian years may be easily
converted into solar years and the methods are explained

by Bhattotpala in the commentaries on St. 1 of Ch. VIII
of *Brihat Samhita*. (*Vide* Translation by Prof. B. V.
Raman in THE ASTROLOGICAL MAGAZINE). The four
yugas (a Mahayuga), Krita, Treta, Dwapara and Kali
contain 4320000 solar years or the Sun would go so many
rounds in the zodiac in one Mahayuga. But for the same
number of years the jovian years would be 4370688. As jovian
years are greater the solar years must be deducted from
them thus : 4370688—4320000=50688 jovian years. When
50688 are gained in one Mahayuga, what would be the pro-
portion to one solar sidereal year. Thus we have $\dfrac{1 \times 50688}{4320000}=$

$\dfrac{50688}{4320000}$ divided by the common factor 2304 we get $\dfrac{22}{1875}$

years $= \dfrac{22 \times 12 \times 30}{1875} = \dfrac{7920}{1875}$ days. For every $170\frac{5}{11}$ solar years

we get 2 jovian years extra. For one solar year we get $\dfrac{7920}{1875}$

days ∴ for $\dfrac{1875}{11}$ solar years what do we get. Thus $\dfrac{7920}{1875} \times \dfrac{1875}{11}$

=720 days or two years measured by jovian movements.
In the *Nasta Jataka* process we have to multiply the
numbers of years obtained by the position of Jupiter by $\dfrac{22}{1875}$

and subtract the same from the number of solar years to get
the solar time. Now he gives hints to find out the seasons
or Rithus. According to Aryan astronomy there are given
6 Rithus. They are :—

   (1) Vasanta=Chaitra and Vaisakha or spring. April
       and May.
   (2) Grishma=Jyeshta and Ashada or summer. June and
       July.

(3) Varsha=Sravana and Bhadrapada. August and
     September—rainy.

(4) Sarat=Aswija and Kartika–October and November
     —clear or bright season.

(5) Hemanta=December and January. Margasira and
     Pushya—dewy or cold season, autumn.

(6) Sisira=Magha and Phalguna—February and March
     —cold season, winter.

If the Prasna Lagna is occupied by the Sun or his
house rises as drekkana, the birth must be predicted in
Grishma. If Saturn is in Lagna or his drekkana rises at the
time, then birth takes place in Sisira. If Venus is in Lagna
or the drekkana falls in his house, birth happens in Vasanta.
If Mars is in Lagna or his house rises as drekkana predict
Grishma. If Lagna rises in the drekkana of Chandra or he
is in Lagna predict Varsha Rithu. If Mercury is in Lagna
or his drekkana rises in it, Sarat. If Jupiter occupies Lagna
or his house rises as drekkana, Hemanta. If there are
many planets in the question lagna, then the season must
be ascribed to him who is the strongest of the lot. When
there are no planets in the lagna, then alone reference must
be made to the rising drekkana. When a Rithu comes in
an Ayana in which it does not fall then predict the Rithu
with reference to the Sun. *These results, observes
Bhattotpala, must be referred to the solar movements and not
to the lunar (Chandramana) which prevails usually in the
world.* Thus if Vasanta is to be predicted then say that
Rithu extends to the season when the Sun moves in Aries
and Taurus. According to Chandramana Chaitra may fall
while the Sun is still in Pisces and it is called Meena,
Chaitra or Chaitra which falls in Meena.

चन्द्रज्ञजीवाः परिवर्तनीयाः
शुक्रारमन्दरयने विलोमे ।
द्रेष्काणभागे प्रथमे तु पूर्वो
मासोनुपाताच्च तिथिर्विकल्प्यः ॥ ३ ॥

Stanza 3.—If a Rithu falls in a wrong Ayana
then, change Moon, Mercury and Jupiter for
Venus, Mars and Saturn respectively.   If the first
half of a drekkana rises the first month of the
Rithu must be predicted, and the day must be
proportionately found out.

NOTES

In this stanza Varahamihira gives suggestions for a
knowledge of the correct Rithu in a wrong Ayana, month
and the day.   There are two Ayanas namely Uttarayana
and Dakshinayana.   Uttarayana contains 3 Rithus, *viz.*
Sisira (Makara and Kumbha), Vasanta (Meena and
Mesha) and Grishma (Vrishabha and Mithuna).   There
is some confusion here.   In the last stanza, it is stated
that Vasanta has to be taken as Aries and Taurus,
while here it is stated as Pisces and Aries.   This is
only to be taken when the Rithu falls in a wrong Ayana
and according to the movements of the Sun.   But our
Rithus always are calculated according to Chandramana and as it is brought up to the Souramana every 2 or
3 years by the addition of an inter-calary month, the
meaning in this stanza only has to be considered in fixing
the month.

Dakshinayana comprises 3 Rithus, *viz.*, Varsha (Kataka and Simha), Sara (Kanya and Thula) and Hemanta (Vrischika ¡and Dhanus). If Varsha Rithu comes in Uttarayana then predict it as Vasanta. Chandra is given rainy season and Sukra, Vasanta and therefore Sukra must be substituted for Chandra. If Sarat rises in Uttarayana then Grishma must be substituted and *vice versa*. Budha governs Sarat and Ravi and Kuja rule Grishma. They must be exchanged. Similarly work out for other Rithus and the lords who govern them. As a Ruthu contains two months the author now takes the readers to find out the correct month. Divide the rising ʹdrekkana into two equal divisions and ascribe the first month of the Ruthu to the first half and the second month to the second half. Each drekkana contains 10 degrees and therefore, the first 5 degrees of it represent the first and the next 5 degrees the second month of the Rithu. All these must be referred to solar movements and not to lunar or Chandramana. Each rasi is composed of 1800 liptas and therefore each drekkana contains 600 liptas. Drekkana represents two months and one half of it or one month is represented by 300 liptas. Each month contains 30 days and therefore each day gets 10 liptas, and the particular day will be found out by the rising lipta at the time of question. Take an illustration. A person puts the question in the commencement of the 10th degree of Mesha with the Sun there. The Rithu therefore will be Grishma. As the last half of the drekkana rises the month will be the second of Grishma or Mithuna (it may fall in Jyeshta and Ashada— June' and July). But as the lagna rises in the first hora of Mesha the Ayana will be Uttarayana. The person was born in Uttarayana Grishma Rithu and Mithuna Masa (month). The question was put at the commencement of the 10th degree. The first five degrees represented the 30 days of the first month in Grishma or Vrishabha. Therefore in the second out of the 5 degrees four degrees have passed and the 5th is just rising. Each degree gets 60 liptas and therefore 4×60 or 240 liptas in the second half of the drekkana have passed. If 30 days get 300 liptas, each day gets 10 liptas. Therefore 241 liptas give 24 days and a balance of one lipta or the commencement of the 25th day in the second month of Grishma.

अत्रापि होरापटवो द्विजेन्द्राः
सूर्यांशतुल्यां तिथिमुद्दिशन्ति ।
रात्रिद्युमंत्रेषु विलोमजन्म-
भागैश्च देलाः क्रमशो विकल्प्याः ॥ ४ ॥

Stanza 4.—The learned Brahmin astrologers predict the thithi by reference to the degree of the Sun. The birth must be predicted reversely in the nocturnal and diurnal signs. By the degrees of the lagna, the time of birth must be acertained.

NOTES

This is a very important stanza, determining the lunar day, the time of the day and the sign of the zodiac in which a person is born. The learned Brahmin astrologers suggest that the lunar day has to be made out by the degrees, etc., the Sun has passed in the rasi at the time of the query and these represent the number of lunar thithies which passed at the time of birth. Suppose the Sun at the

time of the question is found in the 10th degree, then the
lunar day will be the 10th or *Dasami* in the Sukla Paksha
(or bright half). If he is in the 27th degree, then the
lunar day will be the Dwadasi of the Krishna Paksha (or
dark half of the month). Bhattotpala says that if the
month is Makara then convert that into the Magha of
Chandramana, Kumbha for Phalguna and Meena for
Chaitra, etc. In the original there is no authority to say
that the *thithies* must be counted from the Prathama of
Sukla or the 1st day of the bright half of the lunar month.
While in Southern India, the month is calculated from
New Moon to New Moon, in Northern India, it is from
Full Moon to Full Moon and so our Phalguna Bahula will
be their Chaitra Bahula while Chaitra Sudda will be common to both. The calculation presupposes that the Sun
and Moon enter a house together. It is not always
possible that Chandramana will be in the 10th of the
bright half when the Sun is in the 10th degree of any
sign. [For example, the 18th of Meena this year
(31-3-1947) was not Krishna Paksha 3, but Sukla Paksha
(Chaitra) 10th]. Bhattotpala supports his interpretation
by a clear quotation from Manitha. After knowing
the day, he now gives the method for finding out
the birth during the day or the night. Nocturnal
and diurnal signs have been explained in St. 10, Ch. I.
If the rising lagna at the time of query is nocturnal
then the birth must be predicted during the day and *vice
versa*. After knowing the time of birth during the night or
day, the time of birth and hence the correct lagna of birth
will have to be thus ascertained. Take the *cheshaka* gained
over in the lagna at the time of query and multiply the

same by the duration of the day or night of the birth, and divide the result by the *Swadesha Rasi Pramana* and the quotient represents the time after which the birth of the person during the day or the night, has happened. Work out an example. A man questions an astrologer on the 15th of September 1908 at 5 ghatis after sunrise. The solar day is 31 of Simha. The Sun is in the 30th degree of Simha. He has to gain 11 vighaties in Simha. Thus there has passed 11 vighaties in Simha and 4.49 ghts. in Kanya at the time of the question. Bringing these into *cheshakas* or vighaties, we get $4 \times 60 + 49$ or 289 Cheshakas. Kanya measures here (in Madras) 315 cheshakas. Kanya forms a diurnal sign and therefore the birth took place during the night. To find out the correct time of the birth during the night the following method must be pursued. First find out where Guru is at the time of birth. The rising drekkana in Kanya is the 3rd and so Guru was at the time of birth in Vrishabha. Therefore the child must be 3 or 15 or 27 or 39, etc. years. By other circumstances such as personal appearance he is 3 years old. As it is the 2nd Hora the Ayana was Dakshina. Budha is in Kanya and the Rithu was Sarat. The second half of the 3rd Drekkana has risen in Kanya and therefore the second month of the Rithu Sarat or Thula masam. The lunar month will be Karthika. Find out now the solar day. In Kanya each drekkana gets 105 cheshakas and half of it will be $52\frac{1}{2}$ cheshakas. This comprises 30 days or we get for each day $52\frac{1}{2} \div 30 = \dfrac{105}{2} = \dfrac{1}{30} = \dfrac{105}{60}$ cheshakas. As per lagnasphuta 289 cheshakas have expired, of which the first 210 represent the first two Drekkanas. Therefore in the 3rd Drekkana 79 cheshakas have expired of which $52\frac{1}{2}$ form the first half of the 3rd

Drekkana and the first month of the Sarat Rithu. Now in the second half of this drekkana 79-52½ or 26½ cheshakas have expired. Thus $26\frac{1}{2} \div \frac{105}{60} = \frac{53}{2} \times \frac{60}{105}$

$= \frac{318}{21} = 15\frac{1}{7}$ days or the Sun occupies the 16th degree of Thula. As the Sun is in the 30th degree of Simha at the time of question, the lunar day will be the Amavasya of the lunar month Karthika. The duration of night on the birthday was 31-52 ghts. Convert these into cheshakas. We get $31 \times 60 + 52 = 1912$. Multiply this by the number of cheshakas passed in Kanya at the time of question. We get $1912 \times 289 = 552568$ cheshakas. These must be divided by the Swadesha Lagna Pramana (or the extent of Kanya obtained in any particular place) or 315 cheshakas, governed by Kanya here $= \frac{552568}{315} = 1754\frac{58}{315}$ cheshakas. Dividing again this by 60 cheshakas to bring it into ghatis we get $\frac{138142}{4725} = 29\frac{1117}{4725}$ ghatis. So the birth was after 29 ghatis on the night of that day.

Bhattotpala gives a list of the extent of the cheshakas for the various signs, probably to his native place, and they are—

            Meena and Mesha=200 ch. each.
            Vrishabha and Kumbha=240 ch. each.
            Mithuna and Makara=280   do.
            Kataka and Dhanus=320   do.
            Simha and Vrischika=360   do.
            Kanya and Thula=400   do.

From these it seems that Bhattotpala must have lived somewhere near Ujjain, for the extent of rasis applies to that place. (See Chap. I, St. 19).

केचिच्छशाङ्काध्युषितान्नवांशा
च्छुक्रान्तसंज्ञं कथयान्ति मासम् ।
लग्नत्रिकोणोत्तमवीर्ययुक्तं
संप्रोच्यतेऽङ्गालभनादिभिर्वा ॥ ५ ॥

Stanza 5.—Some say that the lunar month
has to be made out with reference to the position
of the Moon in the navamsa. The position of
the Moon must be made out by the most powerful among the *Lagna* and *Trikona* or by the
touching of the organs, etc. of the querist.

NOTES

He gives here a different method to find out the month
and the rasi where the Moon is. Chandra occupies some
navamsa at the time of question. This is indicated by some
constellation. The lunar month will be that in which this
constellation figures on its Pournima. There are some stars
from which some months take their names. In such cases if
the Moon occupies such a constellation, the month must be
made out as per movements of Jupiter detailed by Varahamihira. In Ch. VIII, Sts. 1 and 2 of *Brihat Samhita,*
Varahamihira thus explains :—The two stars Krittika and
Rohini give rise to Karthika ; Mrigasira and Aridra produce
Margasira ; Punarvasa and Pushyami give Pushya ; Aslesha
and Makha produce Magha ; Pubba, Uttara and Hasta
give Phalguna ; Chitta and Swati give Chaitra ; Visakha and
Anuradha produce Vaisakha ; Jyeshta and Moola produce
Jyeshta; Purvashada and Uttarashada give Ashada; Sravana

36

and Dhanista produce Sravana; Satabhisha, Poorvabhadra
and Uttarabhadra produce Bhadrapada and Revati,
Aswini and Bharani give Aswija. Therefore if Chandra is
in the 9th navamsa of Mesha or the first seven navamsas
of Vrishabha, the person must be declared to have been
born in the lunar month Karthika. If Chandra is in the last
two navamsas of Vrishabha or the first six navamsas of
Mithuna the month will be Margasira. If Chandra is in
the last three navamsas of Mithuna or the first five navamsas of Kataka the man will be born in Pushya. If Chandra
is in the last four navamsas of Kataka or the first four of
Simha the month will be Magha. If Chandra is in the last
five navamsas of Simha or the first seven navamsas of
Kanya he will be born in Phalguna. If Chandra is in the
last two navamsas of Kanya or the first six navamsas of
Thula the month will be Chaitra. If Chandra is in the last
three navamsas of Thula or the first five navamsas of Vrischika the month will be Vaisakha. If Chandra is in the last
four navamsas of Vrischika or the first four navamsas of
Dhanus the person will be born in Jyeshta. If Chandra is in
the last five navamsas of Dhanus or the first three navamsas
of Makara the month will be Ashada. If Chandra is in the
last six navamsas of Makara or the first two navamsas of
Kumbha the month will be Sravana. If Chandra is in the
last seven navamsas of Kumbha or the first five navamsas
of Meena the month will be Bhadrapada. If Chandra
occupies the last four navamsas of Meena or the first eight
navamsas of Mesha the month will be Aswija. The original
contains *Suklantha Soungmya Masa* with a purpose. The
lunar month begins with the first lunar day after the New
Moon and not as some erroneously have cried out that the

month begins with *Krishna Paksha*. (*Vide* note on Stanza 4
on this aspect). Find out which of the trikonas, *viz.*,
Lagna, 5th or 9th is most powerful and place therein
Chandra. Yavaneswara clearly supports this view. We
have already given the different organs of the Kalapurusha.
Whichever organ among these is touched by the querist the
Moon may be placed in that sign which is represented by
that organ. The word Adi or etc. is used in the original.
Suppose the querist asks the question when a goat passes
by or bleats. Then the sign occupied by Chandra may be
fixed as Mesha. The reader must be very careful in judging
these matters.

यावान् गतः शीतकरो विलग्रा-
च्चन्द्राद्देत्तावति जन्मराशिः ।
मीनोदये मीनयुगं प्रदिष्टं
भक्ष्याहृताकारहतैश्च चिन्त्यम् ॥ ६ ॥

Stanza 6.—The position of Chandra will be
in that rasi which is equal to the number of
rasis gained by him from the question lagna. If
Chandra is in Meena, then that will be the sign
occupied by him at birth. The position of the
Moon at birth may also be ascertained by the
articles of food, by animals and sounds at the
question time.

NOTES

Another method is sketched here for finding out the posit
-ion of the Moon at the time of birth. Put the lagna at the

time of query and ascertain where Chandra is located. Find
out how many rasis (houses) he is from lagna. Then place
Moon at the time of birth in a house which is removed as many
rasis from Chandra as he is from lagna.   Take an example.
Say the query lagna falls in Cancer and Moon is in Scorpio.
Counting, from lagna to the Moon at the time we find him
in the 5th house. Then count from Moon the 5th house
and it becomes Meena. Predict therefore that the Moon
was in Meena at the time of birth. Suppose at the time of
question, Chandra is in Meena, then place him in that
house at the time of birth also. This is only applicable to
Chandra being in Meena. Though Meena is the 9th from
Cancer, we cannot put him in the 9th from Meena as was
done in the previous case. Probably this is an exception.
Bhattotpala offers some suggestions here which are very
valuable. Different methods have been given above for
finding out the position of the Moon at the time of birth.
Suppose difference in the position of Chandra arises ; then
the reader will be in a fix. The commentator suggests that
at the time of question if any animal is seen or food, etc.,
is brought or the appearance of the querist suggests
some resemblance to animals or the sounds suggest the
nature of the animals, then the Moon may be fixed in
that rasi to which any of these events suggested resemble.
Suppose a cat or a dog appears at the time, then suggest
Simha. If any cattle appears then the Moon will be in
Vrishabha and so forth.

होरानर्वांशप्रतिमं विलग्नं लग्नाद्द्वियाँवति च द्वकाणे ।
तस्माद्देचावति वा विलग्नं प्रष्टुः प्रद्धतावति शास्त्रमाह ॥ ७ ॥

Stanza 7.—The birth lagna will be that represented by the rising navamsa at the time of
the query or it will be that lagna which when
counted from the question time is similar in
number to the drekkanas separating the question
lagna from the Sun at the time.

NOTES

Take the lagna which rises at the question time and
find its navamsa. The birth sign will be that house which
the rising navamsa denotes. Thus if the question time
falls in Mesha when the navamsa of Kataka rises, then
predict that the man was born when Kataka was rising as
lagna. This is easy enough. Another method here suggested
is a little complicated. Find out the rising drekkana at the
question time, and also the drekkana where the Sun will be
located; then count from the Lagna Drekkana to the
drekkana occupied by the Sun at the time of the query.
Take this number and count from the question lagna to a
similar number and predict that sign which falls there as
the birth lagna. Take one example. The 2nd Drekkana
in Mesha rises at the Prasna time. The Sun is found in
the 3rd Drekkana of Dhanus. Each drekkana has 10° of a
sign and so one sign has 3 drekkanas. The 3rd Drekkana
would be the 9th house from lagna. Thus Sun is found
in the 26th drekkana from the drekkana at the time of
question. There are only 12 signs in the zodiac. Divide
26 by 12, we get 2 remainder. Now count from the
question Lagna Mesha and put the birth lagna in the
second from it or Vrishabha. Take another example. The

first drekkana in Kataka rises while the Sun is found in the
2nd Drekkana of Thula at the time of query. Counting
from the drekkana at the time of question to the drekkana
occupied by the Sun we get lagna as the 11th house from
the lagna at the time of question, viz., Kataka and hence
Vrishabha which is the 11th from Kataka.

Varahamihira says that these principles are put forward
by him on the strength of the ancient sciences and not
based on his own intelligence or education. The great
Varahamihira shows the highest respect for the ancient
Maharishis and thus adds dignity to himself and his
works.

जन्मादिशेछ्यगते सत्रीर्यं
छायाङ्गुलघ्नेऽर्कहतेऽवशिष्टम् ।
आसीनसुप्तोत्थितिष्ठतां
जायासुखाब्जोदयगं प्रदिष्टम् ॥ ८ ॥

Stanza 8.—Multiply the sphuta of the planet
in the lagna or that of the most powerful by
chayangula and divide it by twelve. The remainder
denotes the number of the birth lagna from
Mesha or the birth lagna will be the 7th, 4th,
10th or lagna as the querist is sitting or lying
down or rising or standing respectively.

NOTES

He gives here two methods to find out the birth lagna
of the querist. Find out if there is any planet in the

ascendant at the question time or if there is none there,
then find out the most powerful of the planets at the question time and ascertain its sphuta or the correct degree,
minute and second.   Reduce these into kalas.   Get a place
levelled by water and fix the *sanku* or stick which must be
12 angulas.   8 yavas make an *angula*.   *Yava* means a
barley grain or something like it.   Four angulas make a
mushti or fist, and 6 mushtis make a *hasta* or hand.   Four
hastas make a *danda* or danas (bow) and 2000 dandas
or rods make a *krosa*.   Four krosas make a *yojana*.
Hundred yojanas make a *desa* (country) and four desas
make a *mandala*.   One hundred mandalas make a *khanda*
(continent) and the earth contains nine *khandas*.   A hand
is roughly about 18 inches or a foot and a half.   Therefore
one angula roughly means $\frac{3}{4}$ths of an inch.   Danda means
6 ft.   12,000 ft. make a krosa or 2 miles 2 furlongs and 40
yards or 2 miles $2\frac{2}{}$ furlongs.   A *yojana* so often repeated in
Sanskrit works will be 9 miles 8/11 furlongs.   A country or
desa will be about 909 miles, and 4 desas make a mandala
or 3,636 miles.   A khanda contains 100 mandalas or 3,63,600
miles and the earth contains nine khandas or 32,72,400
miles.   (See *Lilavathi*, Stanza 5, *Paribhasha Prakarana* by
Bhaskaracharya.   Also *Suryasiddhanta*).

Twelve angulas will be equal to about nine inches.
Take the shadow cast by this stick and multiply kalas by
this and divide by twelve.   The remainder shows the
number of the birth sign from Mesha.   Thus, if the
remainder is 7, then the birth lagna will be Thula.   If it is
11, then it will be Kumbha.   There is another method to
find out the birth lagna.   If the querist asks the prasna
sitting, then the birth lagna will be the 7th from the Prasna

Lagna. If he asks when lying down, the 4th lagna from the query lagna will represent the birth sign. When the querist is rising, then the birth lagna will be the 10th from Prasna Lagna. When the querist is standing at the time, the birth lagna will be the same as the Prasna Lagna. This view is supported by quotation from other works. Thus, if the man asks the astrologer standing, then his birth lagna will be that which rises at the time of question. Suppose a man comes to an astrologer at midday in the month of Virgo, then the rising lagna will be Dhanus. If this question is asked when he stands, then his birth house will be Dhanus. If this question is put while he is sitting, then the 7th from Dhanus or Mithuna will represent his birth lagna. If the question is asked when he lies down, then the 4th from Dhanus or Meena will be his birth sign. If he puts the query when rising, the 10th from Dhanus or Kanya will represent his birth sign.

[The following horoscope will illustrate this point. A gentleman consulted an astrologer at 10-10 a.m. on Wednesday the 24th Sept. 1947. The planets at the time of query were thus situated.

RASI

		Rahu	Kuja Sani
	RASI		Rahu
Moon	Guru Kethu	Lagna	Ravi Sukra Budha

AMSA

Ravi			Lagna
Sani	AMSA		Guru Kuja Kethu
Rahu			Budha
Moon			

As the query was made rising on the chair, the birth lagna would be the 10th or Kataka and the horoscope was cast for 9-8-11 at 0-15 ghatis in the morning and proved correct.]

RASI

	Rahu Kuja Sani		
Moon	RASI		Ravi Lagna
			Budha
	Guru Kethu	Sukra	

NAVAMSA

	Moon		
Lagna Guru	NAVAMSA		Rahu
Kethu Ravi Sukra			
	Sani	Kuja	Budha

गोसिंहौ जितुमाष्टमौ क्रियतुले कन्यामृगौ च क्रमात्
संवर्ग्यो दशकाष्टसप्तविषयैः शेषाः स्वसंख्यागुणाः ।
जीवारास्फुजिदिन्दवाः प्रथमवच्छेषो ग्रहाः सौम्यव-
द्राशीनां नियतो विधिर्ग्रहयुतैः कार्या च तद्वर्गणा ॥ ९ ॥

Stanza 9.—The signs Taurus and Leo, Gemini and Scorpio, Aries and Libra, Virgo and Capricorn, must be multiplied by 10, 8, 7 and 5 respectively. The remaining rasis (signs) must be multiplied by their own number. Jupiter, Mars, Venus and Mercury must be similarly muliplied. The remaining planets must be multiplied like Mercury. This must be necessarily done with

the signs.   When there is a planet in the lagna, it
must also undergo this multiplication.

NOTES

Here a general summary of the various methods for
calculating lost horoscopes is given. Convert the rising
sign at the time of the question into kalas. When Taurus
or Leo rises, multiply its kalas by 10. When Gemini or
Scorpio rises, multiply its kalas by 8. When Aries or
Libra rises, multiply its kalas by 7. When Virgo or
Capricorn rises, multiply its kalas by 5. The other signs,
viz., Cancer, Sagittarius, Aquarius and Pisces, must be
multiplied by their own number, viz., Cancer represents
four from Aries and therefore must be multiplied by 4,
Sagittarius represents 9 and it must be multiplied by 9,
Aquarius by 11 and Pisces by 12.   Thus multiply the signs
as follows :—

Aries	by	...	7
Taurus	,,	...	10
Gemini	,,	...	8
Cancer	,,	...	4
Leo	,,	...	10
Virgo	,,	...	5
Libra	,,	...	7
Scorpio	,,	...	8
Sagittarius	,,	...	9
Capricorn	,,	...	5
Aquarius	,,	...	11
Pisces	,,	...	12

The lagna at the time of question must be multiplied
by their respective figures. If there is a planet in that

lagna, then the kalas the planet has passed in it must be
multiplied by the number given to it. Thus, when Jupiter
occupies lagna, first multiply the lagna by its number and
then multiply the result by the number given to Jupiter,
viz., 10. When Mars is there, by 8 ; when Venus is there,
by 7; and when the rest of the planets, *viz.*, Mercury, Sun,
Moon and Saturn, by 5.

> Thus :—Jupiter must be multiplied by 10,
>   Mars   ,,   8,
>   Venus   ,,   7,
>   Mercury, Sun,   ,,   5.
>   Moon and Saturn.

If there is more than one planet in the rising sign, then
each must be multiplied by the figures given to them
respectively. The resultant must be kept in one place, for
disposal as detailed in the following stanzas :

सप्राहतं त्रिधनभाजितशेषमृक्षं
दत्वाथवा नव विशोध्य न वाऽथवाऽस्मात् ।
एवं कलत्रसहजात्मजशत्रुमेभ्यः
प्रष्टुर्वदेदुदयराशिवशेन तेषाम् ॥ १० ॥

Stanza 10.—Multiply the result thus obtained
by 7, and divide the total (after adding to or
subtracting 9 from it) by 27; the remainder shows
the number of the star in which the person is
born. From the question lagna, the 7th, 3rd, 5th
and 6th bhavas, may also be indicated and their
stars ascertained.

NOTES

Here he gives hints to find out the constellation at the time of birth of a person and that of any of his relations like children, brothers, wife or enemies.   In the previous stanza a certain process has been named and a resultant is obtained.   This must be multiplied by seven.   We get a result.   To this total we must add 9 when the rising lagna falls in a movable sign.   When it falls in a common sign, 9 must be subtracted from the total.   When the lagna falls in a fixed sign, no addition or subtraction must be made. This is what some authors say.   But Bhattotpala explains it in a different way.   If the 1st Drekkana of the question lagna rises, then 9 must be added to the total.   If it falls in the 2nd Drekkana, there must be no addition or subtraction.   If the rising drekkana is the 3rd, then 9 must be subtracted.   After doing this, take the total and divide it by 27.   Then the remainder denotes the number of the star from Aswini.   Some are of opinion that the grand total, before adding or subtracting 9, must be divided by 27. Take the remainder and then add to, or subtract from or do nothing, as the case may be and predict the constellation from that number.   In the case of children, brothers, wife, enemies, etc., the author advises the readers to consult similarly from the house, which represents that bhava from the question sign.   Take an illustration.   Suppose Mithuna rises at the question time.   The 7th from Mithuna is the house of his wife.   Take that bhava, see how many kalas it has passed and follow the multiplication and division process as recommended above and the number that remains there, will represent the constellation at the time of the birth of his wife.   For other relations and events take

other bhavas (significations) and predict the constellations
working from them as if they are the rising lagnas at the
time of question. The age, lagna, year, etc., for any relations must be worked out as the author has done for the
person himself from their lagnas. Bhattotpala gives preference to his explanation.

वर्षर्तुमासतिथयो द्युनिशंझुड्नि
वेलोदयेर्धनवभागविकल्पनाः स्युः ।
भूयो दशादिगुणिताः स्वविकल्पभक्ताः
वर्षादयो नवकदानविशोधनाभ्याम् ॥ ११ ॥

Stanza 11.—By multiplying the total mentioned in Stanza 9 by 10, etc., and also by adding
to, or subtracting from it and by dividing that
by the various figures already given, the year,
season, month, lunar day, night and day, constellation, time, ascendant, navamsa, etc., may be
ascertained.

NOTES

This stanza is so briefly expressed in Sanskrit that no
English translation could do justice to it unless it is supple-
mented by full and elaborate explanations. Reduce the
rising sign to kalas, and then multiply it by the figures
given to that lagna and any planet which may occupy it.
Keep this total in four separate places. Multiply one
by 10, the second by 8, the third by 7 and the fourth by 5.
Then follow the methods for adding to or subtracting from

them the figure 9.   Then the total must be divided by 120
to get years

> Do—by 6 to get Rithus
> Do—by 2 to get Months
> Do—by 27 to get Constellations
> Do—by 15 to get Lunar days

and these details are clearly given in the next three stanzas.

विज्ञेया दशकेष्वब्दा ऋतुमासास्तथैव च ।
अष्टकेष्वपि मासार्द्धास्तिथयश्च तथा स्मृताः ॥ १२ ॥

Stanza 12.—From the total multiplied by 10
the year, season and month have to be found
out.   From the total multiplied by 8, fortnight
and lunar day have to be ascertained.

NOTES

The total has been desired to be posited in four different places. Take the total multiplied by 10, and divide
it by 120 the *parmayus* or the total length of life mentioned
in the earlier chapter.   The remainder shows the age in
years of the questioning person or the person about whom
he puts the query.   The same figure divided by 6 will give
the Rithu represented by the remainder from the Sisira.
When that total is divided by 2 and the remainder is one,
then it represents the first month of the Rithu already
ascertained.   But when there is no remainder then the 2nd
month of the Rithu must be predicted.   But if a man is
above 120 years then the process named in the lost horoscopes will not apply to such cases.   Then take the total
obtained by multiplying it by 8.   Divide this by 2 and if the

the remainder is one, then the birth has taken place in the
first half of the lunar month. If there is no remainder,
then the birth takes place in the 2nd or dark half of the
lunar month. When the total is divided by 15, the number
of the remainder shows the number of lunar days in the
first or second half of the lunar month.

दिवारात्रिप्रद्धतिं च नक्षत्रानयनं तथा ।
सप्तकेष्वपि बर्गेषु नित्यमेवोपलक्षयेत् ॥ १३ ॥

Stanza 13.—Take the total multiplied by 7
and from it predict the constellation, day and
night times.

NOTES

Take now the total obtained by multiplying the first
by 7. When this total is divided by 2, representing day and
night, if the remainder is one, the birth falls in day, and if
there is no remainder then the birth falls in night. When
this total is divided by 27, the number of constellations,
the remainder shows the number of constellation from
Aswini. As the importance of constellations is very great
for all, the explanation has been repeated twice.

वेलामथ विलयं च होरामंशकमेव च ।
पञ्चकेषु विजानीयान्नष्टजातकसिद्धये ॥ १४ ॥

Stanza 14.—Take the total multiplied by 5
and ascertain the time, sign, Hora, Amsa, etc.

NOTES

Take now the total obtained by multiplying the first by five and if the man was born during the day, then divide it by the duration of that day or if he was born during the night divide it by the duration of the night on that day. The remainder shows the number of ghatikas during the day or the night—as the case may be, when the person was born. Finding the correct ghatis, etc., the divisions of lagna—*viz.*, Hora, Drekkana, Navamsa, etc., may easily be ascertained by correct calculations. Then by mathematical calculations the positions of the planets at the time of birth may be easily ascertained. Then the results detailed in the earlier chapters, *viz.*, of Dasas, Antardasas, Astakavargas can be predicted.

संस्कारनाममात्रा द्विगुणा छायाङ्गुलैः समायुक्ताः ।
शेषं त्रिनवकभक्तान्नक्षत्रं तद्धनिष्ठादि ॥ १५ ॥

Stanza 15.—Take the *matras* of the real name, multiply it by two and add to the result the number of *chayangulas* obtained at the time and divide the total by 27; then take the remainder and count it from Dhanista to get the birth constellation of the querist.

NOTES

Here Varahamihira gives another method to identify or find the birth constellation of the querist. A man may have many or several names, pet, nick or from other cause ; but his real name given at the time of birth must be taken. Consonants represent half *matras* (measure of time) while vowels represent full matra. Take the number of matras contained in his proper name and multiply it by 2. In the previous stanza a process has already been named to get the number of *chayangulas* (shadow) at the time of the question and add this number to the total thus obtained. Then divide the total thus obtained by 27 we get some remainder. This number shows the number of constellation—counting from Dhanista—at the time of birth. Take an illustration. We shall say the name is Ramakrishna. This name is composed of *Ra Ma Kri Shna* $1\frac{1}{2}+1\frac{1}{2}+1\frac{1}{2}+2=6\frac{1}{2}$ matras. This total must be multiplied by 2 and the result is 13. Suppose the chayangula or shadow measurement is 5 angulas. Thus $13+5=18$. This must be divided by 27. As 18 cannot be divided by 27, we must take 18 as the remainder. Count from Dhanista till you get 18 and then name the star you get as that of the birth constellation of the querist. The 18th from Dhanista is Hasta and it becomes the birth star. Take an English name : Edward. It is composed of, Sanskrit letters which give 4 matras. This multiplied by 2 gives 8. Add 5 chayangulas. The total is $8+5=13$. The remainder is 13 ; the 13th from Dhanista is Pushyami and it is to be predicted as the birth star of the querist.

द्विग्निचतुर्दंशदशतितिथिसप्तत्रिगुणानवाष्टचेन्द्राद्याः ।
पञ्चदशघ्नास्तद्दिङ्मुखान्विता भधनिष्ठादि ॥ १६ ॥

Stanza 16.—The figures 2, 3, 14, 10, 15, 21, 9 and 8 from the East, etc., must be multiplied by 15 and the number of persons looking in the same direction as the querist, must be added to the

total; and divided by 27; the remainder shows
the number of constellation from Dhanista.

NOTES

Another method is given here to find out the birth star
of the querist. If the querist faces the East, South, S.W.,
West, North-West, North and North-East are represented
by the figures 2, 3, 14, 10, 15, 21, 9 and 8 respectively.
If he faces East, then take the number 2 and multiply it
by 15. The total is 30. Suppose two persons are also
looking with him towards the East. Then add 2 to the
total 30. The total is 32. This must be divided by 27,
the remainder is 5, or, the star Revati, which is the 5th
from Dhanista, must be identified as his birth star. Suppose the querist faces the South without any company.
14 represents South and this must be multiplied by $15 =
14 \times 15 = 210$. This must be divided by $27 = 210 \div 27 = 7$
and the remainder is 21. The 21st from Dhanista, *viz.*,
Visakha must be identified as his birth constellation.

इतिनष्टजातकमिदं बहुप्रकारं मया विनिर्दिष्टम् ।
ग्राह्यमतः सच्छिष्यैः परीक्ष्य यन्नादयथा भवति ॥ १७ ॥

Stanza 17.—Various methods have been expounded by me about the lost horoscopes. The
real student will accept that which he finds correct after laborious calculations.

NOTES

Varahamihira collected his information about lost
horoscopy from Vasishta, Parasara, Manitha, Yavana, etc.,

and explained in this chapter the various methods by which the birth time, constellation, week day, lunar day, solar day, month and the year can be ascertained. He here concludes by exhorting the diligent student to try all these by proper and laborious calculations and accept that system which agrees best with his practical experience. It may be questioned as to why Varahamihira does not give one method which is the best out of the lot, and which tallied with the experience of that great astrologer. In St. 7, Chap. VII, he has clearly stated the reasons which have been fully dealt with by me in my notes for that stanza. The reader may refer to them.

CHAPTER XXVII

DREKKANA ADHYAYA

त्रैष्काणाध्यायः

कल्यां सितवस्त्रवेष्टितः कृष्णः शक्त इवाभिरक्षितुम् ।
रौद्रः परशुं समुद्यतं धत्ते रक्तविलोचनः पुमान् ॥ १ ॥

Stanza 1.—The 1st Drekkana of Mesha represents a man with a white cloth round his waist, dark complexion, pretending to protect, fearful red eyes and a lifted axe.

NOTES

There are 12 signs in the zodiac and each sign is divided into 3 equal parts called a Drekkana. Thus there are 36 drekkanas, whose individual influences, peculiarities and potencies are distinctly explained in this Chapter by Varahamihira. The uses for these drekkanas are clearly stated in the commentaries of Bhattotpala under St. 36 of this Chapter. Mars rules this drekkana; it is masculine and armed. Since each sign has 3 drekkanas, there are 36 drekkanas and Mesha, Simha, Dhanus form 3 drekkanas for Mesha and Mars, Sun and Jupiter are the lords. Vrishabha, Kanya and Makara are the 3 drekkanas for Vrishabha with Sukra, Budha and Sani as lords. Similarly from every house, the 1st, 5th and 9th form the 3 drekkanas and as the 1st, 2nd and 3rd drekkanas, they have

different shapes and different characteristics, so that Mesha
as 1st drekkana, is not the same as the 2nd drekkana for
Dhanus and is feminine and as the 3rd drekkana for Simha
is masculine.   The lords are no doubt the same.

रक्ताम्रबाभूषणभंक्ष्यचिन्ता
कुंभाकृतिर्वाजिमुखी तृषार्त्ती ।
एकेन पादेन च मेषमध्ये
द्रेष्काणरूपं यवनोपदिष्टम् ॥ २ ॥

Stanza 2.—The 2nd Drekkana of Mesha is
sketched by Yavanas as representing a woman
with red cloth, fond of ornaments and food,
pot-belly, horse-face, thirsty and single-footed·

NOTES

This is a quadruped Drekkana, feminine in nature and
governed by the Sun.   The characteristics are those of a
woman and hence biped.   But Varahamihira classifies this
as quadruped because the face is that of a horse—a quadruped.   Some say that this is a Khaga or bird Drekkana.

क्रूरः कलाङ्गः कपिलः क्रियार्थी
भयव्रतोऽभ्युद्यतदण्डहस्तः ।
रक्तानि वस्त्राणि विभर्ति चण्डो
मेषे तृतीयः कथितस्त्रिभागः ॥ ३ ॥

Stanza 3.—The 3rd Drekkana of Mesha
represents a man, cruel, skilled in arts, yellowish,

fond of work, unprincipled, with a lifted-up stick, angry and covered with purple clothes.

NOTES

This is a masculine Drekkana armed and ruled by Jupiter.

कुंचितलूनकचा घटदेहा
दग्धपटा तृषिताऽशनचित्ता ।
आभरणान्यभिवाञ्छति नारी
रूपमिदं वृषभे प्रथमस्य ॥ ४ ॥

Stanza 4.—The 1st Drekkana of Vrishabha represents a woman with torn ringlets, pot-belly, burnt cloth, thirsty, fond of food and ornaments.

NOTES

This represents a feminine Drekkana, fiery in nature and governed by Venus. The hair will be in ringlets but partly torn and protruding belly resembling a pot.

क्षेत्रधान्यगृहधेनुकलाज्ञो लाङ्गले सशकटे कुशलश्च ।
स्कन्धमुद्वहति गोपतितुल्यं क्षुत्परोऽजवदनो मलवासाः ॥ ५ ॥

Stanza 5.—The 2nd Drekkana of Vrishabha represents a man possessing knowledge of lands, grains, houses, cows, arts, ploughing and carts, hungry, sheep faced, dirty clothes and shoulders like the hump of an ox.

NOTES

Arts include knowledge in music, drums, dancing, writing, painting, etc. This is a masculine Drekkana, quadruped and governed by Mercury.

द्विपसमकायः पाण्डुरदंष्ट्रः
शरभसमांघ्रिः पिङ्गलमूर्तिः ।
अविमृगलोभव्याकुलचित्तो
वृषभवनस्य प्रान्तगतोऽयम् ॥ ६ ॥

Stanza 6.—The 3rd Drekkana of Vrishabha is represented by a man with a body like that of an elephant, white teeth, legs like that of *sarabha*, yellowish colour, and clever in capturing sheep and deer.

NOTES

Sarabha is an animal at which the lion is supposed to get frightened. It has eight legs of great size and strength. Deer is representative of mild animals. This is masculine, quadruped and ruled by Saturn. Amara Simha thus derives the word Sarabha = Srinathi Simbam = Sarabha or that which kills the lion. Referring to Mahabharata, we find Sarabha thus described :—

Ashtapadurdheva nainaha sarabho vanagocharaha— means that it has eight legs, eyes in the top and lives in the forest. Probably this species is now extinct or may be found in forests yet to be discovered.

स्वच्याश्रयं समभिवाञ्छति कर्म नारी-
रूपान्विता भरणकार्यकृतादरा च ।
हीनमजोच्छ्रितभुजर्तुमती त्रिभाग-
माध्यं तृतीयभवनस्य वदन्ति तज्ज्ञाः ॥ ७ ॥

Stanza 7.—The 1st Drekkana of Mithuna represents a female, fond of needle work, handsome, fond of ornamentation, issueless, lifted hands and in menses.

NOTES

This is feminine and ruled by Mercury.

उद्यानसंस्थः कवची धनुष्मा-
ञ्छरोऽस्त्रधारी गरुडाननश्च ।
क्रीडात्मजालंकरणार्थचिन्तां
करोति मध्ये मिथुनस्य राशेः ॥ ८ ॥

Stanza 8.—The 2nd Drekkana of Mithuna represents a man, living in garden, in armour, with a bow, warlike, armed with weapons, face like that of Garuda, and fond of play, children, ornamentation and wealth.

NOTES

Garuda is the vehicle of Vishnu and is represented as having a long nose. This is a masculine and bird Drekkana armed, and ruled by Venus.

भूषितो वरुणवद्धहुरन्नो
बद्धतूणकबचः सधनुष्कः ।
नृत्तवादितकलासु च विद्वान्
काव्यकृन्मिथुनराश्यवसाने ॥ ९ ॥

Stanza 9.—The 3rd Drekkana of Mithuna represents a man, adorned, decked with gems, armoured with quiver and bow, skilled in dancing, drumming and arts, and poet.

NOTES

This is a masculine and armed Drekkana ruled by Saturn.

पत्रमूलफलभृद्द्विपकायः
कानने मलयगः शरभांघ्रिः ।
क्रोडतुल्यवदनो हयकण्ठः
कर्कटे प्रथमरूपमुशन्ति ॥ १० ॥

Stanza 10.—The 1st Drekkana of Kataka represents a man, holding fruits, roots and leaves, elephant bodied, residing on sandal trees in the forest, legs like that of Sarabha, and horse-necked.

NOTES

This is a quadruped masculine Drekkana governed by the Moon.

पद्मार्चिता मूर्द्धनि भोगियुक्ता
स्त्री कर्कशारण्यगता विरौति ।
शाखां फलाशस्य समाश्रिता च
मध्ये स्थिता कर्कटकस्य राशेः ॥ ११ ॥

Stanza 11.—The 2nd Drekkana of Kataka represents a female worshipped on the head by lotus flowers, with serpents, full blown youthfulness, living in forests on the branch of *phalasa* and crying.

NOTES

This is feminine and ruled by Mars.

भार्याभरणार्थमर्णवं नौस्थो गच्छति सर्पवेष्टितः ।
हैमैश्च युतो विभूषणैश्चिपिटास्योन्त्यगतश्च कर्कटे ॥ १२ ॥

Stanza 12.—The 3rd Drekkana of Kataka represents a man covered with serpents, flat-faced, and crossing the ocean in a boat in search of wife's jewels.

NOTES

This is masculine and serpent Drekkana ruled by Jupiter.

शाल्मलेरुपरि गृध्रजम्बुकौ
श्वा नरश्च मलिनाम्बरान्वितः ।
रौति मातृपितृविप्रयोजितः
सिंहरूपमिदमाद्यमुच्यते ॥ १३ ॥

Stanza 13.—The 1st Drekkana of Simha represents a vulture and a jackal on the *Salmali* tree, a dog and a man dressed in dirty raiments, leaving father and mother, and crying.

NOTES

This is masculine, quadruped and bird Drekkana governed by the Sun. Salmali is the Salmalia-Malabearica or the loose cotton tree largely found in S. India.

हयाकृतिः पाण्डुरमाल्यशेखरो
बिभर्ति कृष्णाजिनकंबलं नरः ।
दुरासदः सिंह इवात्तकार्मुको
नताग्रनासो मृगराजमध्यमः ॥ १४ ॥

Stanza 14.—The 2nd Drekkana of Simha represents a man resembling a horse's body with white garlands on the head, wearing krishnajina and kambalam, fierce as a lion with a bow in the hand and bent nose.

NOTES

This is a masculine Drekkana, armed and governed by Jupiter.

There are two readings—Krishnajina Kambala and Krishnajina Chivara. Krishnajina is the hide of a dark deer, kambala means a woollen blanket, and chivara means torn cloth.

ऋक्षाननो वानरतुल्यचेष्टो
बिभर्ति दण्डं फलमामिषं च
कूचीं मनुष्यः कुटिलैश्च केशै-
र्मृगेश्वरस्यान्त्यगतस्त्रिभागः ॥१५॥

Stanza 15.—The 3rd Drekkana of Simha represents a man with a bear's face, acts like those of a monkey, long beard, curbed ringlets and holding a stick, fruit and flesh.

NOTES

This is a masculine, quadruped, armed Drekkana governed by Mars.

पुष्पप्रपूर्णेन घटेन कन्या
मलप्रदिग्धाम्बरसंवृताङ्गी ।
वस्त्रार्थसंयोगमभीष्टमाना
गुरोः कुलं वाञ्छति कन्यकाद्यः ॥१६॥

Stanza 16.—The 1st Drekkana of Kanya represents a female with a pot, full of flowers, covering the body with dirty raiments, fond of money and clothes, and going to the home of the preceptor.

NOTES

This is a feminine Drekkana governed by Mercury.

पुरुषः प्रगृहीतलेखनिः
श्यामो वक्त्रशिरा व्ययायकृत् ।
विपुलं च बिभर्ति कार्मुकं
रोमव्याप्ततनुश्च मध्यमः ॥ १७ ॥

Stanza 17.—The 2nd Drekkana of Kanya
represents a man with a pen in the hand, dark
complexion, the head tied round by a cloth,
counting gains and expenditure, covered over the
body with dense hair and holding a big bow.

NOTES

This is a masculine Drekkana, armed and ruled by
Saturn.

गौरी सुधौताग्रदुकूलगुप्ता
समुच्छ्रिता कुम्भकटच्छुहस्ता ।
देवालयं स्त्री प्रयता प्रवृत्ता
वदन्ति कन्यान्त्यगतास्त्रिभागः ॥ १८ ॥

Stanza 18.—The last Drekkana of Kanya
(observe great authors) represents a female,
yellowish, covered by a white silk cloth, tall,
holding a pot and a spoon, going to a temple
with great sanctity.

NOTES

One reading is Dukula Gupta or covered by a silk
cloth, another reading is Dukula Hasta or holding cloth

in the hand. This is a feminine Drekkana governed by
Venus. These are characteristics explained by the great
Munis or Rishis.

वीथ्यन्तरापणगतः पुरुषस्तुलावा
नुन्मानमानकुशलः प्रतिमानहस्तः ।
भाण्डं विचिन्तयति तस्य च मूल्यमेत-
द्रूपं वदन्ति यवनाः प्रथमं तुलायाः ॥ १९ ॥

Stanza 19.—The 1st Drekkana of Thula,
say Yavanas, represents a man seated in a shop
in the middle of the road, holding balances,
clever in weighing and measuring with a small
scale for weighing gold, diamonds, and thinking
of his capital, and the prices of the articles in the
shop.

NOTES

This is a masculine Drekkana ruled by Venus. Measuring here refers to the measure of grains, etc. The Yavanas here referred to are the *Purana* or old Yavanas.

कलशं परिगृह्य विनिष्पतितुं
समभीष्सति गृध्रमुखः पुरुषः ।
क्षुधितस्तृपितश्च कलत्रसुता-
न्मनसैति तुलाधरमध्यगतः ॥ २० ॥

Stanza 20.—The middle Drekkana of Thula
represents a man with a vulture's face, hungry

and thirsty, holding a pot which is ready to fall
and thinking of his wife and children.

NOTES

The pot is ready to fall because of his weakness by
hunger and thirst. This is a masculine, bird Drekkana
governed by Saturn.

विभीषुयंस्तिष्ठति रत्नचित्रितो
वने मृगान् काञ्चनतूणवर्मभृत् ।
फलामिषं वानररूपभृन्नर-
स्तुलावसाने यवनैरुदाहृतः ॥ २१ ॥

Stanza 21.—The last Drekkana of Thula,
say the Yavanas, represents a man, decked with
gems, wearing golden quiver and armour and
frightening the animals in the wilderness, resembling a monkey and holding in the hand fruits and
flesh.

NOTES

Fruits refer to mangoes, etc. There are two readings :
  (1) Kanchana Thuna Varma Brit=wearing gold
      quiver and armour.
  (2) Kinnara Rupa Brinnaraha=wearing the form of
      Kinnaras, a set of celestial beings with horse-
      like faces.

This is a masculine, quadruped, resembling a monkey
and governed by Mercury.

वस्त्रैर्विहीनाऽऽभरणैश्च नारी
महासमुद्रात्समुपैति कूलम् ।
स्थानच्युता सर्पनिबद्धपादा
मनोरमा वृश्चिकराशिपूर्वः ॥ २२ ॥

Stanza 22.—The 1st Drekkana of Vrischika
represents a woman naked and without ornaments, coming from the middle of a great ocean
to the shore, dislocated from her original place,
the feet bound by serpents and handsome.

NOTES

This is a feminine, serpent Drekkana ruled by Mars.

स्थानसुखान्यामिवाञ्छति नारी
भर्तृकृते भुजगावृतदेहा ।
कच्छपकुंभसमानशरीरा
वृश्चिकमध्यमरूपमुशन्ति ॥ २३ ॥

Stanza 23.—The middle Drekkana of Vrischika represents a woman fond of home and
happiness for her husband's sake and covered by
serpents with a body resembling a tortoise and a
pot.

NOTES

This is a feminine, serpent Drekkana ruled by Jupiter.

पृथुलचिपिटकूर्मतुल्यवक्त्रः
श्वमृगवराहसृगालभीषकारी ।
अवति च मलयाकरप्रदेशं
मृगपतिरन्त्यमतस्य वृश्चिकस्य ॥ २४ ॥

Stanza 24.—The last Drekkana of Vrischika
represents a lion with a broad flat face, resembling a tortoise, frightening dogs, deer, boars and
jackals, protecting localities covered with sandal-
wood trees.

NOTES

This is a masculine, quadruped, lion Drekkana ruled
by the Moon.

मनुष्यवक्त्रोऽश्वसमानकायो
धनुर्विगृह्यायतमाश्रमस्थः ।
क्रतूपयोज्यानि तपस्विनश्च
ररक्ष आद्यो धनुषस्त्रिभागः ॥ २५ ॥

Stanza 25.—The 1st Drekkana of Dhanus
represents a man with a human face and a horse's
body with a bow in hand residing in a hermitage,
protecting sacrificial articles and Maharishis.

NOTES

This is a masculine, quadruped, armed Drekkana ruled
by Jupiter.

मनोरमा चम्पकहेमवर्णा
भद्रासने तिष्ठति मध्यरूपा ।
सम्रुद्ररत्नानि विघट्टयन्ती
मध्यत्रिभागो धनुषः प्रदिष्टः ॥ २६ ॥

Stanza 26.—The middle Drekkana of Dhanus represents a woman, handsome, with the colour of Champaca or gold, picking up the gems from the ocean and sitting in the Bhadrasana fashion.

NOTES

This is a feminine Drekkana ruled by Mars.

There are several postures in which Devotees in the yoga practice are required to sit and contemplate. This is technically called *Asana* which means a position of the body by which steadiness and concentration can be secured in the search of knowledge after Para-Brahma. Sixty-four Asanas are mentioned and even today there are some yogis who can show all the sixty-four. The schools are also teaching some important Asanas to the students and many boys can show more than 16 to 20 Asanas as observed. In 1906, I brought a north Indian yogee to the house, who showed all the 64 Asanas. I kept him for about a week and sent him with rich presents, asking him not to exhibit them in the Moore Market for the sake of a few pice and giving him the healthier aspect of these Yogasanas and their sacred attainments. The most important Asanas for yoga practice are:

(1)	Padmasana	(5)	Kapalasana
(2)	Swastikasana	(6)	Mayurasana
(3)	Bhadrasana	(7)	Kukkutasana
(4)	Gomukhasana	(8)	Simhasana and so forth.

कूर्चीं नरो हाटकचम्पकाभो
वरासने दण्डधरो निषण्णः ।
कौशेयकान्युद्वहतेडजिनं च
तृतीयरूपं नवमस्य राशेः ॥ २७ ।

Stanza 27.—The 3rd Drekkana of Dhanus
represents a man with a long beard, complexion
like that of Champaca or gold, holding a stick,
sitting in a splendid posture and keeping silks and
deer skins.

NOTES

This is a masculine, armed Drekkana governed by the
Sun.

Champaca belongs to the Mangolia family and is called
Michelia champaca.

रोमचितो मकरोपमदंष्ट्रः
सूकरकायसमानशरीरः ।
योक्त्रकजालकबन्धनधारी
रौद्रमुखो मकरप्रथमस्तु ॥ २८ ॥

Stanza 28.—The 1st Drekkana of Makara
represents a man covered with much hair, teeth
like those of a crocodile, body like that of a pig,
keeping yokes, nets and bandages, and with a
cruel face.

NOTES

Bandages include ropes and chains. This is a masculine, Nigala (chains or bandages) Drekkana governed by Saturn.

कलास्वमिज्ञाञ्जदलायताक्षी
श्यामा विचित्राणि च मार्गमाणा ।
विभूषणालंकृतलोहकर्णा
योषा प्रदिष्टा मकरस्य मध्ये ॥ २९ ॥

Stanza 29.—The middle Drekkana of Makara represents a woman, skilled in arts, broad eyes like lotus petals, greenish dark, searching all kinds of articles and wearing iron ear ornaments.

NOTES

This is a feminine Drekkana ruled by Venus.

किंनरोपमतनुः सकम्बल-
स्तूणचापकवचैः समन्वितः ।
कुंभमुद्वहति रत्नचित्रितं
स्कन्धगं मकरराशिपश्चिमः ॥ ३० ॥

Stanza 30.—The last Drekkana of Makara represents a man, with a body like that of Kinnaras, with a Kambalam, with a quiver arrows and bow, and bearing a pot on the shoulder decked with gems.

NOTES

This is a masculine, armed Drekkana ruled by Mercury.

स्नेहमद्यजलभोजनागम-
व्याकुलीकृतमनाः सकंबलः ।
कोशकारवसनोऽजिनान्वितो
गृध्रतुल्यवदनो घटादिगः ॥ ३१ ॥

Stanza 31.—The 1st Drekkana of Kumbha represents a man with a mind disturbed by oils, wines, water and food being brought to him, with a Kambala, silk cloth and deer skin and a face resembling that of a vulture.

NOTES

This is a masculine Drekkana ruled by Sani. It represents a man being sorrowful by oils, food, wine, etc., being brought to him, with Kambala (woollen cloth) Pattasa, silk cloth, and Krishnajina or deer skin. The face resembles that of a vulture or Gridhra.

दग्धे शकटे सशाल्मले लोहान्याहरतेऽङ्गनावने ।
मलिनेन पटेन संवृता भाण्डैर्मूर्ध्नि गतैश्च मध्यमः ॥ ३२ ॥

Stanza 32.—The 2nd Drekkana of Kumbha represents a woman, covered with a dirty cloth in a forest, bearing pots on her head and dragging metals in a burnt cart loaded with cotton trees in it.

NOTES

This is a fiery, feminine Drekkana ruled by Mercury.

श्यामः सरोमश्रवणः किरीटी
त्वक्पत्रनिर्यासफलैर्बिभर्ति ।
भाण्डानि लोहव्यतिमिश्रितानि
संचारयन्त्यन्तगतो घटस्य ॥ ३३ ॥

Stanza 33.—The 3rd Drekkana of Kumbha indicates a man dark, with ears covered with long hair, wearing a crown and wandering with pots filled with iron, skin, leaves, gum and fruits.

NOTES

This is a masculine Drekkana governed by Venus. The author uses *Thwak* which means skin or bark.

खुग्भाण्डमुक्तामणिशङ्खमिश्रै-
र्व्याक्षिप्तहस्तः सविभूषणश्च ।
भार्याविभूषार्थमपां निधानं
नावा ध्रुवत्यादिगतो झषस्य ॥ ३४ ॥

Stanza 34.—The 1st Drekkana of Meena represents a man decked with ornaments, holding in hand sacrificial vessels, pearls, gems, and conch shells and crossing the ocean in a boat in search of jewels for his wife.

NOTES

As the language is plain and simple in the translation notes are necessarily short. This is a masculine Drekkana governed by Jupiter.

अत्युच्छ्रितध्वजपाताकमुपैति पोतं
कूलं प्रयाति जलधेः परिवारयुक्ता ।
वर्णेन चम्पखा प्रमदा त्रिभागे
मीनस्य चैषकथितो मुनिमिर्द्वितीयः ॥ ३५ ॥

Stanza 35.—The 2nd Drekkana of Meena indicates a woman with a colour more beautiful than that of Champaka, surrounded by her attendants, and sailing in a boat decked with long flags in search of the coast of the ocean.

NOTES

This is a feminine Drekkana ruled by the Moon. Champaka is a beautiful yellow strongly scented flower, pertaining to Mangolia species.

श्वभ्रान्तिके सर्पनिवेष्टिताङ्गो
वह्नेर्विहीनः पुरुषस्त्वटव्याम् ।
चौरानलव्याकुलितान्तरात्मा
विक्रोशतेऽन्त्योपगतो झषस्य ॥ ३६ ॥

Stanza 36.—The 3rd Drekkana of Meena represents a man crying in a pit in a forest, naked and covered over his body by serpents and with a mind distracted by thieves and fire.

NOTES

This is a masculine serpent Drekkana governed by Mars. There are twelve signs and each sign has 3 Drekkanas or there are in all 36 Drekkanas. It has already been

explained in several places in the body of this work about
the uses of these Drekkanas. They are especially useful
in travelling. Varahamihira says in his *Yatra patala* thus
—" The results of the rising Drekkana at the time of journey
must be predicted with reference to their form, actions and
nature. If the Drekkana is agreeable, bearing flowers,
fruits, gems or treasures or if they are aspected by benefics,
then prosperity will attend the traveller's march. If the
Drekkanas are armed he will be victorious, if aspected by
malefics, he will be defeated or beaten. If the Drekkana
happens to be serpent or bondage, the traveller will be
disgraced or imprisoned or will die. These Drekkanas also
enable one to know the nature, place and form of the
thieves. Varahamihira's son Prithuyasas thus observes in
his Shatpanchasat. " By the navamsa of the question the
nature of the article lost, by the Drekkana, the nature of
the thieves, by the Lagna, the time, locality and direction
and by the lord of the Lagna, the age and caste of the
thieves have to be known and predicted ". My work
' Chappanna ' gives elaborate details of Prasna.

The matter may be simplified thus. When a question
is put to an astrologer about the loss of an article by theft
or otherwise he will make the necessary calculation and fix
the lagna and navamsa for the time of question. When the
calculations are correct, the Shadvargas *Lagna, Hora,
Drekkana, Navamsa, Dwadasamsa* and *Thrimsamsa* can
easily be ascertained and fixed. After having done this he
must ascertain the nature of the article lost by the rising
navamsa. Each sign has various significations and governs
several articles. The nature of the thieves will have to be
predicted by the Drekkana which rises at the time. By the
Lagna, the time, at which an article has been lost or stolen

away, the direction in which it has been taken and the
place from which it is lost and the locality in which it is
deposited or concealed, and by the lord of the Lagna, the
age and caste of the thieves. In the second and third
chapter of this work all these details are given and the
student is referred to them for ready information.   In
travelling, necessarily the person leaves his house or place
of occupation at some time. The Lagna can easily be
ascertained and the rising Drekkana known. If the
Drekkana is good, he will have a prosperous journey, if it
is evil or malefic he will suffer loss, and if it is very bad he
will even die. The strength, position, conjunction and
aspects must be carefully consulted.   Varahamihira and
his famous son Prithuyasas seem to have confined their
views of Drekkana to lost articles, thieves and their
directions and travellers and their luck or ill-luck on their
journey. But their uses are more comprehensive than has
been stated here. When a person is born in a cruel
Drekkana, he will be bad and miserable. When he is born
in a beneficial Drekkana he will be good and successful.
When the Drekkana is good and evil planets occupy it, or
when it is evil and good planets combine in it the results
will be mixed. But when it is evil, occupied by a malefic
and aspected by an evil planet, the results are very
disagreeable, the person will suffer miseries, defeats,
poverty, losses, disgraces and various diseases. When the
Drekkana is good, occupied and aspected by benefics,
without malefic influence, the person will be eminently
successful, will be happy, will have good and distinguished
progeny and will attain to a good position and command
great respect and influence. (See Vaidyanatha's *Jataka
Parijata*, Sts. 112 to 116, Chapter IX).

A SUMMARY

Rasi	I Drekkana	II Drekkana	III Drekkana	Remarks
Mesha	Mesha Male Mars	Quadruped Feminine, some say bird, Sun	Masculine Man Jupiter	I. Mesha. II. Dhanus. III. Simha. Varaha- mihira classes the 2nd quadruped
Vrishabha	Feminine Venus	Masculine Quadruped Mercury	Masculine Quadruped Saturn	Vrishabha I Kanya II Makara III
Mithuna	Feminine Mercury	Male Bird Venus	Man Armed Saturn	Mithuna I Thula II Kumbha III
Kataka	Man Quadruped Moon	Female Mars	Man Jupiter Serpent	Kataka I Vrischika II Meena III
Simha	Masculine Quadruped Bird, Sun	Masculine Jupiter	Masculine Quadruped Mars	Simha I Dhanus II Mesha III
Kanya	Feminine Mercury	Masculine Saturn	Feminine Venus	Kanya I Makara II Vrishabha III

Thula	...	Male Venus	Masculine Bird Saturn	Masculine Quadruped Mercury	Thula I Kumbha II Mithuna III
Vrischika	...	Feminine Serpent Mars	Feminine Serpent Jupiter	Masculine Quadruped Moon	Vrischika I Meena II Kataka III
Dhanus	...	Man Quadruped Jupiter	Feminine Mars	Masculine Sun	Dhanus I Mesha II Simha III
Makara	...	Masculine Saturn	Feminine Venus	Masculine Mercury	Makara I Vrishabha II Kanya III
Kumbha	...	Masculine Saturn	Feminine Mercury	Masculine Venus	Kumbha I Mithuna II Thula III
Meena	...	Masculine Jupiter	Feminine Moon	Masculine Serpent Mars	Meena I Kataka II Vrischika III

CHAPTER XXVIII

Upasamhara Adhyaya

उपसंहाराध्यायः

(*Concluding Chapter*)

राशिप्रभेदो ग्रहयोनिभेदो
वियोनिजन्माथं निषेककालः ।
जन्माथ सद्योमरणं तथायु-
र्देशाविपाकोऽष्टकवर्गसंज्ञः ॥ १ ॥

Stanza 1.—The first chapter is Rasi Pra-
bheda, the second Grahayoni Bheda, the third
Viyonijanma, the fourth Nishakakala, the fifth
Janma Vidhi, the sixth Balarista, the seventh
Ayurdaya, the eighth Dasa Vipaka, and the ninth
is Ashtaka Varga.

NOTES

Here the author simply quotes the names of the
chapters he has composed from the commencement in this
work and their meanings have been well explained in their
respective places.

कर्मजीवो राजयोगाः खयोगा-
श्चान्द्रा योगा द्विग्रहाद्याश्च योगाः ।
प्रव्रज्याथो राशिशीलानि दृष्टि-
र्भावस्तस्मादाश्रयोऽथ प्रकीर्णः ॥ २ ॥

Stanza 2.—Tenth chapter is Karma Jiva, the eleventh Raja Yoga, the twelfth Nabhasa Yoga, the thirteenth Chandra Yoga, the fourteenth Dwigrahadi Yoga, the fifteenth Pravrajjya Yoga, the sixteenth Rasi sila, the seventeenth Dristi Phala, the eighteenth Bhavadhyaya, the nineteenth Asraya, and the twentieth Prakeerna.

NOTES

Here he repeats consecutively the names of the chapters he has composed.

नेष्ठा योगा जातकं कामिनीनां
निर्याणं स्थानष्टजन्म हकाणः ।
अध्यायानां विंशतिः यज्ञयुक्ता
जन्मन्येतद्यात्रिकं चाभिधास्ये ॥ ३ ॥

Stanza 3.—The twenty-first is Anistayoga, the twenty-second is Strijataka, the twenty-third is Niryana, the twenty-fourth Nastajataka and the twenty-fifth is Drekkana. Thus is Hora Sastra. I have composed 25 chapters, and I am going to name other chapters relating to Yatra or travelling.

NOTES

Varahamihira names only 25 chapters while we have given 28 chapters in this work. In the sixteenth chapter under Rasi sila, there have been divided three chapters, *viz.*, (1) Rooksha sila, (2) Chandra Rasi sila, and (3) Rasi sila.

Thus two more chapters have been added by giving separate names by somebody. But Bhattotpala concludes each of the 17th and 18th chapters with his name. Therefore we have a good authority in this learned commentator to follow in the division and enumeration of these chapters. It matters very little what the number of chapters are, since the same chapter has been converted into 3 chapters dividing the treatment of the subject into (1) results of signs, (2) results of signs occupied by the Moon, and (3) results of constellations.

प्रश्नास्तिथिर्मे दिवसः क्षणश्च
चन्द्रो विलग्नं त्वथ लग्नभेदः ।
शुद्धिर्ग्रहाणामथ चापवादो
विमिश्रकाव्यं तनुवेपनम् च ॥ ४ ॥

Stanza 4.—First Prasna Prabheda, (2) Thithi Bala, (3) Nakshatra Bhedana, (4) Divasa Bala, (5) Vara Bala, (6) Muhurtha, (7) Chandra Bala, (8) Lagna Nischaya, (9) Lagna Bheda, (10) Graha Siddhi, (11) Apavada, (12) Vimisra, and (13) Thanu Vepana.

NOTES

Varahamihira enumerates the names of chapters he has written in his Yatra work, but it is very curious to see why he should name the headings of chapters which go to form altogether a separate work dealing on a different subject and having nothing to do with this book. But the nature of the subjects have inter relations and probably he gave his readers to understand that he has written a

separate book called *Yatra patala* and they must also be
read in order to understand *Brihat Jataka* well. Or it may
be that even if *Yatra patala* is lost by the destructive hands
of time, people may know what its contents are.

अतः परं गुह्यकपूजनं स्यात्
स्वप्नं ततः स्नातविधिः प्रदिष्टः ।
यज्ञो ग्रहाणामथ निर्गमश्च
क्रमाच्च दिष्टः शकुनोपदेशः ॥ ५ ॥

Stanza 5.—(14) Worship of Guhyaka, (15)
Swapna, (16) Snana Vidhi, (17) Grahayagnya,
(18) Nirgama.

विवाहकालः करणं ग्रहाणां
प्रोक्तं पृथक्तद्द्विपुलाथ शाखा ।
स्कन्धैस्त्रिभिर्ज्योतिषसंग्रहोऽयं
मया कृतो दैवविदां हिताय ॥ ६ ॥

Stanza 6.—(19) Shakuna, (20) Vivahakala,
and (21) Graha karma. In this way have been
composed works in the three important branches
of Jyotishya for the benefit of the astrologers by
me, *viz.*, Varahamihira.

NOTES

He also refers here to Vivaha patala or a work he has
composed on marriage. Thus he says his works extend in
the three Skandas (Sections of Jyotishya), *viz.* :

(1) Siddantha (Ganitha or mathematical astronomy) as explained in his Pancha Siddhantika.

(2) Hora or astrology (horoscopy) as shown in *Brihat* and *Laghu Jataka*.

(3) Samhita (treatment of collateral subjects and physical phenomena) as shown in his Brihat and Sama Samhitas, Muhurtha, Prasna and Yatra belong to the horoscopy.

When I was in Cochin in 1910 A.D. an excellent carpenter of a low caste was introduced to me who gave extensive quotations from Grantha Samuchaya by Varahamihira. The genius of Varahamihira was versatile, comprehensive and unrivalled and hence in the enumeration of the nine literary gems in the court of the famous Vikramaditya, Kalidasa adds the adjective Khyato (renowned) to Varahamihira (*vide* ' Life of Varahamihira ' by me). Grantha Samuchaya refers to house building, carpentry and the nature of the materials to be collected for such purposes. His *Brihat Samhita* (which is now being translated by Prof. B. V. Raman) is a monument of Varahamihira's extensive knowledge, and those who read carefully that illustrious work will be immensely benefited by the expansion of their intellects, and by the useful knowledge he has stored in his priceless pages. Modern scientific culture of the highest order in agriculture, commerce, industry, discoveries and inventions has been forestalled and the chapter on the metamorphosing of planets and making them yield fruits and flowers quiet foreign to their nature and growing them in the shortest time possible, is most interesting and worthy of an early trial. (See Chs. VII and VIII, Part 2 of *Brihat Samhita* by the same author).

पृथुविरचितमन्यैः शास्त्रमेतत्समस्तम्
तदनुलघुमयेदम् तत्प्रदेशार्थमेव ।
कृतमिह हि समर्थे धीविषाणामलत्वे
मम यदिह यदुक्तं सज्जनैः क्षम्यतां तत् ॥ ७ ॥

Stanza 7.—Other great Rishis have composed
extensive works on these subjects. I have made
only an abstract of what they have already stated.
Let good people excuse faults, if any, in my works
as my object is to sharpen the intellect.

NOTES

Here Varahamihira is plain and plump. He
pretends no originality. He takes no unnecessary or un-
warranted credit of pride to himself. There are many
important works in the extensive sections (Skanda
Thraya) of astrology, *viz.*, mathematics or astronomy,
Horoscopy or astrology and Samhita or natural
phenomena.

Varahamihira's great credit lies in bringing, in a
small compass, large and comprehensive works of great
difficulty and technical in nature. He has eminently
succeeded in his aim, and the literary world of all nations
is greatly obliged for his labours and the ability which he
brings to bear on his numerous productions. Leaving
aside the great Maharishis who could not easily be
approached in elevation of intellect, or versatility, by any
person, he stands second to none among the numerous
authors on astrological literature for the ability, facility,

capacity, and easy flow of style in his works. Though he flourished 2,000 years ago, and was honoured by Vikramaditya, one of the greatest Sovereigns of the world, who patronised literature, sciences and arts in India, his name is now as familiar, and as honoured, as that of any other author ancient or modern. He is candid in his opinions and excels generally in the brevity of expression which is the soul of all literary compositions.

He has given the suggestive ideas with a view to simplify matters and encourage their easy study. By reading his works Varahamihira rightly says that the human intellect will be sharpened and much useful knowledge will be acquired. He requests the learned men to excuse him, if in his concise expression of extensive ancient works, any errors may have unwittingly crept into them. Here there is a double signification. First the fact that errors creep into works composed by great men and second that humility and not pride should mark the conclusion of a learned work.

ग्रन्थस्य यत्प्रचरतोऽस्य विनाशमेति
लेख्याद्बहुश्रुतमुखाधिगमक्रमेण ।
यद्वा मया कुकृतमल्पमिहाकृतं वा
कार्यं तदत्र विदुषा परिहृत्य रागम् ॥ ८ ॥

Stanza 8.—If the work suffers in its travel and copyings, the reader must set the errors right by referring them to the most learned. They must also correct any errors, which I may have committed, by my negligence, or by misapprehension of the originals without envy or mean jealousy.

NOTES

As time advances, good works in manuscript, as well as printed ones suffer a great deal at the hands of the ignorant copyists and the careless, conceited and ignorant printers. It is also possible to think that the author in his anxiety to be concise and short, may not have paid as much attention to the sketching of the details as was necessary or he may have misapprehended some ideas put forth in the sutra form by the renowned Maharishis. Varahamihira, therefore, begs his readers and the learned men into whose hands these works may fall, to put away envy and mean jealousy [we may also mention staunch bigotry so abnormally prevailing among literary men and correct any errors which may have crept into his books from the various sources enumerated above. His work will sharpen their intellects and they will be benefited by reading what he has so well said.

आदित्यदासतनयस्तदवाप्तबोधः
कापित्थके सवितृलब्धवरप्रसादः ।
आवन्तिको मुनिमतान्यवलोक्य सम्य-
ग्घोरां वराहमिहिरो रुचिरां चकार ॥ ९ ॥

Stanza 9.—Varahamihira, the son of Aditya Dasa, who imbibed his knowledge from his father, blessed with the grace of the Sun in all branches of knowledge, born in Kapitha, a town in the country of Avantica, having carefully read all the extant literature of the Maharishis, composed this excellent work.

NOTES

A learned and holy Brahmin called Aditya Dasa lived in Kapitha, a village in the country of Avantica [Ujjini] or Malva and Varahamihira was his renowned son. The author seems to have been carefully educated by the father as he says that he was instructed by his father in the principles of astrology. Varahamihira appears to have been a great worshipper of the Sun [Savitru], and declares that he obtained all his knowledge and capacity from the grace, the Sun was pleased to bestow upon him, for he distinctly uses the expression *Savitru Labdha Vara Prasada* or the gift of the knowledge from the glorious Sun himself. This must have been the result of ardent devotion and deep contemplation upon the most glorious light which creates, protects and destroys the worlds and which embodies the three characteristics of Brahma, Vishnu, and Maheswara and which is the representation of all terrestrial and celestial knowledge. The father was a very learned Brahmin as declared by Varahamihira himself. We have seen the capabilities and genius of the author and the high proficiency he has exhibited in his valuable works and corroborated and commentated by no less a scholar than Bhattotpala. Varahamihira's son, Prithuyasas (greatly known) is the author of Shatpanchashat, one of the finest works in 56 stanzas. We have on Prasna sastra (horary) his work known as 'Shatpanchasat' and I have translated his 'Chappanna' or 'Shatpanchasat'. Thus for three generations father, son and grandson, this Brahmin family maintained a high order of intelligence and genius and in jataka and prasna, the father and son yield to none in capacity, brevity or clearness in exposition.

दिनकरमुनिगुरुचरणप्रणिपातकृतप्रसादमतिनेदम् ।
शास्त्रमुपसंगृहीतं नमोऽस्तु पूर्वमुनेतृभ्यः ॥ १० ॥

Stanza 10.—This work was composed by me after my intellect was elevated by my prostrating upon the feet of the Sun, Maharishis and my preceptor. I bow in reverence to the Purvacharyas or ancient preceptors.

NOTES

Among all great Sanskrit writers, Mangala (or blissful invocation to Gods and Preceptors) or invocation must be used either in the commencement, in the middle or in the end of their works. Some of the authors use this Mangala thrice, *viz.*, in the commencement, middle and end. In the first stanza he invokes the grace of the Sun and in the middle, he often names Maharishis which is considered to be a Mangala and in the end he invokes their help and blessings. Varahamihira thinks [rightly] that his mind has become pure and elevated by the blessings of the Sun, Maharishis and those of his Preceptor [Guru] Aditya Dasa (his father). By referring to the Sun all other planets, constellations, and zodiacal divisions are implied and by using Maharishis, the greatest intellectual giants of this land, Vasishta, Bharadwaja, Vyasa, Gargi, Atri and others are included, and by referring to Guru, he includes all preceptors including his father who may have instructed him in this as well as in other branches of learning. With these invocations the learned Varahamihira concludes his invaluable work.

Bhattotpala thus brings his priceless commentaries to a conclusion. He observes : " Varahamihira's works represent

a great ocean of knowledge. Utpala has written the commentaries called Vivriti (Chintamani) and those who desire
to possess treasures (real intellectual truths) can use this as
a boat to cross the ocean of knowledge to secure them.
This commentary is called Chintamani (the heavenly gem
which grants all mental desires) and it will be highly
endearing to all learned men.

His commentary contains 7,500 Anustup verses. An
Anustup stanza generally contains 32 letters and is prominently used by all great writers. Bhattotpala says, " Don't
accept this commentary out of any love to me or reject it
out of envy in you. Take all that is useful in my commentaries. Please try and find out those errors which have been
neglected by me, which have been stated by me in con-
sistency with high intelligence, and which have been
explained by me against the real meaning of the
original texts. This commentary was completed by
me in the saka year 888 on a (Guruvasara) Thursday, on
Panchami the 5th lunar day of the bright half of the lunar
month Chaitra. Let the Sun who represents the essence of
the Thrimurties,—Brahma, Vishnu and Iswara—be pleased
with the merit I have obtained by writing these commentaries to this sastra". Here Bhattotpala gives Vaswaswata-
mithay Sakay, 888 saka year as the time at which he
completed his commentaries. There may be some doubt
raised about the meaning of the word saka (Era) as it may
refer to Vikrama or Salivahana. Varahamihira also simply
uses the word saka in his Brihat Samhita (See Ch. XIII, St. 3)
but that refers to Yudhistira saka by adding 2536 years
to the present saka prevailing in his time. About the age
and time of Bhattotpala see note on the chapter on Bhattot-

pala of this work and my article in *The Astrologiccl Magazine*, Pp. 133 of Vol. X of 1908 A.D. It is clearly proved by references that he means Vikramasaka, as his illustrious successor Bhaskaracharya after 180 years also names Nripasaka or Vikramasaka. (See also Stanza 20, Ch. VIII, Brihat Samhita.) Here he clearly explains that saka refers to the era or period, when the *Mlechas* or *Sakas* were completely conquered by the illustrious Emperor Vikramaditya. The famous Kalidasa, one of the nine literary gems who flourished in that Emperor's court, gives clear details of the conquest of these sakas in his *Jyotirvidabharana* a work of great merit on Muhurtha and says that the 14th year of the reign of Vikramaditya was marked by the complete defeat of the 55 lacs of troops brought by the sakas and this grand event, which saved India for some time from the foreign yoke, was marked by institution of the Vikramasaka Era which now counts as 2004 (1948).

These valuable translations and notes on one of the greatest works in astrology, were finished by me, *viz.*, Bangalore Suryanarayana Rao, on Friday the 11th day of the bright half of the lunar month Jyeshta in the constellation, Chitta on the 1st June 1917, A.D. at 15 m. after 10 o'clock in the morning at my own residence in Hunsamaranahalli near Bangalore in S. India and the following is the diagram for the time which may be perused for interest and guidance for fixing the age to which my humble labours would remain as useful and be appreciated by the educated public of all times and nations. I offer these notes with my most humble respects to that final Effulgence and infinite wisdom whose visible manifestation is the glorious Sun and whose divine energy alone can give capacity

and life for writers to finish their works whether, originals
or commentaries.

The astrological diagram for the time at
which I, Bangalore Suryanarayana Rao, finished
the notes on *Brihat Jataka* of Varahamihira with
the help of the invaluable commentaries of Bhattotpala is given here for reference and study.

Vikrama Saka 1974
Salivahana Saka 1839
Cyclic year Pingala
Solar month Vrishabha 16th day
Lunar month Jyeshta
11th day of the bright half,
Christian Era 1st June 1917

Friday, in the constellation Chitta (14th) at 15', after
10 o'clock in the morning or about 12-30 ghatis after sunrise.

	Kuja Budha	Ravi Guru	Sukra Kethu	Kethu	Lagna		Ravi
	RASI Diagram for the time at which I finished the notes		Sani		NAVAMSA Diagram		
			Lagna	Guru			Chandra Sani
Rahu			Chandra	Kuja Budha			Sukra Rahu

As the constellation Chitta ruled at the time, the
period of Mars rules and there is a balance of 5 years, 11
months and 22½ days. The lord of the lagna (ascendant)
is the Sun and he is in the 10th house with the benefic

Guru who owns the 5th. The lord of the 12th or Vraya
occupies the 2nd and is aspected by Guru and Sani. Sukra
lord of 3rd and 10th is in the 11th with Kethu. The lords
of Labha [gains] and Bhagya [9th indicating wealth] Budha
and Kuja are in the 9th, and the 10th or Karyasthana is
hemmed in by two benefics Sukra and Budha in the 2nd
and 12th houses respectively. Besides, the occupation of
the 9th, 10th and 11th houses from lagna by Kuja and
Budha, Ravi and Guru and Sukra and Kethu, is good and
anticipate that these notes of mine written after much
labour and research will have a bright future, will be a
source of instruction and pleasure to students, will live
long in the literary world and will enlighten the learned.
Readers might calculate the Ayurdaya of the child born at
this time. Guru as lord of 8 being in 10, and also as lord of
5 is not likely to kill. Sani though lord of 7 and in the
12th, is in the labha bhava. Except the Moon as lord of
12th, and in the 2nd aspected by Sani in rasi and combined
with him in amsa, others will not make the work forgotten.
It means that it will live for more than 110 years and by
that time probably, the English language would have gone
out of India and not understood as widely as it is now.
The prejudices created by foreign nations about these
valuable Aryan sciences and arts will and must disappear in
the destructive folds of all powerful time, and there will be
a time when the Aryan sciences, Aryan literature and Aryan
genius will appear in their true grandeur and utility.

   May God be pleased with my humble labours in the
field of astrology has always been my earnest prayer, to
Him, who is the fountain head of all mercy, devotion,
faith, energy, protection and final beatitude.

MY GENEALOGY*

I belong to the Mulakanadu Andhra section of the Brahmin Community, and descended from the stock of the venerable Vasishta and claim that Gotra. Twelve generations ago my ancestors resided in Walaja Nagar, under the patronage of the Nawabs of Arcot and the neighbouring Polagars and they had distinguished themselves by performing sacrifices or Yagnas, by simple and holy lives and by the religious fervour of their exemplary and virtuous lives. My family records give me the following names of my ancestors :—

1. Sarana Varjhulu	...	Had performed Yagnas or sacrifices.
2. Konda Varjhulu	...	Do.
3. Naga Varjhulu	...	Do.
4. Mallava Dhanlu	...	Religious and holy Brahmins.
5. Malla Bhatlu	...	Do.
6. Lingappagaru	...	Devoted themselves to public and private business and service.
7. Venkatappagaru	...	Do.
8. Venkatagiriappagaru	...	Do.
9. Parayyagaru		
10. Venkataramaniahgaru		

This was my grandfather who was born in 1747 A.D. and died in 1828 A.D. having lived 81 years. He married first Narasamma and had two sons by her. After her death he married Naranamma when he was nearly 60 years. He commanded 500 horse and a suitable corps of infantry under Hyder and Tippu and changing his life into civil, he was

---

* Prof. Rao has given a summary here while his life has been fully given in his Autobiography a summary of which as appeared in January 1947 issue of THE ASTROLOGICAL MAGAZINE.

an Amildar and became Peshkar of Kikkeri, Channaraya-
patna and Devanhalli, in which last place Hyder first made
his political entry. My grandfather had two daughters and
five sons by his second wife and my father Gopala Rao was
the third son and the most lucky among the lot. My father
was born on the 17th July 1816 on Friday, the 10th lunar
day of the dark half of the month Ashadha, at about
15 ghatis after sunrise when the constellation Bharani ruled
with the dasa of Venus. He was only 12 years when his
father died and had to educate himself, as best as he could.
He was of slender build, energetic, strong and extremely
active in work which I have inherited from him to a large
extent. My mother Rukminiamma was an intelligent,
quiet going and very handsome woman and she died when
I was about 10 years old. My father could read and speak
about ten languages and filled various posts in the Ganjam
District and became Manager or Dewan of Parlakimidi
Zamindari. He was an expert in Mantra Sastras, and
highly religious and obliging. He would never flinch from
doing an obligation and brought me up with great care and
love. The following is his horoscope :

	Chandra	Rahu	Budha
			Sukra Ravi
Sani	RASI		Kuja
	Kethu	Birth Guru	

Mark the positions of planets in all the kendras. In addition to his onerous duties, he completed the gigantic task of completing with his own hand, one crore and twenty-five lakhs of Rama Namas or names of Sri Rama and concluded the religious rites connected with them four months before his death. He died in his 76th year on the morning of 27th August 1891 and was therefore 75 years and 40 days according to English calculations. My mother bore six children, four daughters and two sons, and I am the second. My elder brother Jagannatha Rao entered Mysore Service retired as an Amildar and died in December 1915. I was born on the Rathasaptami, Tuesday, in the month of Magha in Rakshasa at about 14 ghatis after sunrise at Chicacole and the following is my horoscope :—

	Moon Rahu	Birth	Saturn			Birth Jupiter	Rahu	
Mercury Jupiter Sun		RASI				NAVAMSA		
Venus		Mars Ketbu		Mercury	Kethu	Sun Venus Saturn Mars	Moon

An incident occurred in my fifth year which has influenced all my life to a remarkable extent. My first Aksharabhyasa, education, began at Parlakimidi in my fifth year and I slept that night with my father. I dreamt that I was taken to Suryaloka to the presence of the Sun, made to sit on his lap, and given some Payasam (wheat preparation)

by his wife Chayadevi and after a great deal of love,
the Sun putting his hands on my head, observed that I
would live long, be happy and become a great scholar and
author. I awoke and related my dream to my father,
who had already anticipated some ideas of my future greatness. In my boyish days I was extremely intelligent, and
possessed an excellent memory coupled with a piercing
intellect. But as it often happens with intelligent boys,
I was irregular in attendance at school, careless of my
studies, fond of running and other athletic exercises and
was mischievous to a considerable extent. All the while
I felt I would become a great man, and even challenged my
teachers with this idea. While I was in the Senior B.A.
class in the Central College at Bangalore, Mr. Cook, M.A.,
its Principal rebuked me for my want of attention to studies and for not writing notes which he gave very copiously.
I was ready with my impertinent answer. I observed in a
determined tone that copying notes forms the part of dull-
headed students and superficial teachers and that bright
students like myself need no such process. He remarked
that he was a student and amanuensis of Dr. Bains of
Psychological fame and that I should obey him. I told him
that I would become a greater man than both of them with
the result that I was turned out of the class for a day. Mr.
Cook was a generous Scotch gentleman. He sent for me
next day, and asked me whether my behaviour was right.
I said that his treatment of students should be different,
as the intelligent and spirited could not bear calmly, remarks which dull boys may consider as their inheritance.
When I met him after publishing some of my works,
specially History of Vijayanagar, he had the nobility to

address me as a greater man than himself while I modestly
acknowledged his valuable instructions as the basis for all
my scholarship in English. I was intended to take the legal
line and accordingly finished my legal studies and practised
for about 9 years. My astrological instincts were stirred up
by a Sastri while I was in the F.A. class and I picked up
my knowledge in it by reading books on the subject in Sanskrit. I had no high opinion for English astrological publica-
tions and never cared to them. My first work in Astrology*
in a diglot form (English and Kannada) appeared in 1882,
and it sold well. My collegiate studies gave me no leisure
to attend to astrological studies and my Self-Instructor in
English appeared in 1892. The second edition in 1893 and
third in 1900, the interval being taken up by my legal practice, 4th, 5th and 6th editions followed and the 7th is in
print. Soon after my birth an Ooriya Astrologer by name
Brahma predicted my future greatness. I feel I am under
the direct grace of the glorious Sun at every important turn
in my life and his presence in the 10th house along with
Budha and Guru has enabled me to hold the view that I am
destined to become a great man and write valuable works
on a variety of subjects. I married first my maternal uncle's
daughter by name Bhagirathi and she bore 10 children of
whom four died early in life. I have now 6 children by
her, 3 sons and 3 daughters and after her death I married
again Subbi. She has one daughter now and I am leading
a quite honourable and religious life. My second son
Lakshminarayana Rao is a graduate of Philosophy and
Logic and has entered the Mysore Educational Service. My

---

*This is now re-published under the name of *Compendium of
Astrology* omitting the Kannada portions.

eldest son Nanjunda ¦Rao assists me in my office work.
(Dr. B. V. Raman in his eldest son.) I have now 4 grands
sons and 6 grand-daughters. God has been pleased to
place me above want, and though my earnings are great,
my expenses have not been small. I possess generous
instincts and always take delight in helping others who are
in need. I am an admirer of all talent in any form in any
man and my company is always pleasant and instructive.
I possess powers of speech and writing fluently in almost
equal degrees and my familiarity with various Western and
Eastern sciences, gives me a decided advantage to lead the
people wherever I may be. I am a great lover of music and
fine arts, and my residence is generally kept in a very
fashionable manner. My house is open to all classes alike
and I have never withheld my help in any charitable cause
when they sought my help. I have had audience with
Viceroys, Maharaja's and Governors and all of them were
pleased with my behaviour, spirit of independence, and
capacity in conversation and discussion. I have had
suitable Khillats or presents from many Maharajas and the
national predictions I have made about wars, famines,
deaths of royal personages, epidemics, and other phenomena, have been remarkably fulfilled. My prediction
about the present great Anglo-German war, six months
before it happened, in my *Astrological Magazine* has raised
my reputation high and my works and lectures have always
been appreciated and recognised by the educated public.
I am now in my Guru Dasa and Sukra Bhukthi and hope to
pull through it and a portion of Sani, through God's grace.
I have been leading a religious life in this age of false allure-
ments, of false civilisation and have felt strongly in my
innermost heart that God protects all those who entirely

place their confidence in Him and my own independent life is a great illustration of that great principle which lays down complete devotion to God and honest and sincere life under His able and Omnipotent guidance. May He shower His blessings on all and make the world happy and cheerful have been my earnest daily prayers.

THE END

INDEX